T0304912

# LAWLESS REPUBLIC

# LAWLESS REPUBLIC

## THE RISE OF CICERO
## AND THE DECLINE OF ROME

## JOSIAH OSGOOD

BASIC
BOOKS

LONDON

First published in Great Britain in 2025 by Basic Books UK
An imprint of John Murray Press

1

Copyright © Josiah Osgood 2025

Maps copyright © Kate Blackmer 2024

A CIP catalogue record for this title is available from the British Library

Hardback ISBN 9781399811552
Trade Paperback ISBN 9781399811569
ebook ISBN 9781399811583

Typeset in Adobe Garamond Pro

Printed and bound in Great Britain by Clays Ltd, Elcograf S.p.A.

John Murray Press policy is to use papers that are natural, renewable and
recyclable products and made from wood grown in sustainable forests.
The logging and manufacturing processes are expected to conform to the
environmental regulations of the country of origin.

Carmelite House
50 Victoria Embankment
London EC4Y 0DZ

www.basicbooks.uk

John Murray Press, part of Hodder & Stoughton Limited
An Hachette UK company

The authorised representative in the EEA is Hachette Ireland, 8 Castlecourt
Centre, Dublin 15, D15 XTP3, Ireland (email: info@hbgi.ie)

Portrait of Cicero (credit: Musei Capitolini, Rome, Italy, Luisa Ricciarini / Bridgeman Images).

# CONTENTS

# LIST OF MAPS

# INTRODUCTION

"Every trial is a drama," it's been said.[1] In the Roman Republic, criminal trials were especially theatrical. They took place outdoors, in the Forum, the vast open area at the heart of Rome that was ringed around by shops, government buildings, and temples of the gods with great stone columns that seemed to reach up to the heavens. A separate court operated for murder, extortion, and each of the other major crimes recognized by the law, and it would convene whenever charges were to be heard.

As a trial got underway, participants filled the wooden benches where they would sit. Here came the prosecutor, often a young man looking to make a name for himself, neatly groomed, in a freshly cleaned white toga, his head held high in a display of confidence. He would be accompanied by his assistants, and perhaps slaves carrying wooden boxes filled with notes and documents. The defendant aimed for spectacle of a different kind. To stir pity, he shuffled in unwashed, unshaved, dressed in dark rags. In the criminal courts of the late Republic, the usual penalty was exile, which the Romans

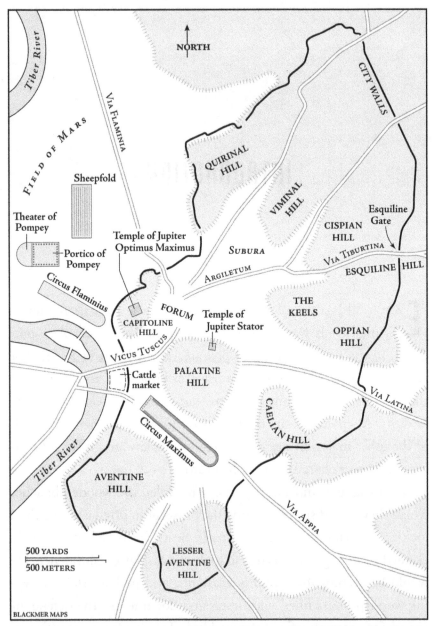

Cicero's Rome, circa 55 BC, showing the hills, the walls built in the fourth century BC, and a few major roads and sites. Cicero spent much of his time arguing legal cases in the Forum. As a young man, he lived on a slope of the Esquiline Hill known as the Keels. Later he moved to a mansion overlooking the Forum on the hugely desirable Palatine Hill. The location of the Temple of Jupiter Stator, where Cicero gave a famous speech denouncing the conspirator Catiline, is approximate.

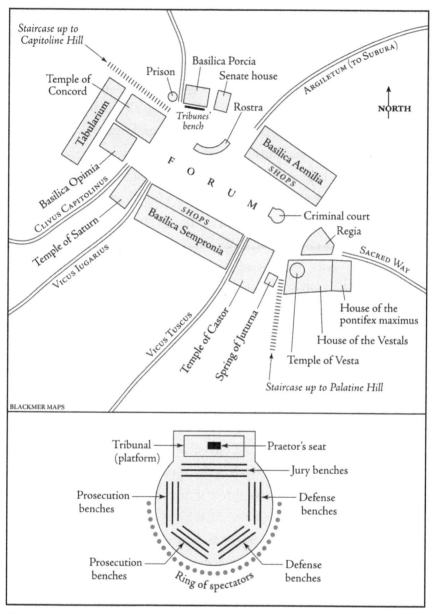

The Roman Forum, circa 80 BC. The schematic representation shows how a criminal court might have been set up: the tribunal (platform) with the praetor's seat, the jury benches in front of the tribunal, the prosecution and defense benches in front of the jury benches, and the ring of spectators around the whole court.

considered practically a form of death, so his family members might trudge along with him conveying an air of bereavement. Also with the defendant were his lawyers and other powerful members of Roman society, ready to testify to his good character.[2]

Milling about the benches were the jurors, all men of high rank, as many as seventy-five at some trials. They might take the chance to carry out some personal business with each other or swap jokes before the proceedings began. Finally, in came the magistrate who presided over the court. Usually this was a praetor, a high-ranking elected official, second only to the consul in authority, and he didn't so much walk through the city as *process*. Wearing a special white toga trimmed with a purple stripe, he was accompanied by six officers who carried tightly bound bundles of rods known as the fasces, a symbol of his office. While everyone else would sit on benches, the praetor alone took his seat on an ivory stool—another insignia of office—that was placed on a high wooden platform. In front of this tribunal were set the benches of the jurors, with the prosecution's benches on one side and the defense's benches on the other. Surrounding the court was a ring of onlookers, often many rows deep, ready to cheer, jeer, clap, hiss, and above all gasp at whatever sensational details were about to be revealed.

A trial would begin with a lengthy speech from the lead prosecutor. He would rise and move into the area between his benches and those of the defendant. As he opened his speech, he would turn and face the jury, his most important audience. The outcome of the trial rested in their hands. As the prosecutor continued to speak, he could move around, like an actor on a stage. At one moment he might be addressing the jury, at another looking up at the praetor; then he could turn and confront the defendant, then pivot again to look at the witnesses he was going to call, who usually sat on the prosecution benches.

After the prosecution finished, it was the defense's turn. A man on trial might have as many as four lawyers to speak for him, each handling different parts of the case. As the defense counsel ranged around the court, he could confront the prosecutor, turn back and look with pity on the accused, then face the jury and plead with them to vote for acquittal, as if they were savior gods. The defendant might stand up and speak for himself, even extend his hands to the jury or fall to his knees and grovel before their benches. His family members would sob.

Last came the witnesses, each one summoned by a herald to the praetor's tribunal to testify under oath. This provided more spectacle for court-watchers. Especially elaborate were the trials of those officials accused of extorting money while on government service abroad. Foreigners, or Roman citizens who lived overseas, would travel hundreds of miles to the city. Before a rapt audience in the Forum they would tell horrifying stories of how a governor had extorted money for military protection, pillaged temples of the gods, or raped and killed innocent men and women. Each side got to cross-examine the other's witnesses. At this stage of the trial, as the lawyers argued about evidence, they might taunt each other too.

At the end of it all, the jurors voted. They did not deliberate in seclusion, as happens in some modern courts. They received no summing up or instructions from the presiding magistrate. Rather, each juror was made to swear an oath to render a conscientious verdict and handed a small wooden tablet, covered with wax, with the letter *A* written on one side and *C* on the other. *A* stood for the Latin word *absolvo*, "I acquit," and *C* for *condemno*, "I condemn." The juror first rubbed out one of the two letters (or both, to abstain), then perhaps held up the tablet for the public to see while concealing his verdict, and finally dropped it into a bronze urn kept on the praetor's tribunal. After everyone had cast a ballot, the votes were tallied: a majority of *C*'s was enough to convict. The procedure shows ordinary people's role as spectators, even watchdogs.[3] They were not jurors, but they witnessed trials and expected the courts to bring to justice powerful men who had harmed the public interest.

People came to court to be entertained as well. It was thrilling to see the high and mighty dressed as if for their own funeral. Who knew what secrets would spill out at the trial? Perhaps stories of drunken politicians at a party, the floor drenched in wine, with wilting garlands and fishbones littered around?[4] In Rome, a city addicted to gossip, street-corner rumors could be cited as evidence in criminal trials. No rules of admissibility operated in a Roman court.

Also to be savored were the performances of the lawyers, the best of whom, like Marcus Tullius Cicero, had spent years training in the art of public speaking. Cicero himself said that if you walked by a trial while it was underway, you could tell how it was going with a quick glance.[5] If jurors were yawning, chatting, or checking the time, the onlooker would see that the case lacked an orator. But if the onlooker saw the jurors watching intently, conveying agreement with their expressions, held in suspense by a speech, like a bird by another's call, or—the chief goal—stirred by pity, hatred, or some other emotion, he would know that an orator was at work.

This book tells the story of Cicero and his rise to prominence as a trial lawyer, from his debut in the courts in the late 80s BC to his death nearly four decades later. Cicero's successful defense of many influential men accused of murder, extortion, and other crimes earned him wealth, favors to call in, and a name for himself, which he parlayed into a career in politics. Quite unusually for one born into a family with no prior electoral success at Rome, he rose to the Republic's top office of consul. Quintilian, a later expert in public speaking, remarked, it was not without reason that Cicero's contemporaries called him the king of the law courts while posterity considered "Cicero as the name not of a person, but of eloquence itself."[6]

The crimes I discuss were all (allegedly) carried out by members of the top ranks of Roman society: senators, who held political office, and the group below them, equestrians, men of demonstrated wealth who had once made up the cavalry in the army but by Cicero's day filled other roles such as military officers and government contractors. The criminal courts of Rome primarily addressed the illegal activities of the ruling class, especially senators. The courts were established in the second century BC to repress offenses deemed threatening to the Republic as a whole. Prior to this, citizens were put on trial before full assemblies of the people.[7] Some criminal courts tried crimes that only officeholders or candidates for office could commit, such as extortion and electoral bribery. Nonofficials could perpetrate other crimes, such as murder, but typically only the upper echelons of society went on trial. In Rome, there was no public prosecutor meant to enforce law systematically. Rather, private individuals had to apply to a magistrate for the right to prosecute, and this limited the cases heard.[8] Lower-class members of society accused of crimes were dealt with more summarily.

The published versions of Cicero's speeches are our best source for crime and its prosecution in the courts in the late Roman Republic. These orations were usually given for the defense but also, on one occasion, for the prosecution. While other Roman lawyers published their speeches, only Cicero's have survived into modern times, largely because they were studied by later generations of students as the best of their kind. This means that for all the trials I discuss, we mainly have Cicero's side of the case, or at least the part of the case he covered when on a team of several lawyers. From his speeches, however, it is possible to deduce something about the opposing counsels' arguments as well as the facts of the case and the larger legal issues.[9]

There are further limitations to our evidence of which it is important to be aware. Speeches made up only part of the trial and its record. We lack the formal transcripts of witness testimony. Furthermore, the published speeches did not necessarily correspond exactly to what Cicero said in court. It was his practice to write out in full the introductions and conclusions of his speeches before a trial; the rest of his case he outlined in notes. After delivering a speech, he would write it up using his own outline, his memory, and perhaps notes made by a secretary while he was speaking. This means it is unlikely we have a perfect transcript of what he said. Sometimes he left out from published speeches discussions he thought would be of little interest to readers, although he did note the omissions. My reconstructions of Cicero's trials depend, then, on Cicero's reconstructions. Still, because he intended the published versions of his speeches to be records of his legal triumphs useful for learners, I share with other scholars confidence that we do have access to the arguments he made.[10]

Along with the speeches, other sources cast light on Cicero's trials and the Roman courts more generally. Cicero himself wrote extensively about oratory. Toward the end of his life he produced an innovative history of public speaking in Rome, titled *Brutus* in honor of his young friend Marcus Brutus, the future assassin of Julius Caesar. In this work, Cicero delivered memorable judgments on the performances of his peers and predecessors. One orator, while articulate, was "so louche and effeminate in his movements, that a dance step came to be named after him."[11] In *Brutus*, Cicero also traced the rise of legal advocacy. It had always been the practice in Rome that less powerful members of society turned for help to the more powerful, their "patrons." With the establishment of the criminal courts, a small group of men from the ruling families with the greatest skill in speaking became much sought after for conducting cases, especially for the defense. Over time, as court business increased, less distinguished members of society took up legal pleading too. All these men were known as *patroni*, and in general they were a separate group from the experts in civil law who also made themselves available for consultation. In another book, *On the Ideal Orator*, Cicero created an imaginary dialogue in which the famous advocates who had taught him in his youth discuss rhetoric and philosophy at a country villa. Again and again, they cite real examples from their own careers.[12]

Among numerous later works written after Cicero's death, three are especially valuable. In the mid-first century AD, a scholar named Asconius prepared a detailed commentary on Cicero's speeches. Using sources now lost to us, he uncovered the surprising backstory of one of Cicero's most important defenses.[13] Slightly later Quintilian produced a massive handbook called *The Orator's Education*. He wrote about all the elements of trials, including the examination of witnesses, which helps to fill in gaps left by Cicero's speeches. Quintilian also discussed how Cicero and other speakers delivered their speeches: their movements, their gestures, their facial expressions, their use of voice. In Cicero's view, delivery was an essential aspect of oratory—"bodily eloquence" he called it—but it is hard to access this in his published speeches.[14] Finally, the Greek Plutarch left us the only complete biography of Cicero that survives from antiquity, though others were written. In his typically moralistic manner, Plutarch praised Cicero's educational achievements but faulted his overconfidence.[15]

At their best, public trials at Rome held to account those who had abused their power. Trials enacted society's commitment to live peacefully together under the rule of law. But at their worst, trials could be highly sensationalized. The courts did not evenly apply one law to everyone, as a modern judicial system tries to do. Participants in trials did not always receive a basic level of dignity from the courts. Sometimes a man would be taken to court by a personal or political enemy. The courts were used to ruin politicians' careers and wreak revenge.

In Cicero's speeches, we recognize arguments and techniques used by trial lawyers today such as establishing criminal intent and discrediting a star witness. We also see sharp differences. In Rome, no real limits were placed on what lawyers could say nor were there strict standards of proof. Lawyers could attack defendants or even opposing counsel for their physical appearance, the way they dressed, or their sexual practices. They appealed to the prejudices of jurors and onlookers, arguing, for instance, "The foreigners testifying against my client are far less likely to be trustworthy because they are foreigners!" While Roman lawyers did not ignore hard evidence, in their speeches they constantly drew inferences from an individual's supposed character. They might posit, for example, "The defendant is known to be a man of loose morals, so of course he committed murder."[16]

Once we grasp how the courts worked, the reasons for Cicero's success become clear. Certainly he mastered the teachings of rhetoric. He knew how to devise arguments based on probability that would convince jurors. He powerfully wielded rhetorical devices. He produced highly rhythmical sentences that almost made his voice sing. He used sharp wit and humor to skewer opponents and win over juries. A secretary of Cicero—a slave of his named Tiro whom Cicero eventually freed—assembled books of Cicero's best jokes, which were by no means reserved for trials. For example, when a woman named

Fabia said she was thirty, Cicero observed, "It's true. I've heard her say that for twenty years now."[17] But most critical to Cicero's success was his skill as a storyteller. He could take some or all of the facts in a case and turn them into a narrative that was not only logically persuasive, but more important, emotionally moving. Speaking for the defense, as he mostly did, he had a special talent for telling counter-stories that undid the prosecution's case. That would be good advocacy in any age, but Cicero went further. In creating heroes and villains, he often relied on stereotypes about social status, ethnicity, and gender.

Much in Cicero's legal speeches may strike a modern ear as irrelevant or offensive. "Objection!" one might cry out repeatedly. But all Roman lawyers made the same character-based arguments that Cicero did; he just did it best. Rome was a highly stratified society. An individual's status was determined by their birth, wealth, and personal reputation. Every year, thousands were born into slavery and were denied all rights. On the other hand, some Romans inherited enormous privilege. Although the Roman form of government was republican, there were "nobles," who descended from consuls through the male line. Nobles had a great advantage when running for political office and arguing cases in the courts. The patricians, a few dozen families, some with several branches, were an even more exclusive group that traced their ancestry back to the earliest days of Rome.

Although the criminal courts sometimes held the powerful accountable, they ultimately reinforced the hierarchy. Enslaved persons were not allowed to give testimony as the freeborn did but had to endure interrogation under torture. Slaves were not allowed to give evidence against their owners. Slaveowners could kill their slaves with impunity; this did not count as murder. Freeborn witnesses who testified might be derided, especially if they were foreigners. Lawyers openly said at trials dealing with extortion in territories under Roman imperial control that the interests of Roman citizens should be put ahead of those of other peoples. Cicero himself once pleaded with jurors that "our fathers" had acquitted one governor, "despite much evidence for many crimes of greed, because he had fought a vigorous war against runaway slaves."[18] Of course, Cicero said that when defending another man accused of extortion; a prosecutor would take a different line. Taken as a whole, the trials Cicero took part in show the difficulty provincial populations faced in upholding their rights.

The aspirational words carved in marble across the entrance to the US Supreme Court, "Equal justice under law," were not a motto for the criminal courts of the Roman Republic. The cases lawyers made often relied less on law and evidence than personal reputations and the precedency of empire. Cicero won cases by diverting jurors' attention and stoking prejudice, and trial procedures allowed this to happen. Romans themselves questioned how fairly the courts worked. During Cicero's years as a lawyer, juries were often suspected of making decisions based on political pressure or bribes. On some occasions, as we shall see, they almost certainly did. The courts' capriciousness and corruption not only sapped public trust, but also emboldened those who were inclined to commit crimes to feel they might get away with it.

Cicero's legal career took place during the last years of the Roman Republic, a time of both great cultural achievements and savage violence. As Cicero reached adulthood in the 80s BC, a vicious civil war shut down the courts. The victor, a brutal general named Sulla, reestablished the courts, which functioned for about thirty years alongside the other organs of republican government. But the civil war's dark shadow hung over everything. To get ahead and survive in that struggle, Rome's ruling class had done nearly unthinkable things. They could do so again, especially if the courts failed to restrain them. As Cicero's legal practice advanced, violence ticked up again in Rome and Italy as a whole. At times, rival gangs fought for control of the streets. Militias rose up in the Italian countryside, ready to march on the capital. Full-scale civil war broke out again in 49 BC. The conflict would drag on for twenty years and claim Cicero himself among its victims.[19] Great public trials in the Forum were never brought back again.

Cicero's career is a mirror to this age, so this book is about not only his most famous cases but also the larger struggle between law and violence. In the first few chapters, we will see Cicero establish himself in the courts. We will also see the relentless pursuit of wealth and power by the upper classes of Roman society. Politicians needed money to pay for ostentatious displays that enhanced their status—mansions in Rome where they received clients, country villas where they hosted friends, gladiatorial games and theatrical shows to entertain the masses of Roman citizens. Leading Romans had always competed, but the civil war of the 80s BC made the rules of the game more brutal. During the conflict, Romans seized the estates of their political enemies or even innocent bystanders. They then looked to exploit the overseas provinces. To Rome's credit, there was an extortion court, which did net some offenders. Some Roman leaders tried to improve governance and pass new laws to remedy such problems as extortion and electoral bribery.[20]

While Cicero would never profit from civil war nor plunder a province, he was certainly not free from the urge for wealth and influence. As his legal career flourished, he began purchasing villas in the most fashionable spots and decorating them with art. He climbed his way up the political ladder by smearing rivals. But just as in the tragedies that Romans enjoyed watching on stage, he underwent a terrible reversal of fortune. During the year he served as consul, 63 BC, a conspiracy to topple the government broke out, spearheaded by a disgruntled senator who cleverly exploited widespread social misery in Italy. Cicero took stern measures to suppress those he deemed as subversive and even executed five of the leading conspirators without a trial. He was engulfed in controversy almost immediately and was himself sent into exile for a year and a half.

Cicero returned to Rome and tried to resume his legal practice. But the city suffered from more political violence, fueled by glaring inequality among citizens and unscrupulous leaders exploiting this gap. Political violence became the Roman crime from hell: it could shut down even the court designed to punish it, making it hard to repress. In the courts and beyond, Cicero began to advance an argument that in response to political violence, it was acceptable to fight back in kind. "In times of war, the laws fall silent," he memorably suggested.[21] Clearly a state may need to use force to repress internal violence, but Cicero's doctrine was open to abuse. This sort of thinking contributed to the renewed outbreak of civil war in 49 BC, which ultimately led to the murder of Julius Caesar five years later. Cicero had no part in planning the conspiracy against Caesar, but immediately afterward he became the assassins' chief defender. There was a higher law, he claimed, that transcended the laws of men.

At the heart of Cicero's story lies a strange irony: the career of Rome's greatest trial lawyer also demonstrates how the rule of law broke down. To an extent, Cicero was directly implicated in the Republic's problems. As a politician who held high office, he bore responsibility for failing to address social inequality. As a lawyer, he sometimes advanced arguments for disregarding the law. But more often, Cicero's legal and political career illustrate problems that went beyond him, which any democratic society may find itself struggling with. How, after an outbreak of violence, do you restore the rule of law? How do you protect against the threat of domestic terrorism without suppressing civil liberties? How do you hold to account those who incite violence? When should voters decide a politician's fate, and when should jurors? Cicero's own extraordinary story and the tumultuous years he lived through provide no simple solutions to these hard questions. But they do help to show what holds up the rule of law, what threatens it, and what happens when law gives way to disorder.

# CHAPTER 1

# Murder by the Baths of Pallacina

It happened after dark, a murder on the unlit streets of Rome, right by the Baths of Pallacina. The victim, Sextus Roscius, was a wealthy man, well-respected in his hometown of Ameria, about fifty miles north of Rome. Life in that little country town was too quiet for him. He preferred the big city, where he enjoyed friendships with some of the highest-ranking families of Rome—the Metelli, the Servilii, and the Scipiones. He was invited to dinners at their grand mansions where he could network with them. Roscius senior was lucky to have his son, Roscius junior, remain in Ameria to manage his thirteen farms.[1]

Life was going well for Roscius senior. The farms, many of them located on the Tiber River, turned a good profit. While it's true that Rome had been locked in a nasty civil war for the last few years, Roscius had backed the winning side. He was seen in Rome celebrating the victory of Sulla and the general's noble supporters with whom

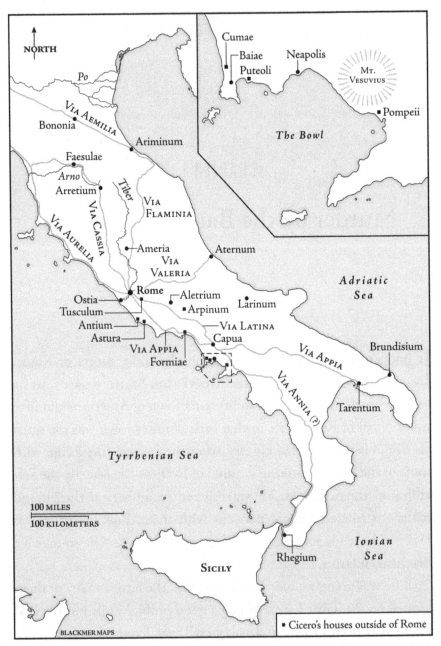

NORTH

Po

VIA AEMILIA

Bononia

Ariminum

Faesulae

Arno

Arretium

Tiber

VIA CASSIA

VIA FLAMINIA

VIA AURELIA

Ameria

VIA VALERIA

Aternum

Rome

Ostia

Tusculum

Aletrium

Arpinum

Larinum

Antium

Astura

VIA LATINA

Capua

VIA APPIA

Formiae

VIA APPIA

VIA ANNIA (?)

Tarentum

Brundisium

Cumae

Baiae

Puteoli

Neapolis

MT. VESUVIUS

Pompeii

The Bowl

Adriatic Sea

Tyrrhenian Sea

100 MILES

100 KILOMETERS

Rhegium

Ionian Sea

SICILY

■ Cicero's houses outside of Rome

BLACKMER MAPS

Cicero's Italy. Over the course of his adult life, Cicero inherited the family property in Arpinum and acquired a number of other houses, mostly along the spectacular Italian coastline that was a popular vacation spot for rich Romans.

he was so close. But one fatal night, Roscius had been at one of the dinners he enjoyed so much and had perhaps been drinking with his powerful friends. As he made his way through the streets afterward with two of his slaves, somebody stuck a dagger in him and fled.

In Rome there were no police to investigate a crime scene. It fell to a victim's family to seek justice. The two slaves with Roscius survived the attack and went to a relative of his in Rome named Magnus. He immediately sent a messenger to Ameria with the blood-stained dagger. Through the night the messenger raced, swapping out horse and carriage several times. It only took him ten hours. You might have thought he would bring the news to Roscius junior first but no, he went to a more distant relative of the victim, Capito. He was a powerful man in Ameria, just as the late Roscius had been. Surely he would know what to do.

The recent civil war had been a bloodbath. Thousands had fallen in battle. And then, late in 82 BC, the victorious general Sulla started posting lists of outlaws. Eighty names reportedly went up the first day, 220 the next, and 220 the day after that.[2] Anyone who brought to Sulla the head of one of the proscribed earned a large reward. Slaves were even allowed to kill their own masters if they were listed: a wealthy Roman's worst nightmare. All the property of the proscribed was confiscated and auctioned off. Soldiers and officers of Sulla grew rich. Names were added to the list—and men subsequently butchered—just to lay hands on their wealth. A grim joke held that one man was killed by his mansion, another by his pleasure gardens, and a third by his thermal baths.[3]

The proscriptions cut asunder the ties that held Roman society together, even the most sacred. Stories were told of terrible betrayals.

One of the proscribed came secretly, with his head covered, to the rear door of the house where his wife was. She refused to let him in. And so he stabbed himself, sprinkling the doorway with his blood, an act of pollution meant to bring the anger of the gods on his spouse.[4]

Atrocities were committed on all sides. Several years before Sulla's final victory, his rival, another general named Marius, had gained control of Rome and launched his own purge. Among those named outlaws was one of Cicero's teachers, the great lawyer Marcus Antonius. His death became legendary. The story goes that Antonius fled to the house of a friend. The man of modest means wanted to entertain the distinguished fugitive as best he could, so he sent a slave to a nearby tavern to buy a better wine than usual. The tavern-keeper asked why. The slave whispered back the reason, paid for the wine, and returned to Antonius. The tavern-keeper, meanwhile, informed Marius, who sent some soldiers to the house. Antonius allegedly used his great powers as a speaker to beg for his life, and the soldiers wouldn't lay a hand on him. Finally the officer in charge, who was waiting downstairs, got concerned about the delay, went up to Antonius, and cut off the orator's head. It was hung, along with those of other victims of Marius, on the Rostra, the lofty speaker's platform in the Forum of Rome, where politicians addressed assemblies of citizens in more peaceful times.[5] Sulla would later nail heads onto the Rostra, too, as if they were trophies.

After all this murder and looting, Romans longed for a restoration of normality. The criminal courts had not functioned well or had been shut down altogether for years. Few men had been brought to justice for their actions. Indeed, during Sulla's proscriptions assassins had won rewards. Ordinary citizens must have missed the great public trials and the entertainment they offered. Cicero, in his early twenties, doubtless did. As part of his training, he would go to the courts to hear the best speakers perform whenever he could.[6]

Even Sulla, for all his brutality, eventually felt it was time to reestablish a more peaceful order. In June of 81 BC the proscriptions ended. Soon afterward, Sulla used his emergency powers as dictator to put in place a new criminal justice system. Seven courts were established to try the crimes of treason, extortion, electoral malpractice, embezzlement, forgery, assault, and murder. The juries would be made up entirely of senators. Sulla hoped to restore the dominance over political affairs that the Senate and its great families had once enjoyed before populists such as Marius had gained power.[7]

A large crowd gathered as the first trial in the new murder court got underway early in 80 BC. After all the unrequited killing of the last few years, people wanted to know whether Lady Justice could balance her scales again. But there was more to it than that. It wasn't just any murder trial about to take place. The defendant, Sextus Roscius junior, was accused of killing his own father, about the most heinous crime possible in Roman eyes.[8]

Seated on the plain wooden bench granted to criminal defendants, gawped at by the gathering crowd, was Roscius junior. Opposite him, on the prosecution bench, sat the kinsman of the late Roscius, Magnus. With Magnus was a full-time lawyer, Erucius. Just as there were no police in Rome, there was no public prosecutor. Private individuals with an interest in a criminal case were expected to bring charges—the relative of a dead man, for instance. If the accuser lacked oratorical ability, he would rely on an advocate—either a politician, or an aspiring politician, who was looking to win fame and favor, or else a man who made a full-time job of pleading in the courts, as Erucius did.

In the murder court especially, it was common to rely on professional prosecutors. While crimes such as extortion could be committed by only a handful of public officials, a wider range of people were prosecuted for murder. There was a need for advocates to take on cases. Professional prosecutors were providing a public service by bringing to justice those who murdered or attempted murder. But they were sometimes looked down on as being driven by personal gain. Advocates were not supposed to collect fees but there were ways around this: a loan, say, interest-free for life. Another complaint about professional prosecutors was that they were malicious and took pleasure in ruining the lives of others. Cicero compared them to watchdogs that bark when a thief comes in the night but may also bite a more peaceful visitor by day.[9]

In Roman murder trials, prosecutors typically focused less on physical evidence—there often wasn't any—and more on the character and motive of the accused. So it was with the case Erucius proceeded to make, after he rose from his bench and turned to face the jurors and, sitting behind them, Praetor Marcus Fannius, who was presiding over the trial.[10] The defendant Roscius junior, Erucius said, was a surly and uncouth man. Over forty years old, Roscius junior had always spent his life in the country and never came to the city. Nobody wanted him at their dinner parties. Worse than that, on at least one occasion he had even been guilty of embezzlement.

Erucius continued that the elder Roscius had always preferred the company of another son, but that son had died. So badly did relations between the father and his surviving son sour that Roscius senior made plans to cut Roscius junior out of his will. Only one way lay open for Roscius junior to save his inheritance. He arranged for his father to be killed. Erucius couldn't definitively identify the actual killer or killers. Roscius junior, everyone agreed, had been in Ameria the night of the murder. But the motive spoke loudly. It had been a lawless time. During the proscriptions, people were sentenced to death by the scratch of a pen. Murderers stalked the streets of Rome. It wouldn't have been hard for the younger Roscius to find men for the job and think he'd get away with it.

Erucius's speech doesn't survive and so must be pieced together from the speech for the defense, which does. It is a good guess that, along with all the points about character and motive, the prosecutor dwelled on the horror of killing a parent. The Romans used a special word for kin-murder, *parricidium*, which is the source of the English "parricide." Tellingly, this word existed in Latin long before the word for simple murder, *homicidium*, meaning the killing of a person (*homo*). For convenience, we speak of the "murder" court established by Sulla, but the enabling statute actually referred to "dagger-men and poisonings." Originally there had been separate courts for violence with the dagger—associated especially with urban gangsterism—and poisoning, both of which were regarded as public menaces. Sulla joined the courts together, and his law marked a step to fuller recognition of the crime of simple murder. Between them, poison and the blade covered the two main ways of killing. Parricide also fell under the statute, but, as Erucius doubtless reminded jurors, it was uniquely abominable, a violation of the laws of men and gods.[11]

So awful was kin-murder in the eyes of the Romans that it entailed a distinctly gruesome penalty: to be sewn up in a sack along with a dog, a snake, a cock, and a monkey, and then dumped into the sea. This was thought to carry off the pollution of the crime and so deflect the anger of the gods away from the human community. Romans occasionally disposed of human hermaphrodites in a similar manner, regarding them also as dangerously unnatural. In Rome's courts, a defendant, even if convicted of murder, could normally go into exile to avoid capital punishment. Not so for a man guilty of parricide, for whom the sack awaited.[12]

As Erucius wrapped up his case, some of the audience might well have started crying out "To the sack!" The penalty could cleanse the city of not just the kin-murder but all the blood spilled in the civil war. It would be cathartic. Little did the onlookers know what the untested lawyer for the defense had in store for them.

All eyes now turned to the defense. Sitting there on the bench with Roscius junior were several young nobles from the families the victim had been close to. But it wasn't any of them who stood up to speak. Instead, another man rose, young, skinny, a near nobody. He'd never spoken in a criminal case before. Like the accused, he came from a country town. It was Cicero.

Erucius seemed to breathe a sigh of relief as the novice lawyer began. "I suppose you are wondering, members of the jury, why is it that when so many distinguished orators and men of the highest rank are sitting here, I in particular should have stood up to speak," Cicero opened.[13] Erucius's mood—at least according to Cicero's later account—only lightened more. The prosecutor started whispering jokes. He was already thinking more about the dinner he would enjoy that night, Cicero suggested, than the case at hand.

But then Cicero said something that nobody had expected. It was like a thunderclap on a clear, bright day. "The property of the father of my client, Sextus Roscius, . . . is worth 6 million sesterces," Cicero told the jurors.[14] That was a fortune far beyond what many of the nobles could count in their account books. And yet, Cicero continued, all that valuable property had been sold for just 2,000 sesterces. The buyer? Lucius Cornelius Chrysogonus. At the mention of the name, according to Cicero, Erucius jumped to his feet, stunned. Men started scurrying from the Forum to get word to Chrysogonus. He was being dragged into a case that no longer looked so open-and-shut.

Chrysogonus, a young man, had been a slave of the dictator Sulla but gained his freedom, which was not uncommon in Rome. He cut a familiar figure in the Forum, where people gathered not just to carry out trials and other public business but also to shop and exchange news and gossip. Since being freed, Chrysogonus had obtained a house on the nearby Palatine Hill, the city's best address, and reportedly filled it with rare and valuable bronze statues confiscated during the civil war. Chrysogonus, Cicero now told the jurors, was "altogether the most powerful man in Rome today."[15] Cicero continued: "He makes the following demand of you, members of the jury. Since he has illegally seized the large and handsome estate of another man, and since the life of Sextus Roscius seems to block him from keeping the estate, he wants you to free his mind of all uneasiness and banish his fears."[16] Chrysogonus, in other words, wanted Roscius convicted so that he could freely enjoy his ill-gotten gains.

Cicero's sensational claim captured the attention of the jurors and the audience. In an instant, he had turned the trial inside out. Far from being a murderer, Cicero's client now was an innocent victim of a civil war profiteer, and now in danger of losing his life. That was why, Cicero explained, the defendant had come to court with a bodyguard, as the jurors had earlier seen with their own eyes.[17] The true criminals were on the prosecution's side, and they planned to use the court as the final step in their diabolical plot to seize the late Roscius's wealth. As Cicero neared the end of his brief introduction, he issued a warning: "Unless you reveal your true feelings in this trial, then greed, crime, and recklessness will break all bounds; murders won't only be committed secretly but also here in the Forum, before your tribunal, Marcus Fannius, before your feet, members of the jury, among these very benches."[18] The court, far from stopping the spate of recent killings, would become a kill zone itself.

In keeping with the standard rules of rhetoric, Cicero next gave a seemingly straightforward statement of the facts that fleshed out his opening assertions. "I will set out for you the story of what happened, from the beginning," he told the jurors.[19]

Cicero started with the victim, Sextus Roscius of Ameria. Roscius had an ongoing feud with two of his relatives. One was Titus Roscius Magnus, who was now sitting on the prosecution bench next to Erucius. The other was an older man, Titus Roscius Capito, currently "in possession of three farms that belong to my client."[20] While Roscius junior farmed in Ameria, Magnus was in Rome, where the nighttime murder had taken place. In fact, it was a freedman (a formerly enslaved person) of Magnus who brought the news of the death to Capito, in Ameria, the next morning.

Just four days later, Magnus and Capito got word to Chrysogonus, who was at the camp of Sulla in Etruria (today's Tuscany). It was a simple matter for the dead man's two kinsmen and Sulla's freedman to get their hands on the farms. The proscription list had been closed a few months before, but the elder Roscius's name could be added retroactively. It was. Then Chrysogonus could buy the farms at auction—or pretend to buy them—without Sulla's knowledge. Capito was ultimately given three of the farms, while the freedman Chrysogonus received the other ten. Magnus was given a job managing the properties. Cicero said that Magnus, who had once been forced to lead an impoverished life, now spent wildly.[21]

People in Ameria, where the murdered Roscius had been in charge, of course were shocked. The local council passed a decree that representatives of the city should go to Sulla to restore the dead man's name and the innocent son's property. But the conspirators dealt with that. When the town's representatives arrived in Sulla's camp, Chrysogonus went out to see them and headed off a meeting with Sulla. The freedman next had a few high-ranking associates of Sulla assure the representatives that Chrysogonus would see that justice was done.

Then came the final step of the conspiracy. The plotters needed to get rid of Roscius junior. Killing him shouldn't have been hard, Cicero said, for "that old and experienced gladiator, Capito," and his pupil, Magnus.[22] Unexpectedly, though, Roscius found a protector. The conspirators had apparently reckoned that none of the dead father's noble friends would want to help Roscius junior. Most had too much at stake and perhaps were too afraid of the power of Chrysogonus and Sulla to protest the clearly fraudulent sale of the farms. But one person felt secure enough in her position to do so: Caecilia Metella, daughter of one of Rome's most powerful families. She gave shelter to Roscius in her house in Rome. Unable to murder him, the conspirators made a different move: they would accuse Roscius of murdering his father instead, with the help of an experienced prosecutor. Rome had gone so long without trials, surely the jurors would want to convict, especially in a case of parricide. What better way to get rid of Roscius than sew him up in a sack and dump him in the sea?

After presenting his summary of events, Cicero heaped on the outrage for a couple of minutes, as any good orator would. "What should I protest first?" he asked, and many indignant questions followed.[23]

He then moved to the next part of a formal speech after the statement of facts, the *partitio*, the "division" of the argument into its main components: "There are three things, as far as I can judge, which are working against Sextus Roscius today: the charge that his opponents have brought, their violence, and their power."[24] He continued, "The prosecutor Erucius undertook the fabrication of the charge; the part involving violence was claimed by Magnus and Capito; and what Chrysogonus, who is the most powerful, brings to the fight is power. About all three of these matters I know that I need to speak."[25]

Cicero's debut in the criminal courts was putting his rhetorical training on glorious display. He was born in 106 BC in the country town of Arpinum south of Rome. His father took him to the city in childhood for education, along with his younger brother Quintus and their cousins. The Ciceros were of equestrian rank and owned a house in a fashionable neighborhood of Rome on the slope of the Esquiline Hill known as the Keels (so named for buildings that resembled ship keels). The family had connections with some of the great nobles, just as the late Roscius did. By his teenage years, Cicero was regularly visiting the swanky Palatine mansion of Senator Lucius Licinius Crassus, which, unusually for its day, was decorated with columns of Greek marble. Crassus had a reputation for luxurious living. He mourned profusely when his favorite pet eel died, as if he had lost a daughter. A colleague in the Senate criticized him for this excess, to which Crassus retorted, "You buried three wives, didn't you, without shedding a tear?"[26]

The witty Crassus was considered one of the finest orators of his day. At his elegant house he hosted Greek teachers of rhetoric, with whom he practiced. Cicero was instructed by these Greek teachers. He learned, too, from Crassus himself, who spoke Greek as fluently as the teachers and possessed a complete command of rhetorical theory himself.

Cicero also visited the senator Marcus Antonius, whose staff Cicero's uncle had served on when Antonius led a war against pirates in Asia Minor. While Crassus excelled in the cut and thrust of senatorial debate, Antonius was better suited for criminal trials. His memory was excellent. It was said that he knew just how to organize his speech, arranging each element as a general lays out his infantry, cavalry, and skirmishers.[27] Above all, he was the master of dramatic gestures. He knew when to stand still, when to pace around, when to stomp his foot down.

Rhetoric, as developed by the Greeks, offered a system of rules for public speaking. Its five main branches were (1) invention, or finding arguments (*inventio*); (2) arrangement of the speech (*dispositio*); (3) style (*elocutio*); (4) memory (*memoria*); and (5) delivery (*actio*). A precocious Cicero began writing a massive work on rhetoric several years before delivering his defense of Roscius. He finished only the first part, on invention, before abandoning it. This treatise, *On Invention*, survives and is useful for understanding how murder cases were argued in the courts of Rome. According to the rhetorical theory Cicero expounded in his book, judicial speeches proceed from one of three issues: was a thing done or not, was it lawful or unlawful, or was it good or bad.[28] In other words, a case is an attempt to answer a question. With a murder, it might be a question of legality or morality, such as an instance of self-defense. But normally with a murder case, the question was whether the deed had been done and by whom.

Cicero gave an example. On a highway, one traveler joined another who had a large amount of money. As the two went along they conversed, and when they stopped at the same inn they agreed to dine together and share a room. After dinner they went to bed. Then the innkeeper—the truth was only found out later, when he had been caught in another crime—came into the room where both weary travelers were sleeping. He drew the sword of the man without money, killed the rich traveler, took the money, replaced the blood-stained sword in its sheath, and went back to bed. Long before dawn, the poorer traveler woke up, addressed his new friend, heard nothing, and set out. Soon, the innkeeper cried, "Murder!" and pursued the traveler, who was caught with the blood-stained sword, brought to the city, and put on trial.[29]

The question in this case is one of fact: Did the traveler commit murder? For both the prosecution and the defense, explained Cicero, arguments would be based on "the reason for the action, the character of the person involved, and the deed itself."[30] Thus the prosecutor would argue that the accused had the motive of stealing his companion's money. Establishing motive is crucial, according to Cicero. No one will believe a crime has been committed unless a reason is given. As for arguments based on character, in this case a prosecutor could argue that the defendant had previously stolen. Cicero explained, "There is little foundation for a motive for a crime unless enough suspicion is cast on the character of the accused that it will not seem inconsistent with such wrongdoing."[31] Finally, there is the "act itself"—the place, the time, the occasion, the opportunity.[32] Here, the accused approached the rich man, dined with him, left the inn alone, and was found with a blood-stained sword.

Motive, character, opportunity: it will all sound familiar to readers of modern detective stories. Speeches in the Roman murder court were often a matter of "Whodunnit?" The difference is that today, while motive, character, and opportunity suggest lines of inquiry, in a detective story or an actual murder trial we seek factual evidence for guilt: a confession by the murderer when confronted by some damning piece of evidence, for example, or a sample of their DNA on the victim. Roman lawyers talked about material evidence, like the blood-stained sword in Cicero's example, and jurors could make decisions on the basis of evidence or a lack of it. But arguments from probability had great weight: so-and-so is the *sort* of person who would do that, and so he did.

Or—if you were speaking for the defense—so-and-so is the sort who would *not* do that.

Cicero's defense was like a spear with three prongs. You could almost picture it as the trident of the sea god Neptune. The first prong was a rebuttal of the case Erucius had made against the accused. "Sextus Roscius is alleged to have killed his father," Cicero began.[33] That is a huge, terrible, extraordinary crime. Only somebody of "unparalleled violence" would kill his own father.[34] Yet, Cicero asked, what kind of man was Roscius junior? A young man, led on by others? No, Roscius was over forty years old. All right, he must be "an old cutthroat, a man prone to violence, often involved in murder."[35] But the prosecution didn't even hint at that. Well, it was his extravagance, debts, and greed that drove him. But Erucius had cleared the accused of extravagance: Roscius never dined out. He had no debts. And how could a farmer who had always lived in the countryside be greedy?

There must be a great motive for a man to kill his father. Erucius had claimed there was: the elder Roscius disliked his son and was going to disinherit him. Cicero now threw back some questions: What reason was there for the father's hatred? If there were such hatred, why had the father turned over all those fine and productive farms to his son to manage? Isn't that what men of country towns most wanted, to have their sons manage the estate?

As Cicero probed the alleged motive, he made a series of arguments that would be inadmissible in a modern lawyer's case but show the ancient orator's art of discovery (*inventio*). Erucius had claimed there was proof of the father's hatred for his son: while the father had two sons alive, he kept by his side the one who had later died. Cicero turned to the prosecutor and said, "Please don't take offense, Erucius, at what I am going to say. I speak not by way of reproach but as a reminder. Even if fortune hasn't allowed you to know who your father is and so to learn how a father feels toward his children, nature at least has endowed you with some human feeling. Along with this is your pursuit of learning, which makes you no stranger to literature."[36] The scurrilous claim that the prosecutor's mother had slept around, shocking as it seems now, was acceptable in a Roman court, where character assassination was part of the legal process. Some of the jurors might have laughed, and if so, Cicero would have paused—a key part of effective public speaking.

He then got to his point. He asked Erucius to recall a famous play, a comedy, in which an old man has two sons, one of whom lives with him in the city and the other in the countryside. Cicero pointed out that anyone familiar with the play knows that the father loves both of the sons.[37]

The defense attorney pressed on: Since when was it a crime to be a farmer? Wasn't farming the most honorable profession one could imagine? It's a good thing Erucius hadn't tried to be a prosecutor back in the days when men were summoned from the plow to hold a consulship. Cicero gave a historical example: a Roman of several centuries earlier, the "famous Atilius," who was found sowing seed with his own hands when summoned to Rome for a military command.[38] Men like that had made the Roman empire flourish, as much as their own fields.

Finally Cicero turned to what would be a concrete reason to kill: the father was intending to disinherit his son. Yet Erucius hadn't proven that, and hadn't even tried to prove it, according to Cicero.

The case was flimsy. And why, exactly, was the prosecutor making it? He had no personal reason to do so. The deceased was not Erucius's own relative. Everyone could see, Cicero said, that Erucius had come before the court for his own financial gain.[39] Here was the usual dig against professional prosecutors, to which Cicero added a threat. Erucius had better watch it, or he'll be tried for having knowingly launched an unfounded prosecution.

Cicero finally moved off motive and onto another line of argument recommended by the rhetorical handbooks: "clear traces of the crime: where the deed was committed, by what means, by whose hand, and at which time."[40] For the atrocious act of parricide, Cicero suggested, proof should abound. Somebody who kills his own father must be visibly disturbed, for example.

To support his claim, Cicero reminded the jurors of a notorious murder that had taken place a few years earlier.[41] A certain Titus Cloelius from the town of Tarracina, a well-known man, had gone to bed after dinner in the same room as his two adult sons. The next morning, he was discovered with his throat slit. There was no slave or free man on whom suspicion obviously fell. The sons who had been sleeping next to their father claimed they had no knowledge of what had happened. In the absence of other suspects, the two sons looked guiltiest. With no police, the matter would have to be investigated in court. The sons were charged with parricide—by the brothers of the deceased (a detail omitted by Cicero but preserved in another source). Cicero gave a taste of the prosecution's arguments: Was it believable that neither of the sons saw anything? Believable that someone would venture into the room when the sons were there, able to see everything and fight back? And what other suspect was there? Yet once it was made clear to the jury that, when the door was opened, the sons were found sleeping, they were acquitted: no juror could believe that anybody could commit parricide and fall asleep afterward.

The intriguing tale shows how trials turned on evidence but also elaborate argumentation and general beliefs about human nature. Murderers of their own parents can never rest in peace, Cicero continued, and he drew again from the well of literature: "The poets have handed down stories to us of sons who exacted punishment from their mothers to avenge their fathers."[42] The reference here is to figures of Greek myth, such as Orestes. He murdered his mother, Clytemnestra, after she had killed her husband, Orestes's father, King Agamemnon. In poetic accounts, parricides, even those who avenged their fathers, were hounded by the Furies, primeval deities who rise up from the underworld after a terrible crime has been committed. The Furies, hags with snakes for hair, brandished flaming torches and metal-studded whips to drive the guilty mad. Romans were familiar with these frightening creatures from the tragedies staged in their theaters. Of course, Cicero said, those were only plays, but his argument reinforced a connection between parricide and madness that would have resonated with his audience.

To conclude his discussion of Erucius's case, Cicero turned to opportunity: How did Roscius commit the crime? He was not in Rome himself, so was it hired assassins? There was no proof. Slaves, then? This second alternative gave Cicero a chance to resume his attack on the excessive power of Chrysogonus.[43]

Rome was a slave society, and slavery's brutality seeped like cold air into every corner of life. It was normal to question the slaves of a slaveowner who was killed. For their evidence to be deemed valid in court, it had to be extracted under torture. Otherwise, it was thought, the slaves could not be relied on to tell the truth. Roscius junior would have consented to such an interrogation, Cicero said, but of course the slaves of his father had been confiscated along with the rest of the estate. Of the victim's large household, not even a single "boy" was left to serve food to Cicero's client: a situation clearly meant to evoke the jurors' pity.[44] By "boy" Cicero could mean an adult: enslaved males in Rome had to endure this epithet as long as they were in bondage. Two of the young nobles helping Roscius junior had asked Chrysogonus to make available the slaves who had been with the elder Roscius when he was murdered. The freedman wouldn't allow it. Perhaps he wanted to protect his property. But Cicero made the most of it, to stir indignation and outrage against the freedman. What could be crueler than not to let a son interrogate slaves about the murder of his father? Cicero asked.[45]

The slaves were not essential for Erucius's case. According to the prosecution's theory, the accused could have relied on some of the many assassins who had collected bounties during the proscriptions. Cicero once more tried to turn the argument upside down. So people were being killed? On whose orders? On the orders of the profiteers, right? Everyone knew that "cutthroats and cutpurses were often the same men."[46] Men like these, who ran around Rome day and night, whipping out weapons, intent on plunder and bloodshed, now wanted to hold poor Roscius junior responsible for all the suffering and wickedness of that time.

Cicero summed up the first part of his case by stating that Erucius's charges lacked foundation and it was time to stop discussing them: "Instead, let us find out where the crime really exists and can be discovered."[47] The crowd's ears must have pricked up at this. They had heard Cicero do his best to demolish the case against his client. Was he going to tell them now who really murdered Roscius senior?

# CHAPTER 2

# The Money Trail

The trial of Roscius came at a critical time for Rome. After bloody victory in civil war Sulla enjoyed absolute power, but with his new courts he was trying to reestablish the rule of law. The question was whether these courts would deliver just verdicts. Long before Sulla, the Romans had been trying to work out how best to prosecute those who had harmed the public interest. There had been frequent controversies over particular trials and, as a result, many reforms: new laws, new courts, new ways of selecting jurors. Sulla's own legislation was more comprehensive than any that came before. But might his courts be highjacked by those who had profited in the civil war and proscriptions? Cicero repeatedly reminded the jurors of their duty not to let that happen. He argued that a vote to acquit Roscius would be a vote for the return of legality. Cicero was not wrong about the stakes of the trial. But good lawyer that he was, he framed the issue in a way most useful to his client.[1]

That's one point to keep in mind about his defense of Roscius. Another is that in a contemporary criminal trial, the object is to weigh the guilt or innocence of one person, and one person alone. Casting sufficient doubt on the prosecution's case may be an adequate defense. This would generally be deemed unsatisfying in the Roman courts. Ideally the defense lawyer would spin a whole new narrative of what happened. In a murder defense, it was practically a requirement to pin the charge on somebody else. Sometimes the defense would even claim that suspicion attached to the prosecution—and suspicion was, of course, a sound basis for argument. The result was a counteraccusation, what Greek teachers of rhetoric termed the *antikategoria*.[2]

This was a key part of Cicero's defense at his debut trial. After doing his best to undermine the arguments of Erucius, he turned to the second prong of his case: the guilt of Magnus and Capito. In essence, Cicero became a prosecutor himself. "You found no motive in Sextus Roscius," he said to Erucius, "but I find one in Magnus."[3]

Cicero shifted his gaze and continued: "For it is with you, Magnus, that I have a problem, since you are sitting on the prosecution benches and you openly profess yourself our enemy. About Capito, we shall see later, if he comes forward as a witness, as I hear he is prepared to do. Then I shall tell him about the other prizes he has walked off with, which he doesn't even suspect that I have heard of."[4]

One of the most famous legal phrases used in Rome, still invoked today, is *cui bono?* or who stands to gain? It was coined by Lucius Cassius Ravilla, a politician active a couple of generations before Cicero who won lasting acclaim for his sternness in judicial matters. One of his signature reforms was the introduction of secret ballots in certain trials, with a view to more honest—and severe—verdicts. As Cicero began his case against Magnus, he recalled the immortal phrase: "The well-known Lucius Cassius, thought by the Roman people to be an extremely conscientious and wise juror, made a habit of constantly asking in trials: *cui bono?*"[5] *Cui bono?* was, and is, a sound basis for a criminal investigation. As Cicero explained to the jurors, "It's the way of the world that no one attempts to commit a crime without hoping for some gain."[6] Often the hope is for financial gain, such as the man who kills his brother to collect an inheritance from him. Or a person might kill for revenge.

Cicero claimed that any juror who asked *cui bono?* in this trial would have only one answer: the prosecution side. All the wealth was now divvied up among them, and Sextus Roscius had nothing—not even one slave "boy" to bring him his meals. Magnus, in particular, had previously been poor, greedy, and locked in disputes with Sextus Roscius senior over property. He was the sort who attacked members of his own family, as his prosecution of Roscius junior showed. Both character and motive told against Magnus. As for opportunity, where was Roscius senior killed? Rome. And where was Magnus at the time? Rome. Cicero recalled Erucius's insistence that at the time of the proscriptions there had been many assassins in the city killing with impunity.[7] And who were those assassins? Either those involved in buying up confiscated property or those who took pay from the buyers. The fact that Magnus and Capito were in possession of confiscated property pointed to their guilt in the murder.

Continuing with his miniature prosecution, Cicero looked at what happened after the murder. This was another set of clues a lawyer might call on in a criminal trial. If a family member failed to mourn for a deceased relative, for instance, that might raise suspicions, and it was up to a lawyer to spell that out. In the trial of Roscius junior, there was for Cicero one clue above all others—a through line for the jurors to follow, like the thread that led the Greek hero Theseus out of the Labyrinth on Crete. It was the wealth of the late Roscius.

Cicero reminded jurors of the narrative he had earlier recounted in his speech. Right after the killing of Roscius senior, a freedman of Magnus had made his speedy journey—to Capito in Ameria. Capito had the news by dawn the next day. Cicero wasn't suggesting that the freedman messenger struck the fatal blow himself—not yet. He joked that he would not search the freedman's clothing now for a weapon.[8] Cicero claimed that it was suspicious that the freedman immediately knew of the murder, and that Capito was the first in Ameria to learn the news. He tried to cover over a lack of proof for his assertions with arguments about Capito's character: "I hear there is no form of murder he hasn't used a number of times, killing many with weapons, many with poison."[9] Once, Cicero claimed, Capito even pushed a man off a bridge into the Tiber River in Rome.[10]

Four days after Roscius was killed, news of the death reached Chrysogonus at Sulla's camp in central Italy. Chrysogonus saw to it that the property was sold off at once. Cicero lacked direct evidence, but he insisted that it was clear who brought the news: those who got a cut in the property. Three farms of great value went to Capito, while Magnus, along with Chrysogonus, got the rest.

Next Capito came to the camp as part of the delegation sent by the council of Ameria to protest what had happened. He warned Chrysogonus that if the matter reached Sulla they would all be in trouble. According to Cicero, it was now that Capito secured possession of the three outstanding farms, while fobbing off the other members of the delegation with excuses to delay their seeing Sulla.[11]

Magnus, Capito, and Chrysogonus each played key parts in the conspiracy. Magnus was in Rome to see that Roscius senior was killed and to get the news to Capito. Magnus and Capito then got in touch with Chrysogonus, who seized the farms from Roscius junior. Finally, Capito prevented the embassy from meeting with Sulla, and Chrysogonus upheld the seizure of the property. Chrysogonus was not directly implicated in the murder, nor was Sulla, as Cicero said repeatedly. But the two kinsmen of the late Roscius, the old "gladiator" and his "pupil," were.

Cicero's case that Magnus and Capito bore responsibility for the murder suffers from certain weaknesses, as many readers have doubtless suspected. How could the two have known that, when Roscius was killed, after the proscriptions had officially ended, Chrysogonus would see to it that the dead man's name was added to the list? Cicero cited no evidence. His own narrative of the various journeys suggests the conspiracy only formed after the murder. Capito's inclusion in the embassy sent by the council of Ameria suggests he was not initially under suspicion. Perhaps he became involved only when he reached Sulla's camp with the other ambassadors and saw a chance to secure some of the late Roscius's holdings for himself.[12]

Furthermore, if we ask Lucius Cassius's question of *cui bono?* the clear answer, at the time of the murder, was Roscius junior. He stood to gain his father's estate, or at least the bulk of it. Only the unforeseen addition of his father's name to the proscription list changed that. This simple point has led some modern scholars to theorize that Cicero's client was guilty of parricide after all.[13]

Roscius junior's motive appears only stronger when some basic facts about Roman society are taken into account. In Rome, unusually among ancient societies, the male head of household held power over his children for life.[14] The *paterfamilias*, as he was known, controlled all the money of those within his power. If a son earned income or gained an inheritance from a friend or relative, legally it belonged to his *paterfamilias*. The *paterfamilias* might give his children an allowance, but he could withdraw it at any time. The *paterfamilias* had to grant permission for his child to marry, regardless of their age. And if that wasn't enough, the *paterfamilias* even enjoyed the "power of life and death." This meant he could punish a child who committed a crime and take the child's life without facing any charge of murder. This power was one reason the charge of simple murder developed so late in Rome. If a son allowed himself to be sexually penetrated by another man, or a daughter slept with another wife's husband, the *paterfamilias* could decide to kill the child as a punishment.

History books told of early Romans who killed their sons for plotting against the Republic.[15] But even in later times, the *paterfamilias* exercised his jurisdiction. In the mid-second century BC, for example, representatives from the people of Macedonia complained to the Senate about the Roman governor who had been sent to rule over them. The governor's father decided to examine the case himself. After hearing arguments from both sides and witnesses, he ruled that his son had taken bribes. As punishment, he banished him from his sight. In shame, the son hanged himself the following evening.[16]

The episode points to one check on the father's power of life and death: he was expected to convene a hearing before exercising his authority. Normally, he would seek the views of others, especially before carrying out a sentence of execution. Also softening the power of the *paterfamilias* was the well-entrenched idea of *pietas*, the loving devotion one member of a family was supposed to show another.[17] Fathers who showed moderation were praised as much as stern ones.

It is not hard to take the facts of the Roscius case as presented by Cicero and envision a different scenario.[18] Quite possibly, Cicero's client, over forty years old and apparently unmarried, chafed under the power of his father, who left him to oversee the farms while he enjoyed life in the city. Perhaps Roscius junior had chewed through his allowance. Perhaps he had—as the prosecutor Erucius indicated—been guilty of embezzlement. Perhaps his workload had been increased by his father as punishment. The power the *paterfamilias* enjoyed made all this possible. Those who believe the son is guilty point to weaknesses in Cicero's case, the father's legal power, and a suspicious circumstance. Cicero's speech of defense makes it clear, in passing, that Roscius senior was married at the time of his death. But his widow—perhaps Roscius junior's mother—lent the accused no support in the trial (if she had, Cicero would have mentioned it). The relative participating most fully in the trial, Magnus, was of course sitting on the prosecution bench.

Yet, appealing as it may be to pronounce Roscius junior guilty, there are some reasons to remain suspicious. First, the accused received help from the elder Roscius's noble friends. Caecilia Metella sheltered him in her own house. True, none of the nobles represented Roscius in the trial, but that can be explained by the political sensitivity of the moment. They found an able defender in Cicero, who, in the interest of making a name for himself, was willing to risk an attack on Chrysogonus. The power of Sulla's freedman, as well as Magnus and Capito in Ameria, could explain the caution of the late Roscius's widow as well. Cicero would have been less likely to publish a copy of his speech if he thought his client were guilty of the heinous crime of parricide. His arguments for the guilt of Magnus and Capito in the murder might seem weak, but after all Cicero was not prosecuting.[19]

When it comes to the "whodunnit?" we are left with a puzzle. Neither the prosecutor Erucius's answer to that question nor Cicero's seems entirely satisfying. One possibility is that Magnus, Capito, *and* Chrysogonus were all implicated in the murder, but Cicero hid the freedman's involvement to limit the attack on him (and by extension Sulla). Or perhaps Roscius senior—who exulted in the victory of his side in the civil war—was killed by some unknown enemy and Magnus, upon learning the news, set in motion the conspiracy. That there was a conspiracy, at least after the murder, is hard to deny. It is damning to the prosecution's case that title to the late Roscius's property rested on his proscription even as Roscius junior was charged with parricide.[20] If Roscius senior had been proscribed, it would not have been a crime to kill him. Erucius, Magnus, Capito, and Chrysogonus must have assumed no defense lawyer would be brave enough to bring up the conspiracy, out of fear of Sulla. For months, Sulla's minions had been getting away with schemes to enrich themselves.

Cicero was brave enough. And as he built toward the powerful climax of his speech, he turned his attention to the conspiracy and the larger questions about the rule of law at stake in the trial.

A successful trial lawyer stirs listeners' emotions. Cicero learned that lesson from his teacher Marcus Antonius.[21] He now put it to use as he tried to clinch his case on behalf of Roscius. The first part of the defense had covered Erucius's charges; the second, the violence, which was the role of Magnus and Capito. Now came the third: "As to Chrysogonus, we maintain that his excessive influence and power is standing in our way, it is entirely unacceptable, and it ought not only be checked by you [members of the jury], but punished, since you have the authority to do so."[22] Chrysogonus's refusal to turn over the slaves of the late Roscius was one abuse. Far worse was how under Chrysogonus's name "the whole partnership lay hidden."[23] The ex-slave had his foot on the neck of Rome.

Cicero harped on the illegal sale of the late Roscius's property. It was Chrysogonus, not Sulla, who bore responsibility. This was a key point. Cicero wanted to assure the jurors and his listeners that he was attacking neither Sulla nor the generals' high-ranking supporters, many of whom had enriched themselves in the recent civil war. Cicero was going after one freedman who had risen to extraordinary heights, a man against whom senatorial jurors would naturally be biased. Leading Romans thought that no ex-slave should have so much money or power.

Roscius junior, claimed Cicero, wasn't concerned about money—just his life.[24] All he wanted was to be freed from suspicion of killing his father. Before Cicero got to his client's fate at the very end of his speech, he said, he wanted to speak with Chrysogonus.[25] Roman lawyers were free to interject themselves into cases like this. Why, Cicero asked, was the late Roscius's property sold? Why so late? Why for so little? Cicero hammered at the point that it would not do to blame Sulla for any of this. After all, Jupiter rules the sky, earth, and sea—but he cannot be held to answer for every wind that blows or every crop that fails.

Many jurors probably shuddered as Cicero offered a savage picture of Chrysogonus and his newly acquired wealth. The advocate conjured up the freedman, "coming down from his house on the Palatine."[26] He also had a country seat outside Rome and many good farms near the city, where produce could be sold at a high profit. The Palatine house brimmed with antique bronze vessels, embossed silver, embroidered textiles, paintings, statues, and marbles—all stolen from illustrious families. There was even an expensive luxury cooker that contained its own heating element, for which Cicero (unusually in his speeches) used a Greek word, *authepsa* (something like a samovar).[27]

He piled on more details: "As for the great number of his household slaves and their many different specialties, what can I say?"[28] It was the mark of a wealthy household to have more than just cooks, bakers, and litter-bearers. Chrysogonus had in his establishment a range of entertainers, "so many of them that the whole neighborhood rings every day with the sound of singing, stringed instruments, and flutes, and at night with partying."[29] And look at Chrysogonus himself, with his hair carefully styled and drenched in perfume, prancing around the Forum, trailed by citizens in their togas. How he looks down on everyone, believing that nobody is a human being except himself, that only he is happy and powerful!

Cicero told the jurors that he had himself supported the victory of the nobles in the recent civil war.[30] True, he hadn't taken up arms himself and had hoped that a reconciliation would have been possible before the final hostilities, just as others had, but that was not to be. The victors exercised their rights in war, rewarding themselves and punishing the losers. But the point of the nobles' victory was not for the "lowest sort of men" to enrich themselves with other people's wealth.[31] Cicero was relying on prejudice against former slaves, but he also was attacking somebody who probably had abused his power and was counting on that power to ruin an innocent man. The lawyer warned that if the jurors convicted Roscius junior, they would prolong the illegality of recent years.

Cicero came to his conclusion, the *peroratio*. This was a standard element of ancient speeches, for which rhetorical handbooks offered many rules. Cicero himself, in *On Invention*, said the speaker's job here was to sum up his points, excite ill will against the opponent, and arouse the audience's pity.[32] There are similarities with the closing statement of a modern court case, but ancient lawyers had more license to appeal directly to the jurors' feelings rather than the evidence and the law. Spare the accused, they might say, out of pity for his poor children or his parents, who would be paraded before the jurors in rags.

In the defense of Roscius, Cicero avoided explicitly ticking off his arguments, instead presenting his client in the most pathetic light. Roscius was "a country farmer, inexperienced in the ways of the world."[33] He had been forced to give to Chrysogonus all his property, his clothes, even the gold ring equestrians wore as an insignia of their status. He had not a single memento of his father. Roscius had been thrown naked off his property, like a shipwrecked man. Was Chrysogonus going to complain that Roscius now sat in court clothed, thanks to the kindness of that great woman Caecilia Metella? One hope now remained for the loyal son: the "goodness and mercy" of the jurors.[34] "If this remains, even now we can all be saved, but if the cruelty which at the present time pervades the Republic should harden and embitter your hearts as well . . . then we are finished. It would be better to pass our lives among wild animals."[35]

At the outbreak of the trial, Roscius had been accused of the savage crime of parricide. But the real cruelty, Cicero said, was exercised by the prosecutors, who wanted their spoils soaked in blood. The jurors had a choice. The newly established court could become a bastion for outlaws, or it could save an innocent man and finally end the cruelty that the Romans, once famed for showing mercy to their enemies, have been inflicting on each other for years. That cruelty had claimed the lives of so many citizens and had even taken away their feeling of compassion: "For when every hour we see or hear of some savage action, even those of us who are by nature most gentle, through the repetition of horrors, we lose all sense of humanity."[36]

With that, Cicero ended his speech. His final line could be a judgment on the whole terrible war the Romans had been living through, in which thousands were killed in battle and innocent men were cut down to get their wealth. Social bonds and law had broken down; one crime spawned another. Cicero was defending Roscius junior, but he was also protesting the rampant brutality and injustice he had personally witnessed.

Years later, Cicero would look back to this, his first criminal case: "Defenses bring the most glory and influence to a speaker, especially if it ever falls to him to come to the aid of a man who appears to be persecuted by some powerful person. I often took on cases like this, for instance when as a young man I defended Sextus Roscius of Ameria against the power of Lucius Sulla who was acting tyrannically."[37] As has often been pointed out, Cicero did not actually speak against Sulla and took care to absolve him at every point. Yet Cicero did expose, first to listeners in the Forum and then to later readers of his speech, the wrongdoing that Sulla and others had failed to stop. In standing up for Roscius, Cicero played a part in restoring the rule of law after civil war.

Because Cicero's speech is the main source, nothing is known of the rest of the trial, such as what the witnesses said or how Cicero cross-examined them. Roscius junior was acquitted but vanishes from history, as do the other protagonists—except for Erucius, whom Cicero would face in a later trial, and of course Cicero himself.[38] Magnus and Capito are not known to have been tried for murder, but one hopes they were forced to return ill-gotten property. For Cicero, the trial launched a career. As he later wrote, "The first criminal case that I pleaded, on behalf of Sextus Roscius, drew such praise that no case afterwards seemed unworthy of my advocacy. Many followed in quick succession, which I brought to court carefully worked out after burning the midnight oil."[39]

Little information survives about the trials Cicero was involved in over the next few years. At least one was of great importance. Sulla stripped some communities of Roman citizenship as punishment for fighting against him in the civil war. It was questionable whether he could do so. Cicero successfully upheld the citizenship rights of a woman (name unknown) from one of these towns, Arretium (today's Arezzo). The verdict not only mattered for her but also indirectly challenged Sulla's disenfranchisement of whole towns.[40] Disenfranchisement made it easier to enslave a man or woman. As in the trial of Roscius, Cicero showed bravery in taking the case. However, it is possible that by this point Sulla had retired from public life and withdrawn to the Bay of Naples, where he spent his final years cavorting with the actors, dancers, and other entertainers whose company he had always enjoyed most.

Nonetheless it was not all smooth sailing for Cicero. By his own account, he was suffering from health problems: "I was, at that time, very skinny and weak, with a long, thin neck: the shape my body was in was thought almost to be putting my life at risk, if one added in the hard work I was doing and the heavy strain on my lungs."[41] Friends and doctors advised him to stop pleading cases. It seems that part of the problem was that he spoke without letup, as loudly as possible, taxing his whole body. Cicero didn't want to abandon the glory he hoped to accrue as a speaker, which he needed to have a political career. In warfare, the other field where a newcomer could distinguish himself, he had little if any talent. Therefore he needed to change his style of speaking: "Although I had been active in

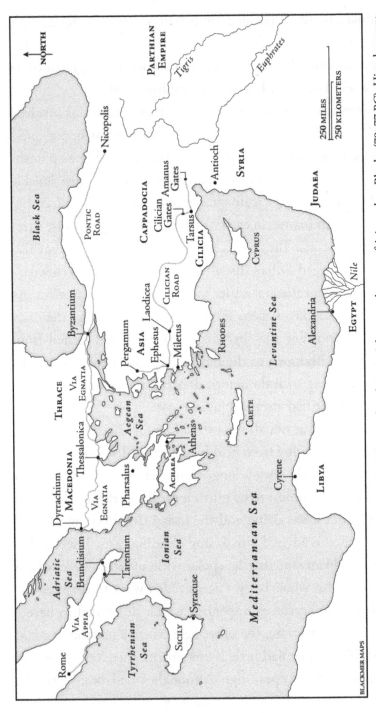

Cicero's journeys to the East. Cicero spent an enjoyable period studying in Athens, on the coast of Asia, and on Rhodes (79–77 BC). His subsequent journeys east were less happy. Penalized with exile, he went to Thessalonica in Macedonia (58–57). In 51–50 he served as governor of Cilicia, where there was fear of a war with Rome's major rival, the Parthian empire. A year later, in flight from Julius Caesar, he returned to Macedonia with other opponents of the dictator.

BLACKMER MAPS

pleading cases for two years and my name was already well-known in the Forum, I left Rome."[42]

Cicero first went to Athens, where he spent six months. The ancient city, its political power long faded, remained a lively intellectual center. Picking up an earlier interest in philosophy he cultivated throughout his life, Cicero began attending the lectures of Antiochus, a leading member of the Academy established centuries earlier by Plato. Cicero would always maintain that study of philosophy enhanced public speaking, though clearly he loved the pursuit in its own right. In Athens, he also trained with a well-established teacher of rhetoric, Demetrius of Syria.

From Greece he moved on to the cities of Asia Minor, where rhetoric flourished. Indeed, there was at this time a so-called Asianic school that distinguished itself from the more austere traditions of Athens by a flamboyant style of speech, marked by aural effects achieved by parallelism of phrases and clauses.[43] Cicero listened to the dominant masters of that time: Dionysius of Magnesia, Aeschylus of Cnidos, and Xenocles of Adramyttium.

But it was something else Cicero needed, and for that he went to the island of Rhodes, where he attached himself to a teacher he had met some years earlier in Rome, Apollonius Molon. An excellent writer and experienced advocate, Molon was also good at spotting faults in others and correcting them. This he now did with Cicero. As Cicero reminisced, "Molon devoted himself, if only he could achieve it, to curbing my overabundance and superfluity and to controlling the flood of speech that overflowed its banks with the unbridled audacity of youth."[44] Careful studies of Cicero's work before and after the stay help to explain what Cicero meant.[45] In the speech for Roscius, Cicero piled up weighty clause after weighty clause, leaving little variety for the listener and requiring himself to maintain a high vocal effort throughout. From Molon, Cicero learned to change tempo more. For emphasis, he still might bring out the bombast. But he mixed in simpler, more staccato passages, where lightness carried him and the listener along. Cicero "simmered down" his style and in doing so relieved the strain he had been placing on himself.[46] He also gained strength and weight through gymnasium workouts. His health improved, although he did continue to struggle with indigestion.

Already in antiquity there was suspicion that it was not a health crisis that led Cicero away from Rome, just as his forensic career was starting to soar. The Greek biographer Plutarch reported that Cicero went to Greece out of fear of Sulla and did not return to Rome until he got news of Sulla's death (from disease, in 78 BC).[47] Cicero had stood up to Sulla in the speeches for Roscius and for the woman of Arretium, which may have added to his stress. Yet his own account should not be dismissed entirely. There was a problem with his speaking that Cicero needed to fix. The journey fits in with his near-obsessive desire to be first. From childhood, he once wrote in a letter, he had taken his watchword from Homer's Achilles: "Far to excel, outtopping all the rest!"[48]

The Rome Cicero got back to was far from tranquil. Sulla was dead, but politicians were agitating against many aspects of his settlement such as his confiscation of lands from Italians who had fought him. A militia in northern Italy briefly rebelled against the government in Rome. On the Iberian Peninsula a tough general named Sertorius, who had fought on the side of Sulla's opponents, established a rival government. Warfare disrupted the food supply of the city of Rome, leading to riots. Cicero largely managed to stay out of the swirling conflicts and controversies. In 75 BC he would be eligible to stand for the quaestorship, the first rung on the ladder of offices. Before then, he would build up his name and make valuable connections by arguing more cases in the courts.

When Cicero returned, he found two orators dominant. One was Gaius Aurelius Cotta, a politically successful noble who would win the office of consul for 75 BC. A physically unimpressive man with weak lungs, Cotta could not move jurors by vehemence and so developed other strengths: he was clever at inventing arguments, organized his cases effectively, and used a clear style.[49] The other star, Lucius Hortensius Hortalus, was, as Cicero later put it, "ornate, intense . . . and quite passionate in his diction and delivery."[50] Sometimes both Cotta and Hortensius were recruited as defense lawyers for the same case, such as the extortion trial of a former governor of Macedonia, prosecuted by a young Julius Caesar. This allowed Cicero to compare the two masters. Though Cotta was the lead counsel, Hortensius ended up playing the bigger role, "because the surge of people and the din of the Forum require a speaker who is intense, fervent, energetic, and loud."[51]

As Cicero began arguing cases again, it was Hortensius he tended to imitate—and wanted to surpass. Hortensius was the flashiest speaker in Rome.[52] Born into a political family, he started pleading in the courts in his late teenage years in the 90s BC. He practiced constantly. If he wasn't appearing at court, he rehearsed at home. A devotee of the Asianic style, he spoke with such rhythm that it sounded like he was making music. He moved his hands so elaborately that he was even compared to a dancing girl. Hortensius also had a secret weapon in the form of his powerful memory: he could easily work up a long speech and repeat it verbatim, without notes. Once, on a dare, he sat through a daylong auction and then without a mistake listed in the right order all the items sold, their prices, and their purchasers.

Although the story sounds incredible, rhetorical handbooks offered a technique for memorization that linked complex information to a series of discrete landmarks or locations, a practice that modern experiments have validated.[53] Poetry can be more easily remembered, for instance, by associating each stanza with a familiar place.

Hortensius made the perfect foil for Cicero in many ways. Cicero was born into equestrian rank and aspired to become what the Romans called a new man, the first in his family to hold political office.[54] Hortensius was a figure of the senatorial establishment. In the civil war he had joined Sulla, and in the 70s BC he defended old associates of Sulla who had gotten into legal trouble. Many, having lost their scruples in civil war, never regained them, and they counted on juries of their own senatorial peers to go easy on them. Like a number of nobles, Hortensius was devoted to sybaritic living. He maintained lavish villas with ornamental fishponds and amassed a large collection of vintage wines. He fussed over his appearance: before leaving his house, we are told, he always looked in a mirror to make sure the pleats of his toga were perfectly arranged.[55]

Only a few details of Cicero's legal career in this period are known, but he was taking cases and winning them.[56] One clear sign of his promise was his successful marriage to a well-connected woman named Terentia, whose half sister was one of the six Vestal Virgins, an exclusive female priesthood. Terentia brought a large dowry to her marriage, which included real estate that yielded rents and produce to support the household. While once wives had passed under the authority of their husbands, by Terentia's day they were legally independent and maintained control of their own assets (unless, of course, they were subject to the power of their own *paterfamilias*). This afforded women considerable power. According to the biographer Plutarch, Terentia kept Cicero under her thumb. But

Cicero's letters suggest that the marriage, at its best, was a partnership, which was the Roman ideal.[57]

Another milestone in Cicero's progress was election to the office of quaestor in 75 BC, which brought him membership of the Senate.[58] Quaestors were financial officers who were typically assigned to handle the public accounts of one of Rome's overseas provinces. Cicero was given responsibility for western Sicily. The island was important because it supplied the city of Rome with much of its grain. While the office normally offered little chance for glory, Cicero executed his duties conscientiously and made sure that food supplies reached Italy.

He could not have known that his time on Sicily would lay the foundation for a stunning legal victory five years later that would make his career.

# CHAPTER 3

# Cover-Up

Gaius Verres couldn't keep his hands off art. A passion, he called it, but even friends of the senator reportedly said it was more like a sickness. His house in Rome overflowed with paintings and statues. In the colonnaded walkway that surrounded the garden, rare and valuable Greek sculptures stood in front of the columns, in the spaces between the columns, and even out in the open air amid the shrubbery. Stories circulated of dinner parties where, if a fine silver dish was brought out, Verres caressed it, like a favorite pet. An especially nice piece? Verres might ask to borrow it and then "forget" to return it.[1]

Verres was lucky when he became governor of the Roman province of Sicily in 73 BC, and luckier still when his one-year term was renewed, not once but twice. Dotted with Greek colonies settled centuries earlier, the island brimmed with artistic treasures. Paintings and sculptures by the most famous Greek masters adorned

Sicily at the time of Verres's governorship, 73–71 BC. Earlier, in 75 BC, Cicero served as one of Sicily's two quaestors (financial officers) and was based at Lilybaeum (modern Marsala). At this time, he established connections with influential Sicilians, especially from the western part of the island.

temples, gymnasia, marketplaces, and government buildings. The prosperous farmers and businessmen of Sicily took pride in entertaining one another, and their Roman overlords, with antique silver dishes and drinking vessels and finely spun fabrics of a rich purple hue. It was later claimed that by the end of Verres's three-year tour of duty, in all of Sicily there was not one vessel of silver, not one fine painting or tapestry, not one statue of bronze, marble, or ivory that he had not examined and—if he had liked it—taken.[2]

In Messana, on the eastern tip of the island, an especially well-appointed house belonged to Heius, a leading man of the town. On display in the family chapel was a small but exquisite collection of art: a delicate marble Cupid; opposite that, a bronze Hercules, bulging with muscles; and also two smaller statues, in bronze, of maidens carrying baskets over their heads with offerings for sacrifice. These works had been crafted by some of the greatest names in sculpture: Praxiteles, Myron, and Polycleitus. Heius had no reason to part with them. He performed religious services in the chapel almost daily. He liked to show the shrine to visitors; it was a standard stop for Roman governors of the island. Heius had no debts, either. He sold the produce of his land—not family heirlooms. Yet he sold the four statues to Verres. As he would testify under oath to a Roman jury in 70 BC, Verres forced him to sell. A Roman governor enjoyed supreme military and judicial powers in his province and could threaten to ruin anyone who refused to meet his demands. Verres's transaction with Heius hadn't really even been a sale, as the laughably low prices for the statues entered into Heius's account books showed. Verres just wanted to make sure there was a record of transfer in case he should be challenged later.[3]

In the gymnasium of Tyndaris, a coastal town to the west of Messana, stood a beautifully made statue of Mercury, the lithe young messenger god to whom athletes prayed for success. Centuries earlier, the Carthaginians of North Africa had plundered the statue, as was the victor's right in ancient warfare. But then a Roman general, after destroying the city of Carthage in 146 BC, returned the statue to the people of Tyndaris, to their lasting gratitude. They revered Mercury and held a yearly festival in his honor. On Verres's first visit to the town, he ordered the statue taken down and brought to Messana, which he was using as a sort of holding area for his loot. Tyndaris officials refused. As Verres departed, he told one of the officials, Sopater, to see to it that the order was carried out. Still the town refused. When Verres later returned, he asked about the statue and was told by Sopater that the town council had declared it a capital offense for anyone to touch the statue without orders from that body. "What's this you say, about religion, a penalty, the council?" Verres thundered back. "I'll have the life out of you. Unless the statue is handed over to me, you'll be flogged to death."[4]

In tears Sopater went back to the council, but the panicked members broke up the meeting without taking action. Verres then summoned Sopater to the governor's official seat of judgment, a folding chair of ivory, the same used by praetors presiding over criminal courts in Rome. Verres had set the chair up in a colonnade overlooking the marketplace of Tyndaris. As Sopater would later tell the same Roman jury in 70 BC, it was a very cold midwinter day with heavy rain. Verres ordered his lictors—the big, strong men who attended a Roman magistrate—to take Sopater into the marketplace and strip him naked.[5]

The predictable punishment would have been a flogging with the fasces that the lictors carried, but Verres had something more inventive in mind. Equestrian statues in bronze of the Claudii Marcelli, a noble family of Rome whose members had been powerful patrons of the towns of Sicily for centuries, stood in the middle of the marketplace. Verres ordered Sopater set astride one of the statues and tied down. To be pressed against the freezing cold metal as the rain poured was an agonizing torture. The large crowd looking on cried out in pity and demanded the council turn over the statue of Mercury to Verres. The gods, they said, would one day avenge their wrongs, but an innocent man must not die, so the council went to Verres and told him he would get the Mercury. Only then was Sopater, nearly frozen stiff, removed from the statue of Marcellus, barely alive.[6]

Perhaps the gods above would avenge the Sicilians' wrongs, but in 70 BC it fell to the extortion court in Rome. Dozens of witnesses journeyed from the island to the Forum to testify about Verres's illegal acquisitions, including Heius of Messana and Sopater of Tyndaris. Two officials from Tyndaris even stated in their testimony that Verres had promised to give back the statue of Mercury in exchange for the town withdrawing all its evidence.[7]

The trial of Verres would turn out to be one of the most famous ever held in Rome. Prosecuting for the first time in his career, Cicero threw himself into the case. The charges against Verres went far beyond extortion. In his prosecution, Cicero would argue that Verres had used money he had wrung out of the Sicilians to offer bribes to jurors, to purchase the date he wanted for the trial, and to bankroll whole political campaigns as part of a conspiracy to ensure his acquittal. At the height of his reputation, Hortensius worked the defense bench, and Cicero accused him of underhanded tactics as well. For years, Cicero would claim, Hortensius had tyrannized the courts. The trial cut to the heart of a mounting scandal in the judiciary system established by Sulla: If a senator had enough money and the right connections, could he place himself beyond the reach of law?

Extortion, the illegal acquisition of money by a Roman official abroad, was a crime where the motive was clear but the opportunities for committing it nearly endless. Governors of the overseas provinces were, first and foremost, military commanders. Their chief duty was to maintain peace within Roman territory and to police the borders. They were also supposed to uphold the interests of Roman citizens living overseas, especially those engaged in commerce. Governors would issue judgments at legal hearings to resolve disputes between citizens and provincials, and sometimes between provincials. Accepting a bribe from a party in a dispute was one way the governor could profit. Others were to require communities to pay for military protection, to demand supplies for the army or require a cash equivalent, and to offer exemptions from the quartering of troops on a town in exchange for a payment.[8]

Verres's desire to acquire rare artistic masterpieces gave rise to some of his crimes but, according to Cicero, he also stole much hard cash, mostly with the usual shakedowns. As soon as he landed on Sicily he sent a letter to the prosperous town of Halaesa, summoning a man named Dio to appear without delay. Verres said that he was looking into a large inheritance that Dio's son had received from a deceased relative. By the terms of the will, the heir was obliged to erect statues in Halaesa's marketplace or else he would forfeit the estate. Verres had somebody ready to testify that Dio's son had failed to comply fully with the will. It would be futile for Dio to argue otherwise, and so he agreed to slip the governor 1 million sesterces—a vast sum, but less than the value of the estate. Verres then insisted on taking away some of Dio's thoroughbred mares as well as the silver and tapestries in his house.[9]

At the trial in 70 BC, Cicero produced copious evidence for what Verres had done to Dio and his family. Dio testified, as did his Sicilian lawyer, Sextus Pompeius Chlorus, who had been honored with Roman citizenship. Most important, a number of high-ranking Romans also testified, among them one of the consuls of 73 BC, whose patronage Dio had long enjoyed. As was often the case in extortion trials, the tables were turned. The men Verres had accused, or had threatened with accusation, were now accusing him.

Because the Romans thought that their governors needed untrammeled power to deal with military threats, the only real check on them was prosecution after they returned to Rome. The extortion court, established in 149 BC, was the first standing court in Rome. Initially it was civil in nature. Romans and non-Romans alike could sue to recover whatever had been taken illegally from them by the governor. The defendant, if found guilty by a jury of his fellow senators, simply had to pay the money back.

Later, as corruption by officials only seemed to worsen, extortion was made a penal offense subject to fines and, eventually, exile. The scope of the crime was broadened to include acts such as the governor or his family members accepting freely offered bribes. Senatorial juries were replaced with juries of equestrians, on the theory that they would be tougher on the guilty. Sulla overturned that reform when he reestablished the extortion court in 81 BC. One earlier innovation he did keep, however, was a requirement to hold an adjournment during the trial. This meant that each side would get to make its case and present written evidence and witnesses, and then each would get a second chance. The evidence in extortion trials was often vast and complex in comparison with the other courts. A criminally convicted defendant would be forced into exile, but the court would also determine precise amounts of damages for each of the complainants. The compulsory adjournment allowed for everything to be gone over twice.

Despite the increasingly elaborate procedures, the courts were unable to hold all offenders to account. One persistent problem was that governors were also generals, and nothing lifted a man's prestige like a great military victory. It could make all the difference in whether a prosecution succeeded, as one of the most famous moments in Rome's forensic history showed. Manius Aquillius, who had served as governor of Sicily for three years, was on trial for extortion in 99 BC. He looked sure to be found guilty until, at the climax of the defense, his attorney, the great Marcus Antonius, grabbed hold of his client and pushed him in front of the jury. Antonius ripped the dingy tunic off Aquillius and revealed battle scars on the front of the general's body. Antonius broke down into tears as he recounted how Aquillius had been wounded in the head by the enemy's leader while fighting on behalf of the Roman people. Aquillius was acquitted.[10]

Even when generals weren't flaunting their scars, another obstacle often blocked provincials' path to justice. The governor could use his vast power to prepare his defense in advance while still serving overseas. One way to do this was to win over a few powerful individuals and communities. On Sicily, Verres exempted the town of Messana from onerous obligations to sell grain to Rome and to offer military service. In exchange, Messana sent a deputation to testify on behalf of Verres at his trial. In the even more important city of Syracuse, which served as the Roman governor's primary place of residence, Verres saw to it that a festival was created in his honor, called the Verria, along with statues. In Syracuse's Senate house, next to a statue of the great Roman general Marcus Marcellus, went up a gilt one for Verres, with an inscription hailing him as "defender of the island."[11] Statues were also raised in Rome itself, "presented by the united people of Sicily."[12] Testimonials like these could muddy even a clear case for conviction.

While under the rule of a corrupt governor, however, provincials weren't entirely powerless. In the first year of his governorship, Verres learned that a certain Diodorus, originally from the island of Malta but then residing in western Sicily, owned some fine silver cups that were crafted by the famed engraver Mentor. Verres summoned Diodorus and asked to see the cups. Diodorus told the governor they were with a relative on Malta and then sent a letter to that relative, instructing him to say that the cups had recently been sent to Sicily. Diodorus then fled Sicily, taking the cups with him. To get him back, Verres arranged for Diodorus to be prosecuted on a capital charge. Diodorus, in the meantime, had traveled to Rome, where, dressed in mourning, he went around to the houses of his powerful friends and related his terrible tale. Soon, Verres's father, a well-connected senator, sent a letter to his son warning him of the ill will he was causing and urging him to back down.[13]

At the time this happened, it looked as if Verres's tenure would be over shortly. The Senate had named Arrius as his successor, and he was on his way. But 73 BC was also the year the gladiator Spartacus, after escaping from a training facility in southern Italy with around seventy other men, launched what would become a massive slave uprising. Several Roman forces were badly defeated by the rebels. The Senate reassigned Arrius to Italy and renewed Verres for another year on Sicily. He was tasked with the important job of preventing the island's many slaves from revolting, as they had in two major wars in the second century BC. When the Sicilians got the news of Verres's renewal, Cicero said, they concluded that they could no longer keep anything locked up safely.[14]

Toward the end of 72 BC, another Sicilian, Sthenius of Thermae, came to Rome with more dreadful stories. Verres took the art from Sthenius's house and then demanded that the town turn over its most prized bronze statues, including one of the lyric poet Stesichorus holding a book and another of a she-goat. Sthenius, a skilled public speaker with a high profile on Sicily, had persuaded the town council not to give in. Verres then arranged for Sthenius to be summoned on a charge of document forgery. While local jurisdiction should have applied in such a case, Verres announced that he would try Sthenius himself. He ordered Sthenius to appear later that same day with his defense ready. Sthenius fled Sicily and was later found guilty in absentia and fined. From the governor's ivory chair, Verres then stated he would allow anyone to prosecute Sthenius on a capital charge in absentia. A volunteer stepped forward.[15]

Sthenius was now in Rome. He reported the attack to his powerful friends there, and the two consuls of 72 BC immediately made a motion in the Senate that prosecutions of persons on capital charges in absentia should be prohibited in the provinces. The consuls related Sthenius's story before the assembled senators. Verres's father urged the senators not to take action prejudicial to his son, but without much success. To prevent the motion from passing, Verres's father had other senators spin out the debate with long speeches until sunset, after which time no decree could be passed. As the meeting disbanded, Verres's father invited all of Sthenius's supporters to see him. "You need not worry about Sthenius," he reportedly told them. "I promise you that I will see to it that no harm comes to him through my son; I will for this purpose send him word in Sicily by reliable messengers, both by land and sea."[16] The father's appeal worked. The Senate dropped the matter.

Despite the message from his father, Verres proceeded to convict Sthenius in absentia. When the news reached Rome, there was an uproar. One of the tribunes—a group of ten annually elected magistrates, each of whom had the right to summon public meetings in the Forum—made a protest. The tribunes resolved, at the urging of Cicero (who had become a patron of the Sicilians during his government service on the island in 75 BC), that Sthenius, despite his conviction, could remain in Rome.

The outrage over Sthenius—like almost everything to do with Verres's governorship—is known mainly from Cicero's prosecution speeches. Obviously these are slanted against Verres, yet even they suggest that Verres had defenders in the Senate. Verres's renewal for a third year in office on Sicily in 71 BC also suggests this. He did not come from one of the great noble families, and his name was not distinguished. *Verres* meant "hog" in Latin, a source of many bad jokes for Cicero.[17] But Verres was not a nobody either.[18] The men in charge of Rome had come to rely on his ruthlessness in recent years. At the start of his career, he had been sent by the Senate with military funds to one of the generals fighting against Sulla in northern Italy in the great civil war. Verres defected to Sulla and brought the funds with him. Sulla rewarded Verres with estates of the proscribed. In the years that followed, Verres built friendships with other men who were climbing the ranks with him, including those from more distinguished backgrounds, such as the Caecilii Metelli. Verres's "sickness" actually helped him here. He lent pieces from his art collection to friends such as Hortensius for public display in the festivals they were in charge of staging while holding political office.[19] And so, while Verres had critics, he also had allies. Whatever he might have been doing wrong, they could point out, he managed to prevent the Spartacus War from spreading to Sicily. At a time of great upheaval in Italy, he increased grain exports from Sicily, throwing the city of Rome a lifeline.[20]

Little of this, of course, counted positively for the Sicilians, who were again in Rome toward the end of 71 BC, and this time in far greater numbers. The Spartacus War had ended, and the Senate appointed Lucius Caecilius Metellus, a member of the powerful family, as Verres's successor. The Sicilians begged Metellus to come as soon as he could. They also presented a petition to the incoming consuls of 70 BC. These were Crassus, the general who had defeated Spartacus using brutal tactics, and Pompey, an old officer of Sulla who early in his career had flushed out Roman opponents of Sulla on Sicily and made many friends there, including Sthenius. In their petition, the Sicilians asked for no more prosecutions in absentia and a ban on promising statues to any governor until he had left the province. They also asked that the governor should not require fixed payments in lieu of demands for grain and that the old system of taxation, which Verres had modified, be reinstated.[21]

The petition put forward genuine requests. The Senate had done little if anything for the Sicilians over the last few years. With Crassus and Pompey in charge, things were changing. Even before taking office, Pompey announced that the provinces had been treated badly and he intended to do something about it.[22] The Sicilians hoped for not only reform but also revenge, and the petition doubled as an indictment against Verres. Delegations from all the major communities except Messana and Syracuse started pouring into Cicero's house on the Esquiline Hill.[23] They wanted him to prosecute.

At first he was reluctant. Back in 75 BC, it is true, Cicero had spent a year on Sicily as quaestor. In charge of the public accounts for the western half of the island, Cicero had won a reputation for fairness and acquired many clients. He had enjoyed touring the province and seeing all the great temples and works of art. Nothing filled him with more joy than rediscovering, in an overgrown thicket outside of Syracuse, the tomb of the great mathematician Archimedes: a column topped not with the usual portrait but a sphere and a cylinder.[24]

Cicero could do his old friends a good deed by taking on the prosecution, but there were reasons to decline. Verres had powerful allies, like the new governor of Sicily, Lucius Metellus, and so there were political risks. Also, prosecuting extortion required lots of time and effort. Anyone who took on such a case had to carry out a thorough investigation, typically involving travel to the province in question. Those who signed on were often either young nobles with free time and a thirst for publicity or more professional prosecutors who had no political aspirations. It was defenses, more than prosecutions, that offered a parade ground for Cicero's cleverness. As the rhetorician Quintilian's handbook put it, "The speech from the prosecution is almost always straightforward and something that can, so to speak, be shouted, whereas the speech for the defense requires a thousand twists and ploys."[25]

And so Cicero told the Sicilians to have another man pursue their case, Quintus Caecilius (no relation to the powerful Metelli). Unlike Cicero, Caecilius, who had served as one of Sicily's quaestors during the first year of Verres's governorship, was keen to prosecute. He claimed that he had been among Verres's victims, which, according to the ethics of the Roman bar, was actually a recommendation: it meant he would not go light on the defendant, nor was he a pawn in somebody else's game.[26] In Rome, courts existed, in part, to enable a man wronged by another to gain revenge.

Then Cicero changed his mind. Though naturally he never said so publicly, he saw that a shift in politics had opened up an opportunity. It had been Sulla's vision that the Senate, dominated by the nobles, should control Rome. For about a decade, that vision held. The main popular assembly, presided over by any of the ten tribunes, was allowed to pass only laws preapproved by the Senate. The tribunes, who were supposed to represent the people's interests, thus had little initiative. Meanwhile, senators entirely manned the juries of the criminal courts. They might not have cared for a freedman like Chrysogonus, but they were not above ignoring one another's crimes in expectation that the favor would be returned. At times, some jurors even accepted outright bribes in exchange for their votes.

The extortion court especially could seem like a giant racket. A governor would go to his province and illegally raise money for himself, his lawyers, and the jury. Hortenius defended a governor of Asia in an extortion trial in 74 BC that became notorious. Allegedly Hortensius arranged for voting tablets of different colors to be handed out to the jurors—to ensure that those men given bribes fulfilled their end of the deal.[27] At the trial of Verres in 70 BC, Cicero would claim that Verres had told people on Sicily that he had "a powerful friend whose help he could count on in plundering the province"—Hortensius.[28] Verres also allegedly said that "he was not trying to make money only for himself, but had the three years of his Sicilian governorship divided up so as to feel he would do very well if he directed the profits of his first year to his own estate, handed over those of the second year to his advocates and supporters, and reserved the whole of the third year—the richest and most profitable of the three—for his jurors."[29]

By early 70 BC, however, efforts were underway to stop small groups of senators from rigging the judicial system.[30] As consuls, Pompey and Crassus passed legislation that restored power to the ten tribunes. Then proposals were put forward to break the senatorial monopoly on juries, either by mixing in equestrian jurors or replacing the senators with equestrians and other wealthy Romans altogether. Suddenly the prosecution of Verres was no longer just another trial for extortion. It offered Cicero a chance to latch on to a popular political issue. It offered a chance to ingratiate himself with Pompey, who wanted to help his old clients on Sicily. Best of all, it offered a chance to dethrone Hortensius as king of the courts and seize the crown for himself.

The first step was to gain the right to prosecute. In January of 70 BC, Cicero applied to the praetor in charge of the extortion court, Glabrio. Verres's former quaestor Caecilius applied as well. As was standard in such a situation, a panel of jurors would decide which of the two advocates was more qualified. Each had to make a petition to the court. Only Cicero's speech in support of his request survives. In it, he made much of the injustices provincials had been suffering for years because of the poor state of the courts. Leading men from all over Sicily desperately wanted Cicero to prosecute, he said, and their deputations were on hand in the court to show their support for him. The extortion law, he continued, was all they had: "This is the foreigners' charter of rights. This is their citadel, somewhat less fortified now, certainly than it once was; but still, if our allies have any hope left with which to comfort their sad hearts, it rests entirely in this law."[31]

Caecilius would make a much poorer prosecutor, Cicero argued. "It has probably never occurred to you," he said condescendingly to his opponent, "how much work it is to carry a criminal trial."[32] You have to set forth in detail the criminal's whole life. It's not enough to appeal to jurors' sense of understanding. The picture must be drawn so vividly that the audience can see it with their own eyes. You need to have some capacity as an advocate and experience in the Forum. It's not enough to learn by heart a phrase or two out of some old speech and think you're well prepared. You must burn the midnight lamps, as Cicero did. In fact, Cicero had never prosecuted. But few of the jurors could have doubted that he could excel Caecilius in creating a compelling story, which is the prosecutor's main job.

Worse than any lack of qualifications, Cicero also claimed, Caecilius was in collusion with Verres.[33] True, the two had fallen out with each other, but since then they had patched things up. Caecilius allegedly was implicated in some of Verres's crimes, such as requisitioning grain and then demanding an inflated sum of money in lieu of it. Caecilius's plan, the Sicilians suspected, was to win the right to prosecute and then, during his investigation on the island, remove documents that implicated Verres—and himself. Cicero suggested that Hortensius wanted Caecilius too.[34] With a weak prosecution, the jurors could vote to acquit without scandal—and Hortensius would continue to reign over the courts.

Cicero might have been exaggerating the cooperation between Caecilius and Verres, but there is no doubt that Verres and Hortensius preferred the less capable Caecilius to be awarded the case and did what they could to ensure it. Cicero's clever speech, not to mention the threat now hanging over senatorial juries, foiled the effort. The jurors selected Cicero to prosecute.

Next, Cicero formally indicted Verres and asked for 110 days to carry out his investigation.[35] As the officially appointed prosecutor, Cicero enjoyed the right to seize documents and compel witnesses to testify in court. Given the transportation and information technology of the day, 110 days really wasn't much time to travel to and from Sicily, gather all the evidence, and put together the case. Cicero asked for a short period because he was planning to run that year for the aedileship, a mid-career political office that oversaw the games, grain supply, and infrastructure of Rome. Elections were set to take place in late July. With an investigation of 110 days, the trial would start around the beginning of May and be over by the time the final burst of campaigning came.

Verres had failed to knock Cicero out of the case, but he had a new move to make. Immediately after Cicero's request for 110 days was granted, Verres had another prosecutor in a different extortion case request a period of 108 days to travel around Greece.[36] This prosecution would start just before Cicero's, which would push Cicero's back on the court docket. The trial of Verres would now commence several months later than Cicero intended due to mandatory court recesses for holidays. This would be just around the time the elections for the aedileship were wrapping up. With luck, and perhaps a few bribes, Cicero might even lose his race, bringing a loss of face. Or perhaps Cicero would be held up on Sicily. If he didn't return to Rome on schedule, Verres could have the Greek prosecution dropped, thereby moving his trial up again. Cicero would lose his case by default if he failed to appear.

If all this seems outrageous, even unbelievable, remember that the state of the courts had become a scandal in Rome. Many of the senators had been installed by Sulla after helping him in civil war; a number of them, like Verres himself, had jumped over to Sulla's side, betraying colleagues. Scruples and survival had not gone together in the civil war. For those who had killed fellow citizens and seized their assets, it was not much of a stretch to render a less than honest vote. Manipulating the court calendar was not much of a stretch either.

Cicero left from Rome at once and spent fifty days investigating on Sicily. Everywhere he went, he later said, evidence lay before him of Verres's crimes.[37] Even the countryside, which just a few years before had been blanketed in golden fields of grain and green pastures for cattle, was a wasteland. Cicero claimed that Sicily looked as if it had been ravaged by a long and cruel war.

In every town he heard tales, some truly terrifying. Others were darkly comic, like one told to Cicero by an old host and friend, Pamphilus, who lived in the western town of Lilybaeum. Verres had seized from Pamphilus a massive silver jug passed through the family for generations. And that wasn't all. "I was sitting sadly at home," Pamphilus reportedly told Cicero, "when a temple slave came running up to me and ordered me to bring my embossed cups to the governor at once. I was very upset; I had a pair of them; I ordered them both to be brought out, so that no further trouble would arise, and to be taken along with me to the governor's house. When I got there, the praetor was resting; but those brothers from Cibyra were pacing up and down, and when they saw me, they cried, 'Where are the cups, Pamphilus?'"[38]

The brothers from Cibyra? These turned out to be two art dealers originally from Asia Minor, who had been driven out of their hometown after plundering a sanctuary of Apollo. As Verres's agents on Sicily, they tracked down works of art for him and gave tips on what was worth keeping. When Pamphilus broke down in tears before the brothers, they asked him what he would pay to stop the cups from being taken. "To cut the story short," Pamphilus told Cicero, "they asked me for 1,000 sesterces, which I promised them. Meanwhile, the governor called for us and demanded the cups." The brothers told Verres that yes, they had heard the cups were valuable, but actually they were cheap stuff, "unworthy of a place in Verres's collection." Verres agreed, and Pamphilus took his two beautiful cups safely home.[39]

Cicero must have been amazed at what he was finding out, but by no means did all go smoothly for him. When the new governor, Lucius Metellus, had arrived on Sicily, he took steps to rescind Verres's unjust acts. He overturned convictions, gave back property, and restored the old system of taxation. But according to Cicero, Metellus changed his course when Cicero appeared on the island to start his investigation, apparently in response to secret instructions from Rome. Metellus began telling everyone that he wished to do everything he could to help Verres. He started asking that

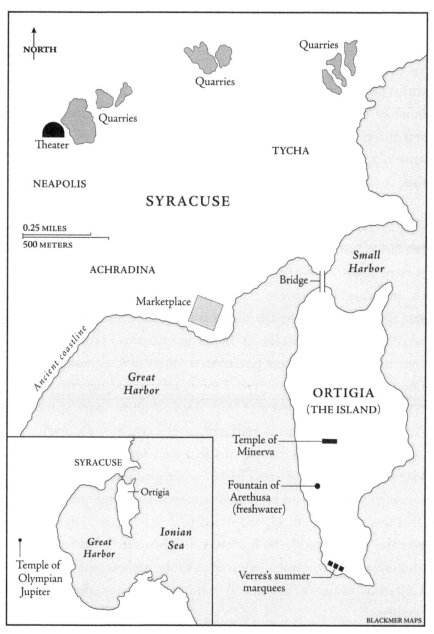

Syracuse at the time of Verres's governorship, 73–71 BC. The Roman governor was based on Ortigia, where no Syracusan was allowed to live because of its strategic importance. In the hot summer months, Verres resided on Ortigia's coast in marquees, the location of which is approximate. Four pirate ships sailed by the marquees and into the Great Harbor in 71 BC, a great humiliation to Verres. The ancient coastline is speculative.

cities provide testimonials on behalf of the defendant. He tried to deter some witnesses from speaking to Cicero.[40] Metellus's behavior was probably more consistent than Cicero alleged. He was close with Verres and wanted to help him. Metellus was trying to undo as much of Verres's damage as he could, to appease the Sicilians. Yet he was also trying to pressure them into giving up their case. It was the same old problem of the governor's overwhelming power, here being used to shield a predecessor.

The most memorable part of Cicero's investigation was his visit to Syracuse. This was by far the largest and loveliest of Sicily's cities, built around two harbors, the heads of which met at a part of town known as the Island because it was separated from the mainland by a narrow strip of sea. Syracuse was so large that it was thought of as four cities joined together. One was the Island, where the great third-century BC king Hiero had built his palace, later used by the Roman governors as their official residence. The finest temples of the city graced the Island, including that of Minerva, famous for its gold and ivory doors. Another part of the city, Achradina, held the main marketplace, the city hall, a spacious city council chamber, the temple of Olympian Jupiter, and many private houses. In a third area, Tycha, named for an ancient temple of Fortune, was the main gymnasium as well as several more temples. This was the most thickly inhabited part of Syracuse. Finally, there was the most recently built New City (*Neapolis*, in Greek, which also gives modern Naples its name). On the highest part of the New City stood the great theater, still in use today, and yet more splendid temples.[41]

According to Cicero's account, he found Syracuse stripped of many treasures he had seen there a few years before. Verres had ransacked the gold and ivory doors of the temple of Minerva. From this same temple, Verres had also removed priceless paintings of the kings of Syracuse, leaving bare and unsightly walls. From the town hall, a precious statue of the lyric poet Sappho was removed; from the Temple of Jupiter, an ancient statue of the god. On and on the catalog went. Tour guides in Syracuse, Cicero grimly joked, used to show visitors what everything was; now they showed visitors what had been taken away.[42]

Cicero arrived under the impression that Syracuse was, at least officially, taking Verres's side. No deputation from Syracuse had asked Cicero to prosecute. And so, at first he focused on collecting information from Roman citizens there and going through their records, which in typical fashion were inscribed with a stylus on the waxed surface of wooden tablets. A few of the Romans helped Cicero understand some anomalies in the records of one of the tax-collecting companies on the island. The documents showed sums of money paid to a certain "Gaius Verrucius." There was always a smudge in the wax wherever the name "Verrucius" appeared. "Verrucius" was really Verres.[43]

Then came a visit to Cicero from a high-ranking Syracusan named Heraclius, one of the city's chief magistrates. Heraclius invited to a meeting of the city council Cicero and Cicero's young cousin Lucius, who was helping with the investigation. As the two Romans entered the chamber, those gathered there rose. The president then asked the distinguished Roman visitors to be seated. The oldest and most influential member of the council, Diodorus, the son of Timarchides, proceeded to make a speech. The thrust of it was that the Syracusans were distressed that Cicero, who had informed all the other Sicilian communities of his mission of help and deliverance, had done nothing of the kind in Syracuse. Cicero replied that, at the meeting of the Sicilians back in Rome, he had been asked to prosecute without any representative of Syracuse being present. He also pointed out that he didn't expect any motion hostile to Verres to be passed in a council chamber that displayed Verres's gilt statue. At this everyone groaned. One by one the councilors told Cicero everything—how Verres had plundered the city, how he had ripped off one of their leading citizens in an inheritance scam, and how the representatives of Syracuse in Rome were his cronies. Cicero urged them to rescind a eulogy that they had been forced to decree a few days before.

The Syracusans wanted to do so. First, they produced secret records from the most private part of their treasury, which listed all the robberies they had suffered. Cicero put his seal on the documents and took them away to use at the upcoming trial. As for the eulogy, they said that Verres had sent a letter asking for one, and they had resisted. Then, just before Cicero had come, Metellus had ordered them to decree one and they felt they had no choice. They had at least tried to write it in a way that would do Verres the least good.

At this point, Cicero and Lucius left the council, so that whatever action it took next would not seem coerced. The council first voted to make Cicero and Lucius official guests of the city. Next, it was unanimously agreed to rescind the eulogy for Verres. After the resolution was entered into the record, a former quaestor of Verres who was on the island made an official protest to Metellus. A hearing followed at the governor's seat. Metellus's view was that the council had no right to rescind its decree. He said that Cicero had behaved quite improperly by going in to the council and speaking to it in Greek. Cicero made a few protests and then, on the suggestion of the Syracusans, tried to seize the tablet on which was written the decree rescinding the eulogy. A Sicilian friend of Verres stopped him, shouting that Cicero was assaulting him. The two took their quarrel back to the governor's seat. Cicero asked for permission to seal up and remove the tablet, while

Verres's Sicilian friend protested. Metellus tried to rule against Cicero but then Cicero recited the law authorizing a prosecutor to possess all records and documents pertinent to the case. Metellus finally gave in.

Cicero would later maintain at the trial that the Syracusans' true feelings had come out in the end. If jurors doubted it, they need only remind themselves that the town had officially abolished the festival decreed in Verres's honor.

Cicero, no doubt exhausted, returned to Italy before his 110 days were over. Consequently, the trial for extortion in Greece proceeded. It ate up several months of the court's time, from May through the start of July, during which Cicero prepared his own case while also campaigning for the aedileship. Only in July did jury selection for the trial of Verres take place under the supervision of Praetor Glabrio.

Following the standard practice, a pool of jurors was chosen by lot. Each side was then allowed to reject some of those selected, perhaps six each. Verres eliminated the most upright men, Cicero claimed.[44] There might be some truth to the remark. Individual jurors could acquire a reputation for honesty or lack thereof. Along with incorruptibility, another factor Verres and Hortensius must have considered was bias. They rejected Peducaeus, the governor of Sicily in the same year Cicero had served as quaestor there, and Cassius Longinus, the consul of 73 BC who ended up testifying against Verres.[45] Whom Cicero rejected is not known, but he purported to be pleased with the final panel, which perhaps numbered fifteen men. Of course, once a jury was in place, it made sense for Cicero to treat its members respectfully. Praetor Glabrio administered the customary oath by which jurors swore to fulfill their duty.[46]

Now came a recess for the elections. Those for the consulship, the highest office, would take place first, followed by the praetorship, and then the aedileship, the race in which Cicero was standing. A small but suggestive episode occurred right after the consular elections, according to Cicero. The winners in the contest were none other than Hortensius himself and an older brother of Lucius Metellus, Quintus. Hortensius was escorted home by a crowd of supporters. An ex-consul caught up with the group and shouted out congratulations not to Hortensius but to Verres. He then went over to Verres, hugged him, and told him not to worry. Echoing the language used to announce a winner at the elections, the ex-consul said to Verres, "I hereby inform you that at today's elections you have been acquitted."[47]

As Cicero would later state at Verres's trial, it was this remark that cracked open the door of suspicion and led Cicero to "all the most secret plans of Verres and his friends."[48] One by one the pieces fell into place, like the tiles of a mosaic. At the ensuing praetorian elections a third Metellus brother, Marcus, gained victory and shortly afterward was assigned presidency of the extortion court for 69 BC. Then, right before the aedilician elections, Cicero learned from various sources, including a bribery agent, that Verres had used some of his illegally acquired funds to finance the election of Hortensius and the two Metellus brothers but had reserved ten chests of silver to defeat Cicero.[49] Cicero was too preoccupied with the case against Verres to pursue any of this in court. He did at least manage to win his race.

Verres's strategy, it was now clear to Cicero, was to spin the trial out into the next year. At that point, the much friendlier Marcus Metellus would take over the extortion court. In addition to that, no fewer than eight of the jurors would have to be replaced, because they had been elected to various political and military posts for the year 69 BC.[50] As president of the court, Marcus Metellus would find a way to select jurors less opposed to Verres and more willing to accept bribes.

The trial was set to start on August 5, months before the end of the year. The problem, for Cicero and his Sicilian clients, was that on August 16, fifteen days of games in honor of Pompey's recent victories would begin. Shortly after that began the annual festival of the Roman Games, which lasted through September 18. Thus there might be time only for Cicero's opening speech before a recess of more than a month. Then, with jurors' memories hazy, the defense would present its opening arguments. More lengthy holidays fell in October, November, and December. It wouldn't be hard for Hortensius to delay proceedings into the new year, at which point he would be holding the consulship but could still handle the case.[51]

Hortensius's defense strategy was extreme, even by the standards of the day, but it points to problems that were to recur in the years to come. Throughout the last years of the Republic, other defendants would try to use delaying tactics to postpone trials. An especially strong reason to do so was that winning an election would grant immunity from prosecution while in office. From high office, you could go straight to an overseas governorship, which also brought immunity. Another barrier to justice was the inability of the courts to limit conflicts of interest. Even those with high ethical standards found it hard to be impartial when the presiding magistrates, lawyers, and members of the jury were active politicians whose friends and family members might be in positions of power. Those bent on gaining or keeping influence for themselves and their allies might actively meddle in cases.

Soon after the elections of 70 BC, both Hortensius and Quintus Metellus summoned the Sicilians in an effort to intimidate them. While the Sicilians stayed away from Hortensius, some did go to Quintus Metellus, wary of his relationship with the current governor of the island. At the opening of Verres's trial, Cicero reported to the jurors what Quintus said to the Sicilians: "I am consul. One of my brothers is governor of Sicily. The other is about to become president of the extortion court. We have gone to great lengths to make sure that Verres comes to no harm."[52] Sometimes in the Roman Republic it was hard to tell a magistrate apart from the head of a criminal gang.

# CHAPTER 4

# Heart of Darkness

As opening speeches in the trial of Verres got underway, on the afternoon of August 5, 70 BC, crowds thronged the court. Many had come to Rome for the recent elections and were staying on for Pompey's victory games, due to start in ten days. The trial would bridge the gap. People had already heard a lot about Verres and his alleged crimes. There he was now, sitting on the defense bench, dressed in mourning to stir pity. At his side were his friends, powerful men in Roman society. Hortensius could easily be spotted in one of his immaculate togas, along with the two nobles who were assisting in the defense. Opposite them, on the prosecution bench, sweated Cicero. He always felt jittery, he said, when he was about to stand up and speak.[1] Although he had no assistant prosecutors, he would have had slaves, freedmen, and perhaps students to haul in the large wooden boxes from which he would produce documents and to help keep track of his case. Also sitting with him on the prosecution benches were crowds of Sicilians—they, too, dressed in mourning.[2]

An onlooker might have reflected that this trial was about more than just Verres and his future. Partisans of Sulla had dominated the Republic for the last decade or so, but that was changing. The powers of the tribunes of the people had been fully restored. Quite possibly, senators were about to lose their monopoly on juries. Meanwhile, calls were mounting for better governance of the empire. While Roman citizens might not have cared much about foreigners' rights, they did care about governors enriching themselves at the expense of citizens. It was one thing for a politician to spend his plunder entertaining the people at public games, but quite another to use his spoils to wallow in private luxury. The trial of Verres tapped into larger anxieties about wealth in the Republic.

Roman courts enforced time limits on lawyers' speeches. Cicero probably had six hours, with additional time allowed for quotation from documents.[3] Very likely, then, his speech would take more than one day. Those watching the trial could expect from Cicero the usual introduction, designed to capture the jurors' attention and win their goodwill. Then would come a discussion of the specific charges against the defendant. Likely Cicero would give a narrative of Verres's early life to show that he was the type of person who committed crimes: greedy, lustful, dishonest. In the peroration, a part of the speech in which Cicero excelled, he would heap abuse on Verres and stir pity for the ex-governor's victims. As Cicero worked himself up to the climax, he might shed a few tears himself.

But it turned out that Cicero had something quite different planned. In a stunningly short speech, not even an hour long, he concentrated on the low reputation of the courts and the growing belief that money could buy acquittals. He ticked through the scandals of the last decade, including Hortensius's use of marked ballots in an earlier extortion trial. Cicero referred to Verres's crimes in Sicily, of course—the shakedowns, the graft, the art heists—but said even more about the ploy to delay the trial to the next year, when a new praetor would take over the court and a number of jurors would be replaced. Cicero told the jurors that hatred burned against the Senate and the only way to hold on to their influence and restore their standing was by voting to convict Verres. He warned that an acquittal might lead to senators being removed from juries altogether: "This is a trial in which you will be passing judgment on the defendant, and the Roman people will be passing judgment on you."[4]

As Cicero reached the end of his brief speech, instead of the usual tearful climax, he told the jurors, "I am immediately calling my witnesses."[5] Normally in an extortion trial, a prosecutor explained in the long opening speech all the often complex charges, the defense lawyers responded at length, and only then came the testimony. Cicero was more or less skipping the first step. He would briefly introduce each charge one at a time during the hearing of the testimony itself, and after each introduction, bring on the relevant witnesses.

This was a clever move that foiled the defense's plan to slow down the trial. Cicero shaved many hours off the court's schedule by foregoing his own speech and by leaving the defense little to say in response. If Hortensius started defending his client on specific charges preemptively, it would only cast more shade on Verres. If Hortensius now tried to delay for any reason, that would also raise suspicion. At the same time, if Cicero handled his examination of the witnesses with skill, he could keep the attention of the large crowds that had gathered. Members of the public would come day after day to find out what the next charge was and learn all the titillating and horrifying details. The rising tide of collective outrage would, Cicero expected, sweep the jurors to conviction.[6]

Hortensius was caught off guard and probably made a brief response. It doesn't survive but the evidence gives hints of what he might have said.[7] His main thrust seems to have been to criticize Cicero's procedure: by not going through all of the charges at the outset, the prosecutor was undermining the requirement of two hearings in extortion trials. Hortensius would get only one chance at defense. He also doubtless made some effort to praise the defendant's record: Verres had bought statues and lent them for display in public festivals, as all Romans knew; he had helped ease grain shortages over the last few years; and as a general he had stopped the Spartacus War from spreading to Sicily and combatted piracy on the island. Hortensius would have probably said that the Sicilians were not credible witnesses. They were Greeks, and, according to Roman prejudice, Greeks had a gift for fast talk, maybe even lying. After all, it was only by a trick, wheeling into the city a great wooden horse with soldiers hidden inside it, that the Greeks had managed to win the war at Troy.

Ingenious as Cicero's plan was, it must have been frustrating for him that Hortensius got to give a fuller speech, punctuated by all his famous hand gestures, while he had to cut his to the bone. In his own opening address, Cicero almost grumbled that he would have to rely on evidence alone to establish Verres's guilt. Such a complaint, unthinkable in a modern court, shows the value an ancient advocate placed on his own rhetoric. Perhaps some of the jurors found Cicero's opening something of a letdown too. And the crowd? Many enjoyed seeing a great speaker make verbal jabs and swing the club of oratory down on the overly rich and powerful. Well, Cicero reminded everyone, there would be a chance for "a full-scale speech for the prosecution" in the mandatory second hearing. For the first hearing, the prosecutor insisted, he had no choice: "I have to counter the trickery of those men."[8]

Nothing caused more stress to a legal advocate than witnesses. So wrote Quintilian, the first-century AD authority on rhetoric, closely familiar with Cicero's speeches.[9] In the criminal courts of Rome, there were two types of witnesses: those who volunteered to testify and those who were compelled to. Only a legally appointed prosecutor could compel testimony, but he did not have the right to interrogate witnesses in advance. That created a great deal of uncertainty for him. Lawyers generally knew what voluntary witnesses would say. But, as Quintilian instructed, care needed to be taken that the witness didn't appear frightened, inconsistent, or foolish. Opposing counsel had the right to cross-examine a witness and could lure them into a trap. Lawyers were well-advised to rehearse with their voluntary witnesses, but it was best that the witness not seem too rehearsed or biased. A good witness was a modest witness.

It took a lot of behind-the-scenes work for Cicero to arrange his witnesses in the trial of Verres. He had to figure out who had the most relevant evidence and the greatest credibility. Another consideration was that witnesses needed to be able to answer in Latin, the only language allowed. In the courts, as everywhere else in Rome, personal authority counted: a prosperous well-born Roman automatically got more credit than a poor Sicilian farmer. Cicero had to decide what point he wanted each of his witnesses to make, coach them on it, and prepare them for cross-examination. He had to decide the order in which to bring on the witnesses.

During the trial, the herald would formally summon each witness up to the presiding praetor's tribunal, where they would swear by Jupiter to speak truthfully.[10] There was no criminal statute against perjury. According to Roman thought, a man who took the name of the gods in vain was doomed to destruction—by the gods themselves. The lawyer who called the witness would start the examination, then the opposing counsel would cross-examine. Witnesses could speak only in answer to a question. The praetor had some discretion to cut off an examination that went on too long, but there were no real limits on the content of testimony. A summary of what each freeborn witness said was recorded—as was, separately, slave testimony.

None of these summaries survive, but there are other sources available such as biographical and historical accounts. Also, Cicero's published speeches from the second hearings of extortion trials provide some insight into the witnesses and their testimony from the first hearings. The Verres trial, as we shall see, never made it to a second hearing, but Cicero published what he had been planning to say (or at least a version of it). From this we can recover the names of dozens of witnesses he called on and something of their testimony. We can also recover the likely order in which Cicero proceeded.[11]

It was standard in an extortion prosecution to review the defendant's career prior to his overseas governorship to establish a pattern of misconduct.[12] As always in the Roman criminal courts, character counted. In extortion trials there was an additional factor at play: misdeeds against fellow citizens typically provoked more outrage than those against foreigners subject to Roman rule. Years before Verres took over Sicily, back in the early 70s BC, he had served as a junior officer on the staff of a Roman governor in Asia Minor. Then, in 74 BC, he held the praetorship—on the ladder of political offices, the rung just below the consulship. Most praetors presided over one of the criminal courts, but Verres drew for his assignment control of civil litigation.[13]

At the trial, Cicero appears to have begun with several witnesses who could speak to Verres's crimes in the East. One witness, a Greek naval captain who had provided military service for Rome, testified that Verres had snatched precious statues and paintings from the sanctuary of Juno on the Aegean island of Samos. Another witness, name unknown, testified that Verres had seized some gold from the Parthenon in Athens. All this made for a strong start. Jurors and audience could grasp these crimes more easily than, say, complex financial fraud. The stories grabbed people's attention. Moreover, they backed up Cicero's key argument in the case: Verres carried out extortion not just for financial gain but also because of his insatiable love for art.[14]

Soon, two other witnesses, Roman military officers, had an even more shocking tale to relate.[15] While on official business for the governor under whom he was serving, Verres tried to abduct a young woman, whom he wanted to rape. The young woman's father would not allow it, and a fight broke out between his slaves and Verres's men. One of the Roman governor's lictors was killed, and Verres helped ensure that the young woman's father and brother were convicted for the murder. The two were then publicly executed. Sexual assault was almost certainly not part of the extortion law, but when the victim was high-ranking, jurors would look down on it. In Roman thinking, lust spoke to a lack of self-control that could lead to the abuse of protected groups, such as Roman citizens. A criminal was a man bent on satisfying his own pleasure rather than the public good.

Verres's case in 70 BC was not helped by the fact that the governor he had served under in Asia Minor, Gnaeus Dolabella, was notorious for corruption. In 78 BC Dolabella had been put on trial for extortion, found guilty, and fined.[16] Verres, showing his usual talent for survival, had agreed to testify against Dolabella in exchange for immunity. But really, Cicero maintained, the two had been partners in crime.[17] When Dolabella's quaestor Malleolus died, it was Verres he chose to take his place.

Jurors must have sat up as the herald summoned to the tribunal the dead quaestor's son along with the boy's mother and grandmother.[18] Young Malleolus was due to inherit a large estate upon his father's death. The elder Malleolus brought much of his liquid capital to the East and lent it out to provincials at high rates of interest. He had also brought with him an entourage of household slaves and a silver dining service. Because the son hadn't reached legal majority at the time of his father's death, he was required to have a guardian to protect his inheritance. The duty fell to Verres, a friend of the deceased. But as young Malleolus, his mother, and his grandmother now testified, Verres managed to keep most of the estate for himself. He confiscated some of the slaves—the better-looking ones, allegedly—and the silver. And what he didn't take for himself, he sold. Altogether 2.5 million sesterces was realized.

When Verres got back to Rome, he rendered no account to his ward or his ward's mother. He claimed that the good-looking slaves he had brought back were his. Young Malleolus's mother and her mother had repeatedly pressed Verres for an accounting of the money, and finally he produced a grossly false record that allowed him to keep much of the estate. Women of high rank were often seen in public worshipping the gods or watching games, but typically stayed away from official gatherings in the Forum. They could not hold political office or even vote. But they could testify in criminal trials. It would have made an impression on the jurors and the audience at Verres's trial to see Malleolus's mother and grandmother, Roman women of high status, tearfully recount how disgracefully Verres had treated the innocent child of a dead friend. Verres, it seemed, would rip off anyone.

There were other miniature dramas for the jurors to watch unfold and be drawn into. When Cicero had a certain Marcus Junius called to the stand, Junius came up with his young nephew.[19] The child was dressed in a shabby toga and, even more striking, had no *bulla*, the protective amulet Roman males wore from birth until they legally came of age, at around fifteen years. The boy's father had successfully obtained the maintenance contract for the Temple of Castor, whose soaring white columns could be seen from where the court was now meeting. When the father died, the contract passed to his son, and the son's legal guardians became responsible for executing it. Among these guardians was the boy's uncle Junius, now on the stand. Cicero's questions unspooled what had happened. Verres was praetor and responsible for reviewing maintenance contracts for the city's public buildings. He saw an opportunity. He insisted that the temple's columns were not plumb and must be straightened. He then issued a fraudulent new contract for this work at a grotesquely inflated cost, most of the profit from which flowed to Verres.

Several more witnesses backed up the uncle's story. And in case any jurors were nodding off, there was a salacious twist. Junius's guardians, outraged to see young Junius's estate swallowed up, had first gone to a member of the powerful Marcellus family, and he in turn went to Verres, but Verres brushed him off. And so the guardians then decided that the best course was to go to Verres's current mistress Chelidon, "the woman who, while Verres was praetor, not only held sway over the Roman people in matters of the civil law and in all private disputes, but even ruled supreme over maintenance contracts."[20] Chelidon told her visitors she would speak with Verres, but not even she could bend him—or so she told them the next day when they returned.

To parade a child in the court was not unheard of. Cicero once, at the climax of a defense, held a baby in his arms as he begged the jurors to acquit. In another case, he had the defendant, a member of the nobility, stand and lift his young son into the air.[21] Romans were so sentimental about children that such displays could practically flood the Forum with onlookers' tears. Hortensius knew Cicero's tactic was effective. As young Junius stood in his dingy toga before the jury, locket missing, the defense attorney loudly protested, claiming that Cicero was pandering to the audience and unfairly stirring up hostility against the defendant.

How thoroughly Hortensius cross-examined all of Cicero's witnesses is unclear. Cicero would later claim that Hortensius tried to ask questions helpful to his client when he could but often stayed silent.[22] That could be an exaggeration. But probably Hortensius did struggle to fight back, since he had little or no idea which witness would be coming next. This was why he complained so much about Cicero's procedure; it robbed Verres of a chance to defend himself. If Hortensius said little much of the time, perhaps he was engaged in a sort of boycott. He wanted to delegitimize the whole proceeding. On at least one day Verres himself claimed to be ill and could not appear in court—again perhaps in protest, or perhaps because he realized he was finished.[23] Not even Hortensius could rescue him. It wasn't for lack of payment—Verres had already given Hortensius a costly bronze sphinx for his troubles, a fact Cicero used to his advantage. At one point during Cicero's examination of the witnesses, Hortensius did say in annoyance, "I don't understand these riddles." Cicero retorted, "You should; you've got a sphinx in your house."[24]

After reviewing Verres's early career, Cicero shifted his narrative to Sicily. Very likely Cicero began with Verres's first crime on the island. Dio of Halaesa, along with his lawyer, Sextus Pompeius Chlorus, and several high-ranking Romans, including an ex-consul, explained how Verres demanded a kickback of 1 million sesterces from Dio to avoid forfeiting an estate.[25] It would be logical for Cicero to start the Sicilian testimony with this initial crime as a preview of the rest. Also, this particular group of witnesses helped Cicero to establish the Sicilians' credibility: after all, high-ranking Romans backed them up.

Cicero appears to have marshalled the subsequent testimony in a manner that allowed him to go through one type of crime at a time, as if each were a chapter of a book. A purely chronological approach would have been harder to follow. The first chapter was Verres's abuses of the justice system in Sicily. As governor of the island Verres enjoyed supreme jurisdiction—and this allowed him many ways to shake others down for money. If he wanted, he could make a lawsuit or prosecution go away. Or, through intermediaries, he could initiate a proceeding and then press his thumb down on the scales of justice. That was how he had slapped a death sentence on Sthenius of Thermae, the old friend of Pompey who had fled to Rome. Several witnesses, including a future consul who was a patron of the Sicilians, testified about the matter of trials in absentia.[26] Then yet more witnesses told jurors, in response to Cicero's questions, of how parties in legal disputes offered Verres bribes in exchange for favorable rulings.[27]

Cities as well as individuals gave testimony in criminal trials at Rome. Typically the city council would put its evidence in writing and have the statement conveyed to the court by an official envoy. The envoy would read out the statement and could also answer questions under oath. As Cicero built his case, he called to the stand a number of official envoys to share testimony relevant for showing abuses of power that harmed whole communities. Some witnesses told of how Verres sold public offices that were supposed to be within the control of the cities. Others told of malfeasance in the tax system.[28] One envoy answered Cicero's questions with such ferocity that Hortensius accused the man of being not a witness but a prosecutor himself.[29] Perhaps not all Sicilians shared the Roman view that a good witness was a modest witness.

Jurors and members of the Roman public present at the trial would care if a governor skimmed off taxes because it lowered state revenue. But by its nature, this was a less graphic crime. Jurors risked glazing over as witnesses read out their statements and unwieldy wooden tablets were produced under the August sun. Cicero livened up this chapter of the story when he requested testimony from envoys from the prosperous town of Aetna, blessed with some of Sicily's most fertile lands.[30] The lead envoy, a man named Artemidorus, told the jury about visits of the tax collector Apronius, a friend of Verres whose breath allegedly always reeked of wine. Accompanied by official slaves, as if he were a Roman magistrate himself, Apronius gave orders for banqueting couches to be set up in Aetna's forum, where he would feast every day at the city's expense. As a band played and slaves poured wine for Apronius in large goblets, he summoned the town's leading farmers and dictated how much grain he expected them to pay in tax. He also demanded an additional bribe for himself. Although he was not on trial, Apronius was present in court, probably to give testimony on behalf of Verres. Cicero used his own witnesses to try to destroy Apronius's credibility.

Cicero pulled off an even bigger stunt when he called Heius of Messana to testify.[31] This was the man whose household chapel had been stripped of its sculptural masterpieces. Heius was the head of the official delegation sent by his home city with a positive testimonial for Verres. Jurors initially would have wondered why Cicero was calling him. Cicero's intent became clear as he began his interrogation. Heius explained how Verres had worked out a deal with Messana, offering the city a break in required military contributions in exchange for its support. Messana had even built a ship for Verres, which he needed to use to transport stolen art from Sicily. Heius also told Cicero how Verres had coerced him into parting with his prized statues. And that wasn't all. Cicero asked Heius if any of his other possessions had passed into Verres's hands. He replied that Verres had instructed him to send his tapestries to Agrigentum, at the other end of the island. Cicero asked if Heius sent them. He replied that he had. Did the tapestries make it to Agrigentum? Yes. How had they come back to him? Thus far, they had not come back. At this the audience chuckled.[32]

It's possible that Heius and Cicero weren't telling jurors the full story. For a time, Heius might have worked more closely with the powerful governor than he cared to let on. Still, you can imagine Hortensius's dismay when his opponent undercut some of the main Sicilian support for the defense. It was probably with Heius that Cicero began the second-to-last chapter of testimony, on the theft of art. There were moments of humor, like Cicero's exchange with Heius about the tapestries, as well as horror, like the harrowing story Sopater of Tyndaris told of nearly freezing to death, bound naked to a bronze equestrian statue. After days of testimony, Cicero needed to keep both the jurors and the audience engaged.

He also needed to end strongly. And so he turned to Verres's military record as governor, the last—but greatest—redoubt for the defense. In the record there was one obvious weakness for Cicero to exploit. As elsewhere in the Mediterranean at this time, piracy plagued Sicily. Pirates lurked off the coasts and regularly seized cargo ships. They kidnapped sailors and passengers and sometimes sold them into slavery. It fell to the Roman governor to organize the island's naval defense, using ships, captains, and sailors supplied by the Sicilians. Verres did so, but in the third year of his tenure pirates managed to raid Syracuse itself, a blow to Roman prestige. Into the Great Harbor they sailed, past the Island, where the governor made his headquarters.[33]

When the Romans suffered military setbacks, it was not their custom to prosecute returning commanders for the defeats, as other ancient states did. In the eyes of Romans, bad luck could be to blame. But that did not account for the raid on Syracuse, Cicero suggested to the jurors. The true cause was Verres's extortion. Two Sicilian sea captains delivered testimony explaining how Verres had sold exemptions from military service to the Sicilians who should have manned the fleet.[34] He had also skimmed off money from the supply budget. The ships did not have their full crews, and the men were underfed.

On top of that, Verres had removed overall command of the fleet from a Roman officer and given it to one of his Sicilian cronies, named Cleomenes. Verres had taken a liking to Cleomenes's wife and wanted Cleomenes gone from Syracuse, while he enjoyed the woman's company during all-night beach parties. After the raid on Syracuse, as outrage built in the city over the disaster, Verres tried to cover up what happened by arranging for some of the ship captains to be put on trial for betraying the fleet to the pirates. After they were found guilty he had them executed. Cicero and his witnesses were claiming that extortion had led to murder.

Not only murder, but the murder of Roman citizens—or so Cicero told the jurors.[35] When ships would arrive in Sicily, filled with perfumes, wines, slaves, and other luxury goods, Verres would claim that the crews on board were pirates, confiscate everything, and throw the sailors into Syracuse's infamous Quarries. These had been hewn out of the rock north of the city centuries earlier, in part by prisoners. Later, one of the tyrants ruling the city turned them into a permanent dungeon. As the equestrian Lucius Suettius testified before a spellbound audience in the Forum, some of those locked up by Verres were Roman citizens and had their necks broken. The cry of "I am a Roman citizen!" was supposed to bring assistance even to the lowliest citizen, but instead it only hastened a man's execution. Verres wanted no credible witnesses to his crimes.

One of those cast in prison, Publius Gavius from Consa in southern Italy, managed to escape from the Quarries and made it to Messana. From there, it was a short sail to the Italian mainland. On a clear day, you could even see across the strait to the walls of Regium, an old Roman colony. Gavius told the people of Messana of how he had been wrongfully imprisoned and was going to Rome to complain. Little did he know that to say such a thing in Messana was akin to saying it in the governor's headquarters. Gavius was seized at once and taken to the chief magistrate. Verres chanced to arrive in Messana the same day.

Then ensued the most unspeakable cruelty, according to Cicero's witnesses, all of whom were high-ranking Romans.[36] Verres ordered Gavius dragged off the ship he had boarded. The poor man was stripped, then tied up in the middle of Messana's forum. The lictors unbound their bundles of rods. Gavius cried out that he was a Roman citizen and had served in the Roman army; a distinguished Roman in the Sicilian town of Panhormus would vouch for his identity. Verres said no, that wasn't true, Gavius had been sent to Sicily as a spy by the leaders of the Spartacus War in Italy. The governor then ordered that Gavius be flogged by several lictors at once. As the blows fell, Gavius kept repeating his appeal: "I am a Roman citizen!"[37] In vain. He was taken for crucifixion, not in the usual spot, a road outside town, but in the part of the town that looked over the strait to Italy. Mockery was a part of Roman executions. A century after Verres, another Roman governor would hang a sneering sign on the cross of an outlaw that read, "Jesus of Nazareth, King of the Jews."[38]

Verres might as well have nailed a citizen to a cross in the Roman Forum itself. The crowd at the trial shouted aggressively upon hearing the story. Precisely because of the horrors regularly inflicted on slaves and provincials, free citizens held dear their right to not be put to death without a legally prescribed trial. In the court Verres jumped to his feet. Yes, he blurted out, Gavius had been yelling that he was a Roman citizen—because Gavius was a spy! A governor had to act harshly to protect the empire. But few seemed to believe Verres's excuse. Before Cicero's witness, the equestrian Gaius Numitorius, could even finish testifying, Praetor Glabrio ordered the court to adjourn for the day.[39] Cicero had stirred the crowd's emotions so deftly that he had nearly caused a riot.

The first hearing ended on August 13, exactly on Cicero's schedule. Because only Cicero's side of the case survives, almost nothing is known of how many witnesses Hortensius called on behalf of Verres, or what they said. What we do know is that the much anticipated victory games of Pompey began and at some point, before the second hearing could get underway in September, Verres fled Rome. By doing so he lost any chance of acquittal. We have one last glimpse of him before his departure, in a story told by Cicero. At a party hosted by Sisenna, who was one of the lawyers helping Hortensius, Verres started pawing the silver. Some of the guests, Cicero remarked, were struck by Verres's folly in increasing suspicion of himself; others, by the lunacy of thinking about silver at all in such a moment. "Sisenna's slaves, I suppose, having heard of the evidence against that man, did not take their eyes off him or move an inch away from the silver."[40]

And so Cicero had won. Not only had he beaten the odds prosecuting a difficult case, but Hortensius's crown as Rome's cleverest advocate now passed to him. Over the next few years, Hortensius would devote less energy to the courts while Cicero enjoyed more legal victories and continued his political rise.[41] He never got to give the full-scale oration against Verres he had spent months preparing. But he did publish, along with his speech against Caecilius and his first speech against Verres, the series of five addresses he would have spoken at the second hearing.[42] As a set, the complete *Verrine Orations* show what Cicero achieved in the first hearing and what heights he could have reached in the second. The art of prosecution, Cicero claimed, is to "draw the picture so vividly that the whole of the audience can see it with their own eyes."[43] In the first hearing, Cicero did that with his parade of witnesses and their answers to his questions. In his publication of the second hearing, he showed how to do it with words alone.

A good example of Cicero's verbal art is the account he gives of the eve of the pirate raid in the last summer of Verres's governorship.[44] Whereas other governors, Cicero said, spent the summer traveling around the province or even set sail themselves to fight piracy, Verres remained in Syracuse. But the old royal palace where Roman governors resided "did not satisfy his luxurious and dissolute tastes." He set up linen marquees on the shore of the Island of Syracuse, "close to the mouth and entrance of the harbor, a pleasant spot, and far-removed from onlookers." There he gave parties every day for his women friends. He was not seen in public for days on end, but he did make one brief appearance as the fleet set sail, under the command of his crony Cleomenes: "He stood in slippers, a governor of the Roman people, wearing a Greek cloak of purple and a tunic down to the ankles, leaning on one of his women." Luxury had corrupted Verres. A proper Roman governor should have been wearing boots and a short tunic, conducting serious staff meetings.

Cicero did not give an objective account of Verres's governorship. Nobody expected him to. Verres's flight from Rome, however, suggests that the evidence against the ex-governor was overwhelming. Why, then, had the Senate kept Verres in office so long? Did the senators not care about the suffering of provincials? Were they just protecting their own? That does seem to be the answer, in part. One also must factor in the sudden emergency of the Spartacus War. With thousands of slaves in revolt, ravaging the Italian countryside, the Senate had little time for other problems. Verres won credit for keeping Sicily out of the war.

He also won credit, at least at first, for enforcing a new system of taxation.[45] The Romans had traditionally collected taxes on Sicily along the lines laid down centuries earlier by King Hiero of Syracuse: most communities paid a simple one-tenth of their grain crops. The Roman governor did not collect the tax himself, but instead the Senate outsourced the job to contractors known as publicans who had to bid in advance what they thought they could collect. Verres modified this system by giving tax collectors more power to declare on the spot what any individual farmer or a whole community owed, and by making the process of appealing assessments harder. Verres thus was able to raise a lot more in taxes and send more grain to Rome—even if he also skimmed off quite a bit for himself, as Cicero claimed.

With or without any fraud, the new system was harder on Sicilians, and it was one of their main complaints when they poured into Rome in 71 BC. Many of the Sicilian farmers had effectively gone on strike earlier that year and refused to work their land—so as to deprive the Romans of grain.[46] This was why, as Cicero said, the landscape looked so barren when he arrived. The strike not only brought Verres himself into opprobrium with the Senate but finally put pressure on the Senate's leaders. Toward the end of 71 BC, the incoming governor Lucius Metellus sent a letter urging the Sicilians to sow their land again and promising to restore the old tax system.[47]

While Verres's closest allies—Hortensius and the Metelli—stuck by him, his reputation must have been considerably tarnished when he returned to Rome. He had somehow let a pirate fleet enter the harbor of Syracuse and then, it seems, dealt with the aftermath terribly. He had also messed up Sicilian agriculture, which affected Rome's grain supply. Meanwhile, Pompey had made the cleanup of provincial government a powerful issue in politics. That rising tide cast Verres further adrift.

On first glance, Verres's flight from Rome would seem to show the effectiveness of the judicial system, at least in the end. He was ruined politically. By going into exile, he lost his Roman citizenship. He could never hold office again. According to Cicero's biographer Plutarch, damages were set at 3 million sesterces.[48] That seems surprisingly low, but perhaps that was all that was left in hard assets for the appropriate official to seize and auction off. According to Cicero, Verres had kept all his Sicilian loot on a cargo ship in southern Italy, awaiting the outcome of the trial. He had also stripped his house in Rome of the art seized earlier in the East. At least some of the collection seems to have ended up with him in Massilia (today's Marseilles), where he settled.[49]

Meanwhile, legislation was passed that ended the senatorial monopoly on juries. Going forward, panels for the criminal courts would comprise only one-third senators. Another third were the equestrians. And the final third were the "treasury tribunes," also men of wealth, who at one point in the Republic's history had served as officials but now enjoyed the title as an honorific. Increasing the pool of jurors meant the size of juries could grow, which would make bribery and favoritism harder.

It was a happy ending for Cicero, and the Sicilians were apparently satisfied with his performance. But problems remained for provincials and Romans alike.[50] The main check on Roman governors was the extortion court. Over the years the law had grown tougher and more comprehensive, a trend that would continue after 70 BC. But in some ways this increasing complexity made the law harder to enforce. The misconduct of senatorial juries that Cicero spoke of at the trial of Verres was only one issue. The bigger problem was that trials were highly onerous and often unfair for provincials. Going to court required a great sacrifice of time and resources. Provincials might only obtain inferior legal representation, as nearly happened to the Sicilians. Defendants had sway in Rome, even if they didn't resort to putting money in jurors' hands. For these reasons, even after the jury reform of 70 BC, exploitation of the provinces continued, and it corrupted politics. Politicians handed out bribes to win elections, then soaked the provinces to pay off debts and buy more support.

At the jury selection for the trial of Verres, Cicero remarked to Praetor Glabrio that the day would come when foreign peoples would send delegations to Rome to ask that the extortion law and court be abolished.[51] If there were no courts, the governor would only need to seize enough for himself and his children. This was an obviously fanciful comment, but it was not entirely wrong. The extortion court gave criminals a sense they might get away with their crimes, and it was hugely difficult for provincials to deal with. Bias against foreign witnesses weighed the scales of justice heavily against them.

A group of unhappy Gauls would encounter that bias the following year, at the trial of their former governor Marcus Fonteius, when Cicero spoke for the defense.

# CHAPTER 5

# The Wine Road

In the ancient world, traveling by land could be treacherous. Dirt roads liquefied into mud during heavy spring floods. In rural areas, bandits lay in wait, ready to strip a man of his coin purse and clothes and to beat him. The biblical Good Samaritan helped a traveler to whom exactly this had happened. Local peoples who controlled a key mountain pass or a bridge might unexpectedly demand a toll or slap a duty on transported goods. Romans fumed about these demands, even though they made them, too, when they took over an area. Rome built great paved highways to hold the empire together, which allowed for soldiers and supplies to be moved at any time of year. To cover costs, Rome imposed taxes.[1]

It was these day-to-day realities of empire, rather than spectacular art heists or executions, that lay behind the extortion trial of Marcus Fonteius in 69 BC. For three years, Fonteius had served as the governor of Transalpine Gaul (today's southern France). A crowd

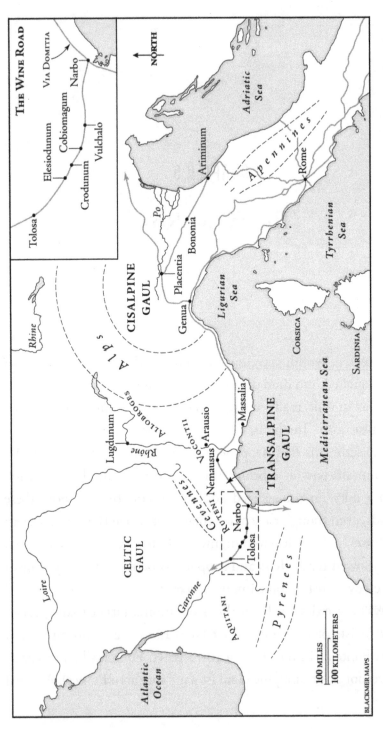

Rome's provinces in Gaul at the time of Fonteius's governorship, circa 75 BC. In the 70s BC Rome governed two provinces known as Gaul. Cisalpine Gaul lies in what is today northern Italy. Transalpine Gaul, in what is today southern France, provided a land route from Italy to the Iberian Peninsula. In the 50s BC Julius Caesar would add to the empire the vast territory to the west and north of Transalpine Gaul.

of Gauls came to Rome to testify that he had made excessive military requisitions, imposed illegal duties on wine, and accepted bribes in exchange for exemption from mandatory roadwork.[2]

Representing Fonteius was Cicero, back in his normal role of defense lawyer. Awkwardly, just a year before he had been fulminating against the abuse of provincials and the laxness of Roman juries. How, after having relied so much on witnesses in the trial of Verres, would he deal with all those testifying against Fonteius? Of course, he tried to rebut the prosecution's specific charges where he could. But his main strategy was to attack the credibility of the Gallic witnesses en masse.

Cicero acted less like a lawyer we might recognize today and more like a demagogue. He invoked ethnic stereotypes, dredging up the most infamous event in all of Roman history: the sack of the city of Rome by Gauls who had swept down from northern Italy in the early fourth century BC. Tradition held that the Gauls, after reaching the city, had murdered senators and looted their houses. Eventually the desperate Romans agreed to pay a price to lift the siege: one thousand pounds of gold. That was disgraceful enough but a further humiliation was added: the scale used by the Gauls to weigh the gold turned out to be unfair. When a Roman officer objected, the chieftain of the Gauls stripped off his sword and, with a sneering laugh, threw it, belt and all, onto the weights. "Woe to the vanquished!" he cried out.[3]

It was happening all over again, Cicero warned. The Gauls had come to Rome not to give truthful testimony but to butcher Fonteius. That was a lie, but not an untypical one in the courts. Other lawyers besides Cicero discredited whole groups of people like this and sought to deny them a fair hearing. In doing so, advocates might have helped their clients, but they undercut the rule of law and in this way destabilized the Republic.

Marcus Fonteius belonged to a well-known family from Tusculum, an ancient town in the hills southeast of Rome that had produced many leaders for the Republic over the centuries. Both Fonteius's father and grandfather appear to have reached the praetorship. His sister Fonteia was a Vestal Virgin, one of the six priestesses who kept watch over a fire in the goddess Vesta's temple—which, so long as it stayed lit, was supposed to guarantee Rome's survival. As a young man, Fonteius held a position in the Roman mint, a stepping stone to political office. He was elected quaestor when Sulla's opponents dominated Rome. During his year in office he worked in the state treasury. However, like Verres, he later defected to Sulla. In the late 80s BC he served as an army officer in Spain. A few years after that he did another tour in Macedonia, where he fought against the Thracians, a people of the northern Balkans with whom the Romans were constantly at war. While Cicero built his reputation through public speaking, Fonteius followed the more traditional path of military service. Probably in 75 BC he was elected to the praetorship, and he was then kept by the Senate in Transalpine Gaul for three years.[4]

By Fonteius's day there were two provinces called Gaul (the name came from the word the Romans used for Celtic peoples, *Gauls*). Cisalpine Gaul—"Gaul on the near side of the Alps"—is what today would be called northern Italy, the area bounded by the Apennine Mountains and the Alps. In the third century BC the Romans conquered this fertile territory and began an impressive program of roadbuilding and colonization. Like other provinces of the empire, Cisalpine Gaul became a patchwork of communities with different types of privileges and burdens. Some inhabitants enjoyed full Roman citizenship.

Transalpine Gaul was a later creation. After the Romans took over parts of the Iberian Peninsula, around the year 200 BC, it became imperative to secure a land route from the Alps to the Pyrenees. And so, they began establishing control of the Mediterranean coast and the Alpine hinterlands. In part, Rome relied on support from the coastal city of Massilia, an old Greek colony with a strong navy. In the later second century, Rome established a colony of its own citizens farther west at Narbo and built a highway from the Rhône River through Narbo to Spain. It was named the Via Domitia, after one of Rome's conquering generals (as Roman highways often were). Transalpine Gaul was predominantly Celtic except for Narbo and Massilia. Indeed, Romans sometimes referred to the region as "Trousered Gaul," after the garment that many Gauls wore but Romans did not. By the 70s BC, however, an increasing number of Romans were engaged in cattle-ranching, slave-trading, and other economic opportunities in the region. In typical fashion, the Romans subcontracted tax collection to private corporations, owned by Roman businessmen known as publicans.[5]

Fonteius had a specific assignment in Gaul. Years before, as Sulla was winning his way to control all of Italy, a number of his high-ranking opponents fled west. One of them, the charismatic general Sertorius, set up a rival government in the Iberian Peninsula, capitalizing on long frustration there with abusive Roman government and inadequate legal protection. In 77 BC the Senate sent the general Pompey to destroy Sertorius. Pompey's first step was to establish firm control of Transalpine Gaul. He fought a number of the Gallic communities there and set in motion a reorganization of the province. In keeping with the standard Roman practice of "divide and conquer," at least some of those communities who had fought Pompey lost territory, while Massilia, the old and faithful ally of Rome, gained new lands. Fonteius's job was to finish this reorganization and support Pompey in Spain. Transalpine Gaul became the staging area for the final push against Sertorius.[6]

In his defense of Fonteius, Cicero at one point summarized the governor's accomplishments. Current enemies "he subdued." Recently defeated enemies "he forced to leave the lands of which they had been stripped. From the rest, who had often been defeated in great wars, so that they might always be obedient to the Roman people, he requisitioned . . . a large number of cavalry, large sums of money for their pay, and a very large quantity of grain to support the war in Spain."[7] The categories Cicero used—current, recent, and ancient enemies—speak to how the Romans viewed the Gauls and foreign peoples more generally. "Woe to the vanquished" was, in truth, the Romans' credo.

Elsewhere in his speech, Cicero noted some of Fonteius's other activities.[8] The governor ordered improvements to be made on the Via Domitia. For one winter, probably 74–73 BC, he hosted Pompey's army during the regular break in campaigning. The force likely numbered into the tens of thousands and would have devoured vast supplies of food. Much or all of this responsibility must have been handed over to the Gauls without compensation. It's no wonder they wanted to take Fonteius to court.

The lead prosecutor was Marcus Plaetorius, a young senator from a political family whose father had been executed by Sulla. He was assisted, Cicero tells us, by Marcus Fabius, perhaps a member of the powerful noble family of the Fabii, who for several generations had been patrons of the Allobroges, a Gallic community living west of the Alps. The leader of the Allobroges, Indutiomarus, was one of the main witnesses against Fonteius.[9]

The prosecution's case can be recovered only from Cicero's speech in the second hearing, which itself is not entirely preserved, because of gaps in the manuscript tradition as well as omissions made by Cicero himself at the time of publication.[10] According to him, no charges were made against Fonteius's character or earliest life.[11] That may be true. When such aspersions were cast, Cicero would take a moment to scoff at them as empty slanders; Rome was a city full of gossipers, he would say.[12] The prosecutors did bring up Fonteius's service as an official in the mint and as quaestor, claiming that he was guilty of embezzlement: a highly relevant allegation in an extortion trial.[13]

As for Fonteius's governorship, the main thrust of the prosecution seems to have been that while making his exactions he was siphoning off money for himself. In doing so, he crushed the province with debt. One charge was that he had profited illegally from road construction. When carrying out improvements to the Via Domitia, he ordered local communities to do the work. It was standard practice for Roman commanders and their soldiers to require civilians to maintain roads and provide transport along them. A famous biblical passage refers to the practice: "If anyone forces you to go one mile, go also the second mile."[14] The crime of Fonteius, the prosecution alleged, was that he had accepted bribes in exchange for exemption from work and for certification of construction that was deficient.[15]

Another charge related to the wine trade. According to Plaetorius, Fonteius set out from Rome with a plan already in place "to establish a duty on wine."[16] Gauls did not produce their own wine at this time, but they had developed a taste for it and imported large quantities of it from Italy. Because the wine was transported in nearly indestructible pottery recoverable in modern excavation, archaeologists can demonstrate the scale of the trade. At some sites, thousands of Italian amphorae—large jugs, holding over twenty-five liters each—have been recovered. At least initially, wine seems to have been a prestige good. According to one Greek traveler, Gallic leaders served it at feasts for high-ranking or even ordinary members of society as a mark of honor.[17] It was also noted that, whereas Greeks and Romans mixed their wine with water to improve its taste, the Gauls usually drank theirs neat. In exchange for the much sought-after wine, Gauls could offer metals, wool, hams, and slaves who were put to work on estates in Italy—even estates that produced the wine. In the late 70s BC, Gauls were one of the main groups that fought alongside Thracians in Spartacus's army of fugitive slaves.

At Fonteius's trial, the prosecutors offered specific information about the governor's wine duty, which was reiterated by Cicero. He listed a series of places in his defense, all of which appear to have been located on a road that went from the Roman colony of Narbo inland to the old Gallic settlement of Tolosa (modern Toulouse).[18] This was a key trade route, giving access to interior markets. From Tolosa, merchants went northwest by river or road to Aquitania, and from there out into the Atlantic, some sailing as far as Britain. For each location mentioned by Cicero, the duty on one amphora of wine is specified. At Tolosa itself, for example, somebody named Titurius demanded "four denarii for each amphora of wine." At Elesiodunum (probably modern Montferrand) the duty was six denarii if you were exporting "to the enemy" (by which Cicero probably meant the people known as the Ruteni).

Without the prosecution speech, it is hard to know how exactly the duties worked and what Fonteius's malfeasance might have been. Was the duty paid at each stop along the way or only at the point of sale? Who were Titurius and the other men named? Were they tax collectors? Or officers of Fonteius? And how exactly would Fonteius have skimmed off money? One possibility is that he introduced an emergency duty to help fund the ongoing war effort but fixed it with the tax-collecting corporation so that both parties would keep some of the new revenue. Another possibility is that, in exchange for preferential treatment for some markets, Fonteius accepted bribes. What is clear is that an illegal duty could be a cash cow, just as legal duties were. Even Cicero acknowledged this.[19] As he snidely remarked, the Gauls thought wine mixed with water no better than poison; if only they drank as civilized peoples did, they wouldn't have owed so much.[20]

Other details in the prosecution case are more poorly known. One charge concerned Fonteius's conduct in his war against one of the Gallic peoples, the Vocontii.[21] Perhaps they had found his exactions too much to bear and fought back—a common cause of provincial revolts. Another charge concerned the way Fonteius quartered his troops in the winter. Perhaps he had relieved some communities of the burden of hosting Roman armies in exchange for bribes—much as Verres favored the town of Messana in Sicily. Still, Fonteius appears to have had no support at his trial from any of the Gallic communities in his province. Apparently all felt put upon. That might seem a weakness of his case, but Cicero would turn it into a strength.

As always when speaking for the defense, Cicero poked holes in the prosecution case where he could, appealing to both evidence and conjecture. There were no witnesses or documents, he said, to prove that Fonteius had done anything illegal when serving as quaestor in the treasury. Not one person had come forward to say they had given a single sesterce to Fonteius, or that Fonteius had removed any money. Yet the treasury, housed in the Temple of Saturn, stood at the edge of the Forum, in full view of everyone. If there had been crime, somebody would have seen it.[22]

As for the roadwork in Gaul, Cicero had several points to make. First, Fonteius did not grant exemptions. He did refuse to certify work for many. Was that what somebody did to extort money? No, Cicero suggested, it was the sign of a firm governor. Second, Fonteius was so pressed with other responsibilities that he delegated oversight of the work to two of his officers, who issued the orders and certifications. The prosecutors should have known this from Fonteius's correspondence, which, following standard practice, had been collected and turned over to the court as evidence. Cicero ordered the court clerk to read out some of the correspondence, for the benefit of the jurors.[23]

Much of Cicero's argument here was shaky.[24] If Fonteius refused to certify work, he could have been trying to intimidate the Gauls. Even if he delegated his duties to others, he was still responsible for the overall outcome. The extortion statute held him liable and nobody else. Otherwise, a corrupt governor would use subordinates to carry out all his crimes. Furthermore, even if you accepted that Fonteius delegated supervision, Cicero did not prove that the legates were innocent of wrongdoing.

At least in what survives of Cicero's defense speech, his refutations of the prosecution case are weak. It is probably no coincidence that some of his arguments are omitted altogether from the published speech, as is indicated by the headings "On the Charge Relating to the Wine Trade. On the War Against the Vocontii. On the Assignment of Winter Quarters."[25] Cicero did sometimes cut out technical discussions from the written versions of speeches. But if his arguments were strong, you would expect them to be here.

More than a detailed refutation of the prosecution charges, Cicero relied on a discussion of the witnesses and the story they told. Perhaps no Gauls would speak up on the governor's behalf. But Cicero repeatedly pointed out that no high-ranking Romans were testifying against him either. Gaul, he reminded the Roman jurors, was full of Roman businessmen, publicans, colonists, farmers, and cattle-breeders.[26] Not one of them could be found to give evidence of a crime carried out by Fonteius.

Again and again, Cicero returned to a kind of map of Transalpine Gaul, based on various peoples' friendliness to the Roman empire. There were three groups of Gauls, he claimed: the communities who had fought bitter wars against Rome years ago, those who had "just now been marked with disgrace by triumphs and monuments," and those who had fought Fonteius himself. And then, separate from the Gauls, there was Narbo, "a colony of our citizens, a lookout post and bulwark of the Roman people." There was Massilia, "the bravest and most faithful of allies." And there were all the other Romans, many high-ranking, "most honorable men."[27]

Fonteius might have had no Gallic supporters, Cicero said, but everyone else supported him, and their views counted far more.[28] The high-ranking Romans supported him. Narbo supported him. Massilia supported him; the ancient and esteemed city had voted its highest honors on Fonteius and sent a testimonial to the court in Rome. The witnesses against Fonteius, on the other hand, were those from whom, "much against their wishes, the requisitions were made."[29] That is, the Gauls.

Not only could the jurors disbelieve the sworn testimony of the Gallic witnesses, Cicero argued, they should. It is a juror's solemn duty to evaluate every single statement.[30] Even Roman witnesses who deserved credit because of their "courage, family, and exploits" might be discounted if they seemed overeager and motivated by enmity. Once, Cicero pointed out, his own beloved teacher Lucius Crassus—whose casual conversation had the weight of sworn testimony—failed to convince jurors of something he said, because it was uttered "with hostile intent." The Gallic witnesses against Fonteius were deeply biased. That was why, Cicero explained, he did not even bother to cross-examine them. He wanted "no opportunity to speak to be granted to an angry witness, no authority granted to a partial witness." Another possibility, of course, is that it was hard to challenge what the Gauls were saying.

You couldn't trust any Gallic witnesses, Cicero continued. With blatant prejudice, he said that even the least distinguished Roman citizen deserves more credence than the most distinguished Gaul.[31] "Does Indutiomarus know what it means to give testimony?" Cicero asked. The Gallic leader kept saying, "I know" instead of "I believe" when speaking from the tribunal, which was not what a careful Roman juror would do. Cicero appealed to an old ethnic stereotype of the Gauls: they were impressive physically, but impulsive and war-like. Here they were in their trousers, swaggering around the Forum of the Roman people, uttering threats in their barbaric language. Even the prosecutors had warned that if Fonteius were acquitted, "some new Gallic war would be whipped up." Murmurings of a Gal-lic uprising always set Romans on edge. A decade after the trial of Fonteius, Julius Caesar used such reports to launch one of the great-est wars of conquest in Roman history, which elevated him to an unprecedented level of power.

But hadn't the Gauls given their testimony under oath, like any other witness in the courts? Cicero had his answer: the Gauls weren't moved by oaths.[32] They had no respect for the gods at all. While other peoples tried to go to war with the gods on their side, the Gauls went to war against the gods. These people, Cicero said, once sacked the oracle of Apollo at Delphi, a site sacred to all Greeks and the whole civilized world. These people once sacked Rome itself and laid siege to the great Temple of Jupiter on the Capitoline Hill overlooking the Forum. It was all-seeing Jupiter, more than any other god, whose name Romans invoked in their oaths. Clearly Jupiter would mean nothing to the Gauls. Why, Cicero said, the Gauls even pollute their own altars and temples with "human victims." No practice appalled Romans more than human sacrifice, and they were quick to accuse the Gauls of it, perhaps with some basis, even though the Romans had done it themselves in the past. Archaeological evidence indicates that human heads were displayed in religious sanctuaries of Gaul and some enemies captured in battle might have been killed as a sacrifice.[33]

Cicero's attack on the Gauls went beyond saying they were unreliable. If these menacing barbarians succeeded in convicting Fonteius, word would spread among them that they could defy the Romans. Future governors would hesitate to impose levies, even though such levies were necessary for the Roman people to be safe. And with Fonteius convicted, the Romans would lose a talented general, a man they would need for the inevitable crises to come. Keep this man, Cicero exhorted the jurors, "rather than surrender him to tribes that are the bitterest foes of the Roman people and most savage."[34] Here was the nub of Cicero's defense: the Gauls were not reliable witnesses in a criminal trial but conspirators plotting the destruction of Fonteius—and Rome.

As he reached the peroration, Cicero began weaving in one of the most familiar pleas of defense in an extortion trial: the strong military record of the defendant. He pointed out to the jurors the delegations that had poured into the court from across the Roman empire to testify on behalf of Fonteius and were sitting with the defense.[35] There was Spain. There was Macedonia, whose cities Fonteius had saved from plundering by the Thracians. Massilia had sent a testimonial. So had Narbo, freed by Fonteius from an enemy siege.

Yet the court, in the heart of Rome, bristled most with Gauls, practically in arms, hemming in Fonteius.

The peroration was always an opportunity for some visually arresting theater. A defendant's elderly father might break down in tears. A prosecutor might brandish a murder weapon or unbandage a victim's wounds. A man who had been illegally flogged might strip to show his scars.[36] The jurors and audience at the trial of Fonteius would not be disappointed by the spectacle Cicero had planned.

On one side of the defendant sat his mother. As she reached over to her son, Cicero asked the jurors if they were going to look on as Indutiomarus and the other Gauls dragged Fonteius from her embrace.[37] On Fonteius's other side sat his sister, the Vestal Virgin, wearing the white robe of a priestess. Fonteia embraced her brother and then stretched out her hands to the jurors. "The Vestal Virgin," Cicero said, "is holding out her hands to you in supplication, the same ones she is accustomed to hold out to the gods on your behalf." Watch out, Cicero told the jurors, or her tears might extinguish the sacred fire in the Temple of Vesta. It was standard for a relative to ask for mercy, but there would have been a special power in seeing Fonteia, who for years had presided at public sacrifices, begging and weeping. Emotion must have overwhelmed the court. Probably Fonteius himself started crying. "Do you see, members of the jury," Cicero asked, "how that heroic man, Marcus Fonteius, immediately burst into tears at my mention of his parent and sister?"

The scene was surely rehearsed and did not last long. As Cicero himself had written years before in his discussion of perorations, "After you have stirred up feelings, you shouldn't linger over the lament." He quoted his old teacher Apollonius: "Nothing dries faster than a tear."[38] And so he reached his conclusion:

Defend from this danger, members of the jury, a gallant and blameless citizen. Take care that you are seen to have placed more credence in our witnesses than foreigners, to have shown more regard for the safety of your fellow citizens than our enemy's selfish desire, to have valued more highly the entreaties of the woman who presides over your sacred rites than of those who have waged wars against the sacred rites and shrines of the whole world. Finally, see to it, members of the jury—here we come to what most affects the standing of the Roman people—that the prayers of a Vestal Virgin are shown to have more weight with you than the threats of the Gauls.[39]

The outcome of the trial is unrecorded. Cicero almost certainly won the case since he went on to publish the speech.[40] But this does not mean Fonteius was innocent. The weak foundation of Cicero's defense suggests the very opposite. Why then would Fonteius have been acquitted? Cicero gave jurors a story that they could make sense of and that appealed to their feelings of patriotism and cultural superiority. And there were further factors. More careful than Verres, Fonteius had made sure to treat well those who had the most clout in Gaul, especially the high-ranking Romans involved in business. Also, his trial was heard after the judiciary reform of 70 BC went into effect. This meant that one-third of the jurors were senators, while the other two-thirds were men from the wealthy classes just below, focused on business.[41] Cicero spoke approvingly of businessmen throughout his speech.

The case was not one of Cicero's biggest successes that he looked back to later, like those of Roscius and Verres. But it reveals much about his forensic technique and the extortion court. Defending a Roman governor by discounting foreign witnesses against him was a viable strategy. Cicero took the same approach in several of his later cases and other lawyers did as well. "We know that orators have made light of the evidence of whole nations," the rhetorician Quintilian observed.[42] In his defense of Fonteius, Cicero did that with panache.

The hierarchies that existed not just within Roman society but throughout the empire, from Spain to Syria, pervaded the courts of Rome. Slaves could not testify except under torture. Foreign peoples could testify but might be sneered at for it. Some foreign peoples were regarded more highly, especially Greeks, because Romans admired Greek literature, art, and architecture. Others, like trousered Gauls, were considered savages, at least at times. Roman citizens won the most credit, though of course they could be demeaned too.

Cicero's defense might have persuaded high-ranking Roman jurors but it would have hardly seemed fair to Indutiomarus and the other Gauls. Cicero claimed that their coming to Rome was an act of war but in fact the Gauls were placing their trust in a legal process, rather than arms, at least in 69 BC.[43] Several years later, a Roman governor went to war with Indutiomarus's people, the Allobroges.[44] Perhaps—as the prosecution had apparently said—armed resistance was the only recourse left to them. In his defense of Fonteius, Cicero inadvertently revealed as much about the brutality of the Roman empire as he did in his prosecution of Verres.

One may still ask, how so soon after the trial of Verres could Cicero justify defending a man who seems to have been guilty? Years later, Cicero would address the general question of what cases an advocate should take on in a book he wrote about the ethics of public life called *On Duties*.

Speeches for the prosecution, Cicero argued, should be undertaken occasionally—and only then with cause. "You must never indict an innocent person on a capital charge." On the other hand, it was all right to defend a guilty man. People accepted this, he said, and tradition sanctioned it. A man on trial was entitled to defense. "It is the juror's duty in a trial," Cicero suggested, "always to seek the truth, while sometimes the advocate's task is to maintain what is plausible, even if it is not strictly true."[45] Rhetoric manuals brimmed with suggestions on how to present arguments that seemed true. This was not license to tamper with the basic facts of a case, however, which it cannot be shown Cicero did.[46]

Cicero's discussion omits the benefits that accrued to lawyers, which influenced their selection of cases. In part, these benefits were political. Defending a powerful man, whether a senator or the leader of an Italian town, could translate into electoral support.[47] Refusing to defend a powerful man could spell trouble later. To stand up for wealthy businessmen, as Cicero did in the trial of Fonteius, won friendship with a whole class of influential people. Support for this class would become a key part of Cicero's profile.[48] And there was a link here with the other benefit advocacy brought: financial gain. While advocates were legally barred from taking direct payment for their work, they could accept legacies and loans. Over time, as grateful clients died, legacies became a major source of income for Cicero. Near the end of his life, he boasted that he had received over 20 million sesterces in inheritances. He also received loans, especially for buying real estate.[49]

A Roman senator, certainly one trying to rise to the top, had to keep up appearances. He needed a large house in Rome to host the morning receptions where he greeted supporters. For more exclusive evening parties, it helped if the house was tastefully decorated and staffed by attractive slaves. Also desirable was a villa in the vineyard-dotted hills east and south of Rome or by the seaside. These properties could generate income, of course. But senators and their families gathered during breaks from public business in the fashionable vacation spots, and all took note of who resided where.[50]

A year after the trial of Fonteius, Cicero lost his father and inherited the family house on the Esquiline Hill in Rome as well as the estate at Arpinum, which brought in rent from tenant farmers. Around this time, he also acquired a villa that had once belonged to Sulla himself at Tusculum, in the Alban Hills, an easy day's journey from Rome. Cicero found pleasure in this refuge, where he could devote time to reading, writing, and meeting visitors. He added to it a house at Formiae, on the coast, eighty miles south of Rome, and then several more—"my little villas, the darlings of Italy," as he later called them.[51] These villas were the fruits of his legal practice.

We can track Cicero's life more fully from 68 BC onward through surviving letters he wrote to a friend from his schooldays, Titus Pomponius Atticus.[52] Atticus was born into a wealthy equestrian family like Cicero but lacked any ambition to hold political office himself. His passions lay in art, literature, and building wealth. His father died early and left him with 2 million sesterces. A rich uncle with a terrible temper whom nobody could stand—except Atticus—left him with 10 million more. When civil war broke out in the 80s BC, Atticus fled with much of his money to Athens, where he lived for the next twenty years. He and Cicero reunited during Cicero's tour in the East and studied philosophy together. Atticus made frequent visits to Rome at election times to help his friends, and the two must have seen each other then as well.[53]

In the earliest letters from Cicero (only his side of the correspondence survives), he asks Atticus to procure art in Greece for the newly acquired villa at Tusculum. Cicero was no Verres. He was not looking for Greek old masters, just reasonably priced statues suitable for the entrance hall and the study that he would come to call the Academy, after Plato's school in Athens.[54] Cicero thrilled as he got news that Atticus had secured marble pillars topped by bronze heads of gods—especially one of Minerva, the goddess of wisdom. She would be "a suitable decoration for my Academy," Cicero gushed.[55] At Cicero's prompting, Atticus also bought a library, probably works in Greek, but Cicero could not reimburse him right away. "I'm setting aside my little harvest to pay for this helper for old age," he promised.[56] Books at this time were handwritten on rolls of Egyptian papyrus, an expensive material. Old books could fetch an especially large price. There is something endearing in seeing how Cicero wished to spend his earnings. Any moment of free time he devoted to rigorous study.

Cicero often shared family news in the letters. His younger brother Quintus was married to Atticus's sister Pomponia. The couple constantly fought, to the distress of their brothers. Pomponia almost certainly brought a large dowry with her, which was useful for Quintus in his pursuit of political ambitions. Quintus avoided public speaking—one rhetorician was enough for a family, Cicero joked—and instead developed a military reputation.[57] In the letters, we catch glimpses of Cicero's own marriage: "Terentia is suffering badly from arthritis. She is very fond of you [Atticus] and your sister and your mother, and sends you best wishes, as does my darling little Tullia."[58] Tullia was Cicero's beloved daughter, who seems to have inherited her father's cleverness. By the end of 67 BC, though not much older than ten years, she was engaged; marriage would come a few years later. That was in keeping with Roman convention, especially among the upper classes, for whom marriage ideally was a source of happiness for spouses but always an alliance of their two families. Tullia's fiancé, Piso, was a young man from a distinguished noble family—a sign that Cicero was on the ascent.

Earlier in 67 BC, Cicero assured Atticus that there was no need for his friend to leave Greece and return to Rome for elections.[59] Cicero was confident that he would win one of the eight praetorships of 66 BC. He did and, what is more, he was the first candidate to get enough votes to be declared winner, a great achievement for a new man.[60] For his year in office, he would preside over the extortion court. This did not stop his work as an advocate, however. In 66 BC, he would return to the murder court, the scene of his first triumph, and put forward one of the most brilliant defenses of his career.

# CHAPTER 6

# Poison Was Detected

For the Romans, poisoning was the most deceitful crime. It reminded them how vulnerable they were. That cup of wine your spouse handed you might have a toxin mixed in. Or the medicine administered by your own doctor. Slaves could kill with poison, and so could women, leaving normally powerful men defenseless. If a poisoner were sly enough, they would never be caught at all. There were no tests to prove somebody had died of this poison or that, which meant it was all too easy to accuse others of the crime.

Anyone who watched the trial of Aulus Cluentius Habitus in 66 BC could see that. Cluentius, a wealthy man in his late thirties from a ranch town in southern Italy, was charged with poisoning three different men. One of the alleged victims was his stepfather, Oppianicus. According to the prosecution, Cluentius arranged for Oppianicus to be given some bread laced with poison. Oppianicus ate the bread and died. Later, Cluentius tried to serve Oppianicus's son poisoned wine at a wedding banquet, but a friend of the intended victim inadvertently drank the wine and he died instead. Oppianicus junior, about eighteen years old in 66 BC, emerged unscathed and brought the case against Cluentius. But the prosecutor was not the only one at the trial who claimed to have survived a poisoning attempt. The defendant maintained that he had once nearly been killed—by Oppianicus senior.

The source for all this is Cicero's defense of Cluentius, his longest surviving speech, filled with more murder and attempted murder than a Roman amphitheater.[1] Nowhere else in his legal career did Cicero tell such a tangled tale. Like so many of his cases, this one reached back to the civil wars of the 80s BC and the orgy of violence that accompanied Sulla's victory. It reopened earlier trials, allegations of cover-ups, and a major judicial bribery scandal. Adding to the complexity, similar names came up repeatedly. The ranch town from which Cluentius and Oppianicus came, Larinum, was dominated by a small group of families, whose habit of marrying and divorcing one another created a dense web of relationships. Their power struggles mirrored those of the ruling families of Rome.

Some of the names would be more familiar to the jurors in 66 BC than they are to us. But even for the jurors and the audience Cicero wanted to create some murk. It was as if he were taking everyone down to the underworld and then illuminating just two figures in the sulfurous dark. One was the stepfather of Cicero's client, Oppianicus senior. He had died back in 72 BC. Cicero would make much of the fact that two years prior, he had been convicted in the murder court.

Cicero's other antagonist was Sassia, both the widow of Oppianicus and Cluentius's own mother. While the case against Cluentius had been brought by Oppianicus junior, it was Sassia, Cicero said, now present in the court and sitting on the prosecution benches, who was the driving force behind the crime.[2] Her first step had been to win over Oppianicus junior to her side by marrying her daughter to him. She then arranged for a clever young lawyer, Titus Attius, to argue the case on behalf of young Oppianicus. She organized all the witnesses and evidence. Near the start of his speech, Cicero pointed her out to the jurors: "a woman daring, rich, and cruel . . . she longs for her son's destruction, she is eager to shed every drop of her blood provided she may see his poured out first."[3]

In his defense of Roscius, Cicero had followed the textbook rules for arranging a speech. By the trial of Cluentius, his art had matured so that he could do something more creative. Like the mythical craftsman Daedalus, he would create a labyrinth, but with words. His legal strategy proved effective, but what Cicero's case also makes clear is how the Roman courts, far from resolving allegations of poisoning, invited them, even when evidence was lacking.

Larinum, the scene of much of Cicero's story, is situated on the eastern side of the Italian peninsula, over the mountains from Rome.[4] Perched among the foothills of the Apennines, it looks down onto a fertile plain that runs out to the Adriatic Sea, about fifteen miles away. The town supported itself by agriculture, especially pastoral farming. Livestock was herded along drove roads that crisscrossed the region. Sometimes fights would break out between armed shepherds who were driving their flocks to and from upland pastures and farmers.[5] So did nasty inheritance disputes. The leading families schemed and fought to acquire land and gangs of slaves to work it.

Especially important for Cicero's case were the family of his client, the Cluentii; the family of Oppianicus, the Abbii; and a third family, the Aurii. In 88 BC the father of Cicero's client Cluentius died. Cluentius was fifteen at the time. Shortly after her father's death, his sister Cluentia married Aulus Aurius Melinus, one of the Aurii and a leading young man of the town. But just two years later, the couple divorced and Melinus took a new wife, Cluentia's mother, Sassia. Cicero played up the scandalous nature of this marriage as he opened his defense of Cluentius. Sassia, he claimed, could barely hold back her lust for her young son-in-law and seduced him. Cluentia, already pained by her husband's unfaithfulness, burned with the added shame that her rival was her own mother. The poor girl could find comfort only in her devoted brother, in whose arms she cried. It was at this point, Cicero said, that Cluentius stopped speaking with his mother. Cicero claimed Cluentius would have preferred to draw a veil of silence over the affair but couldn't because Sassia had worked up the whole case against him.[6]

Having introduced jurors to his villainess, Cicero next turned to his villain, the late Oppianicus. Cicero went through some of the charges that had been brought against Oppianicus at his murder trial in 74 BC, starting with the saga of Dinaea, a rich old woman of Larinum, and her family. From two different husbands, Dinaea had three sons, Marcus Aurius, Numerius Aurius, and Gnaeus Magius, and one daughter, Magia, who was for a time married to Oppianicus. Marcus Aurius disappeared during the great rebellion of the Italian peoples who lacked Roman citizenship that was launched in 91 BC. He was presumed dead. Then, one by one, Dinaea's other children died off: First, Numerius Aurius, who left his property to his brother Gnaeus Magius. Next, Magia, the wife of Oppianicus. And last of all, Gnaeus Magius, who left his estate to his nephew, Oppianicus junior, with an instruction to share it with Dinaea. But then news came to Dinaea that her son Marcus Aurius was alive after all. After being taken captive in the war, he fell into the hands of a Roman senator who threw him into a slave prison on one of his farms along the Adriatic coast, well north of Larinum. Aurius was likely forced to work in a chain gang to prevent him from escaping.[7]

For Dinaea, who thought she had lost all her children, nothing could have brought more joy than to learn that one of her sons was alive. She sent relatives to rescue him but then fell ill. Hastily she made a new will. It was not unusual for wealthy Romans like her to update their wills. The usual procedure was to write down one's wishes on a set of hinged wooden tablets that could fold shut like a book. Then seven or more men needed to witness the document. Each witness used his personal signet ring to affix a wax seal to the tablet. In her new will, Dinaea selected her grandson, the young Oppianicus, as primary heir but also included a bequest of 400,000 sesterces to her lost son. That would be more than enough to help him get back on his feet.[8]

Oppianicus senior sprang into action. First, he located the man who had told Dinaea of her son Aurius's survival and bribed him for information. Then he had Aurius killed. Those who had set out to rescue the lost son, meanwhile, sent a letter back to the other Aurii in Larinum stating that they were having trouble locating the missing man. One of the family members read out the letter publicly and announced he would prosecute Oppianicus if he found out their kinsman had been murdered. When news reached Larinum of Aurius's death, the threats against Oppianicus grew louder. It was now the late 80s BC. Civil war between Sulla and his enemies was raging across Italy. Oppianicus decided to flee Larinum and take refuge in the camp of one of Sulla's generals.

After Sulla's final victory, Oppianicus swooped back down on his hometown with an armed gang. He threw out the magistrates in

charge and announced that he, along with three others, had been chosen by Sulla to replace them. He then saw to it that several members
of the Aurii were proscribed and killed, including Sassia's husband.[9]

Like so many others, Oppianicus used the cover of the civil war
to carry out crimes and gain power. But worse was to follow, Cicero
told the jurors, much worse. After seizing control of Larinum, Oppianicus conceived a desire to marry Sassia. He saw this as a way to get
at her riches and those of the Cluentii. Oppianicus by this time had
already married five times, an unusually high number, which might
support Cicero's claim that he did so with an eye toward money.
Oppianicus had three sons in total from his five marriages: One son,
from a woman named Novia, was an infant. Another, from Papia,
was a few years older. And then there was the son from Magia, who
had come into large inheritances through Dinaea and her family.
He was the future prosecutor of Cluentius.[10]

Around the time Oppianicus started wooing Sassia, two of his
three sons died. According to Cicero, Sassia was refusing to marry
Oppianicus not because he had murdered her husband, but because
he had three sons. This meant both that his fortune might be dis-
sipated and there were former in-laws who could get in the way of
the new couple. And so, said Cicero, the two boys who died—the
infant son from Novia and the older boy of Papia—were murdered
by Oppianicus. Papia was raising her son in a town near Larinum.
Oppianicus summoned him for a visit and the unsuspecting mother
sent him off. How exactly the child was killed, Cicero did not say,
but circumstances were suspicious. Oppianicus pretended to leave
Larinum on a trip south. That same day, late in the afternoon, the
child was seen out in public looking healthy. However, he was dead
by sundown and cremated before dawn the next day. His mother
got the news only later and had to come to Larinum to hold another

funeral for him. Not ten days later, the other son, the infant, was killed, but again Cicero did not say how.[11]

Soon Cicero was onto allegations of poisonings. One of Oppianicus's wives had been the paternal aunt of Cicero's client. Oppianicus, according to Cicero, gave her a cup with his own hands; as she was drinking from it, she cried out that she was in terrible pain and dying. Barely gasping the words out, she dropped dead; afterward, claimed Cicero, indications of poison were found on her body.[12] By similar means, Oppianicus poisoned his brother to inherit his estate. As if that weren't enough, shortly before that he poisoned his brother's wife, Auria, who was pregnant at the time and close to term. Oppianicus did not want her to give birth to a child who would bar him from coming into his brother's property. Cicero observed with ghoulish eloquence that most men are unable to kill off their relatives even one at a time, but Oppianicus, in a single victim, managed to kill more than one.[13]

According to Cicero, Dinaea's son Magius had come to recognize Oppianicus's criminal daring. After Magius fell gravely ill, he prepared a will in which he designated as his primary heir his nephew, the younger Oppianicus. Magius called together his friends and family and, before all these witnesses, asked his wife whether she was pregnant. She replied yes, she was. Magius then asked her to stay with Dinaea until she gave birth. He left her a large legacy in his will, on the condition that she gave birth to a son, who would then replace Oppianicus junior as the primary heir. After Magius died, Oppianicus senior offered to pay the widow a sum equivalent to the legacy if she took an abortifacient. She did, and five months after Magius's death she married Oppianicus.[14]

For anyone in the jury or crowd who had heard enough of poisoning, the next crime of Oppianicus that Cicero recounted offered something different. This was the murder of a wealthy young man of Larinum named Asuvius. Oppianicus saw his chance when a disreputable man in town, Avillius, became friends with the youth. Avillius took the boy to Rome to enjoy the brothels, taverns, and gaming dens that only the big city offered. Oppianicus followed close behind. When Asuvius was spending the night at a prostitute's house, Avillius feigned illness and requested to make a will. Oppianicus brought in men to witness the will who knew neither Asuvius nor Avillius, and he called Avillius by Asuvius's name. After the witnesses affixed their seals, they left. The false Asuvius then staged an instant recovery. Soon afterward, the real Asuvius was invited for a stroll in some pleasure gardens but was actually taken to pits outside the city gates where sand was dug up for use in construction. It was the perfect spot for a stabbing; out in the pits there were fewer people, and the corpse could be hidden under a pile of sand.[15]

After a couple of days, people began looking for Asuvius in Rome. Back in Larinum, Oppianicus reported that the man had recently made a will. When freedmen and friends of the deceased learned that he had last been seen alive with Avillius, they hauled Avillius before one of the junior magistrates in Rome who oversaw public safety. Avillius told the whole story. But before the magistrate—an unsavory man who had risen to power in the civil wars—could get any further in the matter, Oppianicus bribed him to stay quiet. The truth only came out at the trial of Oppianicus in 74 BC, when Avillius's confession was introduced as evidence.

Cicero had nearly reached the end of his list of Oppianicus's victims, but he still had one final surprise: Dinaea hadn't died of natural causes; she had been poisoned too. Oppianicus brought in his doctor to treat her when she had fallen ill, but she didn't care to try any of the quack's cures. Oppianicus then approached a traveling salesman of medicines, who happened to be visiting Larinum at the time, and came to an arrangement for 2,000 sesterces—as was shown by Oppianicus's own accounts. The salesman was busy and had other towns to get to, so he finished the job quickly. It took just one dose of his drug to kill Dinaea. As she tried to revise her will, Oppianicus grabbed it and began rubbing out some of the provisions written into wax on the tablet. In the end he made so many erasures he had to make a fresh copy of the will, for which he forged the seals.[16]

It is a staggering body count, fourteen victims all told. Could one man have gotten away with so many murders before he was ever brought into court? Could he have killed so many of his relatives, even his own sons? The murders of the Aurii seem easier to believe; they were not Oppianicus's own kin, and the proscriptions of Sulla allowed lawful killing. That Oppianicus killed young Asuvius also seems possible. It appears that evidence for that crime did later emerge. And perhaps Asuvius had few if any relatives willing to take on Oppianicus in the courts. For every other murder where Cicero specified the method of killing, poison was used. That was a harder crime to prove, which also made it easier to allege, as the dark history of poisoning trials in Rome shows.

The first poisoning trial in Roman history apparently occurred in 331 BC. The historian Livy, writing a generation after Cicero, gives an account.[17] It was a terrible year, in which leading citizens kept falling ill and dying. One might have thought it was plague, for highly infectious diseases did strike the city periodically. However, an enslaved woman came to one of the magistrates and promised to reveal the cause of all the deaths, if he would grant her legal immunity. The magistrate referred the matter to the consuls, who then referred it to the Senate. By decree of the Senate, the woman was granted the assurance she sought.

She then revealed that the city was suffering through "female crime." The leading women of Rome were preparing poisons, the slave said; if the consuls would follow her, they could catch the women in the act. The consuls went with the informer and found the matrons brewing what appeared to be poisons. The brews were brought into the Forum, along with the twenty women in whose houses they had been found. Two of the women claimed the substances were medicines. The informer said it was a lie and asked the women to drink them to prove her charges false. The women conferred and finally agreed to comply. In the sight of all they drank the poison and, as Livy wrote, "perished by their own wickedness." More slaves informed on more women; in the end, 170 women were found guilty.

The story shows how difficult it could be to prove intentional poisoning. Whereas stabbing or strangulation left clear marks on a dead body, poisoning was harder to detect. Romans might point to physical signs of poisoning, such as inexplicable or sudden illness or even strange coloration of a corpse, but these could easily be contested. Mortality rates were high; Romans of all ages died all the time, from airborne illness, food poisoning, and a litany of other causes. Infants and young children were especially vulnerable. To establish poisoning, it was helpful to have a witness like the nameless slave who went to the magistrate. Slaves heard and saw a lot through their duties in the house, but their low status afforded them less credibility. They were not normally allowed to testify against their owners. It was only when the matrons fell dead in the Forum that everyone could believe the mysterious deaths were caused by poison.

Evidence like that was hard to argue away, but Livy's story hints at another complication. It was widespread illness that first aroused suspicions. But once the explanation of poisoning was accepted, it became possible to blame every death or sickness at the time on the matrons. Even the innocent might be prosecuted. In several subsequent poisoning investigations, the numbers of those convicted, regardless of gender, soared far higher than the 170 in 331 BC. According to Livy, in one inquiry in the early second century BC, two thousand people were condemned.[18] Suspicions were aroused a few years after that when the death toll spiked in the city and one of the year's consuls died, to be replaced by his stepson. Witnesses came forward and implicated the consul's wife; she had been heard telling her son, before the consul died, to be ready to step into office. Further inquiries condemned three thousand more individuals, "through the evidence of informers."[19] Poisoning provided an explanation for sudden death, but weak or empty charges of it were prone to spread in a climate of paranoia. Women were especially vulnerable to accusations. As the rhetorician Quintilian wrote, it was easier to believe banditry was committed by men, poisoning by women.[20] But in fact poisoning seemed to offer a convenient way for either men or women to quietly eliminate anyone standing in the way of an inheritance or some other ambition. This made it a crime associated especially with the ruling class.[21]

What sort of poisons would the Romans have used? Ancient accounts of poisoning such as Cicero's often describe a rapid death after sipping from a cup. Sudden expiry, after all, was about the best sign that a poison was in play. When a toxin enters the bloodstream directly it can kill swiftly, as with snakebites. One Roman historian mentioned a group of murderers who pricked their victims with needles smeared with poison.[22] But a needle left a mark. Mixing poison into sweetened wine or medicine was easier, albeit less efficient. Typically a plant-based poison would have been used. These did not kill instantly. Socrates was famously forced to drink hemlock, which results in paralysis that spreads from the feet and legs to the rest of the body, ultimately causing breathing to stop. This process can take many minutes or even hours. Aconite, also known as monkshood, is an even more fatal poison that, if ingested, can quickly lead to irregular heartbeat, a burning feeling in the mouth, and eventually numbness. Death might come in an hour. Aconite was used in topical treatments as an analgesic but can permeate the skin and by that route fatally poison. Medical and scientific treatises from the ancient world preserve much poison lore. While doctors, drug-sellers, and others must have known plenty, in Roman criminal trials expert testimony was not used.[23] What mattered more was the jurors' general knowledge and beliefs, shaped by stories they read about or heard. For jurors, the idea that a sip of poison could kill immediately seems to have been plausible.

Investigations like the one into the matrons in 331 BC were carried out by magistrates. But by the start of the first century BC a standing court for poisoning had been established. Sulla's legislation then created the joint court for poisoning and knife murders. The statute punished not only the use of poison but also its manufacture, sale, and purchase.[24] Without good methods of detecting poison, this was the only way to prevent its use for murder. However, the law did not solve every problem. Even a medicine in excessive doses might become toxic, and so could accidentally kill. It remained difficult to prove that a poison was used or intended to be used for the purpose of killing. Certainly witnesses could bolster a case. But often prosecutors and defense attorneys had to fall back on the usual arguments from motive, opportunity, and character, which might not be backed up by much evidence at all.

At the trial of Cluentius in 66 BC, Cicero did not need to prove the late Oppianicus's guilt. He was only reminding jurors of the charges made against Oppianicus back in 74 BC. The prosecution on that occasion had been brought by none other than Cluentius himself, and the centerpiece of the case had been a claim that Oppianicus had tried to poison Cluentius. Cicero's narrative of the trial and the events leading up to it reveals a lot about how a Roman prosecutor could build a case for poisoning and how charges could pile up in a way that might seem outlandish to us.

In the town of Larinum, Cicero began, there was a large group of persons known as Martiales. These were publicly owned slaves, notionally in service to the god Mars, but really used as a labor supply. Several years after gaining control of Larinum, Oppianicus announced that the Martiales were all free men. Perhaps this was to gain a new power base for himself. Other leaders in the town chafed at the move and asked Cluentius, now about thirty years old, to take up the case. He accepted the request. Soon the legal dispute moved to Rome, and Oppianicus and Cluentius were openly fighting each other. Cicero claimed that Oppianicus was supported, even incited, by the dreadful Sassia. But unbeknownst to her, Oppianicus had his own secret plan: Cluentius had not yet made a will. If he died, all his property would pass to his mother. At that point, Cicero pointed out, it would not be hard for Oppianicus to remove her. And so he could achieve his dream of laying his hands on her fortunes and those of the Cluentii.[25]

Cicero invited the jurors to learn "how Oppianicus tried to get rid of Cluentius by poison." In Aletrium, a hill town not far from Cicero's own birthplace of Arpinum, lived twin brothers, the Fabricii, with whom Oppianicus was close. As Cicero observed, similarity of interests cements a friendship. The twins were masters of every sort of fraud and treachery. Oppianicus decided to use one of them, Gaius Fabricius, to carry out his plot.[26]

Cluentius was experiencing health problems at the time and was being treated by Cleophantus, a well-known doctor. In Rome there was no medical licensing. Even good doctors did not understand some diseases, so their patients often died, arousing distrust. Cleophantus enjoyed a reasonably good reputation, however. Fabricius approached Diogenes, a slave of the doctor, to give poison to Cluentius in exchange for a bribe. Diogenes immediately went to Cleophantus, and Cleophantus then spoke with Cluentius. Cluentius consulted with a senator of some experience, who advised him to purchase the doctor's slave to make it easier to use the slave's information. Cluentius did so, without the con man Fabricius's knowledge.

Cicero's account is vague about what happened next. It seems that a few days after Cluentius had bought Diogenes, Diogenes met secretly with a freedman of Fabricius named Scamander. When Scamander handed over a sealed packet of money—apparently to pay for the poison—several men sent ahead by Cluentius jumped out of hiding.[27]

Cluentius had sprung a trap. He was now ready to go to court. Using the services of a highly experienced lawyer, Cannutius, he prosecuted Scamander for purchasing poison. Scamander had an even better lawyer, though: Cicero. This was awkward for Cicero to discuss at the trial of 66 BC, when he had flipped sides and was decrying Oppianicus and his associates as a criminal gang. Cicero explained to the jurors that a large delegation from the town of Aletrium had come to his house in Rome to pressure him to help

Fabricius and take on Scamander's case. Though he did not say it, almost certainly Cicero gave his assent with an eye to future elections, in which he would need support from the wealthy men across Italy who came to Rome to ballot.[28]

The trial got underway with Cannutius's speech for the prosecution. His case boiled down to a few simple words: "poison was detected." Scamander had been caught handing over money for poison to the slave Diogenes, and several high-ranking men had witnessed it. Cicero rose to reply and made the strongest defense he could—"as duty required," he later said. He tried to argue that Scamander had no motive and was a person of good character. Cicero also made a counteraccusation. The slave Diogenes, Cicero claimed, had arranged an ambush. Diogenes had told Scamander he was bringing medicine, not poison, and that's what Scamander thought he was buying. The prosecution rebutted Cicero's case with their distinguished witnesses, including the senator in whom Cluentius had confided. The president of the court, Gaius Junius, called on the jurors to vote, the ballots were counted, and by every vote save one Scamander was found guilty.

Cluentius next prosecuted the con man Fabricius, again relying on the services of the skillful Cannutius. By this time, Cicero said, Fabricius had lost the support of his townspeople and Cicero had dropped him too. In desperation, Fabricius had to resort to the brothers Caepasii, two hardworking advocates who would take any case that came their way. After another snappy speech from Cannutius for the prosecution, the elder Caepasius began to answer in a long opening. The jurors sat up, startled by the man's far-fetched arguments. Caepasius blundered even worse when in his peroration he fell back on one of his favorite rhetorical devices. "Look, members of the jury, at the plight of mortal men," he said. "Look at their changing circumstances. Look at the old age of Gaius Fabricius." After many "looks," Caepasius finally turned to look himself at Fabricius, only to discover his client was gone. Head hung low, Fabricius had fled the court, so badly was his case going. He was unanimously convicted.[29]

Finally, before the same court, with the same praetor Junius presiding, Oppianicus went on trial. Once again, while Cluentius formally brought charges, the skilled Cannutius handled the prosecution. Oppianicus was defended by a fiery speaker named Lucius Quinctius, who was currently holding office as tribune of the plebs. According to Cicero, Cannutius's case rested on the joint plot of Oppianicus, Fabricius, and Scamander and so was helped by the recent convictions of the latter two. Cannutius also went through all the earlier crimes of Oppianicus that Cicero himself reviewed at the start of his defense of Cluentius—the murderous intrigues against Dinaea and her family, the killing of Asuvius in the sand pits, all the poisonings.[30]

In the Roman courts, as far as we can tell, prosecutors did not have to specify every relevant charge in a formal indictment, on which jurors would vote separately.[31] Rather, jurors gave a single verdict. This meant prosecutors could include in their cases every crime a defendant might be suspected of. If done skillfully, this helped to establish a pattern. But this style of arguing also meant that baseless charges might be thrown in. At the trial of Oppianicus, Cannutius wanted to show that Oppianicus had killed before for money, with stealth, and so the prosecutor threw in everything he could. A real criminal hardly stops at one crime, Cannutius might have said.

Yet if we step back and critically evaluate the case against Oppianicus, as related to us by Cicero, we can spot weaknesses.[32] How strong were all the charges of poisoning that allegedly took place before the plot against Cluentius? Not strong at all, it would seem. If Cluentius's aunt cried out that she was in pain as she died, that didn't prove she was poisoned. If Oppianicus paid a medical salesman 2,000 sesterces, that didn't mean poison was bought.

As for the alleged attempt to poison Cluentius, wasn't that stronger? After all, as Cannutius had said, "poison was detected." Or was it? According to Cannutius, the freedman Scamander had appeared at a certain time and place, with money, to get the poison. But if the doctor's slave Diogenes were being bribed to poison a patient under medical care, why wouldn't the slave himself administer the poison directly? Why did Scamander need to obtain the poison? Presumably Diogenes had fed Scamander some story—"meet me in such and such a place to pay for the poisoning"—and then perhaps Diogenes brought out the poison for the benefit of the hidden witnesses. Maybe Cluentius felt he had to rely on subterfuge like this to secure proof against his would-be murderer. Poisoning, or attempted poisoning, was hard to prove. But another possibility is that Cluentius was even more craftily entrapping Scamander. Diogenes may have even suggested poisoning to Scamander. Perhaps Cluentius was an even more skillful operator than Oppianicus.

Cluentius's sting operation is not the only hint that he might have played as ruthless a game as Oppianicus. When jurors finally cast their votes, Oppianicus was convicted only by a narrow margin. Many who did not vote to convict abstained. (If a majority voted this way in a trial, it had to go to a second hearing.) Oppianicus's lawyer Quinctius said he could explain the result. In impressive harangues before large crowds in the Forum, he alleged that Cluentius had paid jurors to condemn an innocent man. "Everyone's prosperity is at stake," Quinctius thundered. "Trial by jury is a thing of the past. No man is safe who has a rich enemy."[33] It was at this time that pressure was mounting to restore to the tribunes the powers Sulla had stripped away. Allegations about the corruption of senatorial juries were swirling. Quinctius could therefore explain away his own defeat in court and advance politically by blaming the Oppianicus verdict on corruption. Quinctius had the president of the court, Junius, fined for failing to take a proper oath and for irregularly filling up a vacancy in the jury panel.

Quinctius was almost certainly not telling the whole story. What seems to have happened is that Oppianicus tried to bribe some of the jurors and Cluentius did as well.[34] This was widely suspected at the time. The Senate called for legislation to set up a special inquiry into the matter, but it was never passed.[35] In his prosecution of Verres, Cicero referred to one notorious juror who was believed to have accepted money from Oppianicus to pass on to other jurors, while also taking money from Cluentius to find Oppianicus guilty.[36] Jurors, plaintiff, defendant, and president of the court: all seemed to be implicated in corruption. "Junian court" became a byword for judicial misconduct.

Whatever misdeeds he was guilty of, Oppianicus at least suffered the penalty of conviction for poisoning. He was deprived of Roman citizenship, though not his fortune (or not all of it anyway). And Junius had been forced to pay a fine. Nobody else was punished at the time but some jurors later suffered penalties when they were accused of other crimes, such as extortion. In 70 BC, when calls for reform reached their height, the censors—magistrates appointed every five years to take a census of all citizens—officially stigmatized some of the jurors.[37] This was mainly a symbolic punishment, but a meaningful one in a world where reputation mattered so much. The censors also stigmatized Cluentius. The prosecution would try to make the most of that when Cluentius went on trial in 66 BC.

It was the late Oppianicus's son, who had only recently reached the age of adulthood, who brought charges against Cluentius. But, in one of many parallels between the trials of the late Oppianicus and Cluentius, the case was argued by a clever young lawyer working with him, Attius.[38] Attius accused Cluentius of poisoning three different victims. The first was Vibius Cappadox, whose estate, the prosecutor said, ended up going to Cluentius. The second charge was that there was an attempt to poison Oppianicus junior at a dinner he was giving to celebrate his marriage to Sassia's daughter Auria. Poison was offered to Oppianicus in sweetened wine but a friend of his, Balbutius, grabbed the cup, drank it, and died instantly. Finally, the third allegation: poison was given in bread to Oppianicus senior by a friend of his, at the instigation of Cluentius, a couple of years after Oppianicus's conviction.

Along with all that, the prosecutor threw in a charge of what might be called judicial murder.[39] The Sullan law against dagger-men and poisoning included a provision that prevented the courts from convicting an innocent person on capital charges (i.e., those that resulted in death or exile). Prosecutor Attius claimed that by having offered bribes to the jurors at the trial of Oppianicus in 74 BC, Cluentius was additionally guilty of murder. This was a clever way for the prosecution to highlight Cluentius's role in the notorious Junian court.

Attius also talked about the defendant's predisposition to kill.[40] Cluentius had his slaves beat up his enemies and steal. An innkeeper on the Latin Way, a major road leading southwest from Rome, claimed that he had been assaulted by Cluentius and his slaves. Cluentius had thrown a woman into slavery illegally. He defrauded others of inheritances they were owed. A man who could do all that could poison, especially if he stood to profit. Likely a main part of the prosecution's story was that Cluentius hoped to eliminate both Oppianicus senior and junior to lay hands on their money.

A key part of Cicero's defense strategy was to focus first and at great length on the accusation of judicial murder and rebut it forcefully. This allowed him to give his own version of the notorious trial of 74 BC and turn the alleged criminal Cluentius back into a victim. The long catalog of charges against the late Oppianicus, flimsy as so many of them are, must have overwhelmed jurors, just as they do readers of the published version of the speech. It is hard not to think of Oppianicus as an out-and-out criminal. *He* must have been the one bribing, and *that* explains the scandal at the time.

Cicero also made a narrower legal argument, probably of great weight for many jurors.[41] He emphasized that the Sullan law on murder held only senators liable for judicial murder. When Sulla wrote his legislation, all jurors were senators. The provision made sense since they were the ones who would have to be bribed to give a false verdict. The murder law remained unchanged after the jury reform of 70 BC, despite two-thirds of jurors being nonsenators. Cicero threatened that if the jury convicted Cluentius, equestrians would be liable for charges of judicial murder from that point forward.[42]

Cicero had little to say on the first two poisoning charges. The alleged victim Vibius Cappadox had been staying in the house of a senator, Plaetorius, when he fell ill and died. Plaetorius was on hand in the court, Cicero said, but whether he would testify wasn't made clear.[43] Cicero could not compel him. As for the attempt to poison Oppianicus junior, Cicero denied that his client had motive and opportunity. Cicero said that the ill-fated Balbutius had arrived at the wedding celebration already suffering from indigestion. He overindulged, as young men do. He was then sick for several days and died. The witness for this was Balbutius's own father, who had already given a deposition. Cicero instructed a clerk of the court to read the statement out and asked the grieving parent to stand for the recital: excellent theater.[44]

At last Cicero came to the poisoning of Oppianicus senior and, to give his story a fitting climax, brought the villainess back onto the scene.[45] Cluentius had no motive to poison his stepfather, Cicero said. Yes, they were enemies, but Oppianicus had been ruined in the courts and could do no more harm. It was more satisfying to let him rot in exile. Neither did Cluentius have the opportunity to administer the poison. And poison in bread? What a strange idea! It was far easier and more effective to slip poison in a cup. No, there was a much better explanation for the whole story: it was a lie, invented by a woman of monstrous cruelty.

The true facts, Cicero said, were these: Oppianicus, wandering about in exile after his conviction, finally found shelter at a farm owned by his advocate Quinctius. He fell seriously ill. Sassia was with him but, given her husband's incapacity, began enjoying the company of a strapping farmer. Oppianicus recovered enough to leave but then was thrown from his horse, sustained an injury, and died a few days later.

Afterward, Sassia decided to investigate his death. She purchased a slave who belonged to Oppianicus's doctor to do just what Cluentius had done with Diogenes. She proceeded to hold, in the presence of witnesses, an interrogation of this man—Strato was his name—along with a slave of her own and a slave who had belonged to her late husband. Despite subjecting the slaves to brutal torture, none was willing to falsely implicate Cluentius in the murder of his stepfather, as Sassia wanted them to. Ultimately she had no choice but to give up. The witnesses she had assembled told her she had gone too far. She was trying to get the slaves to confess to non-existent crimes, a problem with brutal interrogations that even the Romans sometimes acknowledged.[46] Sassia took Strato with her back to Larinum and gave him a shop to open a medical practice, most of the profits of which would go to her.

Several years passed. Sassia married her teenage daughter to Oppianicus junior. Around the same time, a theft occurred at her house. A safe in which she kept money and gold had been cut open at the bottom and emptied. Two slaves were missing, and suspicion fell on them. But then one of Sassia's friends recalled having recently seen among the miscellaneous items sold at an auction a small circular saw. Inquiries were made with the auctioneers, and it was determined that Strato had bought the saw.

Sassia now began questioning her slaves, and one of them told her the truth. Doctor Strato had orchestrated the theft. The missing slaves had been murdered by him and he then dumped their bodies into a fishpond. Investigators dragged the bodies out of the pond, Strato was thrown into chains, and some of the stolen money was found in his shop. Sassia then proceeded to question Strato under torture. But what else did she need to know? Cicero asked. That Strato had robbed her was clear. Her true aim was to reopen the case of Oppianicus's death. And so she once again demanded from Oppianicus junior that he make available one of his late father's slaves for torture. This time around Strato told Sassia what she wanted to hear: Cluentius had killed his stepfather. Strato's confession was taken down in writing and sealed by witnesses. Sassia finally had what she needed—evidence that a poisoning had taken place.

But for Cicero there was something fishy about this testimony. Normally when slaves were interrogated for evidence in a criminal trial, this was done in conjunction with the trial, under the supervision of the presiding magistrate. Yet Oppianicus junior had not made his slave available for the court. Cicero demanded to know what had happened to the man. "As for Strato, members of the jury," Cicero said, "I must inform you that he was crucified, after first having had his tongue cut out, as everybody at Larinum knows."[47]

From these ghastly revelations, it was on to the peroration.[48] Cicero thrust the dagger of attack into Sassia one last time. He wept for his client, who was dressed in rags. He pointed to all the men from Larinum and neighboring towns who had come to the court and were sitting with poor Cluentius. Save this honorable man from his monstrous mother, Cicero pleaded. Spare him from the prejudice that had been unfairly roused against him all those years ago. With no apparent irony, he ended by reminding the jurors that "a court of law is the abode of truth."[49]

Cicero boasted years later that at the trial of Cluentius, he cast a cloud of darkness over the eyes of the jurors.[50] This is our only indication of the outcome of the case. Cicero must have won, but what was the cloud he cast? Part of his victory lay in paying so much attention to the least important part of the prosecution case: the charge of judicial murder back in 74 BC. Even more, his success came down to his usual storytelling ability. He gave jurors and other listeners an alternative version of events that was emotionally compelling. Even if many of his allegations about the late Oppianicus and Sassia were unsubstantiated, he inflamed feeling against them. Near the end of his speech, he practically accused Sassia of being a witch. Character assassination like this, in so blatant a form, would be hard to use in a judicial system with stricter rules of relevance and admissibility. The trials of Cluentius and Oppianicus senior alike reveal how unfettered lawyers were.

In addition to all that, Cicero surely won support from nonsenatorial jurors by making clear he would defend their interests and quash any move to make them liable for charges of judicial murder.[51] This was important for reasons beyond the acquittal of his client. In 66 BC Cicero was looking forward to his campaign for the consulship, for which he would need the votes of the wealthy. As a candidate for the top office, he had to work extra hard. He was a new man, the first in his family to enter the Senate, and in the last two decades no new man had won a consulship. Many nobles would not care to support him, and Romans of lower rank might struggle to see him as a credible candidate.

Yet Cicero would win, and with his consulship began a new chapter in his life. After years of prosecuting and defending criminal cases, he was to be confronted with a crime in the making: a conspiracy to topple the elected government of the Republic. Sulla had taken over Rome by armed force, and Oppianicus had taken over his hometown. Others thought they might do the same again.

# CHAPTER 7

# Conspiracy

Night had fallen on Rome, November 6, 63 BC, when the secret meeting got underway on the Street of the Scythe-Makers. At the house of a fellow senator, Lucius Sergius Catiline had gathered the ringleaders of his conspiracy. Catiline, the proud member of an ancient patrician family, had desperately wanted to become consul but twice now lost in elections. On the verge of bankruptcy, he would not be able to run again. His only path to power lay in a military coup. Physically strong with great charisma, Catiline persuaded a small group of senators and equestrians, dissatisfied with their lots in life, to join him.

At the meeting, Catiline began issuing orders to those present, perhaps around fifteen people. Some were to fan out throughout Italy and stir rebellion. Others were to stay behind in Rome and burn down parts of the city. Catiline said that he was about to set off himself, to join an army in northern Italy recruited by one of Sulla's old officers. All Catiline was waiting for was for the consul Cicero to be killed. Two men of equestrian rank, Gaius Cornelius and Lucius Vargunteius, promised that later that night, just before dawn, they would go to Cicero's house as if to pay their respects but really to murder him in his own bed.[1]

No sooner was the meeting over than one of the conspirators, who was working as a spy for Cicero, got word to him of the trap that was being laid. Cicero reinforced the guards protecting his house. When the two men sent by Catiline came, he denied them entry. Probably one day later, on November 8, he called a meeting of the Senate at the Temple of Jupiter Stator, the god who stopped Roman troops from running away in battle. The temple, located on a spur of the Palatine Hill, was more fortresslike than the Senate house in the Forum usually used for meetings. Cicero surrounded the building with armed men. Perhaps unexpectedly, Catiline turned up and took a seat on one of the wooden benches inside the temple where the senators were already seated. Those near where Catiline sat down got up and moved away.

As the presiding consul, Cicero controlled the debate and he launched into a blistering attack against Catiline. He revealed details of the secret meeting on the Street of the Scythe-Makers, though not everything. Cicero felt he couldn't afford to divulge his sources yet. He went over earlier plots of Catiline that had also failed, such as an attempt to kill Cicero at the recent elections. Cicero chided the senators for not having done more to stop Catiline. To Catiline himself, his message was blunt: get out of Rome![2]

Through the published version of Cicero's speech we can observe the Senate meeting in the Temple of Jupiter, and it is a puzzling scene. If Catiline was doing all that he was accused of, why was he allowed to walk free through the city? Cicero may have exaggerated some of Catiline's misdeeds. But as events shortly after the Senate meeting would show, Catiline was prepared to march on Rome with an army. He was conspiring with other high-ranking Romans. Until he took his fatal step of joining up with an army, what protected him was the glory of being a patrician and his friendships with nobles who doubted unsubstantiated reports from the new man Cicero. What's more, Romans did not typically detain citizens, especially those of high rank, even pending a criminal trial. All this meant that Cicero, as he confronted the mounting conspiracy to overthrow the elected government, had to make one hard choice after another. How could he get Romans to take the plot seriously and secure the city before it burned down?

To understand Cicero's contest with Catiline we must go back to its beginning: the elections for the consulship held in 64 BC, in which both Cicero and Catiline were competing.[3] Each of them had climbed the ladder of required offices that led to the top. In 75 BC Cicero had served as quaestor on Sicily. In 69 BC he was aedile, in charge of the games and grain supply of Rome. Three years later, as praetor, he presided over the extortion court. That year, he began giving speeches in formal debates in the Senate and the Forum on the major questions of the day. But history, as Cicero knew, was unlikely to remember much of this. Only with the consulship could Rome's best orator become a true political titan.

Running for office in Rome was a daunting challenge for any candidate. All the magistrates were elected by one of several assemblies of citizens that convened in the city.[4] Voting was done in person. There were no mail-in ballots, even for citizens who lived hundreds of miles away. Citizens were divided into thirty-five voting groups known as tribes. Four of the tribes represented the city of Rome, the other thirty-one the rest of Italy. As the Romans gained control of the peninsula, they assigned new territory to one of the tribes, making them noncontiguous. Cicero's tribe, the Cornelia, covered his hometown of Arpinum and at least four other parts of central and southern Italy.

The Tribal Assembly elected lower-ranking magistrates such as aediles, with each of the thirty-five tribes receiving one vote. The vote was determined by the majority of the tribe's members on the day of the election. Far more complicated was the Centuriate Assembly, which elected praetors and consuls. This assembly had its origins in the army, in which tradition held that a man's role derived from his wealth. The richest Romans formed the cavalry, for instance, since they could furnish their own horses. By Cicero's day the army was organized differently, but the Centuriate Assembly endured. Every male citizen was placed into one of 193 centuries, according to a classification based on the property he owned. Those without significant property—a vast number—were all shunted into a single century. On the other hand, those who met the top property classification of perhaps 100,000 sesterces made up seventy centuries, two for each tribe.

If it sounds dizzying, it was. On the day of a consular election, citizens would gather early in the morning on the Field of Mars, a floodplain of the Tiber River just outside the old city walls. Voting took place in a vast unroofed wooden structure known as the Sheepfold, because it was divided by ropes into aisles. Voters trudged along in single file. As they reached the head of the line, they were handed wooden ballots covered with wax, which they marked with the name of their two choices and then dropped into urns. As the centuries in each property classification voted, starting with the richest, the votes were tallied and announced. When a candidate reached a majority of ninety-seven centuries, he was declared a winner. With two winners announced, the consular election was over. This took hours and often under beating sun since elections commonly happened in summer.[5]

Romans remarked on the unpredictability of their elections. Cicero once said that not even a strait with currents swirling in many directions could compare to the turbulences and tides of a voting assembly.[6] A candidate could not always be sure who would make it to Rome from the country towns to vote. Poorer citizens might not bother to show up since an election could be decided by the top centuries, but in a tight race their vote mattered. A diligent candidate had to make some appeal to them.[7] In general, though, anyone running for the consulship knew that the votes of wealthy Italians counted most and would work to win them over, even years in advance. This was one reason why Cicero took on so many legal defenses for powerful men from outside Rome, such as the younger Roscius and Cluentius, and why he upheld equestrian interests at the trial of Cluentius among others. Quintus Cicero, in a brief handbook on electioneering he wrote for his older brother's campaign, advised Cicero to "show off the large number and variety of your friends . . . all the publicans, practically the whole of the equestrian order, the many towns that are loyal exclusively to you, the many men of every rank defended by you in the courts."[8] In elections, the rich had clout and their votes mattered most.

Candidates were expected to seek, even beg for, support as visibly as possible.[9] To be accompanied by a large retinue of supporters enhanced one's prestige and suggested that one had the ability to lead effectively—and win on election day. Nobody wanted to back a loser. As elections approached, office seekers wore a specially whitened garment, known as the *toga candida* (from which the English word "candidate" is derived). A candidate tried to get as many supporters as possible to crowd into his house each morning and walk with him to the Forum. There, he would shake hands and greet men by name. (Sometimes candidates had slaves present to whisper names in their ears.) Quintus advised Cicero to include in his entourage former clients of high rank and members of the nobility, for the honor they brought.[10] But it was important to include men of the lower orders as well so that the overall number would be impressive. Respect had to be shown to everyone.

Roman politicians did not run on platforms of issues as much as their modern counterparts do.[11] There were no organized political parties. Name and personal fame meant nearly everything, which is one reason candidates from the nobility enjoyed such an advantage. Cicero's oratorical successes had earned him not just the gratitude of others but celebrity. Without his public speaking, he would have stood no chance of winning a consulship. Still, no new man had won the top office for many years. Therefore a simple but effective tactic for Cicero's opponents was to throw his newness in his face. After all, what battles had he or his family ever won for the Republic? Negative campaigning, especially personal attacks, worked as well in Rome as it does today. Fortunately for Cicero, if his opponents went low, he knew how to go even lower.

Cicero faced a crowded field of competitors. Seven men were running. A couple of them came from families that had never won a consulship and could not match Cicero's fame as a speaker. Two others, although from distinguished families, lacked energy, according to Quintus. One of them, Lucius Cassius Longinus, who turned out to be a key player in the Catilinarian drama, was said to be fat and stupid; Cicero in at least one speech mocked Cassius for his girth.[12] As Quintus's handbook noted, only two rivals appeared to pose a danger to his brother: Gaius Antonius and Catiline.

Gaius Antonius was the son of Marcus Antonius, the legendary lawyer admired so much by Cicero. As a young officer of Sulla, Gaius had racked up wealth by plundering Greece. He was expelled from the Senate in 70 BC due to his misdeeds and high level of personal debt. However, he was able to regain his place by winning election to the tribunate. In 66 BC he served as praetor, alongside Cicero, and won renown for the lavish games he staged that year. In the temporary theater he built, he trimmed the stage with silver.[13]

More impressive, in some ways, was Lucius Sergius Catiline. He boasted patrician ancestry and physical toughness on the battlefield. As an officer of Sulla he killed several men during the proscriptions and bought up confiscated land. Yet scandal always seemed to follow him. In 73 BC he was accused of sleeping with a Vestal Virgin, but help from one of his noble friends saved him. As governor of Africa several years later, he plundered the province so extensively that provincials came to Rome to protest before his term was over. In the ensuing extortion trial, he managed to secure an acquittal, allegedly by bribery. As Quintus Cicero later wrote, Catiline "came out of that trial as impoverished as some of the jurors were before it began."[14] It rankled Catiline that, because of the trial, he was forced to delay his run for the consulship, which he felt was his patrician birthright.

The campaign took place against a backdrop of growing political anxiety.[15] Calls had been growing the last few years to correct some of the injustices of Sulla's dictatorship, such as a ban on the sons of the proscribed from holding public office. In 64 BC a high-minded young politician named Cato—soon to be a force in public affairs—used his quaestorship to comb through the official records of the treasury. He demanded that anyone who had collected the reward of 50,000 sesterces for killing one of the proscribed return the money. Another up-and-coming politician, Julius Caesar, went further. As president of the murder court in 64 BC, he allowed prosecutions to go forward against those who had received the bounties.[16] Association with Sulla was becoming a political liability. Still, many had benefited from Sulla's victory and fretted about how far calls for justice might go. Cicero had staked out the middle ground here. He had frequently acknowledged the injustices of Sulla's rule but, in 66 BC, did help foil an effort to put Sulla's son Faustus on trial in the embezzlement court for retaining money seized by his father.[17]

Another major concern was money in politics. Both men elected in 66 BC to serve as consuls for the following year, one of whom was a nephew of Sulla, were put on trial in the criminal court for electoral bribery and both were found guilty. Their penalty was payment of a fine, expulsion from the Senate, and disqualification from office. Replacement consuls were elected before the first pair ever took up their posts.[18] Campaign finance was a contentious issue because the line between generosity to voters and bribery could be hard to draw. For example, a candidate was allowed to host a dinner for members of his own tribe in the run-up to an election, but not for other groups. But what if a friend of the candidate hosted a dinner for *his* tribe, on the candidate's behalf? Some politicians, such as the punctilious Cato, wanted to toughen the bribery laws by enumerating more offenses. Others said the laws should be relaxed. If two candidates who had both won the consulship could be knocked out, weren't bribery prosecutions likely to become just another weapon in the brutal game of politics?[19]

A final cause of unease in the run-up to Cicero's election was widespread indebtedness. Every level of society struggled with this: the urban poor, who had to pay high rents for their rickety tenements; small-scale farmers in the countryside, including both veterans of Sulla given land in recognition of their service and the men they had dispossessed; and senators, who spent lavishly on political campaigns, not to mention houses, villas, and art. After years of warfare, the Roman East was finally settling down and financiers were calling in loans made to Italians so that capital could be reinvested more profitably abroad. With bankruptcy looming for many, cries for debt cancellation or forgiveness grew. The wealthy equestrians, for whom moneylending was a lucrative activity, feared social unrest. They expected any elected consul to enforce loans strictly.[20]

And so, while candidates for office did not typically address such issues directly, Cicero and his supporters could play on them in their smears against Antonius and Catiline. According to Quintus Cicero, both of his brother's rivals, the former officers of Sulla, were "cutthroats from boyhood on." Both were up to their ears in debt. Deeply corrupt, they figured their only way to win high office was to buy it.[21]

As accusations of bribery swirled, the Senate took up the matter and finally proposed new legislation that would stiffen the penalties. One of the tribunes immediately interposed his veto (tribunes alone enjoyed a special power to block almost any government action).[22] There were reasonable grounds for a veto here. The elections were to take place in a few days' time; if a new bribery law had to be passed first, a delay would ensue. But the tribune (probably a relative of Catiline by marriage, and certainly an opponent of Cicero) took the chance to say publicly that Cicero was unworthy of the consulship—even though Cicero had once represented him in a civil suit for theft. The veto gave Cicero the chance to stand up in the Senate and blast his opponents. This speech, which came to be known as *In the White Toga*, survives only in quotations in a commentary written by the well-informed scholar Asconius about a century later.[23] Even in these fragments, the rhetorical brilliance Cicero had honed over so many years in the courts leaps out, as does his frustration over claims of his unworthiness.

Cicero lobbed accusations of bribery straight at Antonius and Catiline. Probably at the start of his speech he said, "It is my contention, senators, that last night, in the house of a certain noble, a person well-known and recognized in this business of bribery, Catiline and Antonius met along with their agents."[24] Catiline and Antonius were coordinating their campaign efforts to defeat Cicero, and almost certainly they had powerful backers willing to assist their campaigns materially. But Cicero left his audience to wonder who the noble was that hosted the secret nighttime meeting. The commentator Asconius thought it might be Crassus, among the wealthiest senators of his day, who had a reputation for dipping into his silver chests to buy politicians.[25]

Even more than in forensic speeches, in senatorial oratory no holds were barred. As Cicero continued speaking, he piled up a list of his opponents' enormities. Catiline "besmirched himself with every sort of sexual crime and disgraceful act, he bloodied himself in unholy slaughter, he plundered our allies, he infringed the laws, the courts, the administration of justice."[26] Cicero made sensational charges, some of which probably lacked any foundation: Catiline slept with his own daughter. During the proscriptions, he carried with his own hands the head of one victim, still showing signs of life, to Sulla in the Temple of Apollo. As for Antonius, he was a brigand in Sulla's army, a gladiator when Sulla entered Rome, and a charioteer when Sulla celebrated victory games after the civil war.

At a time when anxiety gripped well-off Romans, Cicero wanted to show that his two opponents threatened the established order. Revolution was in the air. Antonius, despite selling all his livestock and giving up his grasslands, "retains his shepherds, from whom, he says, he will stir up a war of runaway slaves whenever he wishes."[27] And Catiline, Cicero claimed, had already nearly toppled the Republic. In collusion with a young senator named Gnaeus Piso, later killed in Spain, Catiline had hoped to carry out a massacre of the leading men of the state but failed.[28] Dark forces were stirring, Cicero said. Evil men had tried to use Piso, the "Spanish stiletto," to "slit the sinews of Roman citizens," and now they hoped to unsheathe "two daggers" at once—Antonius and Catiline.[29] It may sound overheated to a modern reader, but charges of collusion and conspiracy were widespread in Rome and have, of course, reared their heads in modern republics too. Cicero would later discover that the unfortunate consequence of such rhetoric is that when a genuine plot does arise, few may believe it.

After Cicero stopped speaking, Catiline and Antonius replied with insults of their own, including slurs about Cicero's newness. One fragment of a speech of Antonius, perhaps given at this time, survives: "But I do not dread him as a prosecutor, because I am innocent. I do not fear him as a rival candidate, because I am Antonius. I do not expect to see him as consul, because he is Cicero."[30]

The bill on electoral malpractice was never put to the people for a vote and the consular election proceeded on schedule. Cicero was declared a winner first, by the smallest number of centuries needed, ninety-seven. Catiline and Antonius duked it out further until finally Antonius prevailed.

Negative campaigning had helped Cicero to win, as had the general feeling of anxiety he exploited.[31] Cries for radical reform and fears of unrest encouraged even some of the haughtiest nobles to hold their noses and back the new man. At Cicero's request his old friend Atticus, who was close with many of these men, had come back from Greece to help win them over.[32] Cicero's victory was also due to his years of hard work building a reputation through speaking and cultivating powerful friends across Italy, who delivered votes for him in 64 BC. To have reached the consulship, in the earliest year allowed to him, at the top of the poll, was a remarkable achievement. But the attack on Catiline, along with the humiliation Catiline felt losing to a new man, left Cicero with an enemy.

Cicero had secured his great prize. On New Year's Day, 63 BC, he put on the purple-edged toga consuls wore and paraded with the consul's twelve lictors carrying the fasces to the great Temple of Jupiter on the Capitoline Hill, where he held an inaugural sacrifice. His family was now noble. The son born to Terentia in the summer of 65 BC would never face the stigma of newness.[33]

But Cicero's year in office was destined to be stormy due to his promises to wealthy supporters, his belief in the established social and political order, and his conviction that property was sacred above all. Quite unusually, all ten of the incoming tribunes agreed to advance some of the reforms for which many were pushing: relief for the sons of the proscribed, debt forgiveness, and aid for the poor more generally.[34] And Cicero's rival and fellow consul, Antonius, was willing to help them. They had been preparing their bills throughout the fall of 64 BC.

The most ambitious proposal was for land redistribution. One of the tribunes, Rullus, began wearing a rough toga and growing out his hair and beard, as if he were a Roman from centuries earlier when the impoverished plebeians first stood up to the dominant patricians.[35]

Now that the recent wars in the East were over, Rullus said, plunder and new taxes raised there could provide land for the poor. Ten commissioners were to be elected to buy up privately owned land in Italy and release publicly owned land, previously rented out for revenue. New farms would be made available to those struggling in the countryside as well as the urban poor. There were to be no confiscations, and the grants Sulla had made would be secure.

At a meeting of the Senate on New Year's Day, 63 BC, Cicero came out against the law. More surprisingly, Antonius, despite his earlier friendliness with the tribunes, said nothing in support of the law nor did he protest Cicero's remarks. While it might not have been widely known at the time, Cicero had agreed to swap the provinces the two consuls were slated to govern after their year in office: Cicero would take Cisalpine Gaul and hand over Macedonia to Antonius, where there were more opportunities for war-making and extortion. Given Antonius's terrible record, Cicero must have foreseen the suffering this would cause for provincial populations. It was a price he was willing to pay to undercut the reformers.[36]

At the same meeting of the Senate, one of Rullus's tribunician colleagues, who was trying to enact his own law relaxing the penalties for those convicted of electoral bribery, announced he was dropping that bill. And, he said, he would veto Rullus's bill. Without the support of the consul Antonius, and with the defection of this tribune, Rullus saw the ground cut from beneath him.[37]

A few days after the Senate meeting, Cicero denounced the land legislation in a speech to the people. He assured the crowd that the proposed commission of ten would rule Italy as tyrannically as the kings of old. Rullus and his friends did not have the people's interests at heart. They were Sullans in disguise, trying to keep the general's profiteers on their land or give them a chance to unload worthless properties. Did city-dwellers really want to give up all the pleasures available in Rome for a life of unending toil in the desolate countryside?[38]

And so Cicero killed the proposal, just as he would other reform measures later in the year. Still, there remained Catiline. Later in 64 BC he had been put on trial in the murder court for his killings during the Sullan proscriptions but acquitted. Now he was preparing a second run for the consulship. The stakes were even higher than the year before. Not only did he need to avenge his defeat to a new man. Like so many others, Catiline had racked up debt. He had probably spent heavily on his last campaign. He also splurged on lavish parties at his Palatine house. Catiline needed the top office and the lucrative command it would bring to settle up with his creditors. Bankruptcy and ruin awaited if he failed to win.[39]

As the elections of 63 BC approached, concerns about bribery mounted, just as they had the year before. Sulpicius Rufus, one of the candidates, was an expert in civil law who had accompanied Cicero on his study tour in the East years earlier. He suspected his rivals of electoral malpractice and demanded stricter regulations. Sulpicius wanted a new law that would increase the penalty for electoral malpractice to exile, add sanctions against bribery agents working for the candidates, and grant prosecutors the right to select jury panels to ensure rigorous judgment. He found warm support from the punctilious Cato and other senators. As consul Cicero was forced to push through the law, although he did succeed in removing the provision for prosecutorial selection of juries.[40]

The consular election was postponed until September. A few days before it was to take place, Cato at a meeting of the Senate threatened to prosecute Catiline for bribery if he won. Catiline's response was menacing. If his fortunes should be set on fire, he said, he would put out the flames not with water but with general destruction. The tenements in which so many of the city's poor lived were firetraps, and it was common to stop a conflagration by destroying a whole block of buildings. Try to ruin me, Catiline was saying, and I will take down Rome.[41]

What kind of threat was this? Catiline was worried that his own prospects were dimming, and he was aware that so many people's cries for help were being ignored. As a result, he began to openly appeal to those in debt, which he had not done the year before. Debt relief, even debt cancellation, had wide support. Indebtedness was always a problem, but so many loans had been called in recently that a full-on credit crisis was underway. Nobles such as Catiline, who were either unwilling or unable to sell their land, silver, or slaves, would welcome loan write-offs. Even more desperate were the small-scale farmers in the Italian countryside—veterans who had failed to make a go of it and the even more wretched souls who had lost their lands altogether. The most powerful backers Catiline found were a group of downcast men in northern Italy who rallied around an old officer of Sulla's named Manlius in the territory of Fiesole (ancient Faesulae), in the hills outside Florence.[42]

Not only the indebted but others with grievances saw possibilities in Catiline's victory. One was Cassius Longinus, the large man who had lost the consulship to Cicero in 64 BC. Another was a patrician named Lentulus Sura, a former consul who had been kicked out of the Senate by the censors in 70 BC and was now serving as praetor a second time to regain membership. Lentulus burned with indignation at the comedown—and took solace in a prophecy that he was fated to rule Rome.[43]

Another group fascinated with Catiline were a group of well-off young men looking for adventure. Later in 63 BC Cicero would sneeringly describe them in a speech to the people: "This is Catiline's very own group, men he has chosen, or should I say embraced closely? You see them, with their carefully combed hair and their glowing skin, either too young to shave or else nicely bearded, with tunics that reach down to their wrists and ankles. . . . These boys, so charming, so dainty, have learned the art not only of sex, active and passive, not only of dancing and singing, but also of wielding the dagger and sprinkling food with poison."[44] This lurid description cannot be taken too seriously, but it is known that one of Cicero's own students, a fashionable young man named Caelius, caused much pain to his teacher by becoming a Catilinarian supporter.

Cicero had grave concerns about Catiline by September 63 BC. Catiline's fondness for vague threats, while perhaps thrilling the young and malcontented, horrified Cicero. So did Catiline's dalliance with the band forming under Manlius in northern Italy. If Catiline lost the election, he might try to march on Rome, as Sulla had done. A mistress of one of Catiline's followers, a noblewoman named Fulvia, grew so worried about what she was hearing from her lover that she went to Cicero or Cicero's wife, Terentia (accounts vary). She, and then her lover, Curius, agreed to keep Cicero informed.[45]

It was probably through them that Cicero learned of a nighttime meeting at Catiline's own house a couple of days before the consular election. According to Cicero's later account, Catiline told those gathered that there could be no true defender of the poor who was not also poor himself; people who were poor and in trouble should not trust the promises of the rich and carefree. Look at the size of my debts, Catiline said; I will be the leader and the standard-bearer of the desperate.[46] This was military language. Frustrated at how Cicero and Cicero's allies had treated him, Catiline was quite possibly preparing to fight his political battles at sword point if necessary. With his great physical strength, he would make a convincing commander.

Cicero summoned the senators and persuaded them to postpone the election to allow time to discuss Catiline's nighttime address. The Senate reconvened the following day. Cicero shared what he had learned (without divulging his source) and called on Catiline to explain himself. Catiline responded with another of his cryptic threats. "There are two bodies in the Republic," he said, "one feeble and with a weak head, the other strong but headless. This [second] body, if it treats me well, will not lack a head so long as I live."[47] Some senators groaned, but the house collectively decided there was nothing to do. After all, Catiline retained powerful friends and the only information the Senate had to act on was Cicero's report of a speech.

The consular election was held soon after. It fell to Cicero to preside over it and he surrounded himself with a group of burly young men he had brought to Rome from a country town. He also put on a well-polished breastplate and made sure to let his tunic slip so that voters would catch a glimpse of the plate and think they were in peril from Catiline.[48] As century after century voted and the ballots were tallied up it became clear that Catiline had lost again. Short of personal ruin, a conspiracy to topple the government and take over Rome was his only option.

Now came the real test for Cicero as consul. Catiline remained in Rome for weeks after the election. In Etruria, meanwhile, the number of men rallying around Manlius swelled. Thanks to the widespread credit crisis, disturbances were flaring up elsewhere in Italy too. It must have been hard for Cicero to discover Catiline's plans, even with moles like Fulvia and Curius. Perhaps Catiline himself wasn't entirely sure. In any case, Cicero needed to protect his sources, and when he did learn something, all he could say publicly was, "I have discovered that . . ." So often did he use the expression that he came to be mocked for it.[49] Cicero required concrete evidence of plans for sedition—before they had gone too far.

One night in mid-October, Cicero seemed to catch a break. The plutocrat Crassus came with several of his friends after dinner to Cicero's house on the Esquiline Hill. They had the doorkeeper wake up Cicero and told him that, earlier that evening, several anonymous letters had been delivered to Crassus's house. Crassus had opened the letter addressed to him, which warned there would be much bloodshed by Catiline and advised Crassus to leave Rome. The other letters remained unopened.[50]

The next morning, Cicero convened the Senate. He handed over the unopened letters to their addressees and asked for the documents to be read aloud. All were similar to Crassus's. The letters' author remains unknown, but modern historians have guessed that Crassus may have sent them himself to tamp down suspicions that he was conspiring with Catiline. Paranoia gripped Rome. Still, the letters were anonymous, not much better than Cicero's "I have discovered that . . ." Much weightier was a report from a former praetor that a militia was forming in Etruria and the old Sullan officer Manlius was only waiting for secret instructions from Rome to activate it.[51]

As it had done before at moments of civil unrest, the Senate passed a decree instructing the consuls "to see to it that the Republic suffer no harm."[52] From the first time it was used, in the later second century BC, this so-called ultimate decree was dogged by controversy. Proponents felt, with some reason, that in an armed uprising top officials needed special military power. According to this view, the consul could raise and employ voluntary forces to watch over the city, as Cicero now did. Critics, on the other hand, saw the potential for abuse. For instance, what if the consul and his forces killed innocent citizens?

A few days later, another report came in from Etruria: on October 27, Manlius had raised the banner of revolt. Once more, the Senate responded and issued instructions. Several former and current magistrates were to go with armed forces to Etruria and other hot spots of unrest. To prevent a mass uprising in Rome, bands of gladiators were to be removed from the city and parceled out among the towns of Italy. Finally, anyone who came forward with information on the plot was to be given a cash reward—and, if the informer were a slave, freedom as well. In Rome, there was no surer sign of a crisis than that.[53]

About Catiline himself the Senate as a body still did nothing, despite warnings from Cicero that Catiline had been planning a massacre of leading citizens. One senator, however, did bring charges against Catiline in the criminal court for public violence. Established only in the 70s BC after Sulla's dictatorship, this court was ill-equipped to deal with an unfolding conspiracy. As with other courts, defendants were not detained, although Catiline offered to go into voluntary custody at Cicero's own house, which Cicero understandably refused.[54]

Through his spies Cicero learned of the secret nighttime meeting on the Street of the Scythe-Makers in early November. He turned away the two men sent to murder him and, probably the following day, gave his speech in the Temple of Jupiter telling Catiline to leave Rome. "And what more is there, Catiline," Cicero asked, "that you are waiting for, if night cannot cover up your wicked plots with darkness, if a private house cannot contain the voices of conspiracy with its walls?"[55]

After Cicero finished speaking and took his seat on the consul's ivory chair, Catiline rose from his bench. He lowered his face and in a humble tone begged the senators to believe nothing they were told about him without good reason. With the family he was born into and the life he had led, his future was bright. The senators should not think that he, a patrician, who like his ancestors had done many good deeds for the people of Rome, had any need to destroy the Republic, especially when it was being protected by Marcus Tullius Cicero, a squatter in Rome![56]

That night Catiline left the city with a few of his followers. Adopting the insignia of a consul, he went to Manlius's camp to assume command of forces about ten thousand strong. When news of this reached Rome, Catiline's guilt was clear, and the Senate declared him a public enemy. The consul Antonius was sent out to fight the rebels while Cicero was to stay in Rome to defend the city.[57]

Cicero's problems were far from over. For one thing, his old friend Sulpicius Rufus, defeated in the consular race earlier in the year, had pressed forward with a prosecution of one of the victors, a popular general named Murena. Joining Sulpicius for the prosecution was Cato. Cicero was appalled. If convicted, Murena would be sent into exile, and Cicero was counting on him to continue the fight against Catiline into the next year. And so, hard-pressed as he was with other matters, Cicero joined Murena's defense team and gave one of the cleverest speeches of his career. He mocked Sulpicius as a pedantic legal scholar and young Cato as a doctrinaire Stoic devoid of common sense. Men like that would be useless in war. Cicero, who was joined for the defense by his old rival Hortensius, won the case. "What an amusing consul we have," Cato sourly remarked after Cicero's performance.[58]

Another problem was the supporters of Catiline who remained in Rome. But here, finally, Cicero had some luck. Late in November, the conspirator Lentulus Sura tried to enlist aid from several ambassadors of the Gallic Allobroges who were in Rome, pleading unsuccessfully in the Senate for help with their community's debts. Lentulus contacted the ambassadors through a businessman who had frequent dealings in Gaul, explained the conspiracy, and invited them to contribute cavalry to Catiline's army. The ambassadors expressed interest but then, after further thought, went to their patron Fabius Sanga, who in turn went to Cicero.[59]

This was Cicero's chance. Through Fabius, Cicero told the ambassadors to demand written pledges of support from the leading conspirators to take back home. Then, the night the Gauls left Rome, Cicero had the men arrested on the outskirts of the city and all their documents seized. The ambassadors were immediately brought to Cicero's house. Upon questioning by Cicero, they supplied him with the names of the conspirators and other information. Cicero sent for five of the conspirators supposed to be in the city, four of whom came (one had already slipped away). Cicero also sent a praetor to the house of one of the five, the patrician senator Cethegus, where a cache of newly sharpened daggers and swords was found. The Senate was summoned to a meeting in the Temple of Concord, at the edge of the Forum.[60]

Cicero was in his element. What was to unfold would have all the theatricality of a Roman criminal trial—and was meant to. He would make the senators see. Cicero personally escorted into the temple one of the four who had answered his summons, the former consul Lentulus Sura. Guards of Cicero led the other three, the patrician senator Cethegus and two equestrians, Statilius and Gabinius, but the equestrians had to wait outside the temple until called in. Cicero asked four senators, skilled in writing, to record what was said.[61]

Time was short and, just as in the trial of Verres, Cicero quickly plunged into evidence. His most important informants were the ambassadors from Gaul, but it would be unwise to start with them. Hadn't Cicero himself, at the trial of Fonteius, harped on the Gauls' unreliability? And so, while the ambassadors waited outside the temple, Cicero first called in a Roman with whom they had been traveling, a conspirator named Volturcius. Initially Volturcius denied any involvement in the plot. Then the Senate offered him immunity, and Cicero asked him to share what he knew. Volturcius explained how he had been admitted into the conspiracy a few days earlier. He had met with Gabinius, one of the equestrians now in custody, who had told him the names of others involved. Lentulus Sura had given him a letter and verbal instructions for Catiline—that Catiline should enlist slaves and march on Rome as soon as possible. The plan, Volturcius said, was that the conspirators in the city would set fires and carry out assassinations to cause chaos and pave the way for Catiline's return.

Then the Gauls were brought in. They explained that they had in their possession written pledges from Lentulus Sura, Cethegus, and Statilius to take back to their people. These three men, as well as Cicero's old electoral rival Cassius Longinus, had given instructions to send cavalry to Italy. The Gauls also reported that the conspirators, or at least some of them, wanted to carry out their arson and assassination during the mid-December festival of the Saturnalia, when the reveling city would be caught off guard. If all this weren't incriminating enough, Cicero had a further surprise for the senators: he revealed the discovery of the cache of weapons at Cethegus's house. When Cicero asked the patrician about it, he answered lamely that he had always been a collector of fine weapons.

Cicero ordered for the letters seized from the Gauls' luggage to be brought forward. These letters were written on wooden tablets that were folded shut, tied with string, and affixed with a seal in wax made by a signet ring. Cicero first showed Cethegus his letter, and Cethegus acknowledged his seal. Cicero then cut the string and read out the contents—a pledge of support to the Allobroges, written in Cethegus's own hand. Cethegus had little to say.

Next Statilius was brought into the temple and shown his letter. He recognized the seal and the handwriting. It was another pledge of support. Then came Lentulus's turn. Cicero showed him the letter and asked if he recognized the seal. He nodded. "It is indeed a famous seal," Cicero said, "a portrait of your grandfather, a most distinguished man who had a singular love for his country and his fellow citizens." Lentulus had also written a pledge to the Allobroges. After it was read out, Lentulus jumped to his feet and asked the Gauls and Volturcius how they could have visited his house. They explained how they met and reminded Lentulus about all his talk of the prophecy that he was fated to rule Rome. Cicero then produced the letter from Lentulus to Catiline that Volturcius had mentioned, which contained this ominous instruction: "Consider if there is anything which you must now do, and take care to gain the help of all, even the lowest." Cicero brought in the equestrian Gabinius last of all and interrogated him. Although there was no letter of his to read out, he was unable to shake any of the earlier testimony.

Whatever doubts senators might have had earlier in the year about Cicero, this time he was believed. After all the testimony was finished, the house voted to thank Cicero, the magistrates who had helped him, and the consul Antonius. The danger was perceived to be so real that Lentulus was compelled to resign his praetorship and he, along with the three other conspirators in the Senate, were taken into custody at the houses of selected senators. Five others were also to be taken into custody, if they could be found—conspirators with whom Volturcius, the Gauls, or both had had face-to-face dealings.[62]

Night was falling by the time this was all decided. The Senate would have to resume its deliberations the next day. After leaving the temple, Cicero explained to a large crowd in the Forum everything that had just happened, no doubt with much satisfaction. As far as he was concerned, he had saved Rome: "I have quenched the fires that were all but set to the whole city, its temples, its shrines, its houses, and its walls, and were about to engulf them. I have blunted the swords that were drawn against the Republic. I have torn away the daggers from your throats."[63]

The Senate reconvened the next day. A new informer, Lucius Tarquinius, was brought in. The Senate agreed to offer him immunity for involvement in the conspiracy in exchange for his testimony. He more or less repeated what Volturcius had said the day before about the plans for arson, assassination, and a march on Rome. Then came a thunderclap. Tarquinius said he had been sent by the wealthy senator Crassus to tell Catiline not to be alarmed by the arrest of the conspirators and to hasten his arrival in the city. To some in the Senate it seemed incredible that Crassus, who lent money widely, would be backing Catiline. And whereas Volturcius and the Gauls had independently confirmed one another's stories, and there was the evidence of weapons found at Cethegus's house and the letters written by the conspirators, nothing corroborated Tarquinius's claim. The Senate decreed that the testimony appeared to be false and Tarquinius should be detained. Separately, personal enemies of Julius Caesar tried to get

Cicero to implicate Caesar but Cicero refused. Both the consul and the Senate were trying to avoid a witch hunt.[64]

On December 4 the senators voted to reward Volturcius and the Allobroges for their testimony. The question remained of what to do about the five conspirators in custody: the four arrested the day before and Marcus Caeparius, who had been caught as he had set off to raise a revolt in southern Italy. Currently they were being held under guard separately at the houses of five senators, and reports were spreading of attempts to rescue them. Cicero ordered increased security throughout the city. Many equestrians, Atticus among them, took up arms and surrounded the Senate when it met again on December 5 in the Temple of Concord.[65]

Cicero viewed the nine conspirators named in the Senate decree of December 3 as public enemies and believed they deserved the traditional punishment for traitors: execution. As the one consul currently in Rome it would fall to him to carry out the punishment, and he wanted the senators' backing before he acted. Cicero opened the debate and began calling on senators according to rank, as was customary.[66] First to speak was one of the consuls-elect for the next year, Silanus. He proposed that punishment should be inflicted on the five in custody as well as the four others if they were caught. The other consul-elect, Murena, backed this proposal, as did all the ex-consuls, who were called on next.

Then it was the turn of the praetors-elect, among whose number was Julius Caesar. He broke with what all the others had said. He warned that if senators voted for the conspirators to be put to death without a trial, they would come to be hated by the Roman people. It violated a right that all citizens, even the humblest, valued. (Recall the outrage Cicero stirred at Verres's crucifixion of a Roman citizen.) A better course of action, Caesar said, was for Cicero to imprison all the conspirators for life in Italian towns of the consul's choosing and confiscate their property. This novel penalty was in many ways well suited to the circumstances. It showed severity to the conspirators while avoiding the irrevocable act of execution. It created an alternative to the more usual punishment of exile, which clearly would be inappropriate when an armed uprising against the Republic was still underway.[67]

After Caesar spoke, a number of senators backed his motion, including Cicero's brother Quintus. Even the consul-elect Silanus flip-flopped and said that he favored life imprisonment. But when Cicero got to the tribunes-elect, the debate unexpectedly took a turn. Cato stood up and in a fiery speech attacked the senators for backsliding. The enemy was inside the city walls, threatening senators' freedom and even their lives. If strong measures weren't taken immediately, the city would burn down. Our ancestors, he said, knew how to deal with traitors, and we must show the same resolve now. The only course of action was a sentence of death.[68]

As Cato sat down, the senators burst into applause and thronged around him. When Cicero put Cato's motion to a vote, it passed overwhelmingly. Cicero at once left the Senate to fetch the five conspirators. Cicero personally escorted Lentulus Sura from the Palatine through the Forum to the small prison next to the Temple of Concord, mainly used for executions. Praetors brought the other four men. In the prison was an underground chamber, dark and foul-smelling, reached only by an opening in its stone ceiling. One by one, the conspirators were lowered into the chamber and strangled by a noose by the public executioners.[69]

Cicero returned to the Forum after nightfall, leaving no time for a speech. And so he made a solemn declaration of just one word, *Vixere*—"They have lived." Which was to say, "They're dead."

According to Plutarch's biography of Cicero (which likely drew on a memoir of his consulship Cicero himself wrote), as he was escorted home afterward, all those he passed welcomed him with shouts and applause, crying that he was the savior of the city. The streets were lit with lamps and torches set up at the doorways, and from the rooftops women shone lights in his honor, as if he were a victorious general.[70] Cicero would never doubt that it was the most glorious moment of his life.

When news of the executions reached Catiline's army, many of his supporters melted away. His remaining force was soon trapped in a mountain pass between two senatorial armies. Catiline had no choice but to fight his way out. The consul Antonius, pleading gout, turned over his army to a highly experienced officer. In a vicious contest, the Catilinarian forces fought bravely but were almost completely wiped out. When Catiline's body was found, it was said, he was still faintly breathing and had on his face the same fierce expression he had always worn in life. His head was cut off by Antonius and sent to Rome as proof of death.[71]

In the meantime, the backlash over the executions that Caesar had warned against had begun. As fears of arson and assassination subsided, the struggling people of Rome faced the reality that Cicero had not alleviated any of their ongoing difficulties. When new tribunes took office on December 10, 63 BC, a few sensed the change in mood and began drubbing Cicero for taking the lives of citizens without a trial. They blocked him from giving any more speeches to crowds in the Forum.[72]

It was the custom for outgoing consuls to give a farewell address on their last day in office and swear an oath that they had obeyed the laws. Again, one of the tribunes stopped Cicero from speaking and said that the consul could only swear the oath. Cicero stepped onto the speaker's platform (the Rostra) and, after obtaining silence, swore not the usual formula but one of his own devising. The city of Rome and the Republic, he defiantly cried out, had been saved by him alone.[73]

Cicero was not without support. The Senate had already heaped honors on him. One of the most distinguished nobles in the Senate even recommended that Cicero should be called the father of his country, a title previously given only to Rome's founder Romulus and then later to Camillus, who rebuilt Rome after its sack by the Gauls in the fourth century. The motion passed. At a gathering of citizens in the Forum, Cato had those assembled acclaim Cicero in the same way. Cato likely prearranged his crowd, which might well have included many equestrians who would be eternally grateful to Cicero for his hard line on debt cancellation.[74]

Cicero deserved credit for taking steps to prevent unrest in the city of Rome, even at risk to himself. When Catiline and his followers took up arms to overturn an election, they were striking at a key principle of the Republic: the peaceful transfer of power from year to year. Cicero and the Senate had to defeat them, though it almost certainly would have been more prudent to follow Caesar's recommendation of life imprisonment for the conspirators caught in Rome. Cicero's executions set a bad precedent. In addition to that, he can be faulted for having shown little consideration for the ordinary people of Rome and their struggles. In a letter to Atticus, Cicero's true views about politics emerge: his wealthy supporters were "the honest men," and with Cicero they stood up to "the dregs of the city populace . . . the wretched hungry rabble that comes to meetings, treasury leaches."[75]

Cicero's consulship reveals him to have been opportunistic. To stop reform, he sacrificed Macedonia to Antonius and made misleading speeches in public. In the face of such pressing problems as the debt crisis, he fanned hysteria rather than try to calm it. He showed more commitment to upholding the interests of the well-off than to maintaining the rule of law. He claimed to be unifying the Republic, but he wasn't. None of this, of course, acquits Catiline, who was an even greater opportunist than Cicero. On both sides of this struggle, we see a lack of foresight regarding the long-term health of the state.

In the years to come, glaring inequality among citizens would persist and fuel more political violence. There would be more unscrupulous leaders like Catiline, ready to exploit the people's misery. All this left both the Republic and Cicero himself in a precarious position. Political violence and its legal quandaries were to dominate the rest of both his life and the life of the Republic.

# CHAPTER 8

# Secrets of the Good Goddess

Early one morning, the first week of December 62 BC, a year after Cicero executed the Catilinarian conspirators, a shocking story spread through Rome. Even the city's most jaded gossips must have thrilled to hear it. Publius Clodius Pulcher, son of one of the Republic's most distinguished families, had committed sacrilege.[1]

The night before, Rome's high-ranking women had gathered for a female-only religious festival held annually in honor of a deity known as the Good Goddess. The rites, which included dancing, prayer, and sacrifice, took place in the house of a leading magistrate but he had to spend the evening elsewhere. No male creature of any sort was allowed to witness the ritual—or the goddess would be offended. Even the animal burned as an offering to her was a sow. And the entertainers who supplied the flute and string music heard wafting out onto the street? They were all women too.[2]

And that, according to the story going around, was how Clodius had gotten in. Wearing a dress and hood and carrying a lute, he had come to the door of Julius Caesar's house, where the rites were being celebrated that year. The woman watching the door admitted him. On a pitch-dark street, the costume would have been effective. Once inside, though, Clodius tried to avoid the lamps and torches. A slave of Caesar's mother, Aurelia, finally came over and asked him to join in the merriment. But when Clodius replied, his voice gave him away. The slave shrieked and ran off to the other women, crying, "I've found a man here!"

Aurelia stopped the ceremony and ordered the doors closed while she searched the house with torches. Clodius was soon found, hiding in the bedroom of a maid of Caesar's wife, Pompeia, named Habra. The women kicked him out, returned home, and angrily told their husbands what had happened. Clodius had done wrong to the women, the city, and the gods—and he must pay for it.

Scandal, which a Roman poet once imagined as a monster that flies on wings through the night and then lights down on the roofs of a city, had come to Rome.[3] Over the next few months, startling stories of sacrilege, adultery, incest, and bribery carried out by Clodius would fill the streets, squares, and taverns. He would be put on trial for his religious offense, and Cicero was dragged into the case—not as a lawyer but as a witness for the prosecution, with disastrous consequences. A cycle of anger and revenge, discord and violence, was set whirring. Clodius had opened a Pandora's box.

Clodius's family, the patrician Claudii, traced their ancestry back to the earliest days of the Republic.[4] Tradition held that just a few years after Rome's last king had been driven from the throne, the family had come to the city with a large band of clients and quickly built up their power. Over the next five centuries, they achieved, by one count, "twenty-eight consulships, five dictatorships, and seven censorships."[5] The city was filled with monuments to the dynasty's success. One ancestor had constructed Rome's first aqueduct as well as the Appian Way, the great paved road that ran from the city gates to the far south of Italy. Another used the spoils of conquest to build a temple for the war goddess Bellona, which was later decorated with portraits of all the famous family members set within shields.

But pride shades easily into arrogance, and alongside their record of service the Claudii gained a reputation for cruelty and contempt. It was said that one Claudius lusted after a young woman and had a hanger-on claim she was his slave; rather than see her raped, the woman's father seized a knife from a butcher's shop and stabbed her to death in the Forum. Another Claudius began a naval battle off the coast of Sicily, even though the sacred chickens on his ship were refusing to eat. Before any major undertaking, the Romans liked to get divine approval of the gods. One way they did this was by watching birds, believed to be messengers of the gods. The sacred chickens were kept hungry in a cage. When they were finally fed, if any food dropped out of their beaks as they greedily ate, this was a good sign. When Claudius's birds wouldn't eat, in a fit of anger he drowned them in the sea, saying, "They will drink, since they refuse to eat." He lost the battle. His sister outdid him when her carriage got stuck in a throng of people on the streets of Rome and she cried out that she wished her brother might come back to life and lose another fleet—to thin out the crowd blocking her way.

Six years before the scandal of the Good Goddess broke, Clodius already had shown that he lived up to his Claudian ancestry.[6] The patrician, then in his mid-twenties, was serving in the East on the staff of his brother-in-law, the great general Lucullus. A war against Armenia had been going well but then bogged down. The soldiers were starting to flag. Clodius felt that his contributions were being overlooked by Lucullus while other officers were being overpromoted. To stop Lucullus from enjoying any more success, Clodius whipped up a mutiny. Would there be no end to the fighting? he asked the soldiers. Would they keep wearing their lives away, warring with every people, wandering through every land? Had they earned nothing more for their service than to escort Lucullus's wagons and camels laden with gold and jeweled goblets? It was a stirring performance and the soldiers refused to go on. Soon thereafter the government back in Rome replaced Lucullus.[7]

Clodius did not stick around and instead moved to the staff of another general, who put him in charge of a fleet to fight the pirates then swarming the coasts of Asia Minor. Lucullus's judgment of his brother-in-law's abilities seemed to be proven right when Clodius was defeated and taken prisoner. His sense of entitlement more intact than his fleet, Clodius sent messengers to the king of Cyprus demanding a large ransom. When only a small amount of silver was sent back, Clodius was incensed. The pirates released him anyway—"after he satisfied their lusts," Cicero would later claim.[8] Cicero probably made that detail up to add to Clodius's embarrassment. In Rome to accuse a man of being sexually penetrated by another was a standard form of insult. It would hardly be the worst of Cicero's slurs against the patrician.

On January 1, 61 BC, Cicero wrote to his friend Atticus, then away from Rome, to catch him up on all the news: "I suppose you have heard that Publius Clodius, son of Appius, was caught in women's clothing at Caesar's house during the sacrifice on behalf of the people . . . it's a most disgraceful matter."[9] When he wrote this, Cicero had no direct involvement in the episode. In recent years he and Clodius appear to have been on friendly terms.[10] Therefore the letter is an indication that the women's story was credible: Clodius had infiltrated the secret rites.

But what motive would he have had? One possible answer is that it had to do with politics. By chance—or divine providence?—the celebration of the festival the year before had come as the conspiracy of Catiline was reaching its climax. Shortly after Cicero had rounded up the cronies of Catiline in Rome and presented the Senate with evidence of their guilt, it fell to his wife, the formidable Terentia, to preside over the nighttime ceremony for the Good Goddess in Cicero's house. At dawn the next day, on the instructions of the Vestal Virgins, who helped carry out the rituals, Terentia brought word to Cicero of a sign the women had witnessed during the sacrifice. The fire on the altar had gone out, but then a great bright flame shot back up from the ash: the Good Goddess was lending support to Cicero![11] Soon afterward, on the Senate's recommendation, he executed the five conspirators. And so, some modern scholars have suggested, perhaps Clodius—with an eye to winning popularity from citizens who had sympathized with Catiline and were worried about the Senate encroaching on their rights—had violated the rites of the goddess to protest the use Terentia and Cicero had made of them.[12]

But that's only a guess. Ancient sources dwell on a much seamier motive: Clodius wanted to have a tryst. He had recently taken a fancy to Caesar's wife, Pompeia, and apparently the desire was mutual. Caesar, perhaps the city's greatest womanizer, was then in the throes of an intense affair with the patrician Servilia, half sister of the priggish senator Cato. During the debate on the Catilinarian conspirators, a note was delivered to Caesar in the Senate. Cato demanded that it be read out, in the hope that it would implicate Caesar. It turned out to be a love letter from Servilia. The problem Clodius faced, according to Caesar's biographer Plutarch, was not Caesar but Caesar's mother, who lived with her son and daughter-in-law and kept a close watch on Pompeia.[13]

Many or even all these reports about Pompeia may be true. Receiving help from her and one of her slaves could explain how Clodius made it into the house so easily and why he was found in the maid Habra's room. Certainly the story spread that Pompeia was unfaithful, which was embarrassing for Caesar. A year before, he had been elected as Rome's chief priest (*pontifex maximus*, the same title later used by popes). Sacrilege in his house called his priestly authority into question. And so, in early 61 BC, he divorced Pompeia. When pressed on whether this was an acknowledgment that a religious offense had occurred, he famously ducked the question by saying that Caesar's wife must be above suspicion.[14]

But even if Clodius itched to see his lover, he still must have known that crashing the women's festival was the riskiest way to do so. The sacrifice for the Good Goddess was held in private, but it was public in the sense that it was made on behalf of all Roman people. For a man to intrude on the secret rites risked bringing the anger of the goddess down on not just himself but the whole city. Much of Roman religion stemmed from the simple idea that for Rome to flourish, the gods had to be treated well.[15] That was why gods got prayers, sacrifices, temples, and games. And so, Clodius was not just flirting with Pompeia; he was flirting with danger. Yet paradoxically, that might have been the point. Even more than Pompeia, danger was his mistress. She had seduced him long ago, when he led a Roman army to mutiny against his brother-in-law.

And what a thrill it would be to try to crash the nighttime ceremony and find out what it was all about. Men knew so little. Even the deity's true name was a secret: "Good Goddess" was only a title. What did the women get up to, with all that seductive music and the wine they drank? Men had prurient fantasies. One writer imagined the seemingly respectable matrons arousing each other in dance and then sending for their male lovers—and if the lovers weren't available, the slaves, and if the slaves weren't available, the water delivery man.[16]

Whatever Clodius's motives, intruding on the ceremony was clearly sacrilege. Soon after New Year's Day, 61 BC, one of the stricter senators finally raised the matter in the Senate, which had ultimate authority in everything to do with the gods. The Senate then referred the matter to the Vestal Virgins and the priests, who pronounced the occurrence sacrilege.[17] The problem was that sacrilege, other than stealing from a temple, was not a legally recognized crime. There was no court to try the case and assign a penalty. If a god were wronged, the Romans tended to think, she could punish the offender herself. But Clodius's behavior seemed so dangerous that the Senate came up with a novel proposal. Legislation would be passed to set up a special court to try Clodius for what was a recognized criminal offense: impurity.[18]

The Latin word for it was *incestum*. It took two very different forms. One was, as its English derivative suggests, incest: sexual intercourse with close kin. Anyone found guilty of that would be thrown to their death from the Tarpeian Rock, a steep cliff on the Capitoline Hill in the center of Rome. The other type of *incestum* was the failure of a Vestal Virgin to stay chaste. This was a grave offense. While a flawed ritual could always be carried out again to appease the god, virginity, once lost, was lost forever. The hearth goddess Vesta was herself a virgin. If her priestesses lacked purity, that spelled danger for Rome: plague, crop blight, and military disaster were only some of the possibilities. A Vestal found guilty of having sex was sentenced to the dreadful punishment of being buried alive in an underground chamber while her lover, or lovers, were beaten to death with rods.[19]

A spectacular case two generations before Clodius showed how sternly the Romans dealt with such impurity.[20] The trouble began in 114 BC, when a Roman equestrian, traveling with his wife and unmarried daughter, was returning to Rome and overtaken by a storm. The girl was terrified. To reach shelter quickly, the family abandoned their carriage and climbed onto horses. While riding, the girl was struck and killed by lightning. Her body was found with her dress pulled up to her waist and her tongue hanging out of her mouth. So hideous a death could only have been a sign of divine anger. When the soothsayers were consulted, as they always were after freakish events, they said the Virgins had trespassed.

All eyes turned to the Vestals. A slave came forward with information. He said that his wealthy master had secretly defiled Aemilia, one of the Vestals. Aemilia, in turn, had led two of the other priestesses, Licinia and Marcia, to have sex with friends of her lover, perhaps to buy their silence.

All three women and some of their alleged lovers were now accused of impurity. As was customary, the trial was held by the chief priest (the *pontifex maximus*) along with all the other priests (the pontiffs), who voted like jurors. Aemilia was the only one of the three women who was condemned. Licinia and Marcia were acquitted. All three belonged to powerful families and the people of Rome suspected a cover-up. Through popular pressure, a law was passed to establish a special court with equestrian jurors to try separately Licinia and Marcia and their lovers. This time, the full truth was sure to come out. Presiding over the court was Lucius Cassius, the famously severe juror who had formulated the immortal question *cui bono?*

Cassius's special tribunal became known as the "reef of defendants" because so many crashed on it.[21] Licinia and Marcia were both convicted, even though Licinia was defended by her kinsman Licinius Crassus, Cicero's teacher. A number of men were also convicted. One of those accused was another of Cicero's teachers, Marcus Antonius. Naturally the skilled lawyer undertook his own defense. While it's not known what he said, some information on his trial is preserved in a collection of stories about the fidelity of slaves toward masters—a favorite subject for slaveowners' sermonizing. Normally slaves couldn't testify against their masters, but an exception was made in cases of impurity because the crime was considered so serious. The prosecutors of Antonius demanded that a slave of his be interrogated, claiming that the slave had carried a lantern in front of his master when he went to commit the deed. The slave underwent the brutal torture of being pressed with hot plates, and even so not a word harmful to Antonius passed his lips. Antonius was acquitted.[22]

Lucius Cassius seems to have brought justice, but unease lingered in the city like a bad stench. The Vestals hadn't just polluted themselves. They had tried to cover it up, luring others into a ring of sex and silence. People still wondered whether everyone had been caught. The Senate ordered that the *Sibylline Books*, collections of Greek prophecies stored in the great Temple of Jupiter on the Capitoline Hill, be consulted. The priests in charge of the books revealed that the Romans had to offer a terrible sacrifice to avert disaster.

Two Greeks and two Gauls were buried alive in the city's old cattle market by the Tiber River.[23]

Clodius might have craved danger, but he probably got a bigger helping than he wanted when the Senate proposed setting up a court to try him for impurity. But the Claudian sense of entitlement would not fail him. This was the secret of patrician success: at the moment of peril, you had to be most brazen.

Before there could be any trial, the assembly first needed to vote the bill proposed by the Senate into law. Clodius was friendly with one of the year's consuls, Piso. Even though Piso had to present the bill to the voters on behalf of the Senate, he started speaking against it. Clodius had another ally in Fufius Calenus, who held the powerful office of tribune, which allowed him to call public meetings at which he attacked the legislation.[24]

The moves of Piso and Fufius were typical in the game of politics. Clodius wanted to play rougher. He started organizing gangs of young men who would show up in public to cheer him on and make trouble for his opponents. They were easily spotted by their neat beards, in keeping with a new fashion. Older Romans, like Cicero and Hortensius, always shaved unless they were in mourning. Back in his consulship of 63 BC, Cicero complained about how a group of well-groomed young men, many with beards, followed the conspirator Catiline. The hair of those boys, Cicero said at the time, seemed a little too well arranged, and he accused them of wanting to get naked with each other at parties and even sleeping with Catiline himself.[25] Actually, the new look was probably more a symbol of youthful masculinity and protest, similar to that of the 1960s and 1970s. Cicero liked to interpret it otherwise, linking gender deviance and political subversion, as he often did in attacking those he deemed a threat to public order.[26]

In 61 BC, as Cicero wrote in horror to Atticus, "Catiline's whole gang" seemed to be reuniting under Clodius.[27] These were not working-class Romans but young men of leading families such as Scribonius Curio, whose father had been consul in 76. As had been true of Catiline and his followers, though, the good looks and charisma of the youths drew support from many quarters. They reminded men on the street that Cicero and the Senate had put citizens to death without a trial. They argued that the Senate was always trying to strip citizens of their most basic rights, and the plan for a new court was just the latest example. As proof of their claims, Clodius and his young bloods latched onto one feature of the law: the praetor who was to convene the new court would be allowed to pick the jurors himself. Ostensibly this was to prevent corruption, but it could be made to look like more of the Senate's rigged justice. All this put Cicero on the defensive. While he joined those demanding that Clodius be put on trial, he also became wary as he saw the strength of Clodius's attack.

Voting day for the bill came. Men crowded into the Forum, where they would hear a final set of speeches and then line up to cast their ballots. Cicero described the raucous assembly meeting in a letter written shortly afterward: "The goateed young warriors were running to and fro, Catiline's whole gang with Curio's little girl in the lead. They begged the people to reject the bill. Consul Piso, the proposer of the law, actually spoke against it. Clodius's toughs had taken possession of the gangways [on which voters walked]. The voting tablets were distributed without any 'ayes.'" But before ballots were cast, Rome's severest senator, the scowling Cato, jumped onto the speaker's platform to protest what was going on. He gave

Consul Piso "a spectacular beating," wrote Cicero.[28] The meeting had to be dismissed and the Senate was summoned to decide how to proceed.

In the Senate, a motion was made to urge the people to accept the bill. Once again Piso fought it. Clodius fell to his knees and begged the senators for their support. In Rome there was no ban against ex post facto laws, unlike the US Constitution, and special courts, such as the one for the Vestals and their lovers, had been established before. Clodius could complain he was being treated unjustly, but he had to ask for mercy too.[29] Yet only about fifteen senators supported him and voted to reject the decree, against four hundred on the other side. Clodius's ally Fufius Calenus then exercised his right as tribune to veto the measure.

Clodius started making angry speeches in public. He claimed that the unprecedented new court in which he was going to be tried had nothing to do with sacrilege. This was a plot for revenge by Lucullus and friends of his such as Hortensius, still angry about the mutiny Clodius had hatched in Armenia. And Cicero had piled on when he saw a chance to relive what he considered his crowning moment, the suppression of Catiline. Clodius devised the perfect put-down. Throughout the year 63 BC, as Catiline's conspiracy unfolded, Cicero would always preface his latest revelation with a signature phrase: "I have discovered that . . ." In 61 BC Clodius said, "Cicero has discovered everything."[30] While Clodius treated Lucullus and Hortensius more abusively, Clodius was activating public opinion against Cicero.

With the tribune Fufius Calenus unwilling to withdraw his veto, the Senate's effort to pass the bill skidded to a halt. At public meetings, Cicero tried to speak up in defense of the Senate's authority and himself. Clodius also spoke often and found that mentioning

Cicero's name increased ill will against the Senate. Cicero then started to punch back verbally, trying to knock down Clodius and his friends while also slamming the immorality of the younger generation. In Rome it was common for a contentious issue to be debated by two powerful champions. But between Cicero and Clodius, a deep personal enmity was forming.

Meanwhile, Hortensius tried to break the deadlock. He suggested that Fufius propose a new version of the law, according to which jurors would not be handpicked by the praetor but drawn by lot. In something of a surprise, Fufius agreed to the compromise. The revision allowed him to save some face. And perhaps Fufius and Clodius felt that they could continue to sway public opinion. Hortensius, and probably Lucullus, on the other hand, believed that no jury on earth would ever acquit Clodius. A sword of lead would be sharp enough to slit Clodius's throat, Hortensius confidently predicted.[31] Cicero, getting increasingly nervous, wasn't so sure.

After the bill passed, preparations for the trial began. Lucius Lentulus Crus, who would later hold the consulship, was appointed as the lead prosecutor. He was assisted by two other members of his noble family—such was the magnificence of the Lentuli that Cicero coined a term to describe it, "Lentulity"—along with a friend of Lucullus named Fannius. Lentulus Crus was, in Cicero's view, a strong orator. He had a smooth voice and spoke with spirit, though he did tend to shirk the toil of thinking: "For the courts you'd perhaps have asked for something better, but for politics you'd judge what he could do adequate."[32]

Gaius Scribonius Curio was entrusted with Clodius's defense. Curio had held the consulship in 76 BC, which brought prestige, but he did not enjoy a high reputation for speaking. His lapses in memory and his odd delivery could even cause belly laughs. He tended to sway around when he orated. "Who's that talking from a boat?" an opponent once quipped. In Cicero's judgment, "Curio was so absent-minded that sometimes when he said he would make three points, he would add a fourth—or vainly try to remember his third."[33] Curio's young son was a friend of Clodius and the leading member of the Clodian gang, so the father would at least get support from the young bloods.[34]

It wasn't looking good for Clodius. As the praetor in charge of the court drew lots for the jury, both sides exercised their right to reject some of those chosen. Cicero claimed that Lentulus Crus threw out the most disreputable men, while Clodius threw out the most respectable. As Cicero put it, Clodius was acting like the trainer of a gladiatorial school, who would sometimes keep his best fighters out of a dangerous contest.[35] In other words, Clodius wanted only the worst thugs, and this made him look guiltier. Besides that, during the preliminaries to trial, Clodius's motions were always denied, while the prosecutor Lentulus Crus was given even more than he asked for. Hortensius seemed to have been right after all. Everybody looked at Clodius as convicted twenty times over.

Once the trial itself got underway, it became clear that the prosecution had not only better legal talent but a better case. Lentulus Crus spelled out for jurors Clodius's earlier record of crime: sowing rebellion in Lucullus's army and then abandoning his post. Other charges were piled on: complicity in electoral bribery, throwing a prosecution, forging wills. But above all, Lentulus Crus developed the case for impurity. The lawyer went on about the age of the cult for the Good Goddess and its long history of secrecy, which had always been safeguarded—until Clodius. And for those who believed Clodius couldn't have done it, there was clear evidence.[36]

As far as we can tell from surviving information, Lentulus made little of Pompeia's role. But he had demanded for interrogation under torture the slaves of both Pompeia and Clodius. From the maid Habra, Lentulus got some information, perhaps concerning how she had helped Clodius the night of the ceremony. Clodius's own slaves could not be questioned because he had sent them away—some to a brother of his in Greece, others to the manager of an estate he owned in Gaul.[37]

For the jurors and audience, Lentulus had far more than the poor maid's evidence. When it came time for freeborn witnesses, Lucullus took the stand. No doubt he talked about the mutiny, but what stuck in everyone's mind was something far more lurid. After he had lost his command and returned to Rome, Lucullus had divorced his wife, Clodius's sister, Clodia.[38] As Lucullus now told the jury, he had found out, from Clodia's maids, that she had been unfaithful. In fact, she had been sleeping with her own brother, Clodius. A man who committed one type of *incestum* could just as easily commit another.[39]

Caesar's mother was also called as a witness. She said in her testimony that she had ordered Clodius out of the house after he had broken in. And if anyone thought the old woman was confused or hard of seeing, her daughter, Caesar's sister Julia, told the same story.[40] Almost certainly the Vestals also testified. They would have made a visual impression as they took the stand wrapped in white robes, their hair parted into six braids—the same style brides wore.

The defense faced a daunting task in working their way out from under the avalanche of evidence. No doubt Curio had points to make—if he could remember them all—about his client's good character and the Claudian family's service to the Republic. But the bulk of the defense rested on one simple claim: Clodius had been far from Rome the night of the sacrifice for the Good Goddess. He had traveled to the house of a friend, the equestrian Causinius Schola, in a town eighty miles from the city. And Schola was ready to testify as much.[41]

It might have worked, except for one thing. The prosecution called Cicero to the stand—not as a lawyer, but as a witness. The Clodian gang, who had been on hand throughout the trial, started shouting menacingly. The jurors themselves then stood up, yelling in Cicero's defense. According to a letter he later wrote, they even pointed to their bare throats, as if to show the gang that it would have to kill the jurors before it could lay a hand on Cicero.[42] Cicero, used to even the most intimidating crowds after years of pleading cases in the Forum, proceeded to answer the questions he was asked. There was no way Clodius could have been out of Rome, he said. Just a few hours before the sacrifice to the Good Goddess began, the patrician had been meeting with Cicero, in a house Cicero had recently bought on the Palatine Hill that was more in keeping, Cicero thought, with his high status as a senior statesman.

Clodius and his lawyer collapsed in despair when they heard the jurors clamoring against him, or so Cicero claimed. The next morning, a large crowd of supporters came to Cicero's house to accompany him to the court. And the jurors, saying they were worried about their safety, asked the praetor in charge of the court for a bodyguard. The praetor took the request to the Senate, and it was overwhelmingly supported. Clodius looked finished.

It's at the moments of most danger that you have to be most brazen. To reconstruct what happened next, once again we have mainly Cicero's account in a letter to Atticus.[43] All the witnesses had spoken. The jurors were soon to vote. But before that happened, a friend of Clodius, "using a single slave (an ex-gladiator at that), settled the whole business. He summoned the jurors to his house, made them promises, co-signed loans, gave them cash. What's more—good gods, it's bad—some jurors received as a top-up of their payment evenings with certain ladies or introductions to young men of noble families." It is unclear who the friend was since Cicero used a nickname, "Baldhead." A good guess is the immensely rich Crassus, who tended to support young men in difficulties with the expectation of getting the favor repaid later. In the same year as Clodius's trial, he paid off Julius Caesar's creditors, allegedly to the tune of 20 million sesterces.[44]

Supporters of Clodius crowded the Forum menacingly as the jurors marked their waxed tablets and dropped them into the praetor's urn. The final vote count was twenty-five in favor of convicting and thirty-one for acquittal. Clodius was free. An elderly senator named Catulus, who had a tongue as sharp as vinegar, ran into one of the jurors afterward. "Why did you ask us for a guard?" he sourly asked. "Were you afraid that your wallets would be snatched?"[45]

Many in the Senate seethed at the acquittal. There was strong evidence that Clodius had infiltrated the rites for the Good Goddess. By the terms of the new law, he was guilty of impurity. Every man and beast knew it, Cicero said.[46] There is also little doubt that Clodius had relied on bribery for acquittal. Not only is Cicero's account confirmed by later sources, but after the trial the demand for tougher antibribery measures mounted.[47] But Clodius had gotten away with it, just as he had gotten away with mutiny, which did little to help the reputation of the courts. Except perhaps for Cato, nobody took it so hard as Cicero. The acquittal made it seem as if *he* had perjured himself, not Clodius, as Clodius himself gleefully pointed out.[48] And the way Clodius had turned the whole case into a trial of the Senate's authority also undermined Cicero's standing.

In private, Cicero blamed Hortensius's compromise on the selection of jurors, the so-called sword of lead. Cicero publicly denounced the corrupt jurors, the consul Piso, and Clodius. At a meeting of the Senate on May 15, 61 BC, Cicero delivered a scorching attack.[49] He reminded Clodius that Catiline and his chief lieutenant in Rome, Lentulus Sura, had both been acquitted in trials more than once, but justice had caught up with them. Execution awaited Clodius too. Cicero went low in his insults. Maybe the jurors were right. Maybe no *man* had trespassed at the ceremony for the goddess. But even with a woman's dress and a hood, Clodius looked a fright. Cicero punned on Clodius's surname, Pulcher: "I trust that, after you were given a mirror, you realized that you were nowhere near beautiful."

The patrician couldn't stand it. He got to his feet and began poking Cicero at his most sensitive spots. The presumptuous new man, Clodius said, had recently been spending time at the fashionable resort of Baiae. "Well," Cicero retorted, "is that the same as saying I intruded on secret rites?"

"You have bought a house," Clodius said, referring to the new mansion on the highly sought-after Palatine Hill.

"You'd think he was saying that I bought a jury."

"They didn't credit your words, even though you were under oath."

"On the contrary, twenty-five jurors did credit my words, whereas thirty-one gave you no credit, taking their money in advance."

On it went for some time. Just as he had earlier in the year, Clodius parodied Cicero again. "How long, I ask, are you going to abuse our patience?" Cicero had asked Catiline at the start of one of his most famous speeches. "How long are we going to put up with this tyrant?" Clodius now cried out.

Finally the two stopped. Cicero reported to Atticus that he had gotten the better of Clodius in the exchange, but even Cicero's own letter showed that Clodius could hold his own. Hector and Achilles they might not have been in military prowess, but the fury of the two Romans' quarrel was becoming just as potent. In due course, it would tilt the whole balance of politics.

Meanwhile, a Roman might have mused, somewhere up in the heavens the Good Goddess was watching it all. The feeble mortals with their crooked court had let the offender go free. The deity herself would deal out punishment to a man who acted impiously. If they wanted, the gods could avenge themselves with a brutality that made the Claudian dynasty look meek. Even Cicero, writing to Atticus, looked heavenward for help: "Unless some god takes pity on us, the settlement of the Republic, which you attribute to my policy and I to divine providence, and which seemed firmly established upon the alliance of all honest men and the authority of my consulship, has slipped through our fingers in this one trial."[50]

# CHAPTER 9

# Sticks and Stones

Although he escaped conviction for violating the rites of the Good Goddess, Clodius seethed with indignation. For Cicero he reserved a special fury. Cicero often wrote to Atticus over the next few years with worries over the possibility of retaliation. He tried every means he could think of to shore up his standing. In speeches to the Senate and people, he defended the controversial actions of his consulship and continued to advocate for the interests of his well-to-do supporters. He wrote memoirs and even an epic poem about his consulship. He kept up his work in the courts. Earlier, legal victories had been a path to political office; now they bolstered his prestige and helped maintain alliances with powerful politicians.[1]

But in March 58 BC Clodius was able to wreak his vengeance. Holding the office of tribune, he passed a law that banished anyone who killed a citizen without a trial.[2] Almost immediately, a mob of Clodius's supporters showed up at Cicero's Palatine house. It was like an army, ready to sack an enemy stronghold after a long war. The men climbed onto the roof, tearing off tiles and throwing them down. They battered the heavy wooden doors in front. Boom. Boom. Boom. The doors started to budge, then burst open. In poured the gang, looking for loot. Probably most of the valuables—Cicero's statues, his furniture, his books—had already been removed. The invaders yelled insults, smashed the house apart, and finally set fires with their torches. From the Forum below, you could look up and see the flames devouring the house of which Cicero had been so proud.[3]

Far from doing anything to stop the onslaught, the two consuls in charge of Rome were feasting in celebration, or so Cicero later complained. Clodius had just awarded both of them extraordinary commands over eastern provinces to last for five years, which were sure to make them rich. One of the consuls was on the verge of bankruptcy and needed money badly. But the two officials didn't have to go to war to plunder. They didn't even have to get off their dining couches. As one of the consuls ate dinner at his mother-in-law's house, the doors were opened to receive carts of marble pillars carried out of Cicero's nearby home.

Cicero had already fled Rome and was on the road to Sicily when the sack began. He would only hear about it later, from friends and family. Just before he left, though, he had found a way to defy Clodius. Among the orator's most cherished possessions was a sculpture of Minerva (Athena, to the Greeks). The patroness of learning, the virgin goddess also had a reputation for preserving cities. Across the Greek world she was worshipped in temples built on the acropolises of cities, most famously in the magnificent Parthenon of Athens. Cicero carried his statue up to the Temple of Jupiter on the Capitoline Hill and dedicated it to the goddess with an inscription,

"For Minerva, guardian of the city." Which was to say, "Goddess, save Rome!"[4]

Clodius's revenge had been years in the making. After his acquittal in the impurity trial of early 61 BC, he had gone to Sicily to serve as quaestor, the first rung on the ladder of offices. He returned to Rome the next year and poured all his effort into winning election to another office, the tribunate. A far more important position than the quaestorship, this would allow him to hold public meetings and pass legislation on the people's behalf. As tribune, Clodius could gain great popularity—and power over his enemies.[5]

There was only one problem. Clodius had been born into one of Rome's patrician families, the exclusive group that traced their ancestry back to the earliest days of the city. And for all their privilege, patricians could not serve as tribunes. The plebs, the ordinary people of Rome, had established the tribunate as their own office to uphold their rights against the powerful patricians. By Clodius's day, many of the men who held the post, ten each year, belonged to some of Rome's greatest political dynasties, but they were not of patrician birth. Clodius tried to get legislation passed that would make him plebeian but was blocked by senators concerned about his intentions.[6]

His chance came in the spring of 59 BC. An extraordinary triple alliance of Julius Caesar, Crassus, and Pompey dominated politics. Each of the three had been thwarted by the Senate in achieving goals key to their political futures. Most urgently Pompey needed to provide veterans of his recent wars in the East with grants of land. As one of the consuls of 59 BC, Caesar pushed through the necessary legislation on Pompey's behalf. To do so, he had to physically remove from the assembly tribunes who tried to interpose their vetoes. Cicero was upset by both the violence and the threat to senatorial authority posed by Caesar. Speaking for the defense at the trial of his consular colleague Antonius, he took the chance to denounce what was going on.[7] That same day, as retaliation, Caesar passed a law allowing Clodius to be adopted by a plebeian. Clodius's new father was much younger than Clodius—about the right age to be a man's sexual pet, Cicero maliciously observed—and after the formalities were completed he legally emancipated his son.[8]

Clodius's path now lay open. In late 59 BC he was elected tribune and proposed a sweeping package of laws that won him the undying support of working Romans. Many of the inhabitants of the city had livelihoods as precarious as their tenement housing. Fires, floods, and plagues all posed threats. A more regular problem was chronic grain shortages and price spikes. One of Clodius's bills would establish, for the first time ever, free distribution of grain to adult males in the city of Rome and its environs.[9]

Another of his proposed laws dealt with the city's many clubs. Organized around professions, neighborhoods, or religious cults, clubs were the bedrock of many Romans' lives. Their members enjoyed community, a safety net, entertainment, and prestige. Elected officials of the clubs, a number of whom were ex-slaves, got to wear special clothing on ceremonial occasions that made them look like the magistrates of the Republic. A boisterous midwinter festival of the Crossroads, celebrated in every neighborhood, was a yearly highlight for working Romans, both free and enslaved. At altars throughout the city, fatted pigs were sacrificed to the gods after which neighbors enjoyed pork roasts.[10]

The clubs offered politicians a way to connect with and mobilize the city's population. Candidates and officeholders made a point of getting to know club leaders and supporting the festival of the Crossroads. One tribune of 66 BC went further and, on the festival itself, tried to force through a law extending voting rights. Concerned that the clubs were becoming a focus for radical politics, the Senate in 64 BC banned a number of them and also put restrictions on the celebration of the Crossroads festival.[11] Now, six years later, Clodius proposed restoring the old clubs, adding new ones, and reinstating the full festival. To pave the way for passage of his laws, scheduled for early January 58 BC, Clodius had one of his henchmen, Sextus Cloelius, organize a boisterous celebration on New Year's Day.[12]

Cloelius had a much lower social status than the fashionable young nobles who had followed the patrician around during the Good Goddess scandal. He was a government clerk—and, according to Cicero, was born a slave, as such salaried officials sometimes were. Clodius's burgeoning friendship with the man highlights his new political strategy. Clodius would continue to gather crowds to rally support for himself and make trouble for opponents, but on a much larger scale. Given Clodius's background, it might seem surprising that he would hang out with men like Cloelius or the slaves and ex-slaves who frequented the clubs. Cicero tended to dismiss them all as lowlifes. But in a way Clodius was making the ultimate patrician move. He was becoming like his ancestors who, centuries earlier, had dominated the city through armies of clients. Clodius's clients looked to him for food, money, entertainment, and recognition of their standing. In exchange, they could offer votes on legislation, support at rallies, and—when needed—muscle.

The power that the tribune had gained was demonstrated at a trial in 58 BC. Vatinius, an associate of Caesar who had served as tribune the previous year, was summoned on a charge of failing to deposit copies of laws in the treasury, as required. Vatinius asked

Clodius to intervene with a veto. Just as the trial was set to start, Clodius appeared in the court with a large gang of men. They threw the praetor off his tribunal, scattered the wooden benches, and overturned the urns. Other courts in session in the Forum had to disperse as well. Clodius could justify his action on the grounds that he was interposing his tribunician veto—he was defending the rights of a citizen wrongly accused—but the violence was unsettling. As Cicero pointed out, the gang had "carried out actions in breaking up a trial which trials were set up to prevent."[13]

After passage of his first set of laws, Clodius moved on to his next goal: settling the score with Cicero. He now proposed his law banishing anyone who had put to death a Roman citizen without a trial.[14] Superficially, this law only affirmed an already-existing right of citizens, which they cherished as the bulwark of their liberty and the privilege that set them apart from slaves. The law did not mention anyone by name, but clearly Cicero was the target. As consul in 63 BC, he had carried out the Senate's recommendation to execute the Catilinarian conspirators. To ensure Cicero got as little support as possible, Clodius included a provision that extended liability to senators who had advised a magistrate to carry out an execution. The clause hung over the senators' heads like a sword of Damocles. The only officials left for Clodius to handle were the consuls, Gabinius and Piso. They had the constitutional power to declare an emergency, raise forces, and resist the tribune and his mob if they chose to. Clodius bought the two men's support by introducing, at the same time as his law on citizen's rights, a bill awarding each of them provinces in the East with large armies and generous budgets for five-year terms.[15] For Gabinius, especially, this was as tempting as the Sirens' song. While serving as an officer of Pompey several years earlier, he had taken forces over the Euphrates River to the Tigris and became involved in intrigue over the Jewish kingdom. As supreme commander, he could expect far more financial gain and glory.

With these two new laws pending, Clodius began to threaten Cicero directly. Cicero was forced to play the part that so many of his clients had in prior years: he changed into dark clothing, stopped shaving, and walked around the city begging the people for mercy. Wherever he went in the streets, Clodius met him with a band of his followers. They jeered at Cicero's change of dress, threw mud at him, and even pelted him with rocks.[16]

Cicero did not entirely lack support. Hortensius, with whom he had been cooperating politically in recent years, stood by him. Lucullus also gave encouragement. Many of the equestrians—Cicero's most loyal allies because he had represented them in court and saved their loan portfolios during the conspiracy of Catiline—also changed into dark attire and accompanied him with their hair untrimmed. Even the Senate stiffened its spine enough to vote to officially declare a period of mourning.[17]

It was all in vain. The consul Gabinius denounced the equestrians and senators for their actions. He hinted to the equestrians that they might suffer for supporting Cicero in 63 BC. He banished from the city one of Cicero's strongest backers among the equestrians on the grounds that he had incited a riot.[18] Then both consuls told the senators they must return to regular attire. Among Cicero's backers, Lucullus thought Cicero should stay and fight it out but Hortensius and others advised giving in.[19] If Cicero remained, there was a chance he would be killed. Once he left, his friends assured him, he would soon be missed and called back. And so it was that just before the new bills were to be voted on, he carried his statue of Minerva to Capitoline Hill and fled. Terentia and the children stayed behind to watch their house be destroyed.

Cicero had bought the house the year after his consulship to con-firm his arrival in politics and society. It was located on the northern slope of the Palatine, just a couple minutes' walk from the Forum. Few residences in Rome were so conspicuous. The ambitious senator who had built it, a generation before Cicero, told his architect to design it so that whatever its owner did would be seen by all.[20] Next to the house stood a portico built by the victorious general Catulus, glittering with shields captured in a war against the Germans.

There had been grumbling when Cicero moved in. Some moaned that a new man like Cicero shouldn't be able to afford so fine a house, right next to Catulus's portico. Indeed, Cicero had had to borrow most of the money to cover the house's astronomical price of 3.5 million sesterces and joked that he would need to join a con-spiracy like Catiline's to get the debt wiped out.[21]

During the exchange of insults with Cicero after the Good God-dess trial, Clodius had mocked the purchase. It made Cicero look like a man with pretensions above his station. But as Clodius harped on Cicero's illegal executions, the house on the hill, looming over the Forum, started to look like something worse than pretension. In Rome, tales were told of how, in the early days of the Republic, arrogant men who sought to become tyrants had built large houses to dominate the city. On one slope of the Capitoline Hill lay an open space, used as a market for sacrificial animals, which the Romans claimed had once been the house of the would-be king Spurius Maelius. After Maelius's fall, the story went, the Senate had ordered the building destroyed.[22]

And so Cicero's house had to be demolished in 58 BC: he was, as Clodius said, a tyrant. The tribune made it all official after Cicero's flight. He passed a bill that outlawed Cicero by name and referred specifically to his execution of the Catilinarians. Cicero was forbid-den, on pain of death, to come within five hundred miles of Italy, and anyone who helped him would also be killed. All of Cicero's property was to be confiscated. And Clodius was authorized to construct a monument on the site of the Palatine house.

Clodius proceeded to build a new portico, three hundred feet long, that absorbed the old war memorial of Catulus and extended it onto what had been Cicero's property. The tribune emblazoned his own name across the structure, visible from the Forum below. But this was no tyrant's building. Where part of Cicero's house had stood, Clodius set up a shrine to the goddess Liberty.[23]

Clodius's attacks on Cicero and his disruption of the trial of Vatinius speak to an ongoing problem in the last years of the Roman Republic: violence in politics. From the late second century BC onward, as political conflict arose over such questions as what share the people should get of land seized in war, angry mobs took up stones, sticks, clubs, daggers, and swords. In the civic spaces of the city, where disputes were supposed to be resolved by debate and by vote, Romans pushed, shoved, slashed, and killed. Politicians, desperate to win elections and pass laws, saw that violence could be a useful tactic and sometimes deliberately incited it.[24]

Romans grappled with what to do. In the eyes of many, some acts of violence were justified. Romans generally agreed that if a tyrant threatened their city, they were allowed to drive him out and tear his house down as a warning to others. But as violence increased, there clearly was a risk that the rule of law would give way to anarchy and domination by the strongest. Yet even if elected officials wanted to stop acts of violence, they had no standing security forces to do so. In fact, the very idea of such forces was antithetical to Roman ideas of liberty. The consuls could get the Senate to pass an emergency decree and raise volunteer forces, but, as Cicero's own experience in his consulship showed, such steps were controversial.

Like other citizens in democratic societies, Romans struggled to balance a desire for security with respect for civil liberties. In 78 BC, as unrest broke out after Sulla's death, a new court was created that would hear charges of violence (*vis*, in Latin).[25] According to the relevant statute, which was directed against politicians rather than ordinary citizens, violence was unlawful if it was undertaken against the public interest. So a brawl that broke out in a bar over a dicing game would not be within the court's purview, nor would actions taken to fend off burglars from a house. Physically attacking a magistrate or besieging the Senate house, on the other hand, would. The statute did allow for the possibility that some acts of violence could be in the people's interest and therefore had to be permitted. Violence, stretching back to the expulsion of the kings, was too much a part of the Republic's heritage to be condemned outright.

To understand the challenge the Romans faced in dealing with escalating political violence in the 50s BC, it is helpful to revisit a famous trial in 95 BC involving Cicero's teacher, the great advocate Marcus Antonius. The story began about a decade earlier, with troubles in the Roman province of Transalpine Gaul. Germanic peoples from northern Europe had begun a migration southward that destabilized Roman control over the province. The people of Tolosa took the chance to rebel against Rome. Quintus Servilius Caepio, patrician consul of 106 BC, was sent to restore order. In the process of taking back Tolosa, he seized a vast treasure of gold and silver bullion, which was an offering by the Gauls to the gods. Caepio had the riches taken under guard to Massilia, on the coast, but the wagons never arrived. The escorts were ambushed and the treasure seized. Many Romans suspected that Caepio himself was responsible.[26]

Then, on October 6, 105 BC, Caepio faced off against the Germans in battle outside Arausio (today's Orange). The patrician refused to cooperate with his fellow commander, the consul Gnaeus Mallius, who was a new man. Some thought it snobbery on Caepio's part, others an unwillingness to share the glory of victory with another. Whatever the explanation, the worst Roman defeat since the war against Hannibal ensued. Thousands of young Roman men were cut down in battle. The Roman camps were looted and the prisoners taken hanged from trees. Caepio was one of only a handful to get away: as his army perished, he fled on horseback.[27]

Citizens were outraged. The people voted to strip Caepio of command and revoke his membership in the Senate. Then he was twice put on trial. His case was first heard in a special court established to hear charges regarding the loss of the gold of Tolosa. Caepio was sentenced to pay a fine. Then came a trial before the whole people in the assembly for the loss at Arausio. It fell to one of the tribunes of 103 BC, Gaius Norbanus, to prosecute Caepio for abandoning his army. Caepio, a man of some eloquence, spoke in his own defense. He said it was due to bad luck, not his own fault, that he lost his army.[28]

Now the violence began. The angry crowds in the Forum would have none of Caepio's excuses. When two tribunes tried to intervene on his behalf, they were driven off by force. The crowd threw stones in fury, one of which hit the most illustrious member of the Senate, who was supporting Caepio. The people were insistent that Caepio not escape justice. The trial went forward, he was convicted, all his remaining property was confiscated, and he went into exile. "Gold of Tolosa" became proverbial for something that looks enticing but, if touched, brings ruin.[29]

Caepio seems a total villain, but a number of senators thought he had been treated unjustly. It was not in the Roman tradition to condemn generals after they lost battles; that's what unsteady peoples like the Greeks and Carthaginians did. Senators might worry that if they were to lose favor with the public, they might fall too. Some said the real problem was the violence stirred up by the rabble-rousing tribune Norbanus, who had prevented other tribunes from exercising their rights.

While the tides of politics may not be as predictable as those of the sea, they always shift eventually. In 95 BC it was the former tribune Norbanus's turn to be prosecuted as retaliation for what he had done to Caepio. There was no crime of violence at this time. But as politicians' struggles heated up, a law had been passed establishing a new court to hear charges of treason against the Roman people. The original intent of the law's sponsors was to punish politicians who tried to obstruct the will of the people. This could include vetoing a law that an overwhelming majority demanded. So capacious was the charge of treason, however, that it could be used against Norbanus. As the fiery young man who handled the prosecution of the ex-tribune claimed, Norbanus had relied on violence to get Caepio convicted, driving off elected officials in volleys of stones.[30]

Then rose Marcus Antonius for the defense. At first he spoke hesitantly, almost stammering. He said he was defending Norbanus out of personal loyalty. Norbanus had served on Antonius's staff years before when Antonius was a provincial governor.

Gradually, almost imperceptibly, Antonius moved to another point. Some violence had taken place at Caepio's trial, yes. The lawyer defended the event not as an insurrection of Norbanus, but as the result of the justified anger of the Roman people. In his speech, Antonius went through the history of civil unrest in the Republic. The expulsion of the kings who had first ruled the city, the plebeians' struggle for recognition, and much else had required disagreement and even violence. Civil discord, he argued, was "always troublesome" but sometimes "almost necessary."[31] The prosecution wanted to talk about treason? Treason was committed "by the man who handed over to the enemy an army of the Roman people."[32] In an emotional climax, Antonius denounced the absent Caepio for his shameful flight and lamented the loss of so many lives.

Cicero himself remained impressed by Antonius's fine performance decades later, which saved Norbanus from conviction. It points to a problem, though: Couldn't much of the violence plaguing Rome be passed off as "the justified anger of the Roman people"? Couldn't politicians who stoked violence always fall back on that line? After the violence court was established in 78 BC, jurors would have to determine whether a politician had acted in the public interest or against it. Clearly it would be hard to keep politics out of the judicial process here, which risked turning trials into little more than power struggles. And not only that: if a politician could incite a riot, he could try to shut down the courts, as Clodius did at the trial of Vatinius in 58 BC. Far from addressing political violence, trials, or the threat of trials, in the 50s BC channeled violence, elevating people who were not interested in stopping it.


Although Cicero had presided over the executions of five conspirators he considered outlaws while he was consul, he normally shrank from violence himself. He liked to win verbal battles.[33] In a letter to Atticus written in 60 BC, just after Clodius's return from Sicily, Cicero described with pleasure how he skewered his opponent with jokes in the Senate.[34] Apparently Clodius had not been welcomed at the city gates by the large crowd he hoped for. He excused the lack of enthusiasm by saying that he had come back unexpectedly, in just one week's time, and entered the city after dark. Nothing new for Clodius, Cicero sniped back. The man had an amazing ability to be in two places at once. Not only that, "a nighttime entry—the same as before."

Later the two rivals found themselves escorting a political candidate to the Forum. Clodius asked whether Cicero was in the habit of providing seats at gladiatorial shows for his Sicilian clients. Cicero said no. "Well," replied Clodius, "I'm their new patron and I'm going to start. But my sister, who has all that consular space available, gives me just one foot." The sister here is not the Clodia who married Lucullus but an older one, married to Metellus Celer, who was serving as one of the consuls in 60 BC. Clodius was bragging to Cicero that he could rely on her to share some of the seating allocated to her husband, even while complaining, probably with mock petulance, that it was less than he liked.

"Don't complain," Cicero responded, "that your sister gives you only one foot. You can hoist up the other one as well." It was "not a very consular thing to say," Cicero admitted, but he couldn't help it. He disliked Clodia Metelli. She and her brother had a close relationship, and she gave him a great deal of help in his political activities against the wishes of her more conservative husband.[35] Partly for this reason, the charge that Clodius had enjoyed incestuous relations with Lucullus's wife gave way to claims that it was Clodia Metelli's bed he really favored. Cicero wasn't the only one to make the accusation, but he did so with gusto. In his letters, he usually referred to Clodia Metelli as "Lady Ox-Eyes," an epithet used by Homer for the goddess Hera. Clodia did have big, bright eyes. The sting was that Hera's husband, Zeus, was also her brother.[36]

As Clodius started to make moves against Cicero in later 59 BC, Cicero hoped to be prosecuted in a trial, which would allow him to fight back the way he knew best. Clodius was too smart to do that and instead passed his bill outlawing anyone who had put a citizen to death without a trial. Defenseless, Cicero had to flee across the Adriatic Sea to Macedonia, from where he wrote family and friends a series of self-pitying letters. "No man has ever lost so much or fallen into such a pit of misery" is a typical line.[37] Intriguingly, Cicero rarely mentioned Clodius in the letters but again and again blamed advisers such as Hortensius for what had happened: "It was not enemies but jealous friends who wrecked my life."[38] In hindsight, Cicero wished he had taken a tougher stance in response to Clodius's first law: "We were blind, blind I say, to put on mourning and beg the people."[39] In short, it would have been better to fight with more than words and gestures.

Cicero was powerless while absent from Rome and had to rely on supporters in the city to bring him back. So long as Clodius held the tribunate that would be impossible, but an opportunity opened when the new magistrates for the year 57 BC entered office. It helped Cicero's cause that Clodius and Pompey had had a falling-out and Pompey now wanted Cicero back.

Eight of the ten new tribunes agreed to support legislation to restore Cicero from exile, and a vote was scheduled for January 23, 57 BC. But instead of a vote, a massacre took place. According to the fullest account, a later speech by Cicero, not just Clodius's usual bands showed up at the voting assembly in the Forum but also gladiators Clodius had borrowed from his brother Appius, who would be putting on games later that year as praetor.[40] The fighters drove off two tribunes who were supporting Cicero and then began looking for Cicero's brother Quintus, who was also on hand to provide support for the law to bring back his brother. Quintus allegedly saved himself by hiding in a pile of corpses.

Cicero's account is only one side of the story. Almost certainly Clodius showed up with heavily armed men because Cicero's supporters were doing the same. That is why there was so much bloodshed. Naturally each side would claim they weren't guilty of violence; rather, they were expressing justified anger in the face of efforts to thwart the people's wishes. However, the presence of professional fighters, who must have been organized in advance, made such assertions unconvincing. This violence far outstripped the demonstrations at the trial of Caepio back in 103 BC, nearly rising to the level of warfare.

Now came onto the scene the most hard-boiled personality of this whole period, which was not exactly short on tough and cynical men. Titus Annius Milo was one of the eight tribunes of 57 BC working for Cicero's return.[41] Almost nothing is known of Milo's career up to this point, which makes it hard to understand his motive. And while Cicero would go on to say a great deal about Milo's later actions, in all that survives of these writings Milo is always hard to read. He must have been that way in reality: cool, even emotionless, driven by a sense of justice, yet prone to brutality. He stood for law and order, except when he didn't. Milo awoke in Cicero a guilty pleasure in winning fights with real punches if that's what it took. He exuded a manliness that the more intellectual Cicero feared was lacking in himself.

At first Milo tried to respond to the massacre of January 57 BC, in which he was not involved, with legal remedies. As tribune he arrested as many of the gladiators as he could. Clodius responded with the sort of assaults he had unleashed on Cicero the year before: his supporters began to attack Milo's house, waylay him on the streets, and try to terrorize him with violence. But Milo could not be intimidated. He entered the Forum and indicted Clodius on a charge of violence. Clodius promptly got his brother (one of that year's praetors) along with one of the consuls and one of the tribunes to issue an edict that suspended all public business.[42]

No trial in the courts? Criminals walking free? Terrorism? Milo decided he had no choice but to raise forces of his own to fight back. He could never hope to compete with Clodius's political machine. Instead he relied on a smaller group of professional fighters, including gladiators, whom he would pay with money supplied by Cicero's wealthy supporters. If anybody complained, Milo could say the men were his personal bodyguards (an increasing trend among Roman politicians).

In a later speech, Cicero offered a defense of Milo's resort to professional fighters that drew on some basic political theory.[43] Cicero argued that man's first state was one of nature. People wandered at random over the earth, possessing solely what they had seized through murder and bloodshed. Only when they gathered in cities, living under laws, did they escape their bestial nature. There is, Cicero said, a stark choice: law or violence. If we don't have law, we have violence. To end violence, we must impose law. When Clodius suspended the courts, the safeguard of law had broken down. That left only violence, and Milo had no option other than to protect himself by force.

Cicero used these arguments to justify Milo's actions, but they provide an alarming commentary on the condition Rome had reached in the mid-50s BC. Rome *was* descending into the state of nature, "the war of every man against every man," as Thomas Hobbes centuries later would define it. Hobbes's even more famous characterization of a life that is "solitary, poor, nasty, brutish, and short" was also becoming a reality in Rome.[44] Cicero appealed to the state of nature to absolve Milo, but this did not resolve the underlying problem. Actually Cicero made it worse: no good was going to come from defending Milo for roaming the streets with gangs of gladiators. Just as the violence that was "the will of the people" could be abused, so could the violence that was "self-defense." Crime was covered up with a label.

Milo built up his forces to counteract the Clodian gangs. Pompey threw himself into bringing back Cicero. He offered Milo reinforcements and rallied support for Cicero throughout the towns of Italy. By luck, or perhaps through the efforts of Cicero's friends in the business community, a grain shortage developed that hurt Clodius's popularity in Rome. On August 4, 57 BC, legislation was passed that recalled Cicero after sixteen months of exile.[45]

Cicero had begun his crossing of the Adriatic confidently before he even knew the bill had passed. He received the news in the southern Italian port city of Brundisium. His daughter Tullia came to welcome him, and the day they were reunited happened to be her birthday, which made it even more special (though she was in mourning due to her husband's recent death).[46] As Cicero made his way back to Rome he was greeted warmly in the towns he passed through. In Rome itself, according to a letter he wrote to Atticus, he received a rapturous welcome.[47] A crowd met him outside the city gate and applauded him. The same crowd followed him as he went to the Forum and the Capitolium, where, one can be sure, he gave thanks to the gods, including his Minerva.

Cicero was to get back all his property by the same law that restored him. But for what he cared most about, the Palatine house that had become the symbol of his position in the city, a problem stood in the way. Clodius had consecrated the shrine of Liberty on its site. If Cicero tore it down, he risked looking more sacrilegious than Clodius himself. Yet Cicero considered the dedication invalid. The Senate referred the matter to the pontiffs, priests with technical expertise in consecration.[48]

A hearing was held before the priestly college on September 29, at which both Clodius and Cicero made their case. Clodius argued that the shrine had been properly dedicated and removing it would bring divine anger down on Rome. His point was solid, and Cicero in his reply had to rely on distracting arguments and personal attacks. Midway through, Cicero invited his listeners to examine Clodius's goddess of Liberty. Where did she come from? "I have made careful inquiry." He claimed that the marble statue Clodius had put in his shrine was actually the portrait of a Greek prostitute looted from her tomb by Clodius's brother. "Who would dare violate this goddess?" Cicero asked sarcastically. And then he went in for the kill: "The likeness of a prostitute, the decoration of a tomb, snatched by a thief, set up by a desecrator. She is the one who is going to drive me from my house?"[49]

The pontiffs decided in favor of Cicero. But at a public meeting Clodius, with his usual brazenness, told his supporters just the opposite. Cicero was trying to seize the shrine by force, Clodius said. He urged everyone to follow him and defend their Liberty.[50] The Senate was not impressed and decreed that all of Cicero's properties must be restored. The consuls issued a contract for the reconstruction of Catulus's portico, which meant the demolition of Clodius's Liberty shrine. Cicero received 2 million sesterces to rebuild his house.[51]

Construction was underway on November 3 when an armed gang sent by Clodius showed up. They drove the workmen off Cicero's site and tore down the partly rebuilt portico of Catulus. Not only that, they pelted with rocks the nearby house of Cicero's brother Quintus, which they then set on fire. All of Rome looked on, Cicero wrote Atticus soon afterward, as the firebrands were thrown: "Even before, Clodius was running around out of his mind, but after this act of madness he thinks of nothing but killing his enemies. He roams the streets, openly offering the slaves the hope of freedom."[52] About a week later, as Cicero was walking along the north side of the Forum, the Clodian gang came after him directly, "shouting, stoning, cudgels, and swords, all out of nowhere." Cicero had to seek refuge in the house of a friend while his escort fended off the enraged mob.[53]

There were calls to bring Clodius to justice immediately. Milo, in particular, considered reviving the effort he had made earlier in the year to prosecute Clodius for violence. Time was running out, though, because Clodius was running for the aedileship. If elected, he would enter office on January 1, 56 BC, and gain immunity from prosecution for the entire year. And so Clodius organized another attack, just one day after the run-in with Cicero. On November 12 he tried to burn down Milo's house, on the northern slope of the Palatine, "leading out some men with drawn swords and shields and others with lighted firebrands, all in full view, shortly before noon."[54] Clodius made another senator's house his base of operations. But then a surprise: out of a second house that Milo owned poured a band of his fighters, who came over and killed a number of Clodius's gang members. Clodius managed to stay safe in the inner recesses of his friend's house.

This was the state of nature indeed. The Senate held tense meetings to find a way out of the crisis. One of the consuls-elect, who had also been one of Clodius's prosecutors in the Good Goddess trial, wanted him tried at once for his attacks on Cicero and the site of Cicero's house. Clodius stayed away from the Senate, but friends and relatives intervened on his behalf and prevented the Senate from issuing any decrees. But when the election was supposed to take place, Milo blocked it through constitutional maneuvers of his own, as well as violence.

Clodius, Cicero wrote in a letter, was losing support throughout the city, and Clodius's friends blamed Cicero for it. But Cicero thought the credit should go to "our hero Milo." Clodius, Cicero was now convinced, was sure to be brought to trial—unless he was killed first. "If Clodius gets in Milo's way in a riot," wrote Cicero, "I expect that Milo will kill him with his own hands. He has no qualms about doing so and boasts about it. He has no fear of the fate that befell me. Never will he follow the advice of any jealous or treacherous individual or put his trust in the sluggish nobility."[55]

But as had happened so often before, Cicero's high spirits made him overconfident. Through December and then into January the deadlock continued, with still no aedilician elections. The same consul-elect who had already called for Clodius's trial redoubled his pleas and loudly denounced Clodius's arsons, killings, and stonings. At a meeting of the Senate, Cicero condemned Clodius's seditions as if he already were on trial. But Clodius countered with more constitutional maneuvers and public protests. Finally, Senate stalwarts such as Hortensius came around to letting Clodius escape trial—partly because they wanted calm, and partly because they feared that the complete ruin of the ex-patrician would give too much power to Pompey. On January 20, 56 BC, Clodius was elected aedile. Milo had to drop the prosecution.[56]

And then a delicious twist, if anything can be called delicious in such a terrible story: Clodius announced that he was prosecuting Milo for having used armed gangs, including gladiators, as tribune in 57 BC. The trial would not take place in the regular violence court, where Milo would find friends among the high-ranking jurors. Instead, Clodius would exercise the right enjoyed by aediles to prosecute before the whole people in the assembly. He would defend the liberty of the Roman people against its new oppressor, Milo.[57]

The trial got underway in February. Milo's most important defender was not Cicero but Pompey. On the second day of proceedings, Cicero wrote in a horrifying eyewitness letter, Pompey got up to speak—"or he wanted to. As soon as he got to his feet, Clodius's gang started roaring; and this happened throughout the whole speech, so he was interrupted not merely by shouting but by insults and abuse."[58] Pompey toughed it out as best he could, and when he wrapped up Clodius rose. It was now Milo's side's turn to heckle Clodius. Insults of every sort burst forth, even obscene verses about Clodius's incestuous relationship with Clodia, Lady Ox-Eyes. Pale with fury, Clodius started a game of question-and-answer. "Who's starving the people to death?" he called out. "Who is a lecherous imperator? . . . What man seeks a man? . . . Who scratches his head with one finger?" (This scratch seems to have been a signal a man in Rome used to indicate he was open to sex with another man.) Clodius had trained his crowd well. After every question he hitched up his toga, which was the signal for everyone to yell, "Pompey!"

The cacophony continued for some time. Then the Clodius men started spitting at the Milo men. "Anger flared up," wrote Cicero. "They pushed hard to dislodge us, our side made an attack. The Clodian gang fled. Clodius was hurled from the Rostra. At that point I, too, fled, afraid what might happen in the riot." Legal proceedings had escalated from a shouting match to a shoving match.

Even Cicero grasped that both sides were playing with dangerous forces. The verbal insults tossed around by Cicero, Clodius, and others, along with the efforts to ruin each other in courts, were leading to physical brutality that endangered everyone. In the end, Clodius's plan to try Milo would come to nothing, just as Milo had failed the year before. The Romans were choosing violence over law.

Amid all the taunting, violence, and murder it was not surprising that people thought they observed signs of the gods' displeasure.

A blaze of light darted from the South across to the North; a wolf entered the city; an earthquake occurred; citizens were killed by thunderbolts. Scariest of all, in fields close to Rome a strange noise was heard emanating from the ground. It sounded like the clashing of arms.[59]

The Senate consulted with the professional soothsayers, who issued a response. Much was frayed, they said, in the relations between gods and men. Expiations were owed to Jupiter, Saturn, Neptune, and others. Games had been incorrectly performed and profaned. Sacred places had been desecrated, ambassadors killed, and ancient and secret sacrifices incorrectly carried out.[60]

Clodius latched onto the report, especially the clause about sacred places being profaned: clearly the gods were outraged over Cicero's restoration of his Palatine house and the destruction of the shrine of Liberty. At a public meeting, Clodius read out the soothsayers' report and tried to get the crowd to join him once more in demolishing the house.[61]

Cicero was away from the city, visiting his country properties, which were also being rebuilt. When he returned, he gave his own speech in the Senate on what the soothsayers had said. He argued that the sacred places that had been profaned were not Clodius's bogus shrine to the hussy Liberty, but rather a walled-up chapel in Clodius's own house and a chapel that one of the consuls of 58 BC had desecrated. Much else in the soothsayers' report also pointed to Clodius, Cicero claimed: the games incorrectly performed were those Clodius had put on as aedile, and the profaned rites were obviously those of the Good Goddess.[62]

"At a public meeting he complains about the neglect of religious observances," Cicero drawled. "So we are now looking forward to his next meeting, on chastity!" What crimes Clodius had committed against himself and against his family! "Whoever showed less mercy to an enemy camp than Clodius did to every part of his body? What public ferryboat has ever been more open to passengers than he was in his youth? What playboy ever rolled around so brazenly with his prostitutes as Clodius with his sisters?"[63]

It wouldn't have been hard for Clodius to anticipate some of Cicero's lines of attack, especially the one about the profaned rites of the Good Goddess. And so already in his speech Clodius had flaunted his acquittal in the trial of 61 BC and even cheekily joked that the Good Goddess was indeed good, for she had pardoned him.[64] No, Cicero now thundered back, Clodius had paid for his sacrilege. The gods had made him mad, like a character in a Greek tragedy. Everyone in Rome could see it, "when you utter frenzied words at meetings . . . when you hurl flaming firebrands into the houses of your neighbors . . . when you do not distinguish between wife and sister, when you have no idea which bedroom you are walking into."[65]

In their ongoing feud, Clodius and Cicero both tried to exploit the soothsayers' report. But the soothsayers had been issuing a broader warning to the Senate. Care must be taken, the religious experts said, or else "through discord and dissension among the best men, death and danger would be created for the Senate and its leaders and they would be left without the help of the gods, as a result of which power might pass to one man."[66]

Back in the 80s BC, quarrels between politicians and their followers had boiled over into civil war, leading to Sulla's dictatorship. The Republic had been restored. But bitter memories of Sulla's brutal victory and widespread anxiety that liberty might be crushed again, along with persistent hardships for many citizens, kept it under strain. Now a younger generation of politicians was rising to power. In their efforts to win elections, advance their favorite causes, and frustrate their opponents, they encouraged angry crowds to pick up stones, they hired gladiators, they fought on the streets. Most senators did not resort to such tactics, but enough did that it further destabilized an already precarious rule of law. Even Cicero, who condemned the atrocities he had witnessed in his youth, was now condoning violence. As the soothsayers saw, the Republic was in danger.

# CHAPTER 10

# The Hidden Hand

In the spring of 56 BC, Cicero's career was at a crossroads. His triumphant return from exile had done much to restore his reputation. So had his victory in the battle over rebuilding his house. Cicero retained the support of the well-to-do, "honest men" throughout Italy. He hoped now to exert influence on their behalf in the Senate, anticipating that he and his supporters would prevail over Clodius, Caesar, and the other populists. More and more, Cicero also looked to the next generation. As Rome's best orator, available for consultation the way Lucius Crassus had been for him, he had much to offer students. He harbored ambitions of molding talented young men in his own image as orators and as politicians.

Among this younger set, none stood out quite like Marcus Caelius Rufus. Always with an entourage, he swaggered through the streets flaunting his good looks and bold fashions. Nobody wore a purple quite so bright as Caelius. He loved to party and to joke. A talented speaker, he won fame for his aggressive and often rather coarse attacks.[1] None of his speeches survives in full, but there are tantalizing quotations and descriptions. Once, in what appears to have been a bribery trial, he started talking about aconite, a poison reputed to be quick-acting, especially if applied to the genitals of a female creature. That was how the defendant killed his wives in their sleep, Caelius alleged, apparently to suggest that one who could poison could also bribe. In his peroration, Caelius said that it all came down to a murderous finger.[2]

Caelius had begun his study of oratory in his mid-teens under the instruction of Cicero, which caused Cicero some embarrassment in later years. Caelius's drinking, pranking, and whoring were bad enough. In the year of Cicero's consulship, the twenty-five-year-old Caelius even supported Catiline.[3] When Caelius was indicted in the violence court in the spring of 56 BC, Cicero might have been expected to have nothing to do with his former pupil. The charges were serious: causing a riot in Naples, assaulting ambassadors from Egypt in the Italian port city of Puteoli, and then killing one of the ambassadors in Rome. But not only did Cicero take the case, he gave what might be the cleverest defense speech of his entire career.[4]

Cicero saw a chance to notch up a legal victory that would only add to his newly restored standing. But he had goals beyond that. By coming to Caelius's aid, he hoped to win back to his side one of Rome's most promising politicians and enlist his support in future battles. Even more satisfying than that, the case allowed him to carry on the attack against enemies who had made his and his family's life a torment during the sixteen months of exile: Clodius and his sister, "Lady Ox-Eyes." Few trials would show as starkly as this one how the criminal courts were used to settle personal scores.

To understand the case against Marcus Caelius, we must go back to where it all began: Alexandria, Egypt.[5] Other than Rome, no place in Cicero's lifetime was known for violence quite like Alexandria. The city, founded by Alexander the Great and later established as the capital of Egypt, had once ruled a prosperous empire that stretched across the Mediterranean Sea and up the fertile valley of the Nile River. Visitors gaped at its brightly painted houses and temples, its vast gymnasium where young athletes worked out naked in the Greek style, and—wonder of the world—the many-storied lighthouse of white marble, atop which a large mirror flashed with the light of the sun.[6] But as the decades wore on, the royal Ptolemy family descended into vicious power struggles. Kings and queens seemed to murder each other as frequently as the breeze changed. Mobs rioted in the city's wide avenues and spacious squares. In 80 BC a young Ptolemy, living in exile, claimed the throne with Roman help. After he reached Alexandria, he married the queen (who was also his stepmother) and, nineteen days later, had her murdered. The outraged Alexandrians immediately dragged him into the gymnasium and lynched him.[7]

As Milo and Clodius battled each other with their gangs, the last thing Rome needed was more violence. But the Alexandrians, as clever as they were quarrelsome, managed to bring their fighting there. King Ptolemy XII—nicknamed the "Flute Player" after his musical hobby—had in 59 BC promised a vast bribe to Julius Caesar and Pompey in exchange for official recognition as "Friend and Ally of the Roman People." The title offered some protection against annexation by Rome, a threat that had long hung over Egypt. To raise the money, Ptolemy imposed punishing taxes on his people. The Alexandrians protested, and their protests grew even louder a year later, when Clodius annexed Cyprus to cover the costs of grain distribution. The island was part of the Egyptian empire but ruled by a separate king, who had been less generous with bribes than his Egyptian counterpart. He would end up dying by suicide. Ptolemy of Egypt, meanwhile, came to Rome to ask for military aid.[8]

As the king well knew, help never came free in Rome. For about a year, the Flute Player stayed in a villa of Pompey in the hills outside the city and doled out bribes to senators. To cover costs, he signed high-interest loans with Roman bankers. Eventually the Senate assigned the task of restoring him as king of Egypt to one of the outgoing consuls of 57 BC. Many had wanted the job, which was sure to offer more payouts.[9]

At first, the Alexandrians had not known where Ptolemy had gone. They placed his daughter Berenice on the throne, and she and her advisers searched for a suitable husband for her. The candidate they settled on, a Syrian prince, was instantly rejected by the Alexandrian mob, who nicknamed him the "Salt-Fish Dealer." A few days later, Berenice had the poor man strangled.[10] After the Alexandrians learned what Ptolemy was up to, they sent a delegation of one hundred men to Rome to defend themselves against the king's charges and plead that the new queen be recognized. At the head of the delegation was one of the city's most distinguished and well-connected men, a philosopher named Dio.[11]

Ptolemy learned of the Alexandrians' plans in time to arrange for the ambassadors to be assaulted when they arrived in Puteoli. Many died. Some of the survivors who made it to Rome were killed in the city, while others were bribed by Ptolemy to keep quiet. Dio at first stayed at the house of a friend, the senator Lucius Lucceius, a scholarly man. Lucceius spent years working on a history of Rome. Cicero once sent him a letter asking that he suspend the history and write a standalone work on the lawyer's career, "from the beginning of the conspiracy down to my return from exile."[12] The work never appeared. Lucceius was close with Pompey, who was of course King Ptolemy's strongest backer, and so Dio decided to move to the house of another senator, Titus Coponius. Coponius had spent time in Alexandria as a student and gotten to know Dio. His house proved even less safe than that of Lucceius. Dio was found dead there one day late in 57 BC, having likely been stabbed.[13]

The Romans considered the killings of the Alexandrian ambassadors to be especially wicked. Among ancient states it was widely agreed that ambassadors were sacred and inviolable. Even to detain an ambassador against his will was an offense against the gods. Kill an ambassador, and plagues, floods, and famine might rain down on you. If Romans were involved in the deaths of Dio and the others, it spelled trouble for the whole Republic.

A scandal was brewing, and politicians were quick to try to control the damage—or exploit it to their advantage. Early in 56 BC the Senate ordered consultation of the books of the Sibyl, the prophetess of Apollo. As with all good oracles, the Sibyl's answers were usually vague. But the priests came upon a passage of amazing clarity: "If the king of Egypt comes requesting aid, do not refuse him friendship, but do not help him with a large force; otherwise you shall know both toils and dangers."[14] Here it was, straight from the god's mouth: no army should be sent to Egypt. Cicero suspected that the oracle had been faked, as part of the ongoing intrigue. But coming after the deaths of Dio and the other ambassadors, the words could not be brushed aside. The Senate rescinded the assignment of last year's consul to restore King Ptolemy to power.[15]

Several months of tension and confusion followed. Anger at Ptolemy's scandalous conduct and suspicions over plans by Romans to pocket Egypt's wealth mixed like fire with sulfur. Friends of Pompey supported his mission to restore Ptolemy. The king, who had left Rome and claimed sanctuary in the Temple of Artemis at Ephesus in Asia Minor, backed this plan as well. Clodius, on the other hand, suggested that Pompey's old rival Crassus should go to Egypt. No consensus could be reached except that the Roman army should not be involved, no matter what happened.[16] But what about Dio and the other slain envoys: Would they get justice?

Everyone knew that Ptolemy was behind the murders but he lay beyond the reach of the Roman legal system, safe in the Temple of Artemis. He must have had helpers, though, and they could be prosecuted. A number of Alexandrians were tried and some convicted, but no details are known. Also put on trial was a Roman named Asicius. He appears to have been an agent of the king and for a time borrowed from him an eight-bearer litter along with a guard of one hundred swordsmen. Asicius was charged with murdering Dio, but because his case involved an ambassador it was heard not in the regular murder court but in the violence court. Little is known of the trial, except that Cicero, perhaps as a favor to Pompey, defended Asicius and secured an acquittal.[17]

Next came the charges against Caelius, once again in the violence court. Born around 88 BC, in the eastern foothills of the Apennine Mountains, Caelius had a background similar to Cicero's. Caelius's equestrian father had a talent for making money and harbored great ambitions for his son. The family had a house on the outskirts of Rome, and around the age of sixteen Caelius was turned over to Cicero for training in public speaking. For years he was at Cicero's side and would have seen firsthand many of the orator's triumphs, such as the defense of Cluentius.[18] Caelius became a brilliant speaker himself, with a wit and forcefulness that were accompanied by flamboyant gestures that made his teacher wince. Cicero joked that Caelius had a strong right hand and a weak left, meaning that he was much better at prosecuting than at defending.[19] Pupil and teacher had much in common, such as a fondness for demeaning nicknames and a thirst for political success.[20] Cicero stuck to certain principles throughout his career, including the defense of property rights, and would make sacrifices for his beliefs. Caelius, on the other hand, was more cynical and cool, making him a near-perfect study in amorality. In politics, he repeatedly shifted sides, the way a skilled rider in the circus could jump from one horse to another.

Tall and strong, with piercing eyes, Caelius had more natural charisma and confidence than Cicero. It wasn't just that he wanted to break into politics; he had his sights set on high society as well. Caelius loved to dance, an activity Cicero considered the height of frivolity, so he fit right in at Palatine dinner parties and picnics in the pleasure gardens noble families had built around the city.[21] He joined the annual rush to the coastal resort town of Baiae during the Senate's spring recess. Set around a sparkling bay dotted with villas, Baiae was famed for its seafood, yachting, concerts, and love affairs. The poet Martial imagined one matron going there and, after dipping into the waters, abandoning her husband for a young man: "A Penelope she arrived, she left a Helen."[22]

Like Cicero before him, Caelius made a name for himself with a spectacular prosecution. In 59 BC he indicted Gaius Antonius, Cicero's colleague in the consulship four years earlier, who had recently returned from governing Macedonia. The main charge was either extortion or treasonous conduct in the province. It was an embarrassing situation for Cicero, since Antonius probably was guilty and had lent some of his ill-gotten spoils to Cicero to help pay for the

new Palatine house, thus obliging Cicero to defend him. From Caelius's speech survives a passage describing how Antonius was found,
right before a battle, "stretched out in a drunken slumber, snoring
with all the force of his lungs, belching continually, while the great
ladies who shared his quarters sprawled over every couch, and the
other women lay all around on the floor." As the enemy approached,
the women tried to rouse Antonius with increasing urgency, first
by shouting his name, then by whispering sweetly in his ear, and
finally by slapping his face: "Half-asleep and in a stupor, Antonius
was thrown around by his centurions and his concubines."[23] Caelius
won the case.

He was now old enough to stand for office. He moved from his
father's inconveniently located house to an apartment on the Palatine. The building was owned by Clodius, with whom Caelius had
become friendly, another slap in the face for Cicero. As Cicero's fortunes sank, it was all "glitter and glamor" for Caelius: dinner parties and picnics, Baiae and love affairs, bright clothes and a growing
entourage.[24]

Always keen to bask in the sunshine of publicity, Caelius
launched another prosecution in early 56 BC. Lucius Calpurnius
Bestia was charged with bribery in the recent praetorian elections, in
which he had failed to win a spot.[25] Probably it was at this trial that
Caelius went on about the murderous finger, perhaps waving one
of his own digits in the air as he made the sensational accusation.
Only a few months before the trial, it appears, Caelius had been on
familiar terms with Bestia and supported him in the election. But
sudden about-faces were no problem for Caelius.[26] Cicero defended
Bestia successfully at a well-attended trial. Caelius then returned for
the attack. He initiated a second prosecution of Bestia, this time for
bribery in the upcoming elections. Bestia had had enough and got

his son, Atratinus, though still only a teenager, to prosecute Caelius on charges of violence.[27]

Because such accusations were so serious, trials in this court moved more quickly than others. Uniquely, the violence court even convened on holidays.[28] If Atratinus could get Caelius convicted, the family's tormentor would be stuck eating oysters with Verres in exile in Marseilles before the second bribery trial could commence. Of course, Caelius was a more than decent speaker and would be sure to put up a defense. What the prosecution didn't count on was that Cicero, who had just lent his services to Bestia, would do an about-face himself and help Caelius. Even less could the prosecution have predicted the defense Cicero would rely on: that the case had nothing to do with violence but rather a woman scorned in love.

Cicero faced many challenges in preparing his defense. The deaths of the ambassadors and Ptolemy's bribes stank. Caelius had a reputation for bad behavior. And quite possibly he had been on the king's payroll: the allowance Caelius received from his father could not support his lavish lifestyle.[29] Beyond all that, there was another coincidental problem that would prove important for the trial. The prosecution was scheduled to begin the case on April 3, followed by the defense on April 4, after which—as was typical—witnesses would testify.[30] April 4, though, was the first day of the Great Mother's Games, a major festival held in honor of an eastern goddess whose worship was brought to Rome in the third century BC.[31] Everyone would have preferred to be there than listen to Cicero's speech.

As part of the games there were six days of stage performances for the goddess. These took a variety of forms. One was tragedy, just like the famous tragedies of Greece. Many of the Roman scripts in fact were adaptations of Greek originals. Ennius's *Medea* was a favorite. It tells the story of a barbarian woman who betrayed her own family to help the Greek Jason steal the Golden Fleece. Jason then dumped her for another woman, and in revenge she killed her children from him. The opening lines of the play, spoken by Medea's nurse, were often quoted by Romans and would be cited at Caelius's trial: if only Jason's ship, the *Argo*, had never set out, "if only in the Pelian grove the fir planks had not fallen to the earth, hewn by axes," then "never would my misled mistress have set foot outside her house, Medea, sick at heart, wounded by savage love."[32]

There were lighter entertainments too. Romans laughed at comedies in the Greek style, which always used the same limited cast of characters: foolish young men in love, angry fathers, clever slaves, and predatory prostitutes. Part of the fun was to see how, using the stock types, the playwright could produce an original plot.[33] There also was the mime, a type of drama that originated in Alexandria. Unlike mime today, it included much speaking and singing as well as dancing. One performer kept time by playing an instrument like castanets attached to clogs. Mime was bawdy and full of slapstick. Actors improvised a great deal. One of the most popular storylines centered around adultery: a woman and her lover would be discovered by the woman's husband, and she would try to hide the lover (in a tub, for instance). Mime was also sexy. Unlike in other types of theater, the actors didn't wear masks or much clothing either.[34]

Romans of every background loved theater, Cicero included. And that was the problem. On the opening day of the Great Mother's Games, jurors might resent having to listen to Cicero, especially if he droned on too long. The crowd that ringed the court and fed him with energy might wander off. But good strategist that he was, Cicero realized there might be a way to turn this liability into an asset. The Roman courtroom was a sort of stage, and trials always had a theatrical quality. If Cicero played that up, he could provide the entertainment his spectators would be missing—and give the jurors a lens through which to view Caelius more sympathetically.

First came the case for the prosecution, which must be reconstructed through Cicero's defense speech. The lead lawyer was Atratinus. It might seem odd to entrust the case to a teenager, but he would win sympathy for coming to the rescue of his father against Caelius. Joining Atratinus was friend of the family Herennius Balbus, a much older man who could be quite severe. Also speaking for the prosecution was a man called by Cicero "Publius Clodius."[35] This almost certainly was not *the* Clodius but probably a distant kinsman of his or a freedman—an experienced courtroom brawler, according to Cicero. While Atratinus and his father, Bestia, were the driving force behind the prosecution, the ex-tribune Clodius must have been lending support. He and Caelius had once been friendly but had recently broken ties. The trial would keep the scandal of the Alexandrian ambassadors in the news and give Clodius a way to weaken his chief opponent at the time, Pompey, who was so thick with King Ptolemy.

Young Atratinus led off. As was typical for the opening of a prosecution, he focused on Caelius's bad character.[36] Drawing a contrast with his own filial piety, Atratinus accused Caelius of treating *his* poor old father with no respect. Jurors who themselves had dealt with wayward sons must have nodded sympathetically. Atratinus continued by saying that Caelius's fellow townsmen back home thought little of him. His sexual morality was disgraceful. In his earlier years, Caelius had even allowed himself to be the love object of other men.

The teenaged prosecutor plowed on: Caelius was a friend of Catiline and probably a member of his conspiracy. He helped distribute
bribes before elections. And his debt! So much extravagance! Too
good for his respectable father's house, Caelius paid a rent of 30,000
sesterces a year for an apartment. What a violent streak he had too.
One senator was going to testify that he had been punched by Caelius
during the pontifical elections. Other witnesses would tell of how their
wives had been assaulted by Caelius when returning from dinner.

In a phrase that would become important later in the trial,
Atratinus called Caelius "a pretty-boy Jason." The combination of
a mythological or historical character with a belittling adjective
was a common form of nickname in Rome. Lucullus was known as
the "togaed Xerxes." The emperor Caligula called his crafty grandmother Livia "Ulysses in a dress." In Petronius's novel *Satyricon*, an
exasperated husband calls his wife "Cassandra in army boots."[37]
"Pretty-boy" hinted at Caelius's alleged homosexual past, but why
"Jason"? To fund his life of luxury, Caelius needed a Golden Fleece.
And King Ptolemy, with his seemingly bottomless treasure chests,
provided it.

After this opening bombardment, the prosecutor Publius
Clodius rolled out even heavier artillery.[38] The old brawler, said
Cicero, threw his weight around the court. Stirred up from the start,
he shouted out harsh words at the top of his voice. He dealt with
some of the most important charges: the assault of the ambassadors
at Puteoli, the riot at Naples, and "the property of Palla." Details are
missing because Cicero later declined to talk about these accusations.
"The property of Palla" is a total mystery. It may have referred to an
attack by Caelius on a villa where the ambassadors were staying.

Herennius Balbus stepped forward to land the death blow. He
delivered a long diatribe on the way young men were behaving: the

luxury, the debt, their fancy grooming and wild sex lives. He lamented the "orgies, love affairs, adultery, Baiae, beach parties, dinner parties, drinking parties, singing, concerts, pleasure cruising."[39] Balbus didn't rant, Cicero said. He spoke calmly and firmly, commanding the jurors' attention. Balbus claimed that Caelius embodied all that was wrong with Rome. Look at how he had stabbed in the back his old friend Bestia, first supporting him for the praetorship, then prosecuting him, now prosecuting him again. Caelius was out of control.

Balbus also developed two criminal charges his colleagues had not covered. Before Dio had been killed, when he had been staying at the house of Pompey's friend Lucceius, Caelius had tried to have Lucceius's slaves poison the ambassador. Balbus explained that the plan had fallen through, but the prosecution had a witness with strong knowledge of it: Clodius's sister, Clodia Metelli.

She had met Caelius through her brother and had lent him some money for the games he was staging. Only later did she discover that the money was being used to bribe Lucceius's slaves. When Caelius realized that Clodia was on to him, he put in place another criminal plan. The jurors must have been on the edge of their benches, as Herennius Balbus made the accusation with a grave face. Caelius had poison at home, and he tried it out on a slave he had bought just for that purpose. The slave's speedy death showed the drug worked. The next step was to turn a jar of it over to Clodia's slaves, who would administer it to their mistress.

Luckily for Clodia, as the great lady was going to testify, she had loyal slaves. They informed her of what Caelius was planning, and she then arranged a trap. A friend of Caelius named Licinius was supposed to turn over the jar of poison. Clodia instructed her slaves to tell Licinius to meet them at the Senian Baths. She hid freeborn men of respectable status there in advance of the meeting to witness the handover. As the prosecutor informed the court, they had done so and were going to testify to what they had seen. However, the prosecution did not have the jar of poison to present as evidence: Clodia's men jumped out a second too early and Licinius, realizing he was caught, got off with the jar.

The attempted poisoning of Clodia wouldn't normally have counted as a charge in the violence court, but the prosecutors could raise it because it supported the other accusations. Balbus was saying that Clodia had secured proof of Caelius's criminal activities at great risk to herself and that every juror would have to accept it.

This gave Cicero his opening.


Up first for the defense was Caelius himself, who needed to show he wasn't as bad as everyone said. Probably at the start of the speech he assured the jurors that he would be on his best behavior. Among the few surviving quotations of his defense is this: "I hope that none of you [members of the jury] and none of all those present at the trial will find my facial expression too offensive, any word of mine too unrestrained, or even—what matters least—my gestures too flamboyant."[40]

But Caelius couldn't resist throwing out his usual insults. It was too bad Atratinus couldn't write his own speeches and had to rely on his tutor, that "barley-blown rhetorician, the coarse old windbag."[41] And as for Atratinus, if Caelius was a "pretty-boy Jason," Atratinus was "a Pelias in curls."[42] Pelias was the unlikable king of Greece who had devised the idea of the quest for the Golden Fleece to get rid of Jason. Atratinus, in other words, was a tormentor, and an effeminate one at that: real men did not curl their hair. Continuing with the mythological allusions, Caelius called Clodia "a two bit Clytemnestra," or more literally "Clytemnestra for a *quadrans*" (a *quadrans* was a low-value bronze coin).[43] Caelius was hinting that Clodia, like the wife of King Agamemnon, had killed her husband, Metellus Celer—he had died unexpectedly, three years earlier—and that she was a prostitute. Probably before the trial, Clodia had gained the nickname "Quadrantaria" when a lover of hers, whether as an insult or a joke, sent her a purse full of bronze coins as if she performed sex acts for small sums of money.[44]

Along with the nicknames, Caelius seems to have included some of his signature horseplay. According to Quintilian's manual on rhetoric, at one point in a speech—surely this one—Caelius brought out a jar, "in a way unsuitable for an orator or indeed any serious man."[45] Cicero would later refer to the jar in his own speech, along with "a most obscene story"—one that he said was the talk of Rome but he would not repeat. A guess is that Caelius told the jurors that Clodia had been sent a jar of something, but that he wasn't the one who sent it. Perhaps it was an aphrodisiac from a frustrated lover. Quintilian also noted that in one speech—again, surely this one—Caelius called Clodia a terrible tease who wore dresses made of nearly see-through silk.

It fell to the next speaker for the defense to delve into the main charges. As a young man, Caelius had studied with both Cicero and the plutocrat Crassus, who was himself an experienced advocate in the courts. From Cicero, we know that Crassus addressed the charges the prosecutor Clodius had focused on: the riot at Naples, the assault on the Alexandrians at Puteoli, and the property of Palla. As to how Crassus did so, Cicero's surviving speech gives only one clue. Crassus talked about the disastrous arrival of King Ptolemy in Rome. Probably by prearrangement with Cicero, Crassus even quoted the famous opening lines of *Medea*: "If only in the Pelian grove the fir planks had not fallen to the earth, hewn by axes." If only Ptolemy had never come to Rome, none of this recent violence would have taken place.[46]

Last to speak was Cicero, just as he preferred. He began his speech by imagining how perplexed a stranger in the Forum might be upon witnessing the trial underway: "He would wonder, I feel sure, what is the enormity of this case, seeing that on a holiday when public games are held, when all legal business is suspended, this court alone should be in session." If you explained the law against violence, the stranger would then ask what charge was being heard: "When he hears that no crime, no shamelessness, no violence has been brought before the court, that a young man of outstanding talent, diligence, and popularity is being accused by the son of a man whom he is prosecuting and has prosecuted before, and that he is being attacked with the financial support of a prostitute, the onlooker would not blame Atratinius's sense of duty, he would think that a woman's selfish desires should be curbed, and he would judge you hardworking, who not even on a public holiday are given time off."[47]

At the words "financial support of a prostitute," the jurors must have jerked their heads like startled geese. Caelius had already taunted Clodia in his speech, and Cicero had been doing the same for years. But it was surprising how coolly Cicero equated the patrician matron to a prostitute and suggested that the case had nothing to do with any crimes Caelius had committed but rather Clodia's passions. It's not hard to imagine that as Cicero teased his whole line of defense, news of his remarks whipped through the Forum and more spectators arrived, jostling against one another for the best view.

Cicero would keep everyone in suspense for a while. None of the prosecutors, he said next, thought they would win this case "without relying on the unbearable passion and fierce hatred of some other person." Then he turned to Atratinus's attack on Caelius's character. If Caelius had treated his own father so badly, Cicero asked, why was the man now in court, dressed in rags and sobbing over the fate of his son? If Caelius was so disliked in his hometown, why had the council sent a delegation on his behalf? As to the criticisms of the defendant's sexual morals, "never will Caelius take these so hard that he would think it better to have been born ugly!" People always said this sort of thing about young men, so Atratinus had better be careful himself. As to Caelius's friendship with Catiline: yes, Caelius did briefly support him, when he was running for office. Catiline fooled many men: "I myself, yes, I, was once nearly deceived by him."[48]

And so it went, as Cicero waved away Atratinus's claims with weak arguments and jokes. The expensive apartment? "Aha! Now I understand. The building of Publius Clodius in which my client rents an apartment for, I believe, 10,000 a year is up for sale." The prosecutor was trying to drive up the price. Caelius moved to the Palatine not for fun and parties, but to be nearer the Forum so that his supporters could visit him:

On this point I can say what the distinguished Marcus Crassus said a little earlier, when he was protesting the arrival of King Ptolemy: "If only in the Pelian grove." And I could continue the play: "Never would my misled mistress" have caused us this distress, "Medea, sick at heart, wounded by savage love." For you will find, members of the jury, what I shall show when I reach that point in my case—that this Medea of the Palatine and the change of residence was the source of all this young man's troubles, or rather of all the rumors.[49]

Cicero must have gestured over toward Clodia, sitting with the other witnesses among the prosecutor's benches, when he said the words "Medea of the Palatine." All the jurors and the spectators, who knew the myth so well, would have understood what the lawyer was insinuating: Clodia was trying to exact revenge on Caelius.

The other witnesses could be disregarded, Cicero continued. The senator who had been assaulted at the pontifical elections: Why hadn't he pressed charges earlier? The men who claimed their wives had been assaulted when they were returning to dinner: what impressive witnesses they would make when they had to swear under oath that they had never done anything about these terrible wrongs. Just about anything could be bought in the Forum these days, even false testimony. Cicero returned to his earlier point: "The accusers of Marcus Caelius are not the same people as those who are attacking him: the weapons hurled at him in public are supplied by a hidden hand."[50]

Soon Cicero was on to the murder of Dio. Everybody knew who was behind it: the king himself. Herennius Balbus's long lecture on morality, worthy of the dreariest uncle, censor, or schoolmaster, was just an attempt to use the bad behavior of others to stir up prejudice against Caelius. Anyone could attack luxurious living. Cicero could talk about it till nightfall. Caelius shouldn't have to pay for the vices of a whole generation. To go out to dinner, to splash on some perfume, to visit Baiae: these weren't crimes.

What mattered to Cicero were the accusations that Balbus had made and their true originator: "There are two charges, one concerning gold and one concerning poison. In both of them, one and the same person is involved. Gold was procured from Clodia, poison was sought to be given to Clodia, so the prosecution says." Caelius took gold from Clodia and was to hold on to it as long as he wanted: "I can detect strong evidence of an unusual intimacy." Caelius wanted to kill Clodia, sought out poison, pestered people for it, and somehow got it: "I can detect that a great hatred took shape after a cruel rupture."[51]

Cicero was claiming that a version of *Medea* was playing out before the jurors' eyes. The older widow Clodia had fallen for Caelius. When Caelius ended the affair, she set out to ruin him. That was why he was on trial today, and the jurors convicting him would fulfill Clodia's plan. "Everything in this case, members of the jury," Cicero said, "has to do with Clodia, a woman not only of noble birth, but of notoriety." The lawyer had no choice but to bring her into it. He could have gone a lot further, he said, but didn't want to seem spiteful: "I am prevented by my enmity with the woman's husband . . . I mean brother, I always make that mistake."[52]

It's hard not to suspect that, amid all the jokes, Cicero was performing the greatest conjuring trick of his legal career. Almost certainly Caelius and Clodia had for a time been lovers. It seems unlikely Cicero would invent an affair out of nothing. The prosecution concealed this relationship because it did not reflect well on Clodia: respectable women in Rome were supposed to have sex only with their husbands. But the prosecutors figured the defense wouldn't mention it either, since Caelius shouldn't have been sleeping with respectable married women or widows.[53] While it is true that Clodia had been mocked in the past for her incestuous relationship with her brother, the prosecution's reliance on her testimony suggests that she wielded authority. Women could be heard sympathetically in the criminal courts. To counter Clodia, Cicero dragged the affair into the open and tied it to two key points in the prosecution's case: first, Clodia and Caelius were close, then they were estranged. Suddenly the case had nothing to do with public violence but "a woman's desires and delights."[54]

Clodia's alleged lust and her hunger for revenge tinged the case with tragedy. But even more, Cicero turned it into a comedy, just like the ones jurors should have been watching at the Great Mother's Games. Humor was the sleight of hand Cicero used to hide the real charges. A mountain was really a molehill.

How should he deal with Clodia? he asked. Would she like the stern, old-fashioned approach or the more easygoing, modern way? If she wanted the severe way, Cicero would call up from the underworld one of those bearded old Romans—"not with one of those neatly trimmed little beards that delight her so much," but the shaggy type you saw on old statues. How about Clodia's great-great-great-great-grandfather, Appius Claudius the Blind, builder of Rome's first aqueduct and the Appian Way? Before the jurors' eyes, Cicero turned himself into the old censor: "Woman, what business do you have with Caelius, with a young man, with a stranger? Why have you been so intimate with him that you lent him gold or so at odds that you feared poison?" It could only have been her "reckless desire." Influenced by "her brother's vices," Clodia had ignored generations and generations of worthy role models in her family tree. Why, Appius asks, did he even bother to build his aqueduct—so Clodia could foul it with her incestuous practices? Why build the Appian Way—so Clodia "could go up and down it, accompanied by strange men?"[55]

Cicero joked that bringing out an old character like Appius Claudius was risky, as he might accuse Caelius too. Cicero would take care of that later, he said. First, another member of Clodia's family would make an appearance: her little brother Clodius. "What's all the fuss about, sister? Why are you acting so crazy? Why such a brouhaha, why are you blowing out of proportion such a minor affair? You saw a boy next door. His fair skin, his height, his face, and his eyes drove you crazy. You wanted to see him more. You found yourselves together at the same pleasure gardens from time to time." Clodia gave Caelius presents, hoping to bind him that way, but he dumped her. Well, move on! "You have pleasure gardens along the Tiber, carefully sited where all the young men come to swim. Every day you are free to pick your partners there."[56]

After the impersonations of Clodia's family members, Cicero said it was Caelius's turn to be lectured. Cicero would now take up the part of a father. But what type of father should he be? Perhaps like the harsh ones who featured in the comedies of the playwright Caecilius? The sort who said things like "Now at last my mind is flaring up, now my heart is filled with anger!" If such a man had Caelius as a son, he would have said, "Why did you move so close to the prostitute? Why didn't you run away when you became aware of her attractions? . . . Scatter and squander, I don't care! If you run out of money, you'll be the one to suffer." Harsh words, but Caelius could answer them: he had not been led astray by a passion, nor had he incurred a lot of debt. There were rumors, but nobody in a city full of slanderers could escape those. For a milder father, on the other hand, the sort who would say that anything can be fixed, Caelius would have a much easier case to make.[57]

Cicero was applying the stock characters of comedy onto the case he was arguing: Caelius was the young man in a scrape, Herennius Balbus the angry old man, and Clodia the prostitute—the character with whom the male audience rarely sympathized.[58] Cicero thus discredited her and won sympathy for Caelius from the all-male jury. And he weakened the prosecution's charges about Caelius's immorality. Few in Rome, few men anyway, complained if a young man had sex with a female prostitute; it was only natural, they would have reasoned.[59] Though many aspects of Cicero's gender politics may appall us, we have to recognize that Cicero was creatively adapting standards that were enshrined in popular culture such as the theater. He was exploiting such attitudes to win his case, just as the prosecution had when it attacked Caelius's sexual morality.

Cicero took a risk by bringing the affair of Clodia with Caelius into the trial, but it gave him a way to ridicule her accusations about the gold and the poison. Clodia and Caelius were so close, he claimed, that she was fetching gold out of her safe for him and even jewelry she had hung on a statue of Venus in her house—the trophies of her conquests. But if the two were that intimate, she must have known what he would be using the gold for. Her story of Caelius's attempt to poison Dio could not stand, as a sworn statement already made by Lucceius also made clear. And if Caelius never planned to kill Dio, the charge about poisoning Clodia fell apart too. He would have had no motive. If anyone were a poisoner it was Clodia: her husband had fallen ill and died with suspicious speed.[60]

Cicero first donned the mask of tragedy, then the mask of comedy. Last of all would come barefaced farce. The prosecution's story was that Caelius handed over to Licinius the poison to kill Clodia, then Licinius was to meet Clodia's slaves in the Senian Baths. It made no sense, Cicero said. Why wouldn't Caelius meet with the slaves privately? Cicero insisted that even if the claim that Clodia had arranged a trap were accepted, it still made no sense. How would you hide all the men in a bathhouse—unless the lady had made friends with the bath attendant beforehand? And who were these male friends of Clodia who claimed to have apprehended Licinius anyway? Were they respectable men? Or the sort of men Clodia entertained at her notorious dinner parties? Apparently the lady was in the habit of staging theatrical entertainments in her own house, which allowed Cicero to get in a dig about the story of the poisoning attempt: "This whole little drama, the work of a seasoned lady poet with many plays to her credit: how devoid it is of plot, how completely at a loss for an ending."[61]

Cicero imagined Licinius in the baths, hesitating and dithering, before finally managing to slip away. But why had Clodia's myrmidons let him go? Why not arrest him on the spot? All of Clodia's young male friends were strapping, and there were so many of them. Cicero could barely wait for cross-examination: "I will ask them how they hid and where, whether it was the well-known tub or some Trojan horse." The "well-known tub" was a reference to a poorly improvised skit that you would have seen in a mime. It was make-believe, and not even good make-believe. Who could accept that Clodia's men had jumped out before Licinius had even turned over the jar? "And so we have the ending of a mime, not a proper play—the kind of thing where, when no satisfactory conclusion is found, someone wriggles free, clatter go the clogs, and—curtain!"[62]

Cicero grew more solemn as he made his usual plea for mercy at the end: save this young man, show pity on his father, think of your own children.[63] With Cicero's speech as the main source of evidence, it is hard to know how the trial played out after that. We can only imagine how Clodia responded to Cicero and what her testimony was like. Caelius was acquitted, though by how wide a margin is also unknown. Was the verdict just? Cicero turned the trial into a showdown between Clodia and Caelius, but that almost certainly wasn't the whole story. Atratinus and Bestia had strong reasons of their own to prosecute Caelius, going back to Caelius's first suit against Bestia. They must have thought they had a chance of winning their case. The prosecution's story of the attempted poisoning was similar to the one Cicero told about Oppianicus in the trial of Cluentius. It is possible Caelius was involved in the attacks on the Alexandrians. After all, he had a good motive: financial need.

Cicero's speech is a model of how a defense lawyer can weaken the prosecution by plucking a few parts from their case and rearranging them into a new and different story. It is also a model of how Roman lawyers used humor and stereotypes to discredit and distract. The trial of Caelius shows, too, how the courts could be put to nonjudicial uses—for young men to make names for themselves, for more experienced politicians to enhance their authority, and, most troublingly, for political rivals to settle scores and even try to eliminate each other. Quite possibly Clodia and Clodius had joined the prosecution to punish Caelius after they had a falling-out. And quite possibly Clodia had a vindictive streak, like her brother. Quite certainly Cicero himself took the chance to exact revenge at the trial.

For years, Clodia had supported her brother in politics—and so harmed Cicero in the process. At one point in his speech Cicero turned directly to Clodia and addressed her. "I forget now the wrongs you have done me, Clodia," he said, using the orator's favorite device of pretending to pass over something, only to mention it. "Your cruel treatment on my family when I was away I overlook."[64] During Cicero's sixteen months of exile, his wife and his two children had suffered. Terentia was forced to seek shelter with her half sister, a Vestal Virgin, after being driven out of the Palatine house. At least once Clodius even demanded that Terentia appear at his official tribunal, a humiliation to a woman of high social standing.[65] In Rome, there was a convention among top-ranking women to help one another in times of trouble by intervening with their kinsmen.[66] Clodia failed to observe that, and it seems she even made Terentia's and her children's lives more difficult. This helps to explain why Cicero was willing to treat Clodia so mercilessly. His defense of Caelius was payback.

That was justice, of a sort, though the actual murderer of Dio never was caught or convicted, as far as is known. And King Ptolemy regained his kingdom, despite all the anger over his bribes and the Sibyl's warning. In the fall of 56 BC, on the instructions of Pompey, a large army under the command of the Roman governor of Syria, Gabinius, came to Egypt and defeated the forces of the king's daughter Berenice at the fortress city of Pelusium. Gabinius then marched along the Nile to Alexandria and took the city for Ptolemy. The king promptly put Berenice to death as well as many other rich citizens, whose money he needed for he had promised a huge fee to Pompey and Gabinius for their help.[67]

Cicero was livid. Gabinius was one of the consuls of 58 BC who had worked with Clodius to exile Cicero. He shouldn't be walking off with the wealth of Egypt. But maybe, Cicero thought, Gabinius's venture provided an opening for revenge, just as the trial of Caelius had. Cicero publicly denounced Gabinius for what he had done and demanded that the *Sibylline Books* be consulted again, to see if they mentioned a punishment for violating their injunctions. It was by now 55 BC. With the support of Julius Caesar, Pompey and Crassus rigged the elections so that they could serve as consuls for a second time this year. They refused to put Cicero's motion to a vote. But after new consuls took office in 54 BC, the books finally were reopened and nothing was found.[68] Still, Cicero helped turn public opinion against Gabinius. When the commander finally returned to Rome in September of 54 BC, he was under a cloud. Few came out to greet him, and charges were filed against him in three different courts: bribery, treason, and extortion.[69]

The treason trial came first. The restoration of King Ptolemy would be the centerpiece of the case. Gabinius violated the Senate's decree by crossing out of his own province with an army. Sorely as Cicero would have liked to prosecute, he was pressured against it by Pompey. Cicero relied on Pompey for ongoing protection against Clodius, so Pompey was able to dictate much of what Cicero did and did not do in the courts at this time. Cicero limited himself to testifying against Gabinius. Gabinius secured a narrow acquittal: only thirty-two out of seventy jurors voted to condemn. In Cicero's view, the prosecutors botched the case. Also, Pompey had worked hard lobbying jurors to acquit.[70]

Soon after the trial, the Tiber River rose so high that it inundated the lower levels of the city. The flimsy apartment buildings became soaked through and collapsed, many animals were swept away, and men, women, and children who didn't take refuge in time drowned. The cause was likely heavy rains upstream, but Romans surmised it was the anger of the gods. According to a letter of Cicero, a few lines from Homer's *Iliad* circulated throughout the suffering city:

> On an autumn day, when Zeus sends down the most
> violent waters
> in deep rage against mortals after they stir him to anger
> because in violent assembly they pass decrees that are
> crooked,
> and drive righteousness from among them and care
> nothing for what the gods think.[71]

The verses seemed to sum up so many of the crimes of the last few years, from the assault on the Alexandrian ambassadors to fraudulent elections to the acquittal of Gabinius. The verses certainly captured the mood of the populace, pummeled not just by natural disaster but also by the politicians' contests for power and money.

The waters ebbed, but not the despair and rage of the people. As Gabinius's trial for provincial extortion approached, crowds demonstrated against him. Cicero meekly complied with Pompey's demand that he speak for the defense, earning himself an unflattering nickname: the turncoat. Nobody believed Cicero when he claimed that he had forgiven Gabinius, and for once his advocacy probably hurt the defendant far more than it helped. Gabinius was convicted. Finally, at least one Roman had paid the price for selling out Roman foreign policy to the king of Egypt. Gabinius went into exile.[72]

Beyond concerns about his own security, Cicero had another reason not to antagonize Pompey in the fall of 54 BC. Milo was preparing to run for the consulship the following year, and Cicero wanted to help him as much as he could. Cicero needed to keep Pompey on his side. As it was, Clodius would provide enough of a challenge. By the end of 54 BC, Cicero could opine in a letter that Milo seemed to be in good shape—"unless utter violence breaks out."[73]

# CHAPTER 11

# Accident

One January afternoon in 52 BC, Senator Sextus Teidius was being carried by litter on the Appian Way to Rome when he and his entourage came upon the body of a dead man. Lying in the middle of the road, it was covered with stab wounds. Armed robberies along desolate stretches of the highway were increasingly common in these unsettled times when the Roman government struggled to maintain order even in the city. But when Teidius recognized the body, he realized that no ordinary crime had taken place. The dead man was Clodius. Teidius told his slaves to bring the corpse to the city, about twelve miles away. He headed in the opposite direction.[1]

The litter made it to Clodius's house on the Palatine in Rome after nightfall. A large crowd gathered in the mansion's courtyard to mourn their fallen hero. To heighten everyone's shock, grief, and anger, Clodia's widow, Fulvia, made sure to display all of Clodius's wounds. She did not follow the custom of washing the corpse, nor did she cover it in a clean toga. She gave full vent to her own sorrow. Roman women, when mourning, would wail, beat their breasts, and let down their normally pinned-up hair. In her call for revenge, Fulvia became a Fury.

At dawn the next day, January 19, an even larger crowd poured into the house. Among them were two of the year's tribunes, Plancus Bursa and Pompeius Rufus. Goaded on by the pair, the mob took the naked body of Clodius into the Forum and placed it high on the speaker's platform for all to see. The two tribunes began to speak before a large crowd. They lamented the loss of the greatest friend the Roman people had ever known. They stoked rage against Milo, claiming it was he who had done this.

Members of the crowd then carried the bruised and bloodstained corpse into the Senate house. Led on by Clodius's friend Cloelius, they heaped up a pyre of benches, tables, and even the large wooden tablets used for recordkeeping. They burned the body, and the Senate house with it. A nearby building used for public business, the Basilica Porcia, was also engulfed in the flames. Then, around the middle of the afternoon, with the fire still smoldering, crowds of Romans met in the Forum to hold the feast that customarily followed a funeral.

Different stories of what had happened to Clodius continued to spread for weeks afterward, causing mayhem. That Clodius had been killed by some of Milo's slaves traveling with their master along the Appian Way not even Milo could deny. But had Milo planned the ambush of his old enemy, as friends of Clodius claimed? Or, as Milo insisted, had Clodius tried to ambush *him* and had Milo only acted in self-defense? And if that were what had happened, how could Milo prove it? When Milo was eventually put on trial, Cicero had to make the case for the defense for his friend, the hardest test he would face in his legal career. But the trial, along with those of others implicated in the violence of 52 BC, had a much greater significance, not just for Cicero but for the state as a whole.[2] The murder of Clodius and its aftermath proved to be a milestone in the final collapse of republican government in Rome.

Even before Clodius's murder, the normal political process had broken down. Shortly before the consular elections of 54 BC, it was revealed that two of the candidates had offered massive bribes to the consuls currently in office to rig the voting. The elections had to be postponed, and only in July of 53 BC were consuls for that year voted into office. Without consuls there were no praetors, and so the courts had remained shut for seven months. Repeated delays also plagued the elections for the next set of magistrates. When the year 52 BC opened again no consuls or praetors were in office, and the courts were paralyzed.[3]

Three candidates were standing for the consulship of 52 BC: Milo, Plautius Hypsaeus, and Metellus Scipio. Milo had been preparing his run for several years. In 55 BC he made an advantageous marriage to Fausta, daughter of the dictator Sulla.[4] Her twin brother Faustus was a darling of the nobles who favored hardline senatorial government, and Milo wanted their support. Fausta was rich and wielded great influence in her own right. Like Clodia, she was accused of promiscuity. According to one story, when she was carrying on affairs with two men at the same time—a launderer's son and a man named Macula (which in Latin means "stain")—her own brother quipped that it was surprising she had a stain when she had her own launderer.[5] One should be skeptical here: a charge against a woman of sexual immorality might really have been an attack on her influence.[6]

Like other candidates, Milo tried to win over all the key groups. With lobbying by Cicero, he shored up the support of wealthy Italians.

He organized lavish gladiatorial matches and theatrical shows to impress the masses. In a letter from late 54 BC Cicero clucked over the amounts Milo was spending.[7] Allegedly Milo used up three whole inheritances on games. Cicero himself had not spent like that to win office, but with such largesse becoming more and more common, perhaps it was necessary. Whatever the case, Cicero was determined to see Milo win.

Of course, Milo faced opposition from his two rival candidates. Plautius Hypsaeus, a former officer of Pompey, had the great general's support. So did Metellus Scipio, who also boasted the best family tree in Rome, made up of generations of consular ancestors among the Scipios as well as the Caecilii Metelli. All three candidates almost certainly engaged in bribery. And each relied on another tactic that had become distressingly common in politics: they or their supporters had gangs disrupt each other's canvassing and even stop voting when it was underway. Because Milo was so indebted, Hypsaeus and Scipio hoped that by delaying elections long enough their rival might be bankrupted and forced out of Rome.[8]

Meanwhile Clodius was evolving his own political plans. He had intended to stand for a praetorship in the year 53 BC, but because of the long delay in elections he decided to run for 52 BC instead.[9] He hoped, once in office, to pass an ambitious package of laws, one of which would distribute freed slaves more evenly across all the voting tribes. Several politicians had tried to make such a reform like this before, which would address a real inequity in the electoral system. But these efforts always met with opposition both from politicians worried about the influence the reformer might gain and from wealthy Italians who did not want their voting power diluted. To carry out his reform, opposed by Cicero, Milo, and their friends, Clodius would need some time.

And so, even though they were running for different offices, Milo and Clodius effectively became opponents. Clodius thought he would be hamstrung by Milo's consulship and threw all his support to Hypsaeus and Scipio. Milo felt he had no choice but to stymy Clodius's campaign. Their gangs brawled with each other on the streets. In the Senate Clodius charged that Milo's debts went far beyond what he admitted. Clodius claimed that if Milo were elected consul, he would raid the state coffers. Cicero happily rebutted the charges in a speech full of his favorite slurs.[10]

According to a long-standing arrangement, when there was no consul a magistrate known as an interrex was selected from among the patrician senators to hold office for five days. The patricians would select a new interrex every five days until consuls were elected. The first interrex was not supposed to hold elections, but any of his successors could. But none of this could happen at the start of 52 BC. Milo, confident of victory, wanted an interrex named. Scipio and Hypsaeus did not—and they had a way to get their wish. Although no consuls or praetors were in office, tribunes, elected separately by the Tribal Assembly, were. One of the tribunes, Plancus Bursa, used his veto to block the patricians from naming an interrex.[11]

And so Rome was stuck in political deadlock when Clodius left the city on January 17 on his fatal journey. Probably accompanied by around twenty-five armed slaves, he was traveling to the little town of Aricia, about fifteen miles down the Appian Way, to address the town council. Before he left he paid a visit to his architect Cyrus, who was dying and wanted his will witnessed. Cyrus also did work for Cicero, who was also summoned to witness the will. It was the last time the two enemies would see each other alive.[12]

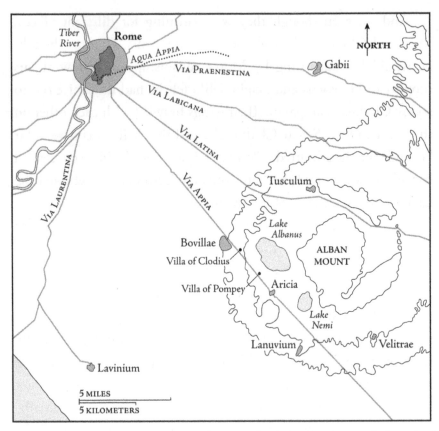

The Appian Way, 52 BC. Cicero's enemy Clodius met his fatal end, in 52 BC, a little south of Bovillae on the Via Appia, the great military highway built by his ancestor Appius Claudius Caecus in the late fourth century BC. Caecus also built the Aqua Appia, Rome's first major aqueduct, which ran largely underground. The aqueduct's path and the location of the villas of Clodius and Pompey are conjectural. This map is based on Richard J. A. Talbert, *Barrington Atlas of the Greek and Roman World* (Princeton, NJ: Princeton University Press, 2000), Map 43.

The next day, January 18, Milo attended a morning meeting of the Senate. He then went home, changed into a hooded riding cloak, and prepared to set off for his hometown of Lanuvium, about nineteen miles down the Appian Way, where he was to preside over the appointment of a priest the next day. Milo was riding in a carriage with Fausta. A train of slaves followed them: gladiators to provide security, personal attendants including maids of Fausta, and musicians of hers, who perhaps came along to entertain her or to participate in the religious ceremony at Lanuvium.[13]

All of this would be investigated in due course. First, somebody needed to take charge of the city. The afternoon of Clodius's funeral, as the fires smoldered and the crowds feasted, the Senate met on the Palatine, probably in the Temple of Jupiter Stator, where Cicero had assembled the senators after he was nearly killed at his house in November 63 BC.[14] At the meeting, the patricians appointed as interrex one of their number, Manius Lepidus.

Almost immediately, crowds of Clodians gathered around Lepidus's house. They wanted him to hold elections straightaway, even though it wasn't customary for elections to be held by the first interrex. Scipio and Hypsaeus were sure to win. Rumors were spreading that Milo wasn't coming back to Rome. Some even said he was going to pull a Catiline, take up arms, and declare war on the Republic. A gang of Clodians rushed to Milo's house on the Palatine and tried to burn it down but were driven off by a barrage of arrows. The group then seized, or perhaps improvised, the fasces that were the insignia of the consulship and took them to the houses of Scipio and Hypsaeus. Neither man was willing to usurp the office. The group also marched to Pompey's villa on the outskirts of the city and shouted for him to become consul or even dictator.[15]

Suddenly Pompey was the man of the hour. It was the part he most enjoyed playing in politics.[16] Nothing stroked his vanity more—and his vanity was immense, in a sense as vast as the Roman empire itself. He had gotten his start back in 83 BC, when he raised troops on his father's estates, appointed himself general, and came to Sulla's aid in the civil war. Two years later, after defeating Sulla's opponents first in Sicily and then in Africa, he demanded—and received—a triumph, the great military parade through the heart of Rome. Sulla even felt he had to start calling Pompey "the Great," as Pompey's soldiers did. One success followed another, each more glittering than the last. Pompey defeated Sertorius in Spain, then Spartacus and the slaves in Italy. Again he rode into Rome in a triumphal chariot. In the 60s BC he fought great wars against the pirates across the Mediterranean and the eastern king Mithridates, the Republic's worst enemy. Pompey reorganized the whole East and upon his return to Rome celebrated a third triumph, at which he wore a cloak said to have belonged to Alexander the Great. He built a vast theater complex on the Field of Mars in Rome to commemorate his conquests. Opened in 55 BC with lavish performances, this was Rome's first stone theater. And it was a massive one, seating perhaps forty thousand. Behind the theater stretched the Portico of Pompey, filled with gardens, fountains, and precious works of art for Romans to admire as they strolled through. There was even a chamber for the Senate to meet in, also named after Pompey and adorned with a statue of the general.

Throughout the 50s BC Pompey remained the first man in Rome, but he had suffered setbacks. For a time he clashed with Clodius, though the two eventually reconciled. As Julius Caesar racked up impressive victories in Gaul, Pompey took a new command in Spain, but he never went there and instead governed through deputies. He craved more distinction than what he could gain by fighting Iberian cattle-rustlers. In 53 BC, as the months dragged on without consuls or praetors, friends suggested that he should assume a dictatorship, the emergency office that conferred supreme power on one man (last held by Sulla).[17] That hadn't happened in 53 BC, but perhaps now in 52 he had his chance.

Milo came back to the city as soon as he learned of the burning of the Senate house. He was hopeful that the rampage of the

Clodians through Rome would swing support to his side, so he resumed campaigning for the consulship.[18] The first interrex, Lepidus, faced mounting pressure to hold an election before Milo could recover his standing. Gangs of Scipio and Hypsaeus laid siege to Lepidus's house. Eventually they smashed into it, even knocking down the weaving that Lepidus's wife was supervising. Milo's gang came to the beleaguered mansion and drove the attackers away.[19] On January 22, four days after Clodius's death, Milo asked to visit Pompey at his villa, but Pompey sent a messenger with instructions not to come.[20] For the moment, it was not in Pompey's own interests to prop up the tottering city.

The next day, one of the two tribunes who had whipped the crowd into a frenzy at Clodius's funeral held a public meeting. This was Quintus Pompeius Rufus, not a close kinsman of Pompey, but a man willing to do his bidding. Rufus claimed in his speech to the people that Milo had planned Clodius's murder and was now plotting to kill Pompey too. "Milo," Rufus said to the citizens, "gave you someone to cremate in the Senate house; he will give you someone to bury on the Capitoline." It is a sign of Pompey's stature that he was deemed worthy of burial in Jupiter's sanctuary on the Capitoline Hill. Rufus told the crowd about Milo's attempt to visit Pompey the day before and Pompey's refusal to see him.[21]

Milo had to respond. Perhaps a few days later, another public meeting was hosted by a tribune friendly to him. This was none other than Caelius, who, over the next few months, was to prove, along with Cicero, Milo's greatest champion. Ever since going on trial in 56 BC, Caelius had been locked in a feud with Clodius and Clodius's family.[22] At the meeting, both Caelius and Milo himself told those gathered that Milo had not planned any attack on Clodius. Nobody would bring his wife along if he were planning to commit a murder, Milo said. It was Clodius who had set an ambush for Milo, and Milo had been forced to defend himself.[23] And so, competing narratives about Clodius's death were taking shape. For weeks to come, along with the stones of rival gangs, mutual accusations flew through the city.

According to the later account of one historian, Caelius's meeting ended in mayhem.[24] The other tribunes together with armed men burst into the Forum. Caelius and Milo were able to escape by disguising themselves as slaves, but those wearing fine clothing and gold rings were killed. The crowd, mostly slaves, then gave free rein to their anger and began to pillage. They broke into houses, looking for anything easy to steal. "For many days," the historian wrote, "Milo was their excuse for burning, stoning, and everything they did." This may be exaggerated. In our sources, we often seem to hear the sensationalized versions of one side or the other in the cacophony of politics. Cicero always claimed that Clodius's supporters had to have been slaves, not real citizens of Rome. That seems to be the viewpoint of the author of our account. Yet perhaps some of those slaves, monstrously abused their whole lives, did take the chance to revolt.

One interrex succeeded Lepidus, then another, but still no elections were held because of ongoing violence and mutual mistrust. Then, starting in February, came a seventeen-day stretch when, by long-standing practice, it was prohibited to hold any assembly meetings, including elections. It was probably with that prospect in view that the Senate, perhaps around February 1, once again took action: it passed its ultimate decree and entrusted the interrex, the tribunes, and Pompey "to see to it that the Republic suffer no harm."[25] Pompey at this time was technically governor of Spain, which gave him the authority to raise troops. And with great speed he did. Perhaps around February 14 he returned to the city. Because he held a governorship he was not allowed to enter the city limits, but he could still meet with the Senate in the chamber that was part of his theater complex. Feeling more confident, the Senate voted to rebuild the main Senate house in the Forum and entrusted the job to Sulla's son Faustus.[26]

Around February 18, the first day a consular election could be held, Milo's rival Scipio delivered a jaw-dropping speech in the Senate accusing Milo of murdering Clodius in cold blood.[27] Cicero must have grimaced as he heard it. Milo's claim of self-defense was a lie, Scipio proceeded to explain. Clodius had set out from Rome with twenty-six slaves to speak to the councilors of Aricia. Milo then left Rome, with more than three hundred slaves, to face him. Just beyond the small town of Bovillae on the Appian Way, Milo attacked Clodius unawares. Clodius, wounded in three places, was carried to an inn in Bovillae. Milo then stormed the inn. Clodius was dragged out and killed on the road itself. As he died, his gold signet ring was ripped off his finger. Milo went to the nearby villa of Clodius on Mount Alba after hearing that Clodius's young son was there. The boy had been whisked away, but Milo questioned the slave Halicorus under torture, cutting him up limb by limb. Milo also slit the throats of Clodius's estate manager and two more slaves. Scipio said that of Clodius's slaves, who had defended their master, eleven had been killed, while only two of Milo's had been wounded. The day after the murder, Milo had manumitted twelve of his own slaves and also begun handing out bribes in Rome to put to rest rumors about himself.

This speech was meant to wreck Milo's chances of winning the consulship. Pompey's troops appeared to be reestablishing order on the streets of Rome, but the contest for the top office was raging on. If an election were held, there was a chance Milo would win, which would confer on him immunity from prosecution. Yet without consular elections there could be no praetorian elections, and without praetors there could be no courts. This meant there would be no way to try Milo. And the tribunes loyal to Clodius's memory, looking to convert the dead man's supporters to their side, could not let Milo escape prosecution.[28]

At public meetings three tribunes in particular lashed out at Milo as a murderer. These were Plancus Bursa, Pompeius Rufus, and an ambitious new man from a country town of Italy named Sallust. Later to become one of Rome's most moralistic historians, Sallust was allegedly caught in bed with Fausta by Milo and promptly flogged.[29] At one meeting the three tribunes brought out Pompey himself and asked him whether Milo was plotting to kill him. Pompey proceeded to tell a sensational story about a certain Licinius, a man whose job was to help kill animals at religious sacrifices and who also seems to have run a tavern near the Circus Maximus, the city's horseracing track. Allegedly some slaves of Milo's had gotten drunk at Licinius's establishment and told him they were being paid by Milo to murder Pompey. Pompey said he could not shake his suspicions, even though Milo had denied the story. More and more, Pompey was staying at his villa, which he surrounded with troops.[30]

It had fallen to two young nephews of Clodius, brothers both named Appius, to press forward with the case against Milo. Clodius's own son was too young to do so himself. With the criminal courts shut, the Appii brought before Pompey the sort of civil suit used against a slaveowner whose slaves had done damage.[31] The brothers demanded that both Milo and Fausta turn over their slaves for interrogation, under torture of course. In retaliation, supporters of Milo then demanded Clodius's slaves and also slaves of

Milo's rival Hypsaeus and the Clodian tribune Pompeius Rufus. An impressive lineup of advocates spoke on Milo's behalf, including Cicero, Hortensius, Cato the Younger, and Faustus Sulla. Hortensius argued successfully that those whose interrogation was being demanded as slaves were in fact free men. Milo granted them freedom after the attack, citing the honorable grounds that they had avenged an attempt on his life. And so Milo's friends were reinforcing his story of Clodius's attempted ambush, which gave Milo a plea for self-defense, a valid reason to kill.

Calls were mounting for Pompey to be made dictator. The only other politician close to him in authority was Julius Caesar, but he had to rush off to Transalpine Gaul to suppress a major uprising that was inflamed by news of the chaos in Rome.[32] There was, however, a difficulty with naming a dictator: Sulla's example had tainted the institution. Also, Pompey's holding it wouldn't solve the underlying problem that Milo might still stand for the consulship and escape trial.

Then came a breakthrough. A Roman year normally had 355 days but periodically a so-called intercalary month of twenty-seven days was added after February, to bring the state calendar into alignment with the astronomical one. In 52 BC an intercalary month began after February. Around the twenty-second day of this month, a proposal was made in the Senate for Pompey to become sole consul for no less than two months, after which time he could hold an election for a colleague as he saw fit.[33] To have only one consul in charge was a breach with the republican tradition of sharing executive power. But it would allow Pompey to hold praetorian elections and reopen the courts, while also ensuring that Milo would have to answer the charges against him before he could hold a consulship. Even Cato the Younger, the most stalwart champion of republican tradition, who had often criticized Pompey before, supported the motion.

And so, on the twenty-fourth day of the intercalary month, Pompey was elected consul for the third time. Two days later, he formally consulted with the Senate about two new laws that he wished to pass, one concerning public violence and the other bribery. After a couple of days of debate, he proposed the laws to the assembly for the customary review period before voting.[34]

Both laws added to, rather than replaced, existing criminal legislation.[35] They set up new courts that could be used to try defendants expeditiously. In a break with established practice, witnesses were to be heard first, over three days. Then, on the final day of the trial, the prosecution would be allowed to speak for two hours, the defense for three. Advocates were forbidden to call on witnesses to give character testimonials irrelevant to the facts of the case. Juries were to be empaneled in an entirely new fashion, to prevent tampering. Pompey would create a new list of 360 jurors. All, it seems, were to hear the evidence, but on the final day of the trial, before the speeches, a random drawing would be held to select a pool of eighty-one. After the speeches, both the prosecution and the defense were allowed to reject fifteen jurors each, leaving a final panel of fifty-one to cast their votes.

The proposal for the new law against public violence worried Milo's supporters. The facts of the case did not favor him, and with the new trial procedure the prosecution would be able to expose them more starkly. Hortensius made a motion in the Senate that the major acts of recent violence should be tried in the regular violence court but given priority over all other cases on the docket.[36] The proposal was voted down.

As the review period for the laws proceeded, Pompey did everything he could to tip the scales against Milo. Caelius complained at public meetings that the new legislation unfairly targeted Milo and that trials were being rushed. As Caelius's attacks grew more fierce, Pompey warned that he would defend the Republic by arms if necessary.[37] Caelius had to shut up. Pompey continued to parade his fear that Milo would ambush him. The general spent much of his time in his villa, surrounded by soldiers. He even dismissed the Senate on one occasion, citing his fear of Milo's arrival. At the next meeting, one senator alleged that Milo had a weapon strapped to his thigh under his tunic and demanded that he bare his leg. Without hesitation Milo lifted his tunic high, practically exposing his whole body: no weapon. Cicero with his usual quickness cried out that the charges leveled against Milo were as false as this one.[38]

The tribunes hostile to Milo held inflammatory public meetings of their own. At one meeting, Tribune Plancus Bursa brought forward a freedman who claimed that he, along with four other men, had been traveling down the Appian Way and saw Clodius being killed. When they raised an outcry, they were kidnapped and kept captive for two months at a villa of Milo's.[39] The tribunes also tried to stir up ill will against Cicero by claiming that the Senate was decreeing not what it truly felt but what Cicero dictated, just as it did during his consulship. One tribune went as far as to say that while Milo's hand killed Clodius, it was Cicero's mind that had plotted the crime. Another said that he planned to prosecute Cicero at a later date.[40] Clearly, as Milo's trial loomed, politicians reverted to seeing criminal trials as a way to score victories over each other. Doubtless this was better than throwing stones or drawing daggers, but it was not a good basis for lasting stability.

Pompey's laws were passed toward the end of March. He proceeded to put forward his list of 360 jurors. A president was chosen for the new violence court by means of a special election. He was Domitius Ahenobarbus, a former consul from a highly distinguished family, well-known for his courage, every ounce of which he would need to keep order in his court. Milo was then formally indicted by the two young Appii Claudii who had earlier demanded his slaves for interrogation. Charges were filed against Milo in other courts as well, but the violence trial would take place first, beginning on April 4.[41]

On that day, the elder of the two Appii made a motion that Milo hand over fifty-four slaves for interrogation. Milo responded that these slaves were not in his possession. Domitius consulted with the jurors and ruled against the prosecution's request. Of course, Domitius said, the prosecution could rely on the evidence supplied by Clodius's own slaves.[42] From Cicero's published speech defending Milo, we learn that the torture of these slaves took place in the Hall of Liberty, which the censors used as their headquarters. It seems grotesque to us. We aren't told by Cicero what the slaves said, only that it was what the prosecutors wanted said.[43] Any Roman lawyer would trot out the well-worn, and not unreasonable, argument that slave testimony could be coerced. It is clear to us that the courts of Cicero's day created a barrier to discovering the truth by the way they dealt with witnesses who were, or had been, enslaved.

We face challenges when reconstructing the rest of the trial. While Cicero's published speech for Milo does survive, it reveals less about the prosecution's case than is usual. What's more, Cicero's published speech isn't the one he gave. Stenographers took down what he said and that was available for consultation by scholars long after he died. But we are told that the speech we read today had been revised by Cicero for publication.[44] From an extensive commentary on the published speech by the scholar Asconius, we learn that, in his spoken version, Cicero hewed to the line that Clodius had tried to ambush Milo and that Milo acted in self-defense.[45] In the published version Cicero drops that argument about two-thirds of the way through and starts proclaiming how much Clodius's murder served the public interest, which he believed justified killing Clodius. Perhaps the first two-thirds corresponds to what Cicero said at the trial, but this is not entirely certain.[46] We are fortunate to have Asconius, who did extensive research into the whole case and consulted records unavailable to us. Through his notes, as well as a few scraps of information preserved elsewhere, we have a general sense of how each side made its case.

According to Asconius, the prosecution held that Milo had set an ambush for Clodius. This is confirmed by an anecdote from the rhetorician Quintilian.[47] According to him, one of the prosecutors claimed that Milo had stopped at the town of Bovillae around 2:30, the afternoon of the killing, to wait for Clodius to leave his nearby villa. Clodius had gotten news that the ailing architect Cyrus had died and decided to return to Rome that day. Milo had learned this by bribing a slave of Clodius. As we shall see, the question of timing was important for the defense too. According to Quintilian, as the prosecutor called out to Milo repeatedly, demanding to know when Clodius was killed, Cicero made one of his jokes, yelling out, "Too late!"

From Asconius we learn about the witnesses the prosecution called over the three days leading up to final speeches, April 5–7.[48] As in other trials, the witnesses seem to have been selected not just for the evidence they could provide but also for their emotional impact. On the first day, Clodius's old friend Causinius Schola, who had provided Clodius's alibi in the Good Goddess trial, took the stand. He said he had been traveling with Clodius the day of the murder and was there when the killing happened. According to Asconius, Schola exaggerated the horror of the deed as much as he could. He would have talked about how Clodius was wounded in the initial encounter, carried off to the inn, and dragged out and killed on the road—the road that Clodius's ancestor, the great Appius Claudius the Blind, had built for the use of the Roman people. One of Milo's lawyers, Claudius Marcellus, a member of the distinguished family and a well-trained speaker, stood up from the defense bench to cross-examine the witness. But the Clodian mob, which ringed the court, shouted so menacingly that Marcellus sought refuge on Domitius's tribunal. Marcellus and Milo himself begged Domitius for an armed guard. Pompey, who was at the nearby Temple of Saturn and could hear the angry chants, promised to bring troops to the court the next day.

He did, and over the following two days the subsequent testimony went more smoothly. Many of the inhabitants of Bovillae testified to what happened there—the inn taken by storm, Clodius's body dragged into the open. Witnesses said that the innkeeper himself had been killed. Priestesses from a shrine near the inn alleged that an unknown woman had come to them, at Milo's request, to seek expiation for the killing of Clodius. The last to give evidence were Clodius's wife, Fulvia, and her mother, Sempronia. Probably they were asked about Clodius's movements on the last days of his life. But their copious tears were the real contribution to the prosecution's case, overwhelming the crowd with feelings of loss and rage. At a public meeting shortly afterward, Tribune Plancus Bursa told those assembled to turn up in force the next day and not allow Milo to escape. It is unknown who testified on Milo's behalf and when. It is also unknown whether the freedman who claimed to have been kidnapped by Milo for two months testified.

The morning after Fulvia's testimony, shops were closed throughout the city. Pompey posted armed guards around the Forum and on the streets leading into it. He himself sat on his consular seat in front of one of the temples, near the court, surrounded by troops. According to the biographer Plutarch, Cicero arrived by litter and waited nervously in it for the jurors to arrive. Milo, on the other hand, showed his usual bravado, refusing to change into grungy clothes and appearing freshly shaved.[49]

After the eighty-one jurors were chosen by lot, the crowds fell silent as the prosecution began. The elder Appius spoke first. He was followed by a friend of Clodius, a vigorous thirty-year-old who was later to become a leading man in politics, Mark Antony. Antony had an impressive physique and a beard that gave him a resemblance to Hercules, from whom he claimed descent. He was a theatrical orator, in the tradition of his grandfather, Cicero's mentor Antonius. Last to speak against Milo was Valerius Nepos, about whom little is known. The three prosecutors spent their two hours telling their story of Milo's premeditated attack.[50]

Then rose Cicero, who alone was to make the case for the defense. Again according to Plutarch, the lawyer was so anxious that at first he could barely speak. Cicero was used to playing off the crowd, but there was no chance of doing that today. Pompey's armed soldiers and embittered supporters of Clodius were not going to be amused. Even Asconius, a great admirer of Cicero, wrote that he "spoke without his usual determination," although in Asconius's telling it was not nerves but the shouting of the Clodians that impeded the advocate.[51]

For months, Milo had been pleading that his slaves had killed Clodius in defense of their master against an ambush, and this forced Cicero to make a case along these lines.[52] To go by the early portions of his published speech, as we will now do, he told the jurors in his opening that he would make it as clear as day that Clodius set a trap for Milo. Milo had defended himself, Cicero argued in a preliminary discussion, and everyone is entitled to the right of self-defense.[53]

Cicero then gave the jurors his narrative of events.[54] Clodius was running for the praetorship, but he knew he would be powerless if Milo were consul at the same time. Therefore he began to declare publicly that Milo had to be killed. Shortly before his own death, Clodius had been heard to say that Milo would be dead within three or four days. Knowing that Milo would be traveling to Lanuvium for the installation of the priest, Clodius set out the day before to set a trap by his own villa at Mount Alba. The next day, Milo went to the Senate and then set out with Fausta, riding in a carriage, accompanied by an unwieldy entourage of slaves. He was met by Clodius, who was traveling light, on horseback, with no coach or baggage. Milo came across Clodius "around 4:00 p.m. or not far off it." Armed men launched an attack on Milo. His coachman was killed. Milo threw off his hooded cloak, jumped down, and defended himself bravely. Some of his slaves were killed, others heard that Milo himself had been killed, and, without his knowledge, they "did what any man would have wished his slaves to do under such circumstances."

Cicero's strategy here was to mention only those facts that backed up his case.[55] What he said about the encounter between Milo and Clodius itself was probably more or less true. Milo's group ran into Clodius's group, fighting ensued, and Milo's slaves wounded Clodius. The one obvious discrepancy on details was the time that Milo and Clodius encountered each other. Cicero tried to place the clash about an hour and a half later, which would weaken the prosecution's claim that Clodius had decided to return to Rome the afternoon of the murder. It was too late in the day to set out, which means Clodius was really lying in wait at his villa. But note that even Cicero said "around 4:00 p.m. *or not far off it.*"[56]

The other main stratagem in Cicero's narrative was to suppress unfavorable facts.[57] Cicero said nothing about Clodius's being taken to the inn nor Milo's attack on the inn. These points were unanswerable, vouched for by witnesses who had made the awful truth clear: after Clodius had been wounded, he was finished off on Milo's orders by Milo's slaves. In omitting any discussion of this, Cicero was following advice laid out in his book *On the Ideal Orator,* written a few years earlier: sometimes the best response to a difficult point was no response; retreat to your own stronghold rather than flail about in the enemy camp.

After setting out his narrative, Cicero proceeded through a series of arguments to prove that Clodius set a trap for Milo, rather than the other way around. Cicero introduced Cassius's famous test: *Cui bono?* Clodius had everything to lose with Milo as consul. Milo gained nothing from having Clodius dead. Milo was sure to win the consulship before Clodius's death, but with Clodius gone Milo's campaign faltered. Arguments from character came next, then opportunity. Clodius attacked good men all the time, whereas Milo's violence was only aimed to stop Clodius's violence. Clodius knew well in advance that Milo would be on the road on January 18, whereas Milo had no way of knowing Clodius would be. On and on the arguments went, audacious if nothing else. Why, Cicero asked, if Clodius was so well prepared, did he not prevail? Well, he was a woman fighting against men.[58]

As Asconius realized, the whole trial was suffused with paradox. If you believed the prosecution, Milo had set an ambush. If you believed the defense, Clodius had set an ambush. Yet almost certainly, neither had done so. The two men ran into each other by pure accident. Sifting through all the evidence available to him, this was the conclusion Asconius reached.[59] As Asconius explained, Milo set out with his carriage for Lanuvium. Clodius, returning from his speech at Aricia on horseback, encountered him near Bovillae, around 2:30 p.m. Among Milo's entourage of slaves were two gladiators, Eudamus and Birria. They were at the back of his column when they got into an altercation with some of Clodius's slaves. Clodius turned back and looked menacingly. Birria pierced Clodius's shoulder with a long spear. A battle broke out, and Clodius was carried off to the nearby inn at Bovillae.

It was a mishap, or at least that's how it began. The death of Clodius, the burning of the Senate house, Pompey's sole consulship, all the armed soldiers in the Forum: none of it would have happened if the two enemies hadn't run into each other. According to Asconius, after Milo learned of Clodius's wounds he took the view that Clodius's survival posed a danger to himself, while Clodius's death would be a relief. And so he ordered Clodius dragged out of the tavern. Chillingly, four years earlier Cicero himself had envisioned that something like this might happen. To Atticus, he had written that Clodius would be brought to trial by Milo, unless Milo killed him first: "If Clodius gets in Milo's way in a riot, I expect that Milo will kill him with his own hands. He has no qualms about doing so and boasts about it."[60] It was not meticulous planning but a chance encounter that gave Milo the opportunity to carry out his crime. Milo was not so much a master criminal as a thug.

But why then did his prosecutors feel the need to claim that Milo had set a trap? The answer is likely that many of Clodius's friends had been saying so for months. If the point were conceded now, it would crack open a door that Cicero could throw wide open. The inflammatory meetings of the last few months had set the terms for the trial, for both sides.[61]

After Cicero finished his speech, the prosecutors and the

defendant each rejected their fifteen jurors, leaving fifty-one to cast their ballots. Milo was convicted by a vote of thirty-eight to thirteen. "The jurors," Asconius wrote, "seem to have been quite aware that Clodius had been wounded initially without Milo's knowledge, but they found that after Clodius had been wounded, he was killed on Milo's orders."[62] Not even Cicero could spin these facts favorably.

The day after Milo's conviction for public violence, he began to be tried for his other offenses, starting with electoral bribery. In absentia, he was convicted on all counts. He set out for exile in Marseilles, where he could dine with Verres and perhaps admire the legendary art collection. Milo's estate was confiscated and auctioned off. Cicero tried to arrange for Milo to keep the many slaves he had taken with him and also honor some financial commitments to Fausta, who did not join her husband. But Milo's creditors had to be paid off first, which left little to nothing.[63]

Milo's trial was not the end of special prosecutions in Pompey's new violence court. The next to be accused was Saufeius, the commander of Milo's slaves, who had taken the lead in storming the inn at Bovillae. Cicero and Caelius together defended him and won his acquittal by a single vote. Asconius commented, "Clearly hatred for Clodius was Saufeius's salvation, since his case was even weaker than Milo's; he had openly led the assault on the inn."[64] Saufeius was then prosecuted a second time, in the regular violence court. Cicero again defended him, in cooperation with a younger protégé, and Saufeius was acquitted by a larger margin.[65] Taken together with Milo's verdict, these verdicts suggest that justice was being applied inconsistently. It was impossible to keep politics and public opinion entirely out of trials, but the lopsided results were not lending much support to the strict and impartial rule of law.

Scipio and Hypsaeus, Milo's rivals for the consulship of 52 BC, both faced charges in Pompey's new court for electoral bribery. Fortunately for Scipio, his attractive daughter had recently been widowed and Pompey married her soon after being named sole consul. To save his new father-in-law, Pompey saw to it that Scipio was elected as consul, which brought immunity from prosecution.[66] The far less distinguished Hypsaeus did not fare so well. Hypsaeus lay in wait one afternoon as Pompey was returning home from the baths to supper. When Pompey appeared, Hypsaeus fell to the ground and begged for help. Pompey passed by Hypsaeus abruptly, informing him that he was achieving nothing except delaying Pompey's supper. Hypsaeus was found guilty. Pompey's favoritism did not enhance his reputation for justice. One later historian commented that "the charms of the marriage bed made him violate the stability of the Republic."[67] Another even more neatly complained that Pompey was "both the author of his own laws and their subverter."[68]

When the tribunes of 52 BC left office in December, they were open to prosecution in the new violence court. The private citizen Cloelius had already been convicted for his role in burning the Senate house by an almost unanimous vote. Now Pompeius Rufus was indicted by the talented prosecutor Caelius and found guilty.[69] Then Cicero himself prosecuted Plancus Bursa. Other than the trial of Verres, this is Cicero's only known prosecution. He took great delight in it. In a letter to a friend, he wrote that he hated Bursa even more than Clodius. Cicero had once represented Bursa in a trial (charge unknown), yet the man showed no gratitude. Also, Clodius at least had political motivations for what he did, "while this little ape chose me to attack for his own pleasure."[70]

At the trial, Pompey tried to practice more of his selective justice. He sent a written testimonial on behalf of Bursa, in violation of his own law banning character witnesses. When the tablet was produced in the court, Cato, sitting as a juror, ostentatiously plugged his ears and then prevented the testimonial from being read.[71] Bursa was convicted unanimously. Cicero, whose speech does not survive, gloated afterward in a letter to his friend: "I took more pleasure in this verdict than in the death of my enemy. I prefer a court to the sword." Of course, as he could freely admit, Cicero was also delighted at how well he had done: the jurors had sided with him, against Pompey. "No citizens were ever so brave as the jurors who dared to find [Bursa] guilty despite the immense power of the man who had empaneled them. They never would have done that unless my grievance was theirs too."[72]

It was perhaps now that Cicero took the chance to debut his new and improved defense of Milo.[73] In the last part of the published speech, which unmistakably hints at Milo's sentence of exile, Milo is imagined as almost basking in pride over the murder of Clodius: "Citizens, please come and listen to me! I have killed Publius Clodius. With this sword and this right hand, I have saved your necks from a man whose madness we were unable to rein in by any laws or courts."[74] Of course the jurors should acquit their savior, Cicero wrote. Indeed, they should honor him. In Greece, those who killed tyrants were elevated to the status of heroes. Hymns were sung in their honor. The true hero is someone who faces death, punishment, or unpopularity, and may not receive any praise—yet still acts to defend his country. As Milo did, and as Cicero did in his consulship when he executed the conspirators.

Cicero argued that Clodius's murder was not a crime that sprang from human planning, but rather showed that the immortal gods cared for Rome. In the end, they would punish those who opposed both the city and the gods themselves. Near the end of his speech,

Cicero added an amazing twist to his narrative of events. It was in front of the estate of a young man named Titus Sertius Gallus where Clodius sustained his first wound, and on that estate was a shrine of the Good Goddess. And so, Cicero said, it was shown that Clodius had not been acquitted by "that wicked verdict" in the sacrilege trial so many years before; rather, he was spared for "this signal punishment."[75]

Cicero argued in his published speech that there was a higher law than human statutes. Clodius's murder was justified because it was in the public interest. It was the will of the gods. But this undermined the purer argument of self-defense Cicero had put forward at the trial, which paid more respect to the laws of Rome. According to a later historian, Cicero sent a copy of his revised speech to Milo, who ironically responded that it was good Cicero had not spoken it or he would not now be enjoying the seafood of Marseilles.[76] The final version of the speech reflected Cicero and Milo's shared belief that sometimes it was necessary to act outside the law. A young friend of Cicero went even further and, in a pamphlet written in the form of a speech on Milo's behalf, dropped the self-defense line entirely and boasted about the killing of a bad citizen. That young friend was Marcus Brutus, the future assassin of Julius Caesar.[77]

With Clodius dead and Milo in exile, order had been restored in Rome. Pompey had ended the anarchy and went on to pass an important law that required ex-praetors and ex-consuls to wait five years before holding an overseas governorship.[78] This was intended to break the nexus between electoral bribery and provincial extortion that was so destabilizing to the Republic. But Pompey's reformed legal system couldn't resolve all of Rome's problems. Pompey and others kept playing politics with criminal trials. He failed to heed his own legislation by holding on to his Spanish governorship, which gave him ongoing access to military power, just as Julius Caesar had his army in Gaul.

In their pursuit of their own ambitions, Roman politicians were increasingly ignoring customary and legal restraints on power such as limited commands, regular elections, and a prohibition on reaching for weapons when passions flared. Cicero himself, especially in the published version of his defense of Milo, showed a willingness to disregard laws when he thought them unjust or inconvenient. Perhaps there are times when one needs to obey a higher law than the laws of men. But as the escalating rancor and violence in Rome shows, there is a grave danger to civil society when that attitude becomes common. Cicero had helped to bring on forces that would ultimately kill him and destroy the Republic.

# CHAPTER 12

# Vengeance

Though he couldn't have known it at the time, Cicero's prosecution of Plancus Bursa would be his last major case in the criminal courts. Questions of justice in Rome increasingly were going to be decided by other means.

Against his wishes, Cicero was sent out in 51 BC by the Senate to govern the province of Cilicia, in southern Asia Minor. No sooner was he back in Italy the following year than a months-long dispute between the former allies Julius Caesar and Pompey flared into civil war. All the horrors of Cicero's early adulthood returned. Armies of Roman citizens met on battlefields and killed each other in the thousands. Political enemies lopped off each other's heads. Houses, villas, and art collections were plundered. In the ongoing struggles, Cicero more than once backed the losing side. Many of his friends were killed, sometimes in scenes as chilling as those of tragedies staged in the theater. Cicero's family, once a refuge for him during his troubles, fell apart, as did so much else during the civil war.

As violence spread, so did a desire for revenge. For the Romans, it was honorable to seek revenge if another citizen attacked you, your family, the gods, or the country. But you were meant to do so in the courts, where penalties were fixed by law. Cicero, of course, had long argued that some men posed such a threat to the Republic that it was acceptable, even glorious, to kill them without a trial. That was a doctrine open to abuse, as Romans learned. Still, most would have agreed that if a tyrant took over, there could never be a judicial proceeding. You would have to take the law into your own hands.

On March 15, 44 BC, a group of senators killed Julius Caesar at a meeting of the Senate on the grounds that he had become a tyrant. Cicero had no part in planning the conspiracy but was close with its leaders, especially Marcus Brutus. In the fractious debate that followed the murder, he became the assassins' strongest defender. Cicero argued that Caesar was a tyrant who deserved to be killed for stealing Romans' freedom. Cicero wanted other enemies of the Republic slain too. Friends of Caesar, on the other hand, thought his killing a heinous crime that demanded the ultimate penalty. Both sides cried out for justice and, like Furies from the underworld, would not rest until they had vengeance in blood.[1]

Cicero had no interest in becoming a provincial governor. Before he left Italy, he called the assignment a "gigantic bore." Day after day he would be required to preside over dull administrative hearings and listen to the provincials pour out their complaints. Worse than that, he might be compelled to fight a war. A couple of years earlier, the rapacious Marcus Crassus had invaded the kingdom of Parthia,

Rome's major rival to the east, and been disastrously defeated in battle. In 51 BC there was a chance that the Parthians would wreak further revenge by overrunning Roman territory. Jupiter help the Romans if they had to rely on Cicero as a general. Wisely, he brought along on his staff his younger brother Quintus, who had served under Julius Caesar in Gaul. Cicero's son Marcus was a teenager now, as was Quintus's son, and they came too, for some military experience. The ever-opportunistic Caelius wrote from Rome to Cicero that it would help Cicero's political fortunes if he could manage a military victory while avoiding a serious clash.[2]

Before leaving Rome, Cicero made Caelius promise to send him political news and gossip so that he would not feel cut off from the city. A number of Caelius's letters survive and are among the most entertaining in the whole Ciceronian correspondence, as lighthearted as Caelius himself must have been in person. They blithely report on the marriages, divorces, and adulteries of the political class; major court cases and heated debates in the Senate; and the growing tension between Pompey and Julius Caesar. Even if Cicero captured the king of Parthia, Caelius wrote once, it wouldn't be so good a spectacle as what was going on in Rome. Caelius passed on all the latest rumors, even a report that Cicero himself had been murdered on the road by one of the tribunes he had clashed with during the Milo case.[3]

Caelius also sent requests. He was elected aedile for the year 50 BC and pressed Cicero to impose a tax on Cilicia to help cover the costs of the games he had to put on. He also begged for some panthers to be captured and sent back to Rome for a staged beast hunt, an increasingly popular form of entertainment. There was always pressure on provincial governors to do favors for friends back in the capital. Fortunately for the people of Cilicia, Cicero felt he would enhance his reputation by sparing them as much as possible. He refused to impose the tax. And as for the panthers, he fobbed Caelius off with a joke: "A good effort is being made by the usual hunters on my orders. But there is a strange shortage of animals and the ones that are here are said to be complaining loudly because the only traps in my province are for them."[4]

Cicero was also asked for favors by the assertive young noble who would become so important to him, Marcus Brutus. Like Cicero, Brutus had an intellectual bent. He studied philosophy as a young man in Athens and would go on to write philosophical works himself. In public speaking he showed talent, though his style was less impassioned than Cicero's. Brutus preferred logic over emotion. And while his seriousness might not always have won over crowds, it impressed senators eager to preserve senatorial power. They saw in Brutus their future leader. What he lacked in charm he made up for with his family tree. On his father's side, he could boast descent from Lucius Junius Brutus, first consul of the Republic, who had driven out the last of Rome's kings around 500 BC. Among his maternal ancestors was Servilius Ahala, reputed to have stabbed to death a politician who was trying to restore kingship generations after it had been abolished.

Before Cicero left Italy, Brutus gave him a memorandum with items of business to take care of in Cilicia. One task was to put pressure on the king of neighboring Cappadocia to pay the money he owed Brutus. Another was to help two associates of Brutus collect on a loan they had made to one of the towns in Cicero's province. Cicero was shocked to learn when he met with the town leaders that the interest rate on the loan was 48 percent, four times the legal limit. It turned out that one of Brutus's associates possessed a decree in the Senate, passed with Brutus's help, granting an exemption for this loan. Cicero, however, was willing only to calculate interest at the rate of 12 percent. Brutus's associate stomped off, then reappeared and thrust into Cicero's hands a letter from Brutus revealing that the real lender was Brutus himself. And now Brutus was asking that Cicero give a staff position to the associate. The associate had enjoyed this rank under Cicero's predecessor and, with the troops under his command, had locked up local leaders of the indebted town's Senate house. Five senators had starved to death. Cicero refused to give the associate a new appointment.[5]

Cicero would never have learned any of this if he hadn't been sent to Cilicia. Exploitation of the provinces was like the Hydra of Greek myth: cut off one head of the monster and a new one grew back. Pass a tougher law and a work-around was found. Cicero found Brutus's behavior offensive and complained more than once to Atticus, a long-standing friend of Brutus: "Brutus, even when he is asking for something, is apt to write me in a stubborn, arrogant, and tactless way."[6] Like so many other Roman nobles, Brutus had a strong sense of entitlement.

Cicero was relieved to return to Rome. He never did have to fight the Parthians. His army had even enjoyed some minor victories over peoples living in the mountains separating Cilicia from Syria. These successes might be enough to get a triumph voted to Cicero, and Caelius threw himself into the task of canvassing senators. Cicero thrilled at the possibility but still wished he'd never set foot in Cilicia. He wrote, near the end of his term, to Caelius, "The city! Stick to the city, my good friend, and live in its light! Residence abroad for any reason . . . is a dim and shabby existence for those whose hard work can shine in Rome."[7]

But the Rome he came back to in January 49 BC was plunged in crisis.

Already in August 50 BC, Caelius had sent a letter warning Cicero that civil war was likely to break out.[8] Julius Caesar's long war in Gaul had finally come to an end, but he refused to surrender his army until he was elected consul for a second time. Old enemies of Caesar like Cato the Younger were determined to stop him, whatever it took, and they had brought Pompey over to their view. The quarrel was dangerous because both sides controlled major military forces. Caesar had the army he had built up in Gaul, ten legions strong—fifty thousand men, if the legions were at full strength. Pompey had seven legions in Spain, two more in Italy, and, because of his long involvement with the grain supply, a navy.

In his August letter, Caelius wrote that he wrestled with what to do. He sympathized with Pompey's position in the dispute but had friends on Caesar's side. And Caesar undoubtedly had a better army, buoyed by years of victories in Gaul. Caelius mused that when a struggle is political, and not by force of arms, a man should take the more honorable side; "but when it comes to war and armies, he should follow the stronger side, and regard as the better cause the safer course."[9]

Cicero faced a tough choice too. Like Caelius, he sympathized with those outraged by Caesar's demands. He felt intense loyalty to Pompey, who had helped him to be recalled from exile. But for some years now Cicero had been friendly with Caesar. Quintus had joined Caesar's staff in Gaul and grown wealthy from his service. Caesar lent money to Cicero, sent him many complimentary letters, and had even written a work on the Latin language and dedicated it to him. Cicero didn't want to have to choose sides, and as soon as he was back in Rome he tried to avert war.[10]

It was in vain. When Pompey learned that Caesar had crossed into northern Italy with armed forces, he insisted that all senators must leave Rome for southern Italy. Two months later he evacuated Italy altogether. With the consuls he sailed across the Adriatic Sea to Macedonia, where he could train an army good enough to take on Caesar. Meanwhile Caesar was busy defeating Pompey's forces in Spain.

Cicero left Rome with Pompey but then for months vacillated over what to do. He didn't want to have to go overseas again, he didn't want to have to fight a war, and Caesar gave him the option of remaining in Italy as a noncombatant. Cicero's daughter Tullia had recently married one of Caesar's officers, a charming though unscrupulous friend of Caelius's named Dolabella. But loyalty to Pompey, and a feeling that Pompey and his allies were more in the right, gnawed at Cicero's conscience. He leaned toward joining them. Caelius, who had joined Caesar, warned Cicero in a letter: "Think, Cicero, think, before you completely destroy yourself and your family and knowingly plunge into a situation from which you see there is no way out."[11] Finally, in May, Cicero made his decision and sailed to Macedonia. Quintus went with him, and they brought their boys. Terentia and Tullia would stay behind to try to manage the family properties.

Cicero made himself an unwelcome presence in Pompey's camp from the start. He criticized Pompey for his earlier mistakes, disapproved of the plans being made, and joked about all the foreign contingents Pompey was relying on. Even in war, Cicero couldn't refrain from wisecracking. After one defeat, an officer pointed out that they should remain hopeful since they still had seven eagles—each Roman legion had a silver eagle as its standard—to which Cicero said, "That would be great, if we were fighting jackdaws."[12]

Cicero usually smiled when he told jokes, but he wasn't smiling now. Not only did he hate military life, but he was getting bad news from Italy. Tullia's husband Dolabella was treating her poorly and she had no money to live on. Then there was what happened to Caelius, who was made one of the praetors for the year 48 BC in exchange for supporting Caesar.[13] The city of Rome seethed with unrest. Civil war had caused food shortages and a collapse of the credit system. Sensing an opportunity, Caelius tried to block the praetor in charge of enforcing loans and proposed legislation that would cancel debts and remit rent payments. Soon Caelius had an armed gang behind him that fought with soldiers of the consul. The consul dragged Caelius off the Rostra in the middle of a public meeting. Caelius then said in a huff that he was leaving to see Caesar, but in fact he had a secret plan: to link up with Milo.

Caesar had invited back to Italy many of those exiled by Pompey's special courts in 52 BC, but not Milo. Milo decided he would return anyway. He still had some of his gladiators. Details are hazy, but it seems that he and Caelius planned to raise additional forces from both the gladiators who trained at schools in southern Italy and from herdsmen in the mountains, just as Spartacus had done. Whatever the old friends had in mind, they failed. Milo died after being hit by a stone that was thrown from the wall of a city he was attacking. Caelius was killed by cavalry under Caesar's command. Violence had finally caught up with both of them.

Cicero played no part in the major showdown between Pompey and Caesar that took place in Pharsalus, Greece, in the summer of 48 BC. He waited things out hundreds of miles away, on the eastern coast of the Adriatic Sea, along with Cato, who was also sour on war. Pharsalus turned out to be a shattering defeat for Pompey. Most of his foreign contingents quickly deserted him afterward. Many of his high-ranking Roman allies took up Caesar's offer of forgiveness, among them Marcus Brutus. After word came of Pompey's defeat Cato asked Cicero to take command, but he refused. Then, through a letter from his son-in-law Dolabella, he received permission from

Caesar to sail back to Italy. He would do so, along with his son Marcus junior, who, though only seventeen years old, had commanded some cavalry at Pharsalus.[14]

In early November 48 BC Cicero arrived in the Italian port city of Brundisium, where he would wait for Caesar's return so that he could make amends in person. A couple weeks after arriving he received some terrible news.[15] After Pharsalus, Pompey had fled to Egypt. He hoped to raise funds from the young adolescent king, Ptolemy XIII, son of Ptolemy the Flute Player, who had died a couple of years earlier. The king's advisers pointed out that accepting Pompey was risky, but so was sending him away. The best course was to put him to death. "A dead man does not bite," the king's rhetoric teacher snappily pointed out. A small rowboat was sent to Pompey's warship off the coast of Egypt to bring him ashore. He got onto the boat. Pompey's wife remained on the warship as the boat was rowed back toward the shore. A soldier then ran him through with a sword from behind. His head was then cut off, to be later presented along with his signet ring as a gift for Caesar. The rest of his body was thrown into the sea. Pompey's wife fled.[16]

In a book about divination Cicero wrote several years later, he asked whether anyone should ever want to know the future. "Do you think that Gnaeus Pompey would have found joy in his three consulships, in his three triumphs, and in the fame of his distinguished deeds, if he had known that he would lose his army and then be savagely killed in an uninhabited spot by the villainy of the Egyptians and that after his death would come those events of which I cannot speak without tears?"[17]

Cicero would end up spending a year in Brundisium waiting for Caesar, who got ensnared in a civil war in Egypt between the young king and the king's older sister, Cleopatra. For Cicero, aside from the sixteen months of exile, this was the most wretched period of his life so far. Everything seemed to go wrong for him personally. Quintus and Quintus's son had stayed behind in Greece to make their peace with Caesar. Cicero learned that both father and son were denouncing Cicero, apparently to ingratiate themselves with the victor. "It is the most unbelievable thing that has ever happened to me," Cicero moaned to Atticus in December 48 BC.[18]

Another woe was Tullia. In late 48 BC she was suffering from poor health and continued to have money problems. And her husband, Dolabella, was sleeping around with other women, Cicero reported to Atticus.[19] Cicero wanted Tullia to divorce, but that might have jeopardized his reconciliation with Caesar. Meanwhile, Cicero's own marriage was also breaking down. He and Terentia had gotten through hard times before, but something was different now. His short letters to her lacked the warmth of earlier ones.[20] Perhaps she resented his less than resolute conduct over the last few years. Why, she might have asked, had Cicero even bothered to leave Italy in 49 BC? Certainly the couple was at odds over money. Cicero felt she was keeping funds from him, and perhaps she was.[21] He had left her with the hard job of handling the family finances during a civil war.

When Caesar made it back to Italy in September 47 BC, he met with Cicero and treated him courteously. Cicero was free to return to Rome. He sent a brusque note to Terentia while on the road, asking her to ready the villa at Tusculum, where he planned to stay awhile.[22]

Finally his spirits started to lift. He took cheer from Brutus's *On Virtue*, a short work of philosophy Brutus had written in the form of a letter to Cicero. In it, Brutus described how he had recently met up with Marcus Marcellus, one of Rome's great nobles, who had helped lead the fight against Caesar. After the Battle of Pharsalus,

Marcellus had refused to ask Caesar's forgiveness and retired to a Greek island where he had taken up the study of philosophy. That, Brutus believed, should be an inspiration for Cicero to renew his pursuit of learning too.[23]

Cicero also found excitement in an impressive work of scholarship Atticus had just completed and dedicated to him. This was a chronology of the whole of Roman history, including important magistrates, laws, and treaties, all contained within just one papyrus scroll. After reading it, Cicero met with Atticus at Tusculum and proposed writing his own history of oratory at Rome.[24] Atticus was enthusiastic. At a time when the courts were shut, a work like this would allow Cicero to look back nostalgically. He could recount his own early triumphs and pay tribute to his former rival Hortensius, who had died just before the outbreak of the civil war.

Cicero wrote his history in the form of a dialogue in which he, Atticus, and Brutus took turns speaking in a conversation set in the garden of Cicero's Palatine mansion. The work was called *Brutus* as a compliment to Cicero's younger friend. Together, the three friends recall the great and not so great orators of Rome, going all the way back to Brutus's ancestor, the first consul. Hortensius was lucky to have died when he did. He would have been pained to see "the Forum of the Roman people, the stage on which he showed his talent, stripped bare of cultured speech worthy of an audience of Romans and Greeks." Brutus, on the other hand, was on the cusp of oratorical greatness when eloquence fell silent. Still, he should keep up with his rhetorical training. Cicero, speaking on behalf of himself and Atticus, said, "We support you [Brutus], we want you to reap the reward of virtue, we want you to have a Republic in which you can renew and add to the glory of two distinguished families."[25] This was the first of many hints to Brutus to live up to his ancestry and fight for the Republic.

For the next couple of years, work after work flowed from Cicero's pen, many dedicated to Brutus. There was more writing on oratory. In one book, Cicero laid out his vision of the ideal orator—a speaker able, like Cicero, to use a variety of styles, from the simplest to the grandest. He produced a whole library of philosophical works, systematically treating epistemology, theology, and what Cicero considered the "most essential part of philosophy," ethics.[26] In none of these writings did Cicero recommend retreating from public life, as Epicurean philosophers did. For Cicero, happiness lay in living for your country—and if necessary dying for it. In one work addressed to Brutus he told the story of the Spartan Three Hundred who fell at Thermopylae, and he translated their epitaph into Latin: "Go tell the Spartans, stranger passing by, / That here obedient to their laws we lie."[27] Again and again, Cicero reminded Brutus of his ancestor the first consul, who fell in battle against the tyrant he had driven out of Rome.[28]

The philosophical works helped Cicero cope with his own diminished role in politics and the end of his legal career. They also brought relief as sorrows pressed in on him. While he did manage to patch things up with his brother, Quintus junior kept criticizing Cicero harshly. Terentia and Cicero divorced acrimoniously. He had to pay back her dowry, and they continued to argue over money. Clucks of disapproval greeted Cicero's choice of a new bride, a girl young enough to be his granddaughter, Publilia. Enemies of Cicero said he married her to clear his debts, and there may have been some truth to the charge.[29]

Then came the greatest sadness of his whole life. Tullia, after divorcing Dolabella, died from complications following the birth of a son, who also died. She had spent her final days at the Tusculum villa and Cicero had to leave, so painful was it to be there. He first sought solace at the house of Atticus in Rome. He then retreated to a property he had recently bought at Astura, on the coast of Italy south of Rome. This villa stood alone on a promontory, with woods behind it. Here Cicero could isolate himself from bothersome callers. "After yourself," he wrote to Atticus, "being alone is my best friend."[30] He sent young Publilia back to her mother, ending the marriage. Friends, including Brutus, wrote supportive letters at first. But as Cicero stayed withdrawn month after month, some complained that he was grieving excessively.[31] A true Roman should be sterner.

Cicero did finally start to heal, but just as the political situation was darkening in his eyes. Pharsalus had not been the last battle of the civil war. While Caesar was detained in Egypt his opponents regrouped in the Roman province of Africa (today's Tunisia), and he had to fight them there in 46 BC. Famously, Caesar's old enemy Cato refused to seek forgiveness and stabbed himself. Afterward, there seemed a chance that Caesar might reestablish order in Rome and return power to the Senate and the popular assemblies. But it wasn't to be. Pompey's two sons raised an army against Caesar in Spain, which Caesar ruthlessly suppressed in a savage war. After he came back to Rome, in the fall of 45 BC, it became clear that he wanted to fight a war against the Parthians. There would be no return to traditional republican government.[32]

Caesar held the supreme office of dictator and was entrusted with all armies and public moneys. He kept tight control over the elections of all the other magistrates. The Senate, stuffed with new members he had personally chosen, showered honors down on him: a purple toga, a golden chair in the Senate house, the right to wear a laurel crown on all occasions. Caesar liked the crown especially because it masked his bald spot (previously he had had to rely on a comb-over). Senators were made to swear an oath to protect his life, as if he were a sacrosanct tribune.

Cicero's letters probably don't reveal his true feelings about what was happening. He knew from his years as a lawyer that it was risky to put such things down in writing because a letter could so easily fall into an opponent's hands. There can be little doubt that, in conversations with Atticus, Brutus, and others, Cicero denounced Caesar as a tyrant. Even in the letters, Cicero several times more or less called Caesar a king—a title Caesar studiously avoided, so hateful was it to the Romans.[33] In his letters Cicero couldn't stop himself from a bitter jest or two. On the last day of 45 BC one of the consuls unexpectedly died. Caesar gave the vacant office for a few hours to one of his old lieutenants, Caninius, who asked for it. In a letter to a friend Cicero joked, "In the consulship of Caninius, you can be certain that nobody had lunch. When this fellow was consul, no crime was committed. His vigilance was extraordinary. Throughout his whole consulship, he didn't sleep a wink!"[34]

Frustration grew in Rome. Senators felt robbed of the chance to compete for office. Even longtime allies of Caesar grew resentful, especially if his decisions didn't favor them. Poorer citizens missed the perks they had enjoyed in political campaigns. According to later sources, malicious gossip spread. Did you hear? Caesar has put soldiers, ex-slaves, and even Gauls into the Senate. Don't show those barbarians the way to the Senate house! Did you hear? After he goes east, Caesar plans to stay there, in Alexandria, with his lover Cleopatra. Italy will be drained of all its troops and money, and Caesar's minions will be in charge of Rome.[35] Marcus Brutus was serving as praetor in 44 BC and, again according to later sources, his tribunal was found covered with such graffiti as "Brutus, you are asleep," and "You are no true Brutus." On the statue of his ancestor, the first consul, were written the words "We wish we had you now, Brutus!"[36]

A few days before he was to set out for Parthia, Caesar called a meeting of the senators for March 15, 44 BC, the Ides of March in the Roman calendar. It was to take place in the Senate house of Pompey, part of Pompey's theater complex. On the agenda was who would serve as consul for the rest of the year. At present, the consuls were Caesar himself and the strapping Mark Antony, who had fought for Caesar in the civil war and, for a time, run Italy in Caesar's absence. Caesar planned to step down as consul but Antony was trying to block Caesar's chosen replacement, none other than Cicero's former son-in-law Dolabella. Antony and Dolabella had been rivals for several years. Each wanted to be the new Clodius. Though born a patrician, Dolabella had converted to plebeian status, as Clodius had done, so that he could become tribune. Antony had married Clodius's widow, Fulvia.[37]

A couple hundred senators gathered in the Senate house the morning of the Ides, among them Cicero.[38] Despite everything that had happened with Tullia, he had stayed on speaking terms with Dolabella and probably supported him over Antony. But Caesar failed to appear. A report came that he would not come that day. He was feeling unwell. Apparently a sacrifice at his house had not gone well. An attendant moved Caesar's golden chair from its platform at the head of the chamber, near a statue of Pompey. Then another report: Caesar was coming after all, by litter. The chair was put back in place.

As Caesar entered the chamber, the senators rose in his honor. Some tried to push petitions into his hands. Caesar moved to the golden chair and sat down. A small group of senators, perhaps a dozen, gathered around him. Among them was Marcus Brutus and his brother-in-law Gaius Cassius. Some of the group made conversation with Caesar, others presented more petitions. But then one of the senators, Tillius Cimber, grabbed Caesar's toga by both shoulders and held him down. Another senator, Casca, pulled out a dagger and stabbed Caesar just below the throat. Casca cried out to his brother, who drove a blade into the dictator. Caesar started to shout in anger but couldn't defend himself. From every side the group closed in and hacked at him furiously with their daggers until he fell dead.

The rest of the senators cried out in shock and ran out of the room, Cicero among them.

The conspiracy had been weeks in the making. At least at first, its driving force seems to have been Brutus's brother-in-law Cassius, a fierce critic of Caesar who had voted in the Senate against some of the honors for the dictator. Cassius believed Marcus Brutus was the ideal figurehead because of his ancestry and pressured him to act. Many others joined them. Several sources indicate that more than sixty men conspired against Caesar. This figure may be too high, but certainly more were in on the plot than those who wielded the fatal daggers. Some of the conspirators were members of Caesar's own circle, which was key to the operation's success. One of Caesar's generals, Trebonius, had the job of distracting Mark Antony in conversation outside the Senate house at the time of the murder. Decimus Brutus, a distant relative of Marcus Brutus who had long been a favorite of Caesar's, lured Caesar to the Senate house when it looked like he wasn't going to attend.[39]

Cicero was not part of the conspiracy, but he participated in the tense negotiations that followed. Immediately after the murder, the assassins marched through the streets of Rome with their daggers lifted high. Freedom was restored, they shouted. They then took shelter in the sanctuary of Jupiter on the Capitoline Hill, where Cicero joined them. Many soldiers of Caesar's were in or near Rome, and the assassins controlled few armed forces themselves.

They needed to proceed with caution. At a meeting of the Senate on March 17, Cicero spoke successfully for compromise.[40] The assassins of Caesar—the Liberators, as they would start to call themselves—were to be granted a full amnesty from criminal prosecution. At the same time, all of Caesar's laws and decrees were to be upheld, as were the appointments he had made. Rescinding these would have caused chaos. Still, many of Caesar's friends and soldiers were outraged. They wanted his murder avenged.

A public funeral for Caesar followed a few days later in the Forum. It fell to Antony the consul to give the eulogy from the Rostra, and he took a page from his grandfather Antonius's book. At the climax of his address, to stir pity, Antony lifted up on the point of a spear Caesar's blood-spattered toga. This was the peroration to end them all. As Quintilian explained, with a touch of rhetorical exaggeration himself, "It was known that Caesar had been killed; his body lay on the bier; but it was the clothing, wet with blood, that made the image of the crime so vivid that Caesar seemed not to have been murdered, but was being murdered there and then."[41] The crowd, which included many of Caesar's soldiers, went wild, just as they had at Clodius's funeral. They moved Caesar's body off the Rostra and set it ablaze on a hastily improvised pyre at the other end of the Forum. An angry mob ran with torches to the houses of the assassins and almost burned those down as well.

In the weeks following the funeral Antony ruled Rome along with Dolabella, who had coolly put on the purple-edged toga of consul right after Caesar's death. Antony busied himself with implementing decisions that Caesar had allegedly made but not enacted before his death. But then Caesar's heir, his grandnephew Gaius Octavius, appeared on the scene. Just eighteen years old, he had been studying overseas at the time of the assassination. He was an attractive young man, with golden curls that made him look a little bit like the god Apollo. More important, by the terms of Caesar's will he gained Caesar's name. For convenience, modern scholars call him Octavian, but he called himself Caesar (and eventually Caesar Augustus). He and especially his advisers began demanding the punishment of Caesar's murderers. This put pressure on Antony to move against the assassins.[42]

As far as Cicero was concerned, the tyrant might have been dead but the tyranny lived on under Antony. In early April 44 BC Cicero left Rome for a tour of his villas. He complained in frank letters to Atticus that Antony and Fulvia were selling political favors. He believed that it would have been better if Antony had been killed on the Ides along with Caesar, as some of the conspirators had wanted. The funeral of Caesar had both whipped up a mob of poor people and slaves and sunk the cause of the Liberators. In late April Cicero met with Octavian and reported to Atticus that the young man treated him respectfully, but "I say that he cannot be a loyal citizen. There are so many around him who threaten death to our friends and say that the current situation is unbearable."[43]

Cicero realized that a new round of civil war was likely, but first armies had to be raised. The Mediterranean world became a giant board game, with one complicated move following another. Soon after the Ides, the assassin Decimus Brutus had taken up command of Cisalpine Gaul (northern Italy), assigned to him by Caesar. In early June 44 BC Antony passed legislation to transfer both Cisalpine and Transalpine Gaul to himself, for five years. Dolabella was given the province of Syria for five years. Marcus Brutus and his brother-in-law Cassius, no longer feeling safe in Rome, made plans to go overseas, where they intended to recruit forces through their connections.[44]

Cicero mulled over what he should do. In July he settled on a plan to set sail for Greece and visit his son. Marcus junior had been sent to Athens a year earlier for study but apparently was spending more time in the city's banquet halls than its lecture rooms. Cicero might also attend the Olympic Games. He made it to Syracuse on August 1 and spent a night with his old friends there. After setting out the next day, he was driven by a contrary wind back to the Italian mainland and held there for several days by the weather. He received a report that the situation in Rome was improving for the assassins. Cicero turned back for the city at once. On his way he met with Brutus, who made clear that the report Cicero had heard was false. Brutus and Cassius were both sailing east. Still Brutus expressed delight that Cicero was returning to Rome, where he could champion the Liberators' cause. Cicero's absence, Brutus added, had been criticized; many felt that it was hardly the time for Cicero to be going to the Olympic Games. He must fight for the Republic too.[45]

Cicero arrived in Rome on September 1 early in the morning. When he was informed that the Senate was to meet that day, to vote on new honors for Caesar proposed by Antony, Cicero sent a note excusing himself. He said he was too worn out from his journey to attend.[46] Antony was furious and threatened to storm Cicero's house. The next day, Cicero came to the Senate but now Antony was absent. Cicero took the chance to make a speech criticizing Antony for passing laws Caesar had never intended as if they were Caesar's own. This was the first of what Cicero would call his *Philippic Orations*, borrowing the name from the speeches the Athenian freedom fighter Demosthenes had delivered against King Philip of Macedon, the father of Alexander the Great.

Antony spent several weeks preparing a diatribe against Cicero, which he delivered in the Senate on September 19. The speech does not survive, but its contents can be gleaned from Cicero's response.[47] Antony accused Cicero of ingratitude, despite having always treated him well. As a young man he had visited Cicero's house to learn oratory. During the recent civil war, when Cicero had been stuck in Brundisium, Antony had helped him. Antony went on to denounce Cicero's entire political career as ruinous for the Roman people. Cicero had acted like a cruel tyrant during his consulship. He had refused to hand over for burial the body of one of the slain conspirators, Antony's stepfather. Cicero had instigated the murder of Clodius and then gloated over it. Cicero had instigated civil war. He had driven Pompey apart from Caesar and then treated Pompey atrociously. Everybody knew about the jokes Cicero made in Pompey's camp. To cap it all off, Cicero had instigated the murder of Caesar too. The moment Caesar was killed, Antony said, Marcus Brutus raised his bloodstained dagger high and cried out Cicero's name and later congratulated him on the recovery of his freedom. It was clear: Cicero was in on the wicked plot.

Cicero took a month or so to craft his response, the *Second Philippic*. Although written as a speech delivered right after Antony's, it was actually a pamphlet in which Cicero defended himself against Antony's charges. Yes, Cicero admitted, he did make jokes: we all have to unwind.[48] Then, at even greater length, he subjected Antony's own life and career to an excoriating review. Antony staggered around Rome drunk. He traveled through Italy on public business with actresses and pimps. After Pompey's death, he moved into that great man's house and trashed it in a few days. After Caesar's death, Antony and Fulvia had done a brisk business in selling fake decisions of Caesar they claimed had been found among his papers. No, Cicero hadn't made Rome's current mess, Antony had. Antony was now maintaining that it was a crime even to have wished Caesar dead.[49]

Of that Cicero was guilty. He admitted as much, though he had never been a member of the conspiracy. If he had been, he wrote, he would have gotten rid of not just the king but kingship itself: "If that pen had been mine, as is alleged, then believe me, I should have finished off not just one act, but the whole play!"[50]


In late 44 BC Cicero embarked on a risky plan to defeat Antony and aid the assassins. He made an alliance with the teenage Octavian. Over recent months Octavian had recruited an army from among Caesar's former soldiers. He needed his position legalized. Antony, meanwhile, had gone to northern Italy to wrest control of the area from the assassin Decimus Brutus. Cicero needed an army to rescue Decimus, who was about to be put under siege by Antony. The plan was for Octavian, along with the two consuls of 43 BC who were Caesarians discontented with Antony, to be authorized to fight Antony. Cicero worked tirelessly to make it happen, booming out in the Senate and Forum more of his *Philippic Orations*. "If now the last chapter of the Republic's history has come," he told the senators on one occasion, "then, just as celebrated gladiators take care to fall honorably, let us, the foremost men of the world and all its nations, take care that we die with distinction rather than serve ignominiously."[51] It was thrilling for Cicero, after so many years in the political wilderness, to play a leading part in public affairs again. He overcame opposition by senators who wanted to negotiate with Antony, and by the spring of 43 BC a full war was on in northern Italy.

Marcus Brutus worried about Cicero's strategy as he learned of the unfolding developments. In the fall of 44 BC Brutus had gone to Athens. In between attending philosophy lectures he secretly prepared for war. He recruited as officers young Romans who were studying in the city, including Cicero's son, and arranged to take over Macedonia, the great land bridge between the two halves of the

Roman empire. Brutus's brother-in-law Cassius, meanwhile, raised soldiers and money in Syria. Another assassin, Trebonius, did the same in Asia. They deemed it better to amass strength in the East, much as Pompey had done at the start of the earlier civil war against Caesar. Brutus thought it unwise for Cicero to keep building up young Octavian. "You seem to me to be placing too much confidence in your hope," Brutus wrote Cicero. "As soon as somebody behaves well, there's no limit on what you'll give him."[52]

The split between Antony and Octavian slowed their plans for avenging Caesar's murder. That pleased Cicero as much as it displeased old friends of Caesar bent on punishment. But in late February 43 BC word reached Rome that Cicero's former son-in-law Dolabella, traveling through Asia on his way to Syria, had taken matters into his own hands by killing Trebonius. Dolabella first feigned friendliness with Caesar's assassin before secretly entering by night the city where Trebonius was staying and capturing him in bed. Dolabella reportedly had Trebonius's head cut off and displayed on the ivory seat where Trebonius conducted public business. Soldiers of Dolabella then rolled the head around the city streets like a ball.[53] These details may have been exaggerated. Enemies of the assassins enjoyed imagining the most horrible fates possible for their foes, taking revenge with their pens as well as their swords. But there can be no doubt that Trebonius was beheaded. Just as in the civil war of Cicero's early adult years, decapitation marked a man as an enemy.

In response to the news, the Senate declared Dolabella a public enemy and confiscated his property. Antony wrote in a letter that, while he was pained by this declaration, he took joy in learning of Trebonius's death: "A heinous criminal had paid the penalty to the ashes and bones of a glorious man." The murderers were worse than assassins, according to him; they were parricides. Among the many honors the Senate had voted to Julius Caesar was the title "Father of His Country." Also, the murderers had broken their oaths to protect Caesar. To kill a parent and to break an oath brought down the anger of the gods. Now, less than a year after Caesar's murder, "the will of the gods has made itself clear."[54] The gods would see the other parricides punished soon. Mortal men were merely the agents of divine justice. This was the sort of thinking Cicero had for years been encouraging, as he justified and even celebrated the summary executions of men he deemed enemies of the Republic.

Cicero's plans unraveled in the late spring of 43 BC. Decimus Brutus was rescued by the senatorial army and Antony was sent reeling to Transalpine Gaul, but Octavian refused to cooperate with Decimus. Octavian had used Cicero only as long as he needed him, to legalize his position and gain enough power to rival Antony's. Cicero had thought he could discard the teenager when the time came. Instead, the teenager discarded Cicero. Octavian sent four hundred soldiers to Rome to demand a consulship for himself, as both the consuls of 43 BC had died in the war in northern Italy. When the Senate balked, he marched on Rome with a full army. Cicero tried to organize a defense of the city, but it was hopeless. Octavian entered Rome and senators rushed to greet him, even Cicero eventually. "Ah," Octavian exclaimed, "the last of my friends to meet me!"[55] Cicero soon fled Rome, after which we have no more letters or speeches from him.

Octavian had himself and his cousin elected as consuls, and together they pushed through a law that set up a special court to prosecute Caesar's murderers. The law was like the one Pompey had passed to deal with Milo, but more extreme. All participants, including those who stabbed Caesar, conspirators who did not wield weapons, and anyone else with knowledge of the plot, were to be tried on a single day. Punishment was set as exile and loss of all property, while rewards were to be given to prosecutors from the estates of the condemned, along with other privileges. The trials were a farce. None of the accused could or would defend themselves in person. Even men who had been far away from Rome at the time of Caesar's murder and had nothing to do with it were indicted and convicted, though Cicero was spared. One juror, a brave senator named Silicius Corona, openly voted to acquit Marcus Brutus. He did not survive long.[56]

Antony could take no credit for securing these judicial punishments, but soon afterward Decimus fell into his hands and was beheaded. And so, as friends of Caesar gloated, Decimus became the next of the murderers to pay the penalty. Caesarians gloated again when, not long after, another assassin, Minucius Basilus, was killed by his slaves, some of whom he had castrated as a punishment. This was seen as more divine justice.[57]

In the fall of 43 BC Octavian and Antony decided to put aside their differences and campaign against Caesar's assassins overseas. Alongside Lepidus, a former officer of Caesar, they agreed to form a triumvirate and take control of Rome. To usher in their rule, the three brought back proscriptions just like Sulla's. The conspirators of Caesar and supporters of theirs such as the juror Silicius Corona were condemned to death. The heads of those caught and killed were nailed to the Rostra. Hundreds more were added to the list to claim their wealth. Among them was Verres, still in exile. Antony allegedly had had his eye on some of Verres's bronzes.[58]

Cicero was condemned for a different reason. Over the last year he had tried to save the Republic, at least as he understood it. He had vigorously attacked Antony with all the eloquence honed over his long career. Meanwhile he had also cultivated the young Octavian, but with obvious insincerity. More than once, Cicero told Octavian one thing but felt quite another. Often in his legal career Cicero had practically convinced jurors that the sun shone at midnight. But rhetoric wasn't going to help him this time. He had shown himself to be unreliable—and also dangerous to the Caesarians. He was still Rome's best orator and could use that power to rally opposition. Antony had every reason to want Cicero gone. There are reports of Octavian asking Antony to spare Cicero but probably this is a later distortion, meant to make Octavian look better. With all the other supporters of the assassins being condemned, Caesar's heir could not go easy on Cicero.

And so Cicero, his son, his brother, and his nephew were all proscribed. We have many accounts of their final days, but they contradict each other in some details and contain embellishments.[59] According to Plutarch, Cicero and Quintus were at the villa at Tusculum when they learned of their proscriptions. They planned to go to Cicero's villa at Astura on the coast and then from there sail to Macedonia, where they could join Brutus and Marcus junior. The brothers began their journey, but Quintus realized he had no money with him and decided to return home first. He and Cicero hugged each other in tears, then parted. A few days later Quintus's slaves turned him over to one of the triumvirs' killing squads and he was put to death along with his son.

According to Plutarch, Cicero made it to Astura and sailed southward along the coast. But then he vacillated. Either in fear of the winter sea crossing or because he still placed some hope in Octavian, he went back ashore. He started to travel in the direction of Rome. But he then changed his mind again and spent a restless night at Astura. Finally he embarked by sea again for his villa at Formiae, where he stopped to rest. There, Plutarch wrote, came a band of soldiers, one of whom had once been defended by Cicero on a charge of parricide. It is really too good to be true that

Cicero was murdered by a man he got off for murder: this was a later fabrication.

It appears that Cicero's slaves were carrying him in a litter from the villa to the sea when soldiers caught up with him. According to the Augustan historian Livy, Cicero ordered the slaves to set the litter down. From his seat he leaned out and offered his neck without flinching.[60] The soldiers cut off his head and also one or, more likely, both of his hands—the hands that had written the *Philippic Orations* that had so viciously attacked Antony. The head and hand (or hands) were sent to Rome and hung up on the Rostra.

There are many awful stories of Antony laughing over the head when he saw it and even placing it in his dining room to gaze on while he feasted. One historian also claims that Fulvia took the head into her hands and, after cursing and spitting at it, set it on her knees, pried open the mouth, and tore out the tongue, which she stabbed with pins taken from her hair.[61] Most likely that never happened, but the story perhaps captured a larger truth about the furious last years of both Cicero and the Republic: without law, there is no limit on revenge.

# CONCLUSION

# "White Toga Crime"

Verres and his art collecting, Fonteius's extra duties on wine, the conspiracy of Catiline, Clodius's murder by Milo's gang on the Appian Way: these and all the other stories of high-class crime recounted in this book are each distinctive, but what underlies them all is the leading Romans' grinding struggle for wealth, power, and honor. The terrible civil war of the 80s BC and Sulla's victory especially fostered a play-for-keeps style in politics and beyond. When you have confiscated your fellow citizens' property and then auctioned it off as the plunder of war, or you have turned in a fellow citizen's head for a cash reward, what wouldn't you do? Verres and Fonteius, men who began their political careers during the years of war, would not have succeeded if they had not betrayed one set of allies for another. Cutthroats got ahead. Of course, politicians in Rome had long competed with one another, just as politicians in the towns of Italy did on a smaller scale. The trials of Roscius and Cluentius reveal the life in these towns and how partisans of Sulla exploited his victory. Violence did not stop with the end of the proscriptions.

Overseas governorships offered Roman politicians a unique opportunity for illegal enrichment. In many ways extortion was the ultimate high-class crime. In senators' houses you might find statues, chests full of silver, and even bevies of slaves seized abroad. Cicero wrote late in life that governance of the provinces deteriorated after Sulla.[1] If you stole from citizens, you could just as easily do so from foreigners. To the Romans' credit, they tried to toughen up the law against extortion. But the statute was a hard tool for provincials to use in their fight for justice. Misrule in the provinces obviously hurt provincials, but it also destabilized politics in Rome by unleashing floods of cash for bribery to buy jurors and voters. Like the extortion law, the jury reform of 70 BC, which significantly increased the number of jurors at trials, was an effort to improve governance.

All human systems of justice are imperfect and make mistakes. Flaws in the Roman system are clear for us to see. Witnesses could be discredited based on their ethnicity or social status. Arguments put forward by lawyers often focused less concretely on evidence and law, and more speculatively on motive, opportunity, and character. In criminal trials in any system there will be arguments from probability. But Roman courts allowed lawyers to stoke prejudices blatantly, making society overall less equitable. The courts could try to hold the powerful to account, but the powerful sometimes held enough sway to overwhelm the courts. A clear example is Clodius, both at his trial for sacrilege in 61 BC and then in later years, when he could not be prosecuted for violence. Even thinking that you have a decent chance of winning in court, when you have committed wrong, weakens the rule of law. If courts become capricious in their verdicts, the justice system becomes a game of chance. Why not throw the dice? It's not surprising that Romans, in moments of frustration with the courts, looked to the gods for justice. But a widespread belief that there is a higher power than human law that justifies murdering your enemy spells trouble for civil society.

Among the worst problems the Roman Republic faced during Cicero's years in public life was a resurgence of political violence. The precedent of Sulla was always there. If you didn't get your way, why not take up arms? Sulla justified his first march on Rome by saying that he was going to deliver the city from tyrants who had taken over.[2] Catiline and his followers taunted Cicero as a tyrant. There was a tradition of heroic tyrannicide in Rome. By reckless demagoguery, politicians could turn their enemies into tyrants and justify their own acts of violence. Clodius did this, and so did Milo and his supporters, including Cicero.

The court for political violence was poorly equipped to prosecute this crime successfully. The court could be easily overwhelmed by force. Such trials would almost inevitably be politicized, and what counted as violence "against the public interest" could be contested. At the trial of Caelius for political violence, Cicero gave what is for many readers today one of his most entertaining speeches. It displays all his storytelling skill. Cicero was able to divert jurors' attention from the question of political violence by focusing on the fact that Caelius's trial was just one in an ongoing cycle of retaliation. High-ranking Romans who were engaged in disputes with one another used the judicial system to wreak their revenge. The court was a way for a dispute to be settled without violence. But when criminal proceedings became more like tests of power between groups, they might stoke the partisan furies rather than calm them. Sometimes legal proceedings, or the prospect of them, invited armed violence.

At his best, Cicero fought against those who threatened to undermine the Republic by subverting free elections and the rule of law through their excessive power. At the trials of Roscius and Verres, he stood up to men who were abusing their positions. In the year of his consulship, Cicero correctly spotted the threat Catiline and his supporters posed when they refused to accept Catiline's electoral loss. In later years, Clodius with his gangs, Caesar with his armies, and Caesar's heirs with their armies also challenged peaceful self-government. At great personal cost, Cicero combated them all in his speeches and writings.

Yet Cicero did the long-term health of the Republic no good by his lack of sympathy for the less privileged members of society. During his consulship he showed no interest in trying to strike any compromise with those pushing for reform. As a politician, Cicero failed to articulate a clear vision for how all Roman citizens could achieve a basic level of dignity. He was much happier to attack his opponents. In both legal and political speeches, he often played on popular prejudices and emotions to position himself and his well-off backers for power.

Cicero came to embrace violence over the course of his political career. In his first defense, the speech on behalf of Roscius, he warned jurors that when human beings are exposed to prolonged cruelty they risk losing their sense of compassion. In a sense, that is what happened to Cicero himself. Near the end of his consulship, he went along with the Senate's vote to execute the five Catilinarian conspirators caught in the city. After the ordeal of exile, he justified Milo's assembling a gang of gladiators. He excused Milo's murder of Clodius. He exalted the assassins of Julius Caesar and called for the deaths of others. To save a republic, a war might be necessary. But if you go to war, you must be ready to win it on the battlefield. Cicero was ill prepared in 44 BC, just as the diehard enemies of Julius Caesar were five years earlier. Cracking jokes about those fighting on your own side, as Cicero did in Pompey's camp, is less than helpful.

Yet if there was a streak of cruelty in Cicero, as his critics charged, this does not negate his achievements as a public speaker. Cicero knew that courts and law offer a better chance for accountable government and justice than does violence. He tried to use the word to persuade, rather than the sword to arbitrate. Long after his own violent death, Cicero's speeches have remained valuable examples of how to convince others to follow a course of action you believe is right. Oratory in the style of Cicero has been put to ends Cicero himself never could have imagined.

To give just one example, in 1856 the abolitionist senator from Massachusetts, Charles Sumner, delivered on the floor of the United States Senate a five-hour speech, "The Crime Against Kansas." Sumner attacked senatorial colleagues for trying to extend slavery into the territory of Kansas. Of Senator Andrew Butler from South Carolina, Sumner said, "Of course he has chosen a mistress to whom he has made his vows, and who, though ugly to others, is always lovely to him; though polluted in the sight of the world, is chaste in his sight—I mean the harlot Slavery." Famously, two days afterward, Sumner was brutally caned at his desk in the Senate by Senator Butler's nephew, Representative Preston Brooks. What is less remembered today is how Sumner sprinkled echoes of Ciceronian oratory throughout his speech. At one point, Sumner described the Slave Power with a personification: "There, sir, stands the criminal—all unmasked before you—heartless, grasping, and tyrannical—with an audacity beyond that of Verres." Sumner even structured the speech as a Ciceronian oration, with all of the requisite parts, from the exordium at the start to the peroration at the end. Just as Cicero would often appeal to the gods as he finished an address, Sumner called on his God: "In the name of the Heavenly Father, whose service is perfect Freedom, I make this last appeal."[3] Cicero's speeches should still be studied today for their limitations but also their rhetorical power. We shall be able to better understand the achievement of later orators such as Charles Sumner by doing so, even as Sumner's caning reminds us of the problems a republic faces when it denies equality to all.

Cicero's speeches also continue to be read and enjoyed today because they are entertaining. Cicero's speeches offer the same satisfactions as true crime stories, mystery novels, and legal and political thrillers. They provide tales of cunning criminals and courtroom dramatics, as well as narratives that raise questions about justice. How well do human systems of law work? And when their verdicts are flawed, what should you do about it? How far can you go to protect your country? Does effective counterintelligence and counterterrorism require that you sink as low as your enemy? Modern novelists such as Steven Saylor and Robert Harris have tapped Cicero's writings to produce enjoyable and convincing historical fiction that raises questions like these. Saylor's mysteries, recounted by the fictional detective Gordianus, powerfully capture the blood sport of Roman politics, as well as one injustice that Cicero never questioned at all: slavery. Harris has his Cicero trilogy narrated by Cicero's onetime slave and secretary Tiro, who makes clear to us Cicero's burning ambition as a politician and a writer. What will any of us achieve for ourselves and our societies, Harris's novels ask, without ambition? Ambition pushes us forward but also leads us astray.

It was common for ancient historians, whenever they related the death of a great man, to end with an epitaph summarizing the man's whole life. It is suitable, then, to finish with the verdict delivered by Livy on Cicero:

He lived for sixty-three years so that, if there had been no violence, his death could not be thought untimely. His talent was fortunate in its achievements and their rewards; he himself long enjoyed favorable circumstances. But in that long run of good fortune, from time to time he was struck with blows—exile, the downfall of his party, the death of his daughter, and his own dark and bitter end. He bore none of these ills as a man should except for death. And his death, to one judging fairly, might have seemed less undeserved since he suffered nothing crueler from his victorious opponent than what he would have done, if he had enjoyed the same success. Still, if one weighs his good qualities against his bad, he was a great and memorable man, and to sing his praises one would need a Cicero as eulogist.[4]

# ACKNOWLEDGMENTS

As I researched and wrote this book, I reflected often on how much I owe to so many people, going back to Mary O'Brien, my high school Latin teacher, who instilled in me a love of Cicero's language along with a knowledge of Latin grammar. At Yale University, Professor A. Thomas Cole gave a more critical portrait of Cicero, which only increased my appreciation for the orator's talents. I have learned much from many other teachers along the way, as well as my colleagues and students at Georgetown University. I especially thank the students in my spring 2022 seminar on Cicero and the courts.

Marissa Koors at Basic Books, along with my literary agents Emma Parry and Rebecca Carter and Emma's assistant Ali Lake, helped me develop an initial idea for a book on true crime in Rome into the book you are now reading. I am grateful to them all, and to Emma for much additional support throughout the writing process. Brandon Proia and Sarah Caro read the final manuscript for Basic Books US and UK respectively, and both gave invaluable advice that helped me see Cicero more fully. Thanks also go to the rest of the team at Basic, including Alex Cullina, production editor Melissa

Veronesi, and copyeditor Nicholas Taylor, who cleaned up my manuscript. Cartographer Kate Blackmer drew the exquisite maps and was so much fun to work with.

Two good friends, Ron Bleeker and Kit Morrell, read an earlier version of the manuscript and sent me notes, for which I am thankful. The members of the online Working Group in Roman History also helpfully commented on portions of the manuscript. I have gained much from conversations or correspondence with Harriet Flower, Carsten Hjort Lange, Maya Jasanoff, Tom Kerch, Jesper Majbom Madsen, Andrew Meshnick, Danny O'Sullivan, John Ramsey, Matthew Roller, Carole Sargent, Susan Treggiari, and Kathryn Welch. My partner Adam Kemerer and the rest of my family have provided much encouragement. Another debt is to previous scholars, among whom I count a number of brilliant novelists.

Finally, I thank the Office of the Vice President for Global Engagement at Georgetown for the opportunity to spend the fall of 2022 as a resident at Campion Hall, Oxford. Everyone at Campion Hall welcomed me warmly and made it so easy to spend the months of my stay reading in Oxford's splendid libraries. I also thank colleagues at the University of Queensland in Brisbane for the invitation to visit as R. D. Milns Visiting Professor of Classics and Ancient History in the spring of 2023. I received many helpful questions from audiences there while also enjoying marvelous hospitality and scenery.

# NOTES

## Introduction

1. Kathleen Freeman, *The Murder of Herodes and Other Trials from the Athenian Law Courts* (London: MacDonald & Co., 1946), 9. Freeman's book, especially her introduction, has helped me in writing my Introduction.

2. My composite sketch of a typical trial is based, in part, on A. H. J. Greenidge, *The Legal Procedure of Cicero's Time* (Oxford, UK: Clarendon Press, 1901); D. H. Berry, *Cicero: Defence Speeches* (Oxford, UK: Oxford University Press, 2000), xi–xxx, a superb introduction to a superb translation; Jonathan Powell and Jeremy Paterson, eds., *Cicero the Advocate* (Oxford, UK: Oxford University Press, 2004), especially the thorough introduction by the editors and the chapter by Andrew Lintott, "Legal Procedure in Cicero's Time" (61–78); Charles Guérin, *La voix de la vérité: Témoin et témoignage dans les tribunaux romains du Ier siècle av. J.-C.* (Paris: Belles Lettres, 2016); and Jean-Michel David, *Le patronat judiciaire au dernier siècle de la République romaine* (Rome: École française de Rome, 1992), esp. 463–495. David's discussion of the theatrical qualities of the trial is fundamental. I have also learned much from Jon Hall, *Cicero's Use of Judicial Theater* (Ann Arbor: University of Michigan Press, 2014).

3. The procedure is most fully attested in a second-century BC extortion law inscribed on a bronze tablet. For details, along with a discussion of the people's role as watchdog, see A. N. Sherwin-White, "The *Lex Repetundarum* and the Political Ideals of Gaius Gracchus," *Journal of Roman Studies* 72 (1982): 18–31.

4. This was the description Cicero gave of a party in his lost speech *For Gallius*, quoted in Quintilian, *Orator's Education* 8.3.66.

5. For this and what follows, see Cicero, *Brutus* 200; another evocative passage is *Brutus* 290. My paraphrase here is indebted to Robert A. Kaster, *Cicero: "Brutus" and "Orator"* (New York: Oxford University Press, 2020).

6. Quintilian, *Orator's Education* 10.1.112. There are a number of good biographies of Cicero, often focused on his political career, e.g., H. J. Haskell, *This Was Cicero: Modern Politics in a Roman Toga* (New York: Alfred A. Knopf, 1942); D. L. Stockton, *Cicero: A Political Biography* (London: Oxford University Press, 1971); and Kathryn Tempest, *Cicero: Politics and*

*Persuasion in Ancient Rome* (London: Continuum, 2011). Elizabeth Rawson, *Cicero: A Portrait* (Ithaca, NY: Cornell University Press, 1975) and, more briefly, Charles Guérin, *Cicéron: Un philosophe en politique* (Paris: Calype, 2022), cover Cicero's intellectual achievements. I have drawn on all these works throughout my book.

7. See Andrew M. Riggsby, *Crime and Community in Ciceronian Rome* (Austin: University of Texas Press, 1999); David, *Le patronat*, 31–36.

8. On nonfinancial rewards for prosecutors, see Michael C. Alexander, "*Praemia* in the Quaestiones of the Late Republic," *Classical Philology* 80, no. 1 (1985): 20–32, with a different view in David, *Le patronat*, 508–525.

9. See, above all, Michael C. Alexander, *The Case for the Prosecution in the Ciceronian Era* (Ann Arbor: University of Michigan Press, 2002).

10. For discussions leaning to this view, see, e.g., Riggsby, *Crime and Community*, 178–184; Alexander, *Case for the Prosecution*, 15–22; Powell and Paterson, *Cicero the Advocate*, 53–58, with a good discussion of publication on which I draw here. Note also my discussions below of the prosecution of Verres (Chapters 3–4) and the defense of Milo (Chapter 11).

11. Cicero, *Brutus* 225, describing Sextus Titius; translation from Kaster, *Cicero: "Brutus" and "Orator,"* an excellent edition I have relied on greatly.

12. An excellent annotated translation is James M. May and Jakob Wisse, *Cicero: "On the Ideal Orator"* (New York: Oxford University Press, 2001). On the development of advocacy, see David, *Le patronat*.

13. R. G. Lewis, ed. and trans., *Asconius: "Commentaries on Speeches by Cicero"* (Oxford, UK: Oxford University Press, 2006). On Asconius, see Thomas J. Keeline, "The Working Methods of Asconius," in *The Scholia on Cicero's Speeches*, ed. Christoph Pieper and Dennis Pausch (Leiden: Brill, 2023), 41–68.

14. See, e.g., Cicero, *On the Ideal Orator* 3.213–237, *Brutus* 141–142, 234–235, *Orator* 54–60 ("bodily eloquence"). A splendid translation of Quintilian can be found in the Loeb Classical Library edition of Donald A. Russell: *Quintilian: "The Orator's Education,"* 5 vols. (Cambridge, MA: Harvard University Press, 2001).

15. For a translation of Plutarch's biography of Cicero with helpful commentary, see Andrew Lintott, *Plutarch: Demosthenes and Cicero* (Oxford, UK: Oxford University Press, 2013).

16. Andrew M. Riggsby, "The Rhetoric of Character in the Roman Courts," in Powell and Paterson, *Cicero the Advocate*, 165–185; James M. May, *Trials of Character: The Eloquence of Ciceronian Ethos* (Chapel Hill: University of North Carolina Press, 1988).

17. Quintilian, *Orator's Education* 6.3.73–74. For Tiro's books of jokes, see Macrobius, *Saturnalia* 2.1.12. Many Ciceronian jokes are found in Macrobius, *Saturnalia* 2.3; and Plutarch, *Cicero* 25–27, 38.2–6.

18. Cicero, *For Flaccus* 98. On extortion, see, e.g., Riggsby, *Crime and Community*, 120–150; Alexander, *Case for the Prosecution*, 55–58; and, more generally, Kit Morrell, *Pompey, Cato, and the Governance of the Roman Empire* (Oxford, UK: Oxford University Press, 2017).

19. For one general history of the late Roman Republic, emphasizing both cultural achievement and frequent political violence, see Josiah Osgood, *Rome and the Making of a World State, 150 BCE–20 CE* (Cambridge, UK: Cambridge University Press, 2018). Two wonderfully

perceptive narratives are Tom Holland, *Rubicon: The Last Years of the Roman Republic* (New York: Doubleday, 2003); and Edward Watts, *Mortal Republic: How Rome Fell into Tyranny* (New York: Basic Books, 2018).

20. On these efforts, see especially Morrell, *Pompey, Cato, and the Governance of the Roman Empire*. For the application of philosophy to the Republic's ongoing problems, see Katharina Volk, *The Roman Republic of Letters: Scholarship, Philosophy, and Politics in the Age of Cicero and Caesar* (Princeton, NJ: Princeton University Press, 2021).

21. Cicero, *For Milo* 11.

## Chapter 1: Murder by the Baths of Pallacina

1. This opening narrative depends on Cicero, *For Sextus Roscius* 15–29. Throughout this and the next chapter, I have made much use of the commentary on the speech by Andrew R. Dyck, *Cicero: "Pro Sexto Roscio"* (Cambridge, UK: Cambridge University Press, 2010); and the translation, with introduction and notes, by D. H. Berry, *Cicero: Defence Speeches* (Oxford, UK: Oxford University Press, 2000), 3–58. My translations of *For Sextus Roscius* owe much to Berry as well as Michael Grant, *Cicero: Murder Trials*, rev. ed. (London: Penguin, 1990).

2. Plutarch, *Sulla* 31.3. The major sources for the civil war of the 80s BC are Plutarch's biographies, *Sulla* and *Marius*, along with Appian, *Civil Wars* 1.1–108; and Livy, *Periochae* 77–90. On the proscriptions, see François Hinard, *Les proscriptions de la Rome républicaine* (Rome: École française de Rome, 1985).

3. Plutarch, *Sulla* 31.5.

4. For C. Papius Mutilus, see Livy, *Periochae* 89; Granius Licinianus 32F; Hinard, *Les proscriptions*, 390–391.

5. Plutarch, *Marius* 44.1–4; Appian, *Civil War* 1.72.

6. Cicero, *Brutus* 311.

7. On the history of the courts and Sulla's reforms, see Berry, *Cicero: Defence Speeches*, xxv–xxx; and more fully, Duncan Cloud, "The Constitutional and Criminal Law," in *The Cambridge Ancient History*, vol. 9: *The Last Age of the Roman Republic, 146–43 BC*, 2nd ed., ed. J. A. Crook, Andrew Lintott, and Elizabeth Rawson (New York: Cambridge University Press, 1994), 491–530; T. Corey Brennan, *The Praetorship in the Roman Republic* (Oxford, UK: Oxford University Press, 2000), 416–424.

8. For the crowd, see Cicero, *For Sextus Roscius* 11. Our picture of the trial derives almost entirely from Cicero's speech.

9. Cicero, *For Sextus Roscius* 56–57, 90. On the murder court and its prosecutors, I draw especially on Andrew M. Riggsby, *Crime and Community in Ciceronian Rome* (Austin: University of Texas Press, 1999), 50–78; Michael C. Alexander, *The Case for the Prosecution in the Ciceronian Era* (Ann Arbor: University of Michigan Press, 2002), 145–147; Andrew Lintott, "*Delator* and *Index*: Informers and Accusers at Rome from the Republic to the Early Principate," *Accordia Research Papers* 9 (2001–2003): 152–166.

10. Erucius's case is reconstructed through Cicero's speech. For more detail, see Alexander, *Case for the Prosecution*, 149–172.

11. On parricide and the crime of murder more generally in Rome, see, in addition to the works on the murder court mentioned above (n. 9), Dyck, *Cicero: "Pro Sexto Roscio,"*

1–2; Duncan J. Cloud, *"Parricidium*: From the *Lex Numae* to the *Lex Pompeia de Parricidiis*," *Zeitschrift der Savigny-Stiftung für Rechtsgeschichte: Romanistische Abteilung* 88, no. 1 (1971): 1–66; Cheryl L. Golden, "The Role of Poison in Roman Society" (PhD diss., University of North Carolina, 2005); Emma Southon, *A Fatal Thing Happened on the Way to the Forum* (New York: Abrams, 2021).

12. On penalties, see Berry, *Cicero: Defence Speeches*, xxx; and, more fully, A. H. J. Greenidge, *The Legal Procedure of Cicero's Time* (Oxford, UK: Clarendon Press, 1901), 502–516.

13. Cicero, *For Sextus Roscius* 1.

14. Cicero, *For Sextus Roscius* 6.

15. Cicero, *For Sextus Roscius* 6.

16. Cicero, *For Sextus Roscius* 6.

17. Cicero, *For Sextus Roscius* 13; Jon Hall, *Cicero's Use of Judicial Theater* (Ann Arbor: University of Michigan Press, 2014), 33–35.

18. Cicero, *For Sextus Roscius* 12.

19. Cicero, *For Sextus Roscius* 14. What follows summarizes Cicero's statement of the facts (*narratio*), 15–29. For rules on the *narratio*, see, e.g., Cicero, *On Invention* 1.28, *On the Ideal Orator* 2.80.

20. Cicero, *For Sextus Roscius* 17.

21. Cicero, *For Sextus Roscius* 23.

22. Cicero, *For Sextus Roscius* 17.

23. Cicero, *For Sextus Roscius* 29.

24. Cicero, *For Sextus Roscius* 35. For rules on the *partitio*, see, e.g., Cicero, *On Invention* 1.31–33, *On the Ideal Orator*, 2.80.

25. Cicero, *For Sextus Roscius* 35.

26. Aelian, *Characteristics of Animals* 8.4; more generally on Crassus, see especially Cicero, *Brutus* 139–165, 183–200, *On the Ideal Orator* 2.1–11; and the full collection of testimony and fragments in Gesine Manuwald, *Fragmentary Republican Latin: Oratory, Part 1* (Cambridge, MA: Harvard University Press, 2019), 427–483. On Cicero's early years and education, see his own account, *Brutus* 301–329; Plutarch, *Cicero* 1–5; and modern biographies, e.g., Elizabeth Rawson, *Cicero: A Portrait* (Ithaca, NY: Cornell University Press, 1975), 1–28.

27. Cicero, *Brutus* 139. On Antonius, see especially Cicero, *Brutus* 139–165, *On the Ideal Orator* 2.1–11, *Tusculan Disputations* 2.57; and the full collection of testimony and fragments in Manuwald, *Fragmentary Republican Latin: Oratory, Part 1*, 381–427.

28. See Quintilian, *Orator's Training* 3.6.45, citing Marcus Antonius; and note, e.g., Cicero, *On Invention* 1.10–16. An excellent introduction to Roman rhetorical theory and practice on which I draw is M. L. Clarke, *Rhetoric at Rome: A Historical Survey*, rev. D. H. Berry (London: Routledge, 1996).

29. Cicero, *On Invention* 2.14–15.

30. Cicero, *On Invention* 2.16.

31. Cicero, *On Invention* 2.32, with slightly modified translation from H. M. Hubbell, *Cicero: "De inventione, De optimo genere oratorum, Topica"* (Cambridge, MA: Harvard University Press, 1949).

32. Cicero, *On Invention* 3.38.

33. Cicero, *For Sextus Roscius* 37.
34. Cicero, *For Sextus Roscius* 38.
35. Cicero, *For Sextus Roscius* 39.
36. Cicero, *For Sextus Roscius* 45–46.
37. Cicero, *For Sextus Roscius* 46.
38. Cicero, *For Sextus Roscius* 50.
39. Cicero, *For Sextus Roscius* 55, cf. *For Sextus Roscius* 57; on prosecutors more generally, see Alexander, *Case for the Prosecution*, 7–8; Jean-Michel David, *Le patronat judiciaire au dernier siècle de la République romaine* (Rome: École française de Rome, 1992), 497–569.
40. Cicero, *For Sextus Roscius* 62.
41. Cicero, *For Sextus Roscius* 64–65; the story is also told by Valerius Maximus, *Memorable Deeds and Sayings* 8.1. absol. ("acquitted") 13.
42. Cicero, *For Sextus Roscius* 66.
43. For what follows (Erucius's case for opportunity), see Cicero, *For Sextus Roscius* 74–81.
44. Cicero, *For Sextus Roscius* 77; on the epithet, see, e.g., Richard P. Saller, *Patriarchy, Property, and Death in the Roman Family* (Cambridge, UK: Cambridge University Press, 1994), 147. On slavery in the Roman world, two valuable introductions are K. R. Bradley, *Slavery and Society at Rome* (Cambridge, UK: Cambridge University Press, 1994); and Sandra R. Joshel, *Slavery in the Roman World* (Cambridge, UK: Cambridge University Press, 2010). For the interrogation of slaves under torture, consult Greenidge, *Legal Procedure*, 491–493; Olivia Robinson, "Slaves and the Criminal Law," *Zeitschrift der Savigny-Stiftung für Rechtsgeschichte: Romanistische Abteilung* 98, no. 1 (1981): 213–254; Kathleen M. Coleman, "The Fragility of Evidence: Torture in Ancient Rome," in *Confronting Torture: Essays on the Ethics, Legality, History, and Psychology of Torture Today*, ed. Scott A. Anderson and Martha C. Nussbaum (Chicago: University of Chicago Press, 2018), 105–119.
45. Cicero, *For Sextus Roscius* 78.
46. Cicero, *For Sextus Roscius* 80.
47. Cicero, *For Sextus Roscius* 83.

**Chapter 2: The Money Trail**
1. On the stakes of the trial, see the discussion in Erich Gruen, *Roman Politics and the Criminal Courts, 149–78 B.C.* (Cambridge, MA: Harvard University Press, 1968), 248–278.
2. See especially Quintilian, *Orator's Education* 7.2.9–11, 7.2.18–27. For murder defenses in general, see Andrew M. Riggsby, *Crime and Community in Ciceronian Rome* (Austin: University of Texas Press, 1999), 50–78. Christopher Craig, "Means and Ends of *Indignatio* in Cicero's *Pro Roscio Amerino*," in *Form and Function in Roman Oratory*, ed. D. H. Berry and Andrew Erskine (Cambridge, UK: Cambridge University Press, 2010), 75–91, discusses Cicero's strategy of counteraccusation.
3. Cicero, *For Sextus Roscius* 84.
4. Cicero, *For Sextus Roscius* 84.
5. Cicero, *For Sextus Roscius* 84. On Lucius Cassius, see also Cicero, *On Laws* 3.35, *Philippics* 2.35; Asconius, *Commentaries* 45C. Note that, as is standard, I refer to Asconius by

the pages in the Latin text of A. C. Clark, which is included in R. G. Lewis, ed. and trans., *Asconius: "Commentaries on Speeches by Cicero"* (Oxford, UK: Oxford University Press, 2006).

6. Cicero, *For Sextus Roscius* 84.

7. Cicero, *For Sextus Roscius* 93.

8. Cicero, *For Sextus Roscius* 97.

9. Cicero, *For Sextus Roscius* 100.

10. Cicero, *For Sextus Roscius* 101.

11. Cicero, *For Sextus Roscius* 110.

12. The weaknesses of Cicero's counteraccusation are widely discussed in the scholarly literature, which I draw on here, especially T. E. Kinsey, "Cicero's Case Against Magnus, Capito, and Chrysogonus in the *Pro Sex. Roscio Amerino* and Its Use for the Historian," *L'Antiquité Classique* 49 (1980): 173–190; T. E. Kinsey, "The Case Against Sextus Roscius of Ameria," *L'Antiquité Classique* 54 (1985): 188–196; Andrew R. Dyck, "Evidence and Rhetoric in Cicero's *Pro Roscio Amerino*: The Case Against Sex. Roscius," *Classical Quarterly* 53, no. 1 (2003): 235–246; and Michael C. Alexander, *The Case for the Prosecution in the Ciceronian Era* (Ann Arbor: University of Michigan Press, 2002), 149–172.

13. See especially Dyck, "Evidence and Rhetoric."

14. My discussion of *patria potestas* follows J. A. Crook, *Law and Life of Rome, 90 B.C.– A.D. 212* (Ithaca, NY: Cornell University Press, 1967), 107–113; and Richard P. Saller, *Patriarchy, Property, and Death in the Roman Family* (Cambridge, UK: Cambridge University Press, 1994), 102–180.

15. For instance, L. Iunius Brutus, first consul of the Republic, killed his two sons: e.g., Livy, *History of Rome* 2.2–5; Valerius Maximus, *Memorable Deeds and Sayings* 5.8.1.

16. Valerius Maximus, *Memorable Deeds and Sayings* 5.8.3.

17. Saller, *Patriarchy, Property, and Death*, esp. 102–132.

18. See the works cited above, n. 12.

19. For arguments against the guilt of Cicero's client, see further Andrew Lintott, *Cicero as Evidence: A Historian's Companion* (Oxford, UK: Oxford University Press, 2008), 425–427; and, in depth, R. Seager, "The Guilt of Innocence of Sex. Roscius," *Athenaeum* 95 (2007): 895–910.

20. D. H. Berry, *Cicero: Defence Speeches* (Oxford, UK: Oxford University Press, 2000), 6.

21. Cicero, *On the Ideal Orator* 2.185–234; Friedrich Solmsen, "Cicero's First Speeches: A Rhetorical Analysis," *Transactions and Proceedings of the American Philological Association* 69 (1938): 542–556.

22. Cicero, *For Sextus Roscius* 122.

23. Cicero, *For Sextus Roscius* 124.

24. Cicero, *For Sextus Roscius* 128.

25. Cicero, *For Sextus Roscius* 130–131.

26. Cicero, *For Sextus Roscius* 133.

27. Cicero, *For Sextus Roscius* 133.

28. Cicero, *For Sextus Roscius* 133.

29. Cicero, *For Sextus Roscius* 134.

30. Cicero, *For Sextus Roscius* 135.

31. Cicero, *For Sextus Roscius* 137.

32. Cicero, *On Invention* 1.98; see also his whole discussion, 1.98–109; Michael Winterbottom, "Perorations," in *Cicero the Advocate*, ed. Jonathan Powell and Jeremy Paterson (Oxford, UK: Oxford University Press, 2004), 215–230.

33. Cicero, *For Sextus Roscius* 143.

34. Cicero, *For Sextus Roscius* 150.

35. Cicero, *For Sextus Roscius* 150.

36. Cicero, *For Sextus Roscius* 154.

37. Cicero, *On Duties* 2.51.

38. On Cicero's victory in the trial of Roscius, see Plutarch, *Cicero* 3.6. For Cicero's subsequent contest with Erucius in the trial of Varenus, see Jane W. Crawford, *M. Tullius Cicero, the Fragmentary Speeches: An Edition with Commentary* (Atlanta: Scholars Press, 1994), 7–18.

39. Cicero, *Brutus* 312.

40. Cicero, *For Caecina* 97; Elizabeth Rawson, *Cicero: A Portrait* (Ithaca, NY: Cornell University Press, 1975), 24.

41. Cicero, *Brutus* 313.

42. Cicero, *Brutus* 314. On Cicero's travels, see, in addition to his accounts (*Brutus* 313–316, *On Ends* 5.1–8), Plutarch, *Cicero* 3.5–4.

43. See Cicero's (not unbiased) account at *Brutus* 325–326; also Quintilian, *Orator's Education* 12.10.16–26.

44. Cicero, *Brutus* 316, with translation, slightly modified, from Robert A. Kaster, *Cicero: "Brutus" and "Orator"* (New York: Oxford University Press, 2020); see also 245, 307, 312.

45. See especially J. C. Davies, "Molon's Influence on Cicero," *Classical Quarterly* 18, no. 2 (1968): 303–314; further on Cicero's style, see Andrew R. Dyck, *Cicero: "Pro Sexto Roscio"* (Cambridge, UK: Cambridge University Press, 2010), 12–17.

46. Cicero, *Brutus* 316.

47. Plutarch, *Cicero* 3.6.

48. Cicero, *Letters to Quintus* 3.5.4 (SB 25). Here and throughout the rest of the notes, when I cite a Ciceronian letter, I include a parenthetic reference to the numbering of D. R. Shackleton Bailey in his authoritative editions, which are most conveniently available in the Loeb Classical Library series.

49. Cicero, *Brutus* 201, 317.

50. Cicero, *Brutus* 317.

51. Cicero, *Brutus* 317.

52. My account of Hortensius draws on Andrew R. Dyck, "Rivals into Partners: Hortensius and Cicero," *Historia* 57, no. 2 (2008): 142–173; key sources are Cicero, *Brutus* 301–329, *Against Caecilius* 44–46.

53. L. A. Post, "Ancient Memory Systems," *Classical Weekly* 25, no. 14 (1932): 105–110; for Hortensius at the auction, see Seneca the Elder, *Controversiae* 1 praef. 19.

54. On Cicero's status as new man, see Henriette van der Blom, *Cicero's Role Models: The Political Strategy of a Newcomer* (Oxford, UK: Oxford University Press, 2010).

55. Pliny, *Natural History* 9.172, 14.96; Macrobius, *Saturnalia* 3.13.4–5.

56. For one (unsuccessful) case of Cicero's that is known, his defense of C. Fabricius Scamander in 74 BC, see Chapter 6 below.

57. Plutarch, *Cicero* 20.3, 29.4; on Terentia, and Cicero's family life more generally, see the thorough and sensitive study of Susan Treggiari, *Terentia, Tullia and Publilia: The Women of Cicero's Family* (London: Routledge, 2007).

58. See especially Cicero, *Brutus* 318, *For Plancius* 64–65, *Tusculan Disputations* 5.64; Plutarch, *Cicero* 1.6, 6.

## Chapter 3: Cover-Up

1. Verres's passion: Cicero, *Against Verres* 2.4.1; Verres's house: 2.1.51; Verres at parties and "forgetting": 2.2.36, 2.4.33. In this and the next chapter, translations of the Verrine orations are based closely on those from L. H. G. Greenwood, *Cicero: "The Verrine Orations,"* 2 vols. (Cambridge, MA: Harvard University Press, 1928); for translations of *Against Verres* 1 and 2.5, I am also indebted to D. H. Berry, *Cicero: Political Speeches* (Oxford, UK: Oxford University Press, 2006). I have also relied, sometimes extensively, on major studies by Frank Hewitt Cowles, *Gaius Verres: An Historical Study* (Ithaca, NY: Cornell University Studies, 1917); R. G. C. Levens, *Cicero: "The Fifth Verrine Oration"* (London: Methuen, 1946); Michael C. Alexander, *The Case for the Prosecution in the Ciceronian Era* (Ann Arbor: University of Michigan Press, 2002), 1–53, 255–262; T. N. Mitchell, *Cicero: "Verrines II.1"* (Warminster, UK: Aris and Phillips, 1986); C. E. W. Steel, *Cicero, Rhetoric, and Empire* (Oxford, UK: Oxford University Press, 2001), 22–47; Thomas D. Frazel, "The Composition and Circulation of Cicero's *In Verrem*," *Classical Quarterly* 54, no. 1 (2004): 128–142; Berry, *Cicero: Political Speeches*, 3–12; Andrew Lintott, *Cicero as Evidence: A Historian's Companion* (Oxford, UK: Oxford University Press, 2008), 81–100; Margaret Melanie Miles, *Art as Plunder: The Ancient Origins of Debate About Cultural Property* (New York: Cambridge University Press, 2009); Ann Vasaly, "Cicero, Domestic Politics, and the First Action of the Verrines," *Classical Antiquity* 28, no. 1 (2009): 101–137; and A. M. Stone, "Gaius Verres Troubleshooter," in *Institutions and Ideology in Republican Rome: Speech, Audience and Decision*, ed. Henriette van der Blom, Christa Gray, and Catherine Steel (Cambridge, UK: Cambridge University Press, 2018), 299–313. There is a well-informed and enjoyable re-creation of Verres's trial in Robert Harris's novel *Imperium* (New York: Simon & Schuster, 2006).

2. Cicero, *Against Verres* 2.4.1.

3. For the story of Heius, see Cicero, *Against Verres* 2.4.3–28.

4. Cicero, *Against Verres* 2.4.85; for Sopater's full story, 2.4.84–92.

5. For a recent study of the curule chair of the magistrate, see Kaius Tuori, "Breaking Chairs: *Sella Curulis* in Roman Law, Identity and Memory," *Arctos–Acta Philologica Fennica* 54 (2020): 257–284.

6. On Gaius Claudius Marcellus and the conquest of Syracuse in 211 BC, see, e.g., Miles, *Art as Plunder*, 60–73.

7. Cicero, *Against Verres* 2.4.92.

8. The works on the trial of Verres cited above (n. 1) often deal extensively with extortion and the legislation against it. I have drawn on these, as well as Richard Orlando Jolliffe, *Phases*

*of Corruption in Roman Administration in the Last Half-Century of the Roman Republic* (Menasha, WI: Banta Publishing Company, 1919); Andrew M. Riggsby, *Crime and Community in Ciceronian Rome* (Austin: University of Texas Press, 1999), 120–150; Kit Morrell, *Pompey, Cato, and the Governance of the Roman Empire* (Oxford, UK: Oxford University Press, 2017); and Josiah Osgood, *Rome and the Making of a World State, 150 BCE–20 CE* (Cambridge, UK: Cambridge University Press, 2018), 144–159.

9. Cicero, *Against Verres* 2.2.17–24.

10. Accounts of the trial of Aquillius include Cicero, *Against Verres* 2.5.3, *On the Ideal Orator* 2.194–196; Jon Hall, *Cicero's Use of Judicial Theater* (Ann Arbor: University of Michigan Press, 2014), 18–20; on arguments from the defendant's military conduct, see Riggsby, *Crime and Community*, 146–149.

11. Cicero, *Against Verres* 2.2.154. See further Jonathan R. W. Prag, "Provincials, Patrons, and the Rhetoric of *Repetundae*," in *Community and Communication: Oratory and Politics in Republican Rome*, ed. Catherine Steel and Henriette van der Blom (Oxford, UK: Oxford University Press, 2013), 267–283.

12. Cicero, *Against Verres* 2.2.154.

13. Cicero, *Against Verres* 2.4.38–41.

14. Cicero, *Against Verres* 2.4.42. A good account of the Spartacus War is Barry Strauss, *The Spartacus War* (New York: Simon & Schuster, 2009).

15. Sthenius's travails are recounted by Cicero, *Against Verres* 2.2.83–118.

16. Cicero, *Against Verres* 2.2.96.

17. An example: after acting properly for once, Verres quickly turned back into a hog, as if he had drunk from Circe's goblet (which turned the companions of the Greek hero Odysseus into swine) (Cicero, *Against Caecilius* 57).

18. Verres's early career is the subject of Cicero, *Against Verres* 2.1. I also draw on Cowles, *Gaius Verres*, 1–26; and especially the brilliant account of Stone, "Gaius Verres Troubleshooter."

19. Stone, "Gaius Verres Troubleshooter," with Cicero, *Against Verres* 2.1.58, 2.3.9; and the ancient commentary in Thomas Stangl, *Ciceronis Orationum Scholiastae* (Hildesheim: Georg Olms, 1964), 238.

20. For Verres's achievements, see, e.g., Cicero, *Against Verres* 2.2.48–49, 2.5.1–8, 2.5.52–58; Sallust, *Histories* 4.32M.

21. On the petition of the Sicilians, see especially Cicero, *Against Verres* 2.2.10, 2.2.103, 2.2.146–148.

22. Cicero, *Against Verres* 1.45, with discussion by Morrell, *Pompey, Cato, and the Governance of the Roman Empire*, 22–56.

23. Cicero, *Against Caecilius* 1–4, *Against Verres* 2.2.10, 2.4.138.

24. For Cicero's experience of Sicily, see Cicero, *Tusculan Disputations* 5.64–66, *Against Caecilius*, 2, *Against Verres* 2.2.117–118, 2.3.182, 2.4.74, 2.5.35; Plutarch, *Cicero* 6.1–2.

25. Quintilian, *Orator's Education* 5.13.2, as translated by Alexander, *Case for the Prosecution*, 39. On the role of prosecutors—necessary, but dangerous and even devalued—see Jean-Michel David, *Le patronat judiciaire au dernier siècle de la République romaine* (Rome: École française de Rome, 1992), 497–569.

26. For Caecilius's claim, see *Against Caecilius* 52–58. On the ethics of prosecution, see, e.g., Jonathan Powell and Jeremy Paterson, *Cicero the Advocate* (Oxford, UK: Oxford University Press, 2004), 10–29.

27. Cicero, *Against Caecilius* 24, *Against Verres* 1.17, 1.40; also the ancient commentary in Stangl, *Ciceronis Orationum Scholiastae*, 193.

28. Cicero, *Against Verres* 1.40.

29. Cicero, *Against Verres* 1.40.

30. For a detailed discussion, see Morrell, *Pompey, Cato, and the Governance of the Roman Empire*, 22–56.

31. Cicero, *Against Caecilius* 18. On the procedure of initiating a prosecution, see, e.g., Lintott, *Cicero as Evidence*, 84–85; David, *Le patronat judiciaire*, 498–508.

32. Cicero, *Against Caecilius* 27; more generally, 27–30, 35–43.

33. Cicero, *Against Caecilius* 27–35, 55.

34. Cicero, *Against Caecilius* 23–24, 44–46.

35. Cicero, *Against Verres* 2.1.30. In general, the major source for the preliminaries of Cicero's prosecution is *Against Verres* 1.

36. Cicero, *Against Verres* 1.6, 1.9.

37. Cicero, *Against Verres* 1.6, 2.3.46–47.

38. Pamphilus's story is told by Cicero, *Against Verres* 2.4.32.

39. For more on Tleopolemos and Hieron, the brothers from Cibyra, see Cicero, *Against Verres* 2.3.69, 2.4.30–31, 2.4.96.

40. On Lucius Metellus, see especially Cicero, *Against Verres* 2.2.62–64, 2.2.138–140, 2.2.160–164, 2.3.122–128, 2.3.152–160, 2.4.147–149, 2.5.129.

41. My account of Syracuse follows Cicero, *Against Verres* 2.4.115–121.

42. Cicero, *Against Verres* 2.4.122–132.

43. The account of Cicero's investigation at Syracuse, including his confrontation with Lucius Metellus, is from *Against Verres* 2.4.132–151.

44. Cicero, *Against Verres* 1.16, 2.1.18. On the procedure, and the likely size of the Verrine jury, see Berry, *Cicero: Political Speeches*, 7; Lintott, *Cicero as Evidence*, 87–88.

45. Cicero, *Against Verres* 2.1.18, 2.3.97.

46. This was separate from the oath jurors swore directly before giving their verdict. On the jurors' oaths, see Gérard Freyburger, *Fides: Étude sémantique et religieuse depuis les origines jusqu'à l'époque augustéenne* (Paris: Belles Lettres, 1986), 213–217.

47. Cicero, *Against Verres* 1.19.

48. Cicero, *Against Verres* 1.17; more generally, 1.16–30.

49. Cicero, *Against Verres* 1.22–23.

50. See the list of names provided by Cicero, *Against Verres* 1.29–30.

51. For the prosecution's strategy, see Cicero, *Against Verres* 1.31–32.

52. Cicero, *Against Verres* 1.27, trans. Berry, *Cicero: Political Speeches*.

**Chapter 4: Heart of Darkness**

1. For example, Cicero, *Against Caecilius* 41, *For Cluentius* 51.

2. Cicero, *Against Verres* 2.5.128.

3. T. N. Mitchell, *Cicero: "Verrines II.1"* (Warminster, UK: Aris and Phillips, 1986), 174.

4. Cicero, *Against Verres* 1.47.

5. Cicero, *Against Verres* 1.55.

6. In approaching the first stage of Cicero's prosecution as a spectacle, I am much influenced by the superb article of Ann Vasaly, "Cicero, Domestic Politics, and the First Action of the Verrines," *Classical Antiquity* 28, no. 1 (2009): 101–137.

7. Michael C. Alexander, "Hortensius' Speech in Defense of Verres," *Phoenix* 30, no. 1 (1976): 46–53. Also useful is Donald Murray Ayers, "The Speeches of Cicero's Opponents: Studies in *Pro Roscio Amerino, In Verrem*, and *Pro Murena*" (PhD diss., Princeton University, 1950), 24–88.

8. Cicero, *Against Verres* 1.55.

9. Quintilian, *Orator's Education* 5.7.1. My account of witnesses here draws on Quintilian's fascinating chapter (5.7), along with A. H. J. Greenidge, *The Legal Procedure of Cicero's Time* (Oxford, UK: Clarendon Press, 1901), 481–491; Michael C. Alexander, *The Case for the Prosecution in the Ciceronian Era* (Ann Arbor: University of Michigan Press, 2002), 44–51; J. G. F. Powell, "Court Procedure and Rhetorical Strategy in Cicero," in *Form and Function in Roman Oratory*, ed. D. H. Berry and Andrew Erskine (Cambridge, UK: Cambridge University Press, 2010), 21–36; and Elizabeth A. Meyer, "Evidence and Argument: The Truth of Prestige and Its Performance," in *The Oxford Handbook of Roman Law and Society*, ed. Paul J. du Plessis, Clifford Ando, and Kaius Tuori (Oxford, UK: Oxford University Press, 2016), 270–282.

10. Greenidge, *Legal Procedure*, 273–274, 300, 481; Gérard Freyburger, *Fides: Étude sémantique et religieuse depuis les origines jusqu'à l'époque augustéenne* (Paris: Belles Lettres, 1986), 218–222.

11. Alexander, *Case for the Prosecution*, 255–262, usefully lists the witnesses and documents; I follow Alexander's argument (26–28) on the likely order in which Cicero called the witnesses.

12. See Andrew M. Riggsby, *Crime and Community in Ciceronian Rome* (Austin: University of Texas Press, 1999), 136–139.

13. Verres's career prior to his governorship of Sicily is the subject of Cicero, *Against Verres* 2.1.

14. Cicero, *Against Verres* 2.1.45, 49–52.

15. Cicero, *Against Verres* 2.1.62–85.

16. On Dolabella and his trial, see Erich S. Gruen, "The Dolabellae and Sulla," *American Journal of Philology* 87, no. 4 (1966): 385–399.

17. Cicero, *Against Verres* 2.1.46, 2.1.72–77.

18. Cicero, *Against Verres* 2.1.91–94.

19. Cicero, *Against Verres* 2.1.129–154.

20. Cicero, *Against Verres* 2.1.136.

21. Cicero, *Orator* 131.

22. Cicero, *Against Verres* 2.1.71.

23. Cicero, *Against Verres* 2.1.20.

24. Quintilian, *Orator's Education* 6.3.98; also see Plutarch, *Cicero* 7.8.

25. Cicero, *Against Verres* 2.2.17–24.

26. See especially Cicero, *Against Verres* 2.2.102–105.

27. See, e.g., Cicero, *Against Verres* 2.2.80, 2.2.118–119.

28. Sale of offices: e.g., Cicero, *Against Verres* 2.2.120. Malfeasance in tax system: e.g., 2.2.120, 2.3.73. On the evidence of cities, see Greenidge, *Legal Procedure*, 489–490.

29. Cicero, *Against Verres* 2.2.156.

30. Cicero, *Against Verres* 2.3.31, 2.3.105–108.

31. Cicero, *Against Verres* 2.4.3–28.

32. Cicero, *Against Verres* 2.4.27.

33. Cicero, *Against Verres* 2.5, deals with Verres and the pirates; for the raid on Syracuse, see especially 2.5.80–135; Orosius, *History Against the Pagans* 6.3.5.

34. They were Phylarchus of Haluntium and Phalacrus of Centuripae; see Cicero, *Against Verres* 2.5.90, 116, 122.

35. For this and what follows, see Cicero, *Against Verres* 2.5.139–170.

36. Cicero, *Against Verres* 2.5.158, 2.5.163, 2.5.165.

37. Cicero, *Against Verres* 2.5.162.

38. John 19:19.

39. Cicero, *Against Verres* 2.5.163.

40. Cicero, *Against Verres* 2.4.33.

41. Cicero, *Brutus* 319–324; see the next chapter for more on Cicero's career after 70 BC.

42. An excellent treatment of this issue is Thomas D. Frazel, "The Composition and Circulation of Cicero's *In Verrem*," *Classical Quarterly* 54, no. 1 (2004): 128–142.

43. Cicero, *Against Caecilius* 27, trans. Greenwood, *Cicero: "The Verrine Orations"*; see also *On Invention* 1.104.

44. Cicero, *Against Verres* 2.5.80–91.

45. For the tax reform, see A. M. Stone, "Gaius Verres Troubleshooter," in *Institutions and Ideology in Republican Rome: Speech, Audience and Decision*, ed. Henriette van der Blom, Christa Gray, and Catherine Steel (Cambridge, UK: Cambridge University Press, 2018), 299–313; Cicero explains the taxation system in *Against Verres* 2.3, on which see Frank Hewitt Cowles, *Gaius Verres: An Historical Study* (Ithaca, NY: Cornell University Studies, 1917), 59–94.

46. Stone, "Gaius Verres Troubleshooter," 309.

47. Cicero, *Against Verres* 2.3.44–46, 2.3.122–128.

48. Plutarch, *Cicero* 8.1.

49. The ship: Cicero, *Against Verres* 2.5.44. Stripping of Verres's house: Cicero, *Against Verres* 2.1.50–51. Verres in exile: Pliny, *Natural History* 34.6; Seneca, *Suasoriae* 6.24; Lactantius, *Divine Institutes* 2.4.37.

50. My discussion here is indebted to Jonathan R. W. Prag, "Provincials, Patrons, and the Rhetoric of *Repetundae*," in *Community and Communication: Oratory and Politics in Republican Rome*, ed. Catherine Steel and Henriette van der Blom (Oxford, UK: Oxford University Press, 2013), 267–283; and Kit Morrell, *Pompey, Cato, and the Governance of the Roman Empire* (Oxford, UK: Oxford University Press, 2017), 36–49, 129–152.

51. Cicero, *Against Verres* 1.41.

**Chapter 5: The Wine Road**

1. For travel, I draw on Lionel Casson, *Travel in the Ancient World* (Baltimore: Johns Hopkins University Press, 1974), 163–218. The story of the Good Samaritan is told at Luke 10:29–37.

2. The major source is Cicero's partly preserved speech *For Fonteius*. Throughout this chapter, I make much use of the excellent edition by Andrew R. Dyck, *Marcus Tullius Cicero: "Speeches on Behalf of Marcus Fonteius and Marcus Aemilius Scaurus"* (Oxford, UK: Oxford University Press, 2012) (hereafter Dyck, *Cicero: "On Behalf of Marcus Fonteius"*); also Michael C. Alexander, *The Case for the Prosecution in the Ciceronian Era* (Ann Arbor: University of Michigan Press, 2002), 59–77. There is also a helpful commentary on the speech in Guido Clemente, *I romani nella Gallia meridionale, II–I sec. a. C.: politica ed economia nell'età dell'imperialismo* (Bologna: Pàtron, 1974). My translations of *For Fonteius* owe a great debt to those of Dyck.

3. Livy, *History of Rome* 5.39–48; Plutarch, *Camillus* 20–28.

4. On Fonteius's career, with the chronology I follow here, see Dyck, *Cicero: "On Behalf of Marcus Fonteius,"* 11–12.

5. On Transalpine Gaul, see Dyck, *Cicero: "On Behalf of Marcus Fonteius,"* 9–10; Clemente, *I Romani nella Gallia meridionale*; Charles Ebel, *Transalpine Gaul: The Emergence of a Roman Province* (Leiden: Brill, 1976); A. L. F. Rivet, *Gallia Narbonensis: Southern France in Roman Times: With a Chapter on Alpes Maritimae* (London: B. T. Batsford, 1988); Greg Woolf, *Becoming Roman: The Origins of Provincial Civilization in Gaul* (Cambridge, UK: Cambridge University Press, 1998).

6. In addition to the works cited in the previous note, see Charles Ebel, "Pompey's Organization of Transalpina," *Phoenix* 29, no. 4 (1975): 358–373.

7. Cicero, *For Fonteius* 13.

8. Cicero, *For Fonteius* 16, 17–18.

9. For Indutiomarus, see Cicero, *For Fonteius* 27, 29, 36, 46. On the prosecutors (mentioned in *For Fonteius* 2, 19, 36, frag. 13), see Dyck, *Cicero: "On Behalf of Marcus Fonteius,"* 13; Alexander, *Case for the Prosecution*, 62–63.

10. Dyck, *Cicero: "On Behalf of Marcus Fonteius,"* 12–13; Alexander, *Case for the Prosecution*, 59–77.

11. Cicero, *For Fonteius* 37, 40.

12. See, e.g., Cicero, *For Caelius* 6, 38, cf. *For Fonteius* 37.

13. Cicero, *For Fonteius* 1–5.

14. Matthew 5:41.

15. Cicero, *For Fonteius* 17.

16. Cicero, *For Fonteius* 19.

17. Athenaeus, *Learned Banqueters* 4.151e–152f, quoting the traveler Poseidonius; see also Julius Caesar, *Gallic War* 2.15.4, 4.2.6; Diodorus, *Library of History* 5.26. For wine consumption in Gaul, I draw especially on André Tchernia, "Italian Wine in Gaul at the End of the Republic," in *Trade in the Ancient Economy*, ed. Peter Garnsey, Keith Hopkins, and C. R.

Whittaker (Berkeley: University of California Press, 1983), 87–104; Woolf, *Becoming Roman*, 174–185.

18. Cicero, *For Fonteius* 19, with useful discussions by Dyck, *Cicero: "On Behalf of Marcus Fonteius,"* 52–54; Alexander, *Case for the Prosecution*, 70–71; Clemente, *I Romani nella Gallia meridionale*, 130–137; and Ella Hermon, "Pouvoir et revenus en Transalpine au Ier siècle av. J.-C.: Un aspect du rapport centre-périphérie," *Revue des Études Anciennes* 97, no. 3/4 (1995): 565–574.

19. Cicero, *For Fonteius* 20.

20. Cicero, *For Fonteius* frag. 10.

21. For this and the next charge, see Cicero, *For Fonteius* 20.

22. Cicero, *For Fonteius* 1–5.

23. Cicero, *For Fonteius* 17–19.

24. For this and what follows, see Alexander, *Case for the Prosecution*, 67–70.

25. Cicero, *For Fonteius* 20.

26. Cicero, *For Fonteius* 12.

27. Cicero, *For Fonteius* 12–13.

28. Cicero, *For Fonteius* 14–15.

29. Cicero *For Fonteius* 14.

30. For this and the following remarks on witnesses, see respectively Cicero, *For Fonteius* 21, 23, 24, 22.

31. For this and the following remarks, see respectively Cicero, *For Fonteius* 27, 29, 33. On the stereotype of the Gauls, see Benjamin Isaac, *The Invention of Racism in Classical Antiquity* (Princeton, NJ: Princeton University Press, 2004), 411–426.

32. For this discussion of oaths, see Cicero, *For Fonteius* 30–31 (quotation from 31).

33. Miranda Aldhouse-Green, *Dying for the Gods: Human Sacrifice in Iron Age and Roman Europe* (Stroud, UK: Tempus, 2001), 97–106, 150–151. For the Roman view of human sacrifice, and the Romans' own practice of ritual murder, see Celia E. Schultz, "The Romans and Ritual Murder," *Journal of the American Academy of Religion* 78, no. 2 (2010): 516–541.

34. Cicero, *For Fonteius* 43.

35. For this and what follows, Cicero, *For Fonteius* 44–46.

36. On the theatricality of perorations, see especially Quintilian, *Orator's Education* 6.1.30–31; Jon Hall, *Cicero's Use of Judicial Theater* (Ann Arbor: University of Michigan Press, 2014), 18–20, 64–98, 144–152.

37. For this and what follows, see Cicero, *For Fonteius* 46–48 (with quotations from 48).

38. Cicero, *On Invention* 1.109.

39. Cicero, *For Fonteius* 49.

40. For fuller discussions, see Dyck, *Cicero: "On Behalf of Marcus Fonteius,"* 15–16; Alexander, *Case for the Prosecution*, 76–77.

41. D. L. Stockton, *Cicero: A Political Biography* (London: Oxford University Press, 1971), 49–51; D. H. Berry, *"Equester ordo tuus est*: Did Cicero Win His Cases Because of His Support for the Equites?," *Classical Quarterly* 53, no. 1 (2003): 228–229.

42. Quintilian, *Orator's Education* 5.7.5; on the strategy, see, e.g., Alexander David Kurke, "Theme and Adversarial Presentation in Cicero's 'Pro Flacco'" (PhD diss., University

of Michigan, 1989), 163–177; Ann Vasaly, *Representations: Images of the World in Ciceronian Oratory* (Berkeley: University of California Press, 1993), 191–217; Andrew M. Riggsby, *Crime and Community in Ciceronian Rome* (Austin: University of Texas Press, 1999), 129–136.

43. Michel Rambaud, "Le *Pro Fonteio* et l'assimilation des Gaulois de la Transalpine," in *Mélanges de littérature et d'épigraphie latines, d'histoire ancienne et d'archéologie: hommage à la mémoire de Pierre Wuilleumier* (Paris: Belles Lettres, 1980), 301–316.

44. For C. Calpurnius Piso, see Cicero, *Letters to Atticus* 1.13.2 (SB 13); Cassius Dio, *Roman History* 36.37.2.

45. Cicero, *On Duties* 2.51, with translation slightly modified from P. G. Walsh: *Cicero: "On Obligations"* (Oxford, UK: Oxford University Press, 2000). On the ethics of Roman advocacy, see further Jean-Michel David, *Le patronat judiciaire au dernier siècle de la République romaine* (Rome: École française de Rome, 1992), 497–654; Jonathan Powell and Jeremy Paterson, *Cicero the Advocate* (Oxford, UK: Oxford University Press, 2004), 19–29.

46. Powell and Paterson, *Cicero the Advocate*, 26.

47. Berry, "*Equester ordo tuus est*," 226.

48. Berry.

49. Powell and Paterson, *Cicero the Advocate*, 15; D. H. Berry, *Cicero: "Pro P. Sulla Oratio"* (Cambridge, UK: Cambridge University Press, 1996), 30–33, 39–42. Cicero's boast is at *Philippics* 2.40. For a more thorough discussion of Cicero's finances, see Israel Shatzman, *Senatorial Wealth and Roman Politics* (Brussels: Latomus, 1975), 403–425.

50. On senators' properties, and Cicero's in particular, I draw on Elizabeth Rawson, *Roman Culture and Society: Collected Papers* (Oxford, UK: Clarendon Press, 1991), 204–222; D. R. Shackleton Bailey, *Cicero* (New York: Scribner's, 1971), esp. 20–26; and Elizabeth Rawson, *Cicero: A Portrait* (Ithaca, NY: Cornell University Press, 1975), esp. 20–26.

51. Cicero, *Letters to Atticus* 16.6.2 (SB 414).

52. D. R. Shackleton Bailey, *Cicero's Letters to Atticus*, 7 vols. (Cambridge, UK: Cambridge University Press, 1965–1971), is an outstanding edition, with translation, on which I have relied much in this book, especially in my translations, along with his translations *Cicero: Letters to Friends*, 3 vols. (Cambridge, MA: Harvard University Press, 2001); and *Cicero: "Letters to Quintus and Brutus," "Letter Fragments," "Letter to Octavian," "Invectives," "Handbook of Electioneering"* (Cambridge, MA: Harvard University Press, 2002). On Atticus, see also the ancient biography of Cornelius Nepos, available in a good edition by Nicholas Horsfall, *Cornelius Nepos: A Selection, Including the Lives of Cato and Atticus* (Oxford, UK: Clarendon Press, 1989); and Kathryn Welch, "T. Pomponius Atticus: A Banker in Politics?" *Historia* 45, no. 4 (1996): 450–471.

53. Cornelius Nepos, *Atticus* 1–5, 13–14; Shackleton Bailey, *Cicero's Letters to Atticus*, 1:3–4.

54. See Cicero, *Letters to Atticus* 1.6 (SB 2); Rawson, *Cicero*, 47–51.

55. Cicero, *Letters to Atticus* 1.4.3 (SB 9).

56. Cicero, *Letters to Atticus* 1.10.4 (SB 6).

57. Cicero, *On the Ideal Orator* 2.10; on Cicero's family life in these years, see Rawson, *Cicero*, 47; Susan Treggiari, *Terentia, Tullia and Publilia: The Women of Cicero's Family* (London: Routledge, 2007), 40–44.

58. Cicero, *Letters to Atticus* 1.5.8 (SB 1).

59. Cicero, *Letters to Atticus* 1.10.6 (SB 6).

60. Cicero, *On the Command of Gnaeus Pompey* 2.

**Chapter 6: Poison Was Detected**

1. Throughout this chapter, I draw on William Ramsay, *Cicero: "Pro Cluentio,"* 3rd ed., ed. George G. Ramsay (Oxford, UK: Clarendon Press, 1876); W. Yorke Fausset, *M. Tullii Ciceronis Pro A. Cluentio Oratio* (London: Rivington's, 1887); W. Peterson, *The Speech of Cicero in Defense of Cluentius* (London: Macmillan, 1895); Gabriele S. Hoenigswald, "The Murder Charges in Cicero's *Pro Cluentio,*" *Transactions and Proceedings of the American Philological Association* 93 (1962): 109–123; Philippe Moreau, "Structures de parenté et d'alliance à Larinum d'après le *Pro Cluentio,*" in *Les "bourgeoisies" municipales italiennes aux IIe et Ier siècles av. J.-C.,* ed. M. Cébeillac-Gervasoni (Paris: Éditions du Centre national de la recherche scientifique, 1983), 99–123; Andrew M. Riggsby, *Crime and Community in Ciceronian Rome* (Austin: University of Texas Press, 1999), 66–78; Michael C. Alexander, *The Case for the Prosecution in the Ciceronian Era* (Ann Arbor: University of Michigan Press, 2002), 173–188; and Elizabeth C. Robinson, *Urban Transformation in Ancient Molise: The Integration of Larinum into the Roman State* (New York: Oxford University Press, 2021). My translations and paraphrases of *For Cluentius* are much indebted to H. Grose Hodge, *Cicero: The Speeches ("Pro Lege Manilia," "Pro Caecina," "Pro Cluentio," "Pro Rabirio," "Perduellionis")* (London: William Heinemann, 1927).

2. Cicero, *For Cluentius* 18.

3. Cicero, *For Cluentius* 18.

4. On Larinum, see the excellent study of literary and archaeological sources in Robinson, *Urban Transformation in Ancient Molise*; I also draw on Alexander, *Case for the Prosecution,* 176–177.

5. Note especially Cicero, *For Cluentius* 161, 198.

6. Cicero, *For Cluentius* 11–18.

7. Cicero, *For Cluentius* 19–21.

8. Cicero, *For Cluentius* 22. On Roman wills and how they were written and witnessed, see the fine study of Edward J. Champlin, *Final Judgments: Duty and Emotion in Roman Wills, 200 B.C.–A.D. 250* (Berkeley: University of California Press, 1991), esp. 64–81. On the distinctive documentary form of tablets, see Elizabeth A. Meyer, *Legitimacy and Law in the Roman World: Tabulae in Roman Belief and Practice* (Cambridge, UK: Cambridge University Press, 2004).

9. Cicero, *For Cluentius* 23–25. Note the inscription found in Larinum calling Sulla "patron": Robinson, *Urban Transformation of Ancient Molise,* 209.

10. Cicero, *For Cluentius* 26. Oppianicus's marriages are discussed by Moreau, "Structures de parenté et d'alliance."

11. Cicero, *For Cluentius* 27–29.

12. Cicero, *For Cluentius* 30.

13. Cicero, *For Cluentius* 31–32.

14. Cicero, *For Cluentius* 33–35.

15. The story of Asuvius is told at Cicero, *For Cluentius* 36–39. An excellent short story based on the Ciceronian account can be found in Steven Saylor, *The House of the Vestals: The Investigations of Gordianus the Finder* (New York: St. Martin's Press, 1997), 43–65.

16. Cicero, *For Cluentius* 40–42. On salesmen of medicine, see Laurence M. V. Totelin, "Pharmakopōlai: A Re-evaluation of the Sources," in *Popular Medicine in Graeco-Roman Antiquity*, ed. W. V. Harris (Leiden: Brill, 2016), 65–85; on Roman medicine and doctors in general, Elizabeth D. Rawson, *Intellectual Life in the Late Roman Republic* (Baltimore: Johns Hopkins University Press, 1985), 30, 84–86, 170–184.

17. Livy, *History of Rome* 8.18, discussed by Dan-El Padilla Peralta, "Pharmapolitics and the Early Roman Expansion: Gender, Slavery, and Ecology in 331 BCE," *Classical Antiquity* 42, no. 1 (2023): 159–194. Other works on the history of poisoning I draw on in this section are David B. Kaufman, "Poisons and Poisoning Among the Romans," *Classical Philology* 27, no. 2 (1932): 156–167; Terence McLaughlin, *The Coward's Weapon* (London: Hale, 1980); Bev-Lorraine True and Robert H. Dreisbach, *Dreisbach's Handbook of Poisoning: Prevention, Diagnosis, and Treatment*, 13th ed. (Boca Raton, FL: CRC Press, 2002); Cheryl L. Golden, "The Role of Poison in Roman Society" (PhD diss., University of North Carolina, 2005); Deborah Blum, *The Poisoner's Handbook: Murder and the Birth of Forensic Medicine in Jazz Age New York* (New York: Penguin, 2010); Evelyn Höbenreich and Giunio Rizzelli, "Poisoning in Ancient Rome: The Legal Framework, the Nature of Poisons, and Gender Stereotypes," in *History of Toxicology and Environmental Health: Toxicology in Antiquity II*, ed. Philip Wexler (London: Elsevier, 2014): 42–51; and Kathryn Harkup, *A Is for Arsenic: The Poisons of Agatha Christie* (London: Bloomsbury Sigma, 2015).

18. Livy, *History of Rome* 39.41.

19. Livy, *History of Rome* 40.37, 40.43.

20. Quintilian, *Orator's Education* 5.10.25.

21. McLaughlin, *Coward's Weapon*, 37–52.

22. Cassius Dio, *Roman History* 67.11.6.

23. For poison lore and the courts, see Golden, "Role of Poison," 107–137, esp. 136–137.

24. For the development of law against poisonings, see, e.g., Riggsby, *Crime and Community*, 50–55.

25. Cicero, *For Cluentius* 43–45.

26. Cicero, *For Cluentius* 46–47.

27. Cicero, *For Cluentius* 47, 49, 50, 53.

28. On the trial of Scamander, see Cicero, *For Cluentius* 49–55. I discuss Roman consular elections in the following chapter.

29. On the trial of Fabricius, see Cicero, *For Cluentius* 56–59.

30. On the trial of Oppianicus senior and its aftermath, see Cicero, *For Cluentius* 59–87.

31. Alexander, *Case for the Prosecution*, 184–185. On the implications for Cicero's strategy in *For Cluentius*, see also Riggsby, *Crime and Community*, 66–78.

32. Some discussions making this point are Peterson, *Speech of Cicero in Defense of Cluentius*, ix–xxix; Hoenigswald, "Murder Charges"; and Alexander, *Case for the Prosecution*, 178–181.

33. Cicero, *For Cluentius* 77.

34. This has been frequently pointed out, e.g., Peterson, *Speech of Cicero in Defense of Cluentius*, xxi–xxix.

35. Cicero, *For Cluentius* 136–138.

36. Cicero, *Against Verres* 1.39; note also 1.29, 2.1.157, 2.2.78.

37. Cicero, *For Cluentius* 117–134. And for the penalties other jurors paid, see *For Cluentius* 88–116.

38. On Attius's oratory, see Cicero, *Brutus* 271. On his case, see, in addition to *For Cluentius* 161–166, 169, Hoenigswald, "Murder Charges"; Alexander, *Case for the Prosecution*, 173–188.

39. For a discussion of Attius's argument, see Alexander, *Case for the Prosecution*, 181–187; on the statute, see Riggsby, *Crime and Community*, 52–54.

40. For what follows, see Cicero, *For Cluentius* 161–164.

41. Cicero, *For Cluentius* 143–160.

42. Cicero, *For Cluentius* 157–158.

43. Cicero, *For Cluentius* 165.

44. Cicero, *For Cluentius* 166–168.

45. For what follows, see Cicero, *For Cluentius* 169–194.

46. See, e.g., *Rhetorica ad Herennium* 2.10; Cicero, *For Milo* 60.

47. Cicero, *For Cluentius* 187.

48. Cicero, *For Cluentius* 195–202.

49. Cicero, *For Cluentius* 202.

50. Quintilian, *Orator's Education* 2.17.21.

51. D. H. Berry, "*Equester ordo tuus est*: Did Cicero Win His Cases Because of His Support for the Equites?," *Classical Quarterly* 53, no. 1 (2003): 229–230.

## Chapter 7: Conspiracy

1. On the meeting, see Cicero, *Against Catiline* 1.8–10, *For Sulla* 52; Sallust, *War Against Catiline* 27.2–28.3 (also 17, for an earlier meeting); Cassius Dio, *Roman History* 37.32.3–37.33.1. Scholarship on the conspiracy of Catiline is extensive. Among major studies, I have drawn on the superb account in D. H. Berry, *Cicero's "Catilinarians"* (Oxford, UK: Oxford University Press, 2020); Gianpaolo Urso, *Catilina: Le faux populiste* (Bordeaux: Ausonius, 2019); John T. Ramsey, *Sallust's "Bellum Catilinae,"* 2nd ed. (Oxford, UK: Oxford University Press, 2007); and Andrew R. Dyck, *Cicero: "Catilinarians"* (Cambridge, UK: Cambridge University Press, 2008). Standard biographies of Cicero have important discussions, e.g., H. J. Haskell, *This Was Cicero: Modern Politics in a Roman Toga* (New York: Alfred A. Knopf, 1942), 151–198; D. L. Stockton, *Cicero: A Political Biography* (London: Oxford University Press, 1971), 64–142; Elizabeth Rawson, *Cicero: A Portrait* (Ithaca, NY: Cornell University Press, 1975), 60–88; and Kathryn Tempest, *Cicero: Politics and Persuasion in Ancient Rome* (London: Bloomsbury, 2011), 71–100. Also helpful has been the annotated translation of Cicero's Catilinarian speeches in D. H. Berry, *Cicero: Political Speeches* (Oxford, UK: Oxford University Press, 2006). In Josiah Osgood, *Uncommon Wrath: How Caesar and Cato's Deadly Rivalry Destroyed the Roman Republic* (New York: Basic Books, 2022), 79–99, I give an account, focused on the roles of Caesar and Cato, from which I occasionally borrow here.

2. For the details mentioned here, see especially Cicero, *Against Catiline* 1.10–11, 16, 21.

3. These elections, in which Cicero competed for the consulship, are discussed in most of the works mentioned above (n. 1). A major source is a campaign handbook written by Cicero's younger brother, for which see the superb edition of W. Jeffrey Tatum, *Quintus Cicero: "A Brief Handbook on Canvassing for Office"* (Oxford, UK: Oxford University Press, 2018). My account of canvassing for office, as well as Cicero's own campaign, relies heavily on Tatum's thorough introduction (1–109). Work by Lily Ross Taylor is of enduring value, e.g., her *Party Politics in the Age of Caesar* (Berkeley: University of California Press, 1949), esp. 50–75; and *Roman Voting Assemblies from the Hannibalic War to the Dictatorship of Caesar* (Ann Arbor: University of Michigan Press, 1966).

4. Taylor, *Roman Voting Assemblies*, on pages 4 and 5, includes a helpful table summarizing the different assemblies; see also Josiah Osgood, *Rome and the Making of a World State, 150 BCE–20 CE* (Cambridge, UK: Cambridge University Press, 2018), 33.

5. On the timing of consular elections, see the important study of John T. Ramsey, "The Date of the Consular Elections in 63 and the Inception of Catiline's Conspiracy," *Harvard Studies in Classical Philology* 110 (2020): 213–269.

6. Cicero, *For Murena* 35.

7. Tatum, *Quintus Cicero: "A Brief Handbook on Canvassing,"* 17–19.

8. Quintus Cicero, *Brief Handbook on Canvassing* 3.

9. On canvassing, see Tatum, *Quintus Cicero: "A Brief Handbook on Canvassing,"* 19–49.

10. Quintus Cicero, *Brief Handbook on Canvassing* 38, 50.

11. Tatum, *Quintus Cicero: "A Brief Handbook on Canvassing,"* 43–45.

12. Cicero, *Against Catiline* 3.16. On the seven competitors, see Asconius, *Commentaries* 82–83C; for Quintus's discussion of the field, see *Brief Handbook on Canvassing* 7–8.

13. On Gaius Antonius, see especially Quintus Cicero, *Brief Handbook on Canvassing* 8, with the notes of Tatum; also Asconius, *Commentaries* 82–94C passim.

14. Quintus Cicero, *Brief Handbook on Canvassing* 10. On Catiline's early life, see especially 9–10, with the notes of Tatum; Asconius, *Commentaries* 82–94C passim; Sallust, *War Against Catiline* 5.1–8, 14–16; and the general works cited above (n. 1).

15. The account of the political situation that follows is much indebted to Stockton, *Cicero*, 64–83; see also Tatum, *Quintus Cicero: "A Brief Handbook on Canvassing,"* 91–92, 102–105.

16. For Cato's and Caesar's actions in 64 BC and the backlash against Sulla, see Osgood, *Uncommon Wrath*, 59–77.

17. Asconius, *Commentaries* 73C; Cicero, *For Cluentius* 94–95.

18. For the prosecution of the consuls-elect of 66 (P. Cornelius Sulla and P. Autronius Sulla), see, e.g., Cicero, *For Sulla* 1, 49–50, 88–91; Sallust, *War Against Catiline* 18.2; Asconius, *Commentaries* 75C, 88C; Cassius Dio, *Roman History* 36.44.3. Many details on consular elections, as well as major criminal prosecutions of the 60s and 50s BC, can be found in Erich S. Gruen, *The Last Generation of the Roman Republic* (Berkeley: University of California Press, 1974).

19. A valuable source on Roman views of electoral bribery (*ambitus*), including Cato's attitudes, is Cicero's defense *For Murena*, discussed below (for Cato, see especially *For Murena* 51, 62, 67–77); on the various legislative efforts, see, e.g., Gruen, *Last Generation*, 212–224.

20. The extent of the credit crisis, which peaked in 63 BC, is attested to by brief but revealing mentions in Cicero, *On Duties* 2.84; Sallust, *War Against Catiline* 33.2; Valerius Maximus, *Memorable Deeds and Sayings* 4.8.3.

21. Quintus Cicero, *Brief Handbook on Canvassing* 8, 55–57.

22. On the proposed law, and the veto of Q. Mucius Orestinus, see Asconius, *Commentaries* 83C, 85–86C.

23. A full text can be found in R. G. Lewis, ed. and trans., *Asconius: "Commentaries on Speeches by Cicero"* (Oxford, UK: Oxford University Press, 2006), with helpful commentary, on which I draw.

24. Quoted by Asconius, *Commentaries* 83C. My translations of Cicero's speech borrow from Lewis, *Asconius.*

25. Asconius, *Commentaries* 83C; for a different view, see A. M. Stone, "A House of Notoriety: An Episode in the Campaign for the Consulate in 64 B.C.," *Classical Quarterly* 48, no. 2 (1998): 487–491.

26. The quotation and citations from Cicero's speech here are from Asconius, *Commentaries* 86C, 88C, 90C, 91C. On speeches in the Senate, see John T. Ramsey, "Roman Senatorial Oratory," in *A Companion to Roman Rhetoric*, ed. William Dominik and Jon Hall (Malden, MA: Wiley-Blackwell, 2007), 122–135.

27. Quoted by Asconius, *Commentaries* 87C.

28. Quoted by Asconius, *Commentaries* 92C. Many modern scholars have been skeptical of this "first Catilinarian conspiracy," on which see, e.g., Berry, *Cicero's "Catilinarians,"* 15–17.

29. Quoted by Asconius, *Commentaries* 93C.

30. Quintilian, *Orator's Education* 9.3.94; Asconius, *Commentaries* 93–94C.

31. For further evaluation of Cicero's success, see Tatum, *Quintus Cicero: "A Brief Handbook on Canvassing,"* 101–105; on the vote electing him, see Cicero, *On Duties* 2.59, *Against Piso* 3.

32. See Cicero's request in *Letters to Atticus* 1.2 (SB 11).

33. On the birth of Marcus junior, see Cicero, *Letters to Atticus* 1.2.1 (SB 11).

34. Cassius Dio, *Roman History* 37.25.3–4; Cicero, *On the Agrarian Law* 2.11–12, with valuable discussion in A. M. Stone, "Was Sallust a Liar? A Problem in Modern History," in *Ancient History in a Modern University: Early Christianity, Late Antiquity, and Beyond*, ed. T. W. Hillard, R. A. Kearsley, C. E. V. Nixon, and A. M. Nobbs (Grand Rapids, MI: Eerdmans, 1998), 230–243.

35. The major source for Rullus's proposals is Cicero's three speeches on the law, for which see the edition of Gesine Manuwald, ed. and trans., *Cicero: "Agrarian Speeches"* (Oxford, UK: Oxford University Press, 2018). For Rullus, see Cicero, *On the Agrarian Law* 2.13.

36. Cicero, *On the Agrarian Law* 1.26, 2.103; Sallust, *War Against Catiline* 26.4; Plutarch, *Cicero* 12.4–6.

37. Cicero, *For Sulla* 62–66.

38. Cicero, *On the Agrarian Law* 2. For more detailed accounts of Cicero's consulship, which I must compress, see, e.g., Stockton, *Cicero*, 84–142; Rawson, *Cicero*, 60–88.

39. Catiline's trial: Asconius, *Commentaries* 91C; Cassius Dio, *Roman History* 37.10.3. His financial troubles, after the elections of 63 BC: Cicero, *Against Catiline* 1.14; Sallust, *War Against Catiline* 35.3.

40. Cicero, *For Murena* 43–47; Gruen, *Last Generation*, 220–223.

41. Cicero, *For Murena* 51. For the chronology, see Ramsey, "Date of the Consular Elections in 63."

42. The backers of Catiline to whom debt cancellation appealed are scathingly described by Cicero, *Against Catiline* 2.18–23; see also Cicero, *For Murena* 49; Plutarch, *Cicero* 14.1–3.

43. L. Cassius Longinus: Cicero, *Against Catiline* 3.9, *For Sulla* 36–39; P. Cornelius Lentulus Sura: Cicero, *Against Catiline* 3.9; Plutarch, *Cicero* 17.

44. Cicero, *Against Catiline* 2.22, with borrowing from the translation of D. H. Berry, *Cicero: Defence Speeches* (Oxford, UK: Oxford University Press, 2000). For Caelius, see Cicero, *For Caelius* 11–14.

45. Sallust, *War Against Catiline* 23.1–4, 26.3; Diodorus Siculus, *Library of History* 40.5; Plutarch, *Cicero* 16.2; Appian, *Civil War* 2.3.

46. Cicero, *For Murena* 50.

47. Cicero, *For Murena* 51.

48. Cicero, *Against Catiline* 1.11, *For Murena* 52; Plutarch, *Cicero* 14.7–8; Cassius Dio, *Roman History* 37.29.4–30.1.

49. See, e.g., Cicero, *Letters to Atticus* 1.14.5 (SB 14), *Letters to His Friends* 5.5.2 (SB 5). For the aftermath of the consular elections of 63 BC, see especially Sallust, *War Against Catiline* 27.1–2, 36.1.

50. For the episode of the letters, see Plutarch, *Cicero* 15.1–4; *Crassus* 13.3; Cassius Dio, *Roman History* 37.31.1.

51. Sallust, *War Against Catiline* 28.4–29.1; Plutarch, *Cicero* 15.5.

52. Cicero, *Against Catiline* 1.4; Sallust, *War Against Catiline* 29.2; Asconius, *Commentaries* 6C; Plutarch, *Cicero* 15.5; Cassius Dio, *Roman History* 37.31.1–2. On the so-called *senatus consultum ultimum*, see Andrew Lintott, *The Constitution of the Roman Republic* (Oxford, UK: Oxford University Press, 1999), 89–93.

53. Sallust, *War Against Catiline* 30.

54. Cicero, *Against Catiline* 1.19; Sallust, *War Against Catiline* 31.4; Cassius Dio, *Roman History* 37.31.3–32.1. I discuss the court in Chapter 9 below.

55. Cicero, *Against Catiline* 1.6.

56. Sallust, *War Against Catiline* 31.7–9 (probably incorrectly assigning to this occasion Catiline's remark on putting out the fire with destruction).

57. Sallust, *War Against Catiline* 36.1–3; Plutarch, *Cicero* 16.6; Cassius Dio, *Roman History* 37.33.2–3.

58. Plutarch, *Cato the Younger* 21.5. Cicero's speech *For Murena* can be read in Berry, *Cicero: Defence Speeches*, 59–106.

59. For Lentulus Sura, the Allobroges, and Cicero, see Cicero, *Against Catiline* 3.3–6, *On His House* 134; Sallust, *War Against Catiline* 39.6–45; Plutarch, *Cicero* 18.4–7; Cassius Dio, *Roman History* 37.34.1.

60. Cicero, *Against Catiline* 3.6–8; Sallust, *War Against Catiline* 46.1–5; Plutarch, *Cicero* 19.1–2.

61. For the senatorial scribes, see Cicero, *For Sulla* 41–42. The account of the meeting that follows is based on Cicero, *Against Catiline* 3.8–15; and Sallust, *War Against Catiline* 47. A fundamental study on which I draw is Duane A. March, "Cicero and the 'Gang of Five,'" *Classical World* 82, no. 4 (1989): 225–234; further insights are added by Shane Butler, *The Hand of Cicero* (London: Routledge, 2002), 85–102.

62. March, "Cicero and the 'Gang of Five.'"

63. Cicero, *Against Catiline* 3.2.

64. March, "Cicero and the 'Gang of Five,'" 233–234. On the attempts to implicate Crassus and Caesar, see Sallust, *War Against Catiline* 48–49.

65. Cicero, *Against Catiline* 4.5, *Letters to Atticus* 2.1.7 (SB 21); Sallust, *War Against Catiline* 49.4–50; Cassius Dio, *Roman History* 37.35.

66. For a fuller discussion of the debate and its organization, see Osgood, *Uncommon Wrath*, 93–99. A. J. Woodman, "Cicero and Sallust: Debating Death," *Histos* 15 (2021): 1–21, argues that discussion of what to do with the conspirators began on December 4.

67. For Caesar's speech, see especially Cicero, *Against Catiline* 4.7–10; Sallust, *War Against Catiline* 51; Plutarch, *Caesar* 7.8–9, *Cato the Younger* 22.4–5; Suetonius, *Divine Julius* 14; Cassius Dio, *Roman History* 37.36.1–2.

68. For Cato's speech, see especially Sallust, *War Against Catiline* 52; Plutarch, *Cato the Younger* 23; Cassius Dio, *Roman History* 37.36.2–3.

69. Sallust, *War Against Catiline* 55; Plutarch, *Cicero* 22.1–3.

70. Plutarch, *Cicero* 22.4–8.

71. Sallust, *War Against Catiline* 56–61; Plutarch, *Cicero* 22.8; Cassius Dio, *Roman History* 37.39–40.

72. Cicero, *Letters to His Friends* 5.1–2 (SB 1–2); Plutarch, *Cicero* 23.1–2; *Cato the Younger* 26; Cassius Dio, *Roman History* 37.38, 37.42.

73. Cicero, *Against Piso* 6.

74. Cicero, *Against Piso* 6; Plutarch, *Cicero* 23.

75. Cicero, *Letters to Atticus* 1.16.11 (SB 16).

**Chapter 8: Secrets of the Good Goddess**

1. The story of Clodius's sacrilege is told mainly by Plutarch, *Cicero* 28–29, *Caesar* 9–10. My translations of the latter borrow from the superb edition of Christopher Pelling, *Plutarch: "Caesar"* (Oxford, UK: Oxford University Press, 2011). I discuss below the key evidence of Cicero's letters to Atticus, my translations of which are much indebted to D. R. Shackleton Bailey, *Cicero's Letters to Atticus*, 7 vols. (Cambridge, UK: Cambridge University Press, 1965–1971); and P. G. Walsh, *Cicero: Selected Letters* (Oxford, UK: Oxford University Press, 2008). Two major accounts of Clodius and the Good Goddess scandal I rely on throughout this chapter are Philippe Moreau, *Clodiana religio: Un procès politique en 61 av. J.-C.* (Paris: Les Belles Lettres, 1982); and W. Jeffrey Tatum, *The Patrician Tribune: Publius Clodius Pulcher* (Chapel Hill: University of North Carolina Press, 1999), 62–86.

2. On the ceremony for the Good Goddess, see, in addition to the works noted above, T. P. Wiseman, "The Good Goddess," in *Cinna the Poet, and Other Roman Essays* (Leicester, UK: Leicester University Press, 1974), 130–137; H. H. J. Brouwer, *Bona Dea: The Sources and a Description of the Cult* (Leiden: Brill, 1989).

3. Virgil, *Aeneid* 4.174–195.

4. A history of the family is given early in the biography of the emperor Tiberius by Suetonius, *Tiberius* 1–2. Among valuable modern accounts are T. P. Wiseman, *Catullus and His World* (Cambridge, UK: Cambridge University Press, 1985), 15–26; and Tatum, *Patrician Tribune*, 32–36.

5. Suetonius, *Tiberius* 1.2.

6. "Clodius" seems to have been an updated spelling for "Claudius," in keeping with a wider trend in the Latin language. Clodius's third name "Pulcher," meaning "handsome," was one used by the family for centuries.

7. Plutarch, *Lucullus* 34; Cassius Dio, *Roman History* 36.14.4; Tatum, *Patrician Tribune*, 44–49.

8. Cicero, *On the Answers of the Haruspices* 42. The main sources for Clodius at this time are Appian, *Civil War* 2.23; and Cassius Dio, *Roman History* 36.17.2–3, 38.30.5; see also Tatum, *Patrician Tribune*, 49–53.

9. Cicero, *Letters to Atticus* 1.12.3 (SB 12). A good discussion of Cicero's reports to Atticus at this time is given by Andrew Lintott, *Cicero as Evidence: A Historian's Companion* (Oxford, UK: Oxford University Press, 2008), 154–159.

10. Plutarch, *Cicero* 29.1.

11. Plutarch, *Cicero* 20.1–3; Cassius Dio, *Roman History* 37.35.4.

12. See, e.g., Michael H. Crawford, *The Roman Republic*, 2nd ed. (Cambridge, MA: Harvard University Press, 1993), 166.

13. Plutarch, *Caesar* 9.1–3. For the letter from Servilia to Caesar, see Plutarch, *Cato the Younger* 24.1–2; *Brutus* 5.3–4.

14. Cicero, *Letters to Atticus* 1.13.3 (SB 13); Plutarch, *Caesar* 10.6. For more on Caesar and Cato at this time, see Josiah Osgood, *Uncommon Wrath: How Caesar and Cato's Deadly Rivalry Destroyed the Roman Republic* (New York: Basic Books, 2022), 117–123.

15. For one guide, see Mary Beard, John North, and Simon Price, *Religions of Rome*, 2 vols. (Cambridge, UK: Cambridge University Press, 1998).

16. Juvenal, *Satires* 6.314–345; see also the discussion of Tatum, *Patrician Tribune*, 85–86.

17. Cicero, *Letters to Atticus* 1.13.3 (SB 13).

18. See the *Scholia Bobiensia*, as quoted in Thomas Stangl, *Ciceronis Orationum Scholiastae* (Hildesheim: Georg Olms, 1964), 89; Moreau, *Clodiana religio*, 81–98; Tatum, *Patrician Tribune*, 74–75.

19. On *incestum*, see Moreau, *Clodiana religio*, 84–87; Tatum, *Patrician Tribune*, 74–75.

20. The major sources are Cicero, *Brutus* 160; Valerius Maximus, *Memorable Deeds and Sayings* 3.7.9, 6.8.1; Asconius, *Commentaries* 45–46C; Plutarch, *Roman Questions* 83; Cassius Dio, *Roman History* frag. 87; Orosius, *History Against the Pagans* 5.15.20–22; Julius Obsequens, *Book of Prodigies* 37; Macrobius, *Saturnalia* 1.10.5. I also draw on the accounts of Erich

S. Gruen, *Roman Politics and the Criminal Courts, 149–78 BC* (Cambridge, MA: Harvard University Press, 1968), 127–131; and Beard, North, and Price, *Religions of Rome*, 1:137.

21. Valerius Maximus, *Memorable Deeds and Sayings* 3.7.9.

22. Valerius Maximus, *Memorable Deeds and Sayings* 6.8.1.

23. Plutarch, *Roman Questions* 83.

24. The main source for the proposed law, and Clodius's efforts to block it, is Cicero, *Letters to Atticus* 1.13–14 (SB 13–14); some details are added by the *Scholia Bobiensia* on Cicero's lost speech *Against Clodius and Curio*, in Stangl, *Ciceronis Orationum Scholiastae*, 85–91.

25. Cicero, *Against Catiline* 2.4, 2.22–23.

26. As in the attacks he made in the last years of his life against Mark Antony, e.g., Cicero, *Philippics* 2.44–46, 55–58.

27. Cicero, *Letters to Atticus* 1.14.5 (SB 14); also Tatum, *Patrician Tribune*, 69–70.

28. Cicero, *Letters to Atticus* 1.14.5 (SB 14).

29. Protests were sometimes made against the procedural injustice of ex post facto laws in Rome, e.g., Cassius Dio, *Roman History* 38.17.1–2.

30. On Clodius's attacks, see especially Cicero, *Letters to Atticus* 1.14.5 (SB 14).

31. Cicero, *Letters to Atticus* 1.16.2 (SB 16).

32. Cicero, *Brutus* 268. The main source for the trial is Cicero, *Letters to Atticus* 1.16 (SB 16); and the *Scholia Bobiensia*, in Stangl, *Ciceronis Orationum Scholiastae*, 85–91; details are added by other sources, e.g., Cicero, *Letters to Atticus* 2.24.3 (SB 44), for Fannius. I have drawn much on the detailed reconstruction by Moreau, *Clodiana religio*, 131–225.

33. Cicero, *Brutus* 210–220.

34. Cicero, *Letters to Atticus* 1.14.5 (SB 14).

35. Cicero, *Letters to Atticus* 1.16.3 (SB 16).

36. Cicero, *On the Answers of the Haruspices* 37; Plutarch, *Cicero* 29.4–5; Cassius Dio, *Roman History* 37.46.2.

37. *Scholia Bobiensia*, as quoted in Stangl, *Ciceronis Orationum Scholiastae*, 90–91.

38. In keeping with Roman practice, she and her two sisters were all called Clodia. To distinguish the three, Romans could add the husband's name. So this Clodia was Clodia Luculli ("Clodia, wife of Lucullus"). Another of the sisters, Clodia Metelli ("wife of Metellus"), becomes more important later in the story.

39. Cicero, *For Milo* 73; Plutarch, *Cicero* 29.4.

40. Suetonius, *Divine Julius* 74.2; *Scholia Bobiensia*, as quoted in Stangl, *Ciceronis Orationum Scholiastae*, 89, 90.

41. Cicero, *For Milo* 46; Asconius, *Commentaries* 49C; Quintilian, *Orator's Education* 4.2.88; *Scholia Bobiensia*, as quoted in Stangl, *Ciceronis Orationum Scholiastae*, 85.

42. Cicero, *Letters to Atticus* 1.16.4 (SB 16); on Cicero's testimony, see also Plutarch, *Cicero* 29.1–4; and *Scholia Bobiensia*, as quoted in Stangl, *Ciceronis Orationum Scholiastae*, 85–86.

43. Cicero, *Letters to Atticus* 1.16.5–8 (SB 16).

44. Plutarch, *Caesar* 11.1.

45. For Catulus's quip and the vote, see Cicero, *Letters to Atticus* 1.16.5 (SB 16).

46. Cicero, *Letters to Atticus* 1.16.6 (SB 16).

47. See, e.g., Cicero, *Letters to Atticus* 1.18.3 (SB 18); Plutarch, *Cicero* 29.6; Valerius Maximus, *Memorable Deeds and Sayings* 9.1.7; for antibribery proposals, see Cicero, *Letters to Atticus* 1.17.8 (SB 17), 2.1.8 (SB 21).

48. Cicero, *Letters to Atticus* 1.16.10 (SB 16). On the damage to the courts' reputation, see 1.19.6 (SB 19).

49. Cicero's account of the meeting survives in *Letters to Atticus* 1.16.9–10 (SB 16); quotations from his speech against Clodius are also preserved in the *Scholia Bobiensia*, in Stangl, *Ciceronis Orationum Scholiastae*, 85–91.

50. Cicero, *Letters to Atticus* 1.16.6 (SB 16), trans. D. R. Shackleton Bailey, slightly modified.

## Chapter 9: Sticks and Stones

1. For Cicero's political fortunes after the trial of Clodius, see especially *Letters to Atticus* 1.17–2.25 (SB 17–45). Among Cicero's legal successes was his defense of L. Valerius Flaccus, prosecuted in 59 BC for extortion in the province of Asia. Cicero drew heavily on ethnic stereotypes to discredit the prosecution witnesses.

2. In this chapter, focused especially on Cicero's rivalry with Clodius, I rely greatly on W. Jeffrey Tatum, *The Patrician Tribune: Publius Clodius Pulcher* (Chapel Hill: University of North Carolina Press, 1999), 87–213; another study of use is A. W. Lintott, "P. Clodius Pulcher— Felix Catilina?," *Greece and Rome* 14, no. 2 (1967): 157–169. Also valuable are the many discussions of Cicero's politics, e.g., D. L. Stockton, *Cicero: A Political Biography* (London: Oxford University Press, 1971), 161–226; Andrew Lintott, *Cicero as Evidence: A Historian's Companion* (Oxford, UK: Oxford University Press, 2008), 159–211; and the edition of a key speech, Robert A. Kaster, *Cicero: "On Behalf of Publius Sestius"* (Oxford, UK: Oxford University Press, 2006). For translations, I have drawn on D. R. Shackleton Bailey, *Cicero: Back from Exile: Six Speeches upon His Return* (Chicago: American Philological Association, 1991). For Clodius's law, see below.

3. The looting of Cicero's house is described by himself extensively, in *For Sestius* 53–54, *After His Return in the Senate* 18, *On His House* 60–62, *Against Piso* 26. On the location of Cicero's house, see T. P. Wiseman, "Where Did They Live (e.g., Cicero, Octavius, Augustus)?," *Journal of Roman Archaeology* 25 (2012): 657–672; and on its symbolic importance, see, e.g., Shelley Hales, "At Home with Cicero," *Greece and Rome* 47, no. 1 (2000): 44–55; Elisabeth Begemann, "*Ista tua pulchra libertas*: The Construction of a Private Cult of Liberty on the Palatine," in *Public and Private in Ancient Mediterranean Law and Religion*, ed. Clifford Ando and Jörg Rüpke (Berlin: De Gruyter, 2015), 75–98.

4. Cicero, *On the Laws* 2.42, *Letters to His Friends* 12.25.1 (SB 373); Plutarch, *Cicero* 31.6; Cassius Dio, *Roman History* 38.17.5; Walter Allen Jr., "Cicero's House and *Libertas*," *Transactions and Proceedings of the American Philological Association* 75 (1944): 1–9.

5. Tatum, *Patrician Tribune*, 87–99.

6. Cicero was watching closely; see *Letters to Atticus* 1.18.4 (SB 8), 1.19.5 (SB 19), 2.1.4–5 (SB 21).

7. Cicero, *On His House* 41; Suetonius, *Divine Julius* 20.4; Cassius Dio, *Roman History* 38.10.4. For a more detailed account of Caesar's first consulship, see Josiah Osgood, *Uncommon*

*Wrath: How Caesar and Cato's Deadly Rivalry Destroyed the Roman Republic* (New York: Basic Books, 2022), 135–151.

8. Cicero, *On His House* 36; on the adoption, see Tatum, *Patrician Tribune*, 99–111.

9. For the legislative program, see, e.g., Cicero, *For Sestius* 55–56; Asconius, *Commentaries* 8C; Cassius Dio, *Roman History* 38.13; a detailed discussion is given by Tatum, *Patrician Tribune*, 114–149. I also draw on Lintott, "P. Clodius Pulcher"; and Josiah Osgood, *Rome and the Making of a World State, 150 BCE–20 CE* (Cambridge, UK: Cambridge University Press, 2018), 135–136.

10. On the Compitalia, see Harriet I. Flower, *The Dancing Lares and the Serpent in the Garden: Religion at the Roman Street Corner* (Princeton, NJ: Princeton University Press, 2017), 162–174.

11. Proposed law of 66 BC: Asconius, *Commentaries* 45C, *For Cornelius* 64–65C; Cassius Dio, *Roman History* 36.42. Senate ban in 64 BC: Cicero, *Against Piso* 8; Asconius, *Commentaries* 6–7C, 75C; Cassius Dio, *Roman History* 38.13.2; Tatum, *Patrician Tribune*, 25–26, 117–119; Flower, *Dancing Lares*, 234–249.

12. Cicero, *Against Piso* 8; Asconius, *Commentaries* 7C; on Cloelius, see Cynthia Damon, "Sex, Cloelius, *Scriba*," *Harvard Studies in Classical Philology* 94 (1992): 227–250.

13. Cicero, *Against Vatinius* 33–34; *Scholia Bobiensia*, as quoted in Thomas Stangl, *Ciceronis Orationum Scholiastae* (Hildesheim: Georg Olms, 1964), 150; Tatum, *Patrician Tribune*, 140–141.

14. On the law, see, e.g., Cicero, *Letters to Atticus* 3.15.5 (SB 60), *For Sestius* 25, 53–54; Livy, *Periochae* 103; Velleius Paterculus, *Roman History* 2.45.1; Cassius Dio, *Roman History* 38.14.4–5. Clodius's moves against Cicero and related measures are discussed by Tatum, *Patrician Tribune*, 150–175.

15. For the law on the consular provinces, see, e.g., Cicero, *For Sestius* 24–25, 53–55, *On His House* 23; Plutarch, *Cicero* 30.1–2. For Gabinius's earlier career, see, e.g., Josephus, *Jewish Antiquities* 14.37, 14.56; Cassius Dio, *Roman History* 37.5.2.

16. Plutarch, *Cicero* 30.6–7; Appian, *Civil War* 2.15; Cassius Dio, *Roman History* 38.14.7.

17. Cicero, *For Sestius* 25–27, 32, *For Milo* 37; Plutarch, *Cicero* 31.1–2; Cassius Dio, *Roman History* 38.16.2–3

18. Cicero would later endlessly denounce these actions of Gabinius, e.g., *Speech of Thanks in the Senate* 12, 32, and *For Sestius* 28–29; see also Cassius Dio, *Roman History* 38.16.4–6.

19. Cicero, *Letters to Atticus* 3.9.2 (SB 55), *Letters to Quintus* 1.3.8 (SB 3); Plutarch, *Cicero* 31.5; Cassius Dio, *Roman History* 38.17.4.

20. Velleius Paterculus, *Roman History* 2.14.3; on Cicero's house, see above (n. 3).

21. Cicero, *Letters to His Friends* 5.6.2 (SB 4); for criticisms of his purchase, *Letters to Atticus* 1.13.6 (SB 13), 1.16.10 (SB 16).

22. See, e.g., Livy, *History of Rome* 4.13–16 (and Cicero, *On Divination* 2.39 for the market); on the destruction of tyrants' houses, see Matthew B. Roller, "Demolished Houses, Monumentality, and Memory in Roman Culture," *Classical Antiquity* 29, no. 1 (2010): 117–180; and, in general, Harriet I. Flower, *The Art of Forgetting: Disgrace and Oblivion in Roman Political Culture* (Chapel Hill: University of North Carolina Press, 2006).

23. On Clodius's second law, see, e.g., Cicero, *Letters to Atticus* 3.1 (SB 46), 3.4 (SB 49); Plutarch, *Cicero* 32.1. On the shrine for Libertas, see the works on Cicero's house (n. 3); Tatum, *Patrician Tribune*, 158–166; Roller, "Demolished Houses," 156–163; Flower, *Art of Forgetting*, 102–103.

24. The classic study is A. W. Lintott, *Violence in Republican Rome* (Oxford, UK: Clarendon Press, 1968). Also of great value is Wilfried Nippel, *Public Order in Ancient Rome* (Cambridge, UK: Cambridge University Press, 1995), a work that places more emphasis on violence in the late Republic as a distinct phenomenon, arising from political conflict and growing neglect of conventions.

25. On the law against public violence, see Cicero, *For Caelius* 1, 70; Lintott, *Violence in Republican Rome*, 107–124; Nippel, *Public Order*, 54–56; Andrew M. Riggsby, *Crime and Community in Ciceronian Rome* (Austin: University of Texas Press, 1999), 79–119.

26. For Q. Servilius Caepio and the disappearance of the gold, see Cassius Dio, *Roman History* frag. 90; Strabo, *Geography* 4.1.13; Justin, *Epitome of the Philippic History of Pompeius Trogus* 32.3.9–11; Orosius, *History Against the Pagans* 5.15.25. A valuable account of Caepio I draw on is Susan Treggiari, *Servilia and Her Family* (Oxford, UK: Oxford University Press, 2019), 30–35.

27. Livy, *Periochae* 67; Cassius Dio, *Roman History* frag. 91; Eutropius, *Abridgment of Roman History* 5.1.1; Orosius, *History Against the Pagans* 5.16.2–7.

28. For the trials of Caepio, see the sources in the previous two notes and *Rhetorica ad Herennium* 1.24; Cicero, *On the Nature of the Gods* 3.74, *On the Ideal Orator* 2.197; Asconius, *Commentaries* 78C, *On Famous Men* 73; Erich S. Gruen, *Roman Politics and the Criminal Courts, 149–78 BC* (Cambridge, MA: Harvard University Press, 1968), 161–166.

29. Aulus Gellius, *Attic Nights* 3.9.7.

30. On the new court for treason, see, briefly, Gruen, *Roman Politics and the Criminal Courts*, 167–168. The trial of Norbanus in 95 BC is known mainly through Cicero's *On the Ideal Orator*, esp. 2.89, 2.107–109, 2.124, 2.164, 2.167, 2.188, 2.197–204. On the trial, see Gruen, *Roman Politics and the Criminal Courts*, 196.

31. Cicero, *On the Ideal Orator* 2.199.

32. Cicero, *On the Ideal Orator* 2.164.

33. Allen, "Cicero's House," 7–8.

34. Cicero, *Letters to Atticus* 2.1.5–6 (SB 21).

35. Clodia's help to her brother is well explored in Marilyn B. Skinner, *Clodia Metelli: The Tribune's Sister* (Oxford, UK: Oxford University Press, 2011). For Clodia, I have also made use of T. P. Wiseman, *Catullus and His World* (Cambridge, UK: Cambridge University Press,1985), 15–53.

36. For "Lady Ox-Eyes," see, e.g., Cicero, *Letters to Atticus* 2.9.1 (SB 29), 2.12.2 (SB 30), cf. *For Caelius* 49; for the charge of incest by enemies of Clodius other than Cicero, see *Letters to Quintus* 2.3.2 (SB 7).

37. Cicero, *Letters to Atticus* 3.15.2 (SB 60), translated by D. R. Shackleton Bailey, *Cicero's Letters to Atticus*, 7 vols. (Cambridge, UK: Cambridge University Press, 1965–1971). Cicero's exile is discussed more fully in studies of Cicero and his family, e.g., Elizabeth Rawson,

*Cicero: A Portrait* (Ithaca, NY: Cornell University Press, 1975), 116–121; Susan Treggiari, *Terentia, Tullia and Publilia: The Women of Cicero's Family* (London: Routledge, 2007), 56–70.

38. Cicero, *Letters to Atticus* 3.9.2 (SB 54).

39. Cicero, *Letters to Atticus* 3.15.5 (SB 60).

40. Cicero, *For Sestius* 75–78; on this meeting, and the efforts to restore Cicero more generally, see Tatum, *Patrician Tribune*, 168–187.

41. On Milo, see, e.g., Cicero, *Speech of Thanks in the Senate*, 19, *For Sestius* 85–95. A helpful study of Milo is Andrew W. Lintott, "Cicero and Milo," *Journal of Roman Studies* 64 (1974): 62–78.

42. For these events, see, e.g., Cicero, *Speech of Thanks in the Senate* 19, *For Sestius* 87–89, *For Milo* 35, 38, 40; also the works mentioned above (nn. 2, 24).

43. Cicero, *For Sestius* 91–92; on the financial support of Cicero's friends, see *Letters to Atticus* 4.2.7 (SB 74).

44. Thomas Hobbes, *Leviathan*, ed. J. C. A. Gaskin (Oxford, UK: Oxford University Press, 1996), 84, 130.

45. Cicero, *Letters to Atticus* 4.1.4 (SB 73), *Speech of Thanks to the Citizens* 16–17, *For Sestius* 107–108, *Against Piso* 35–36.

46. Cicero, *Letters to Atticus* 4.1.4 (SB 73), *For Sestius* 68, 131.

47. Cicero, *Letters to Atticus* 4.1.5 (SB 73).

48. Cicero, *Letters to Atticus* 4.1.7–8 (SB 73), *On His House* 69.

49. The quotations are from Cicero's speech to the pontiffs on September 29, *On His House*, 111–112; see also Cicero, *Letters to Atticus* 4.2.2–3 (SB 74). A valuable discussion of the speech is given by Wilfried Stroh, "*De domo sua*: Legal Problem and Structure," in *Cicero the Advocate*, ed. Jonathan Powell and Jeremy Paterson (Oxford, UK: Oxford University Press, 2004), 313–370. For Cicero's (and Milo's) struggles with Clodius after Cicero's return, I also draw on Tatum, *Patrician Tribune*, 185–213; and Erich S. Gruen, *The Last Generation of the Roman Republic* (Berkeley: University of California Press, 1974), 287–310 passim.

50. Cicero, *Letters to Atticus* 4.2.3 (SB 74).

51. Cicero, *Letters to Atticus* 4.2.3–5 (SB 74).

52. Cicero, *Letters to Atticus* 4.3.2 (SB 75).

53. Cicero, *Letters to Atticus* 4.3.3 (SB 75).

54. Cicero, *Letters to Atticus* 4.3.3 (SB 75); for Milo's attempt to revive the prosecution, see *Letters to Atticus* 4.3.5 (SB 75), *For Sestius* 95, *For Milo* 40; cf. Cassius Dio, *Roman History* 39.7.4.

55. Cicero, *Letters to Atticus* 4.3.5 (SB 75); this letter recounts the clashes between Milo and Clodius.

56. Cicero, *Letters to Quintus* 2.1.1–3 (SB 5), 2.2.2 (SB 6), *For Sestius* 95, *Letters to His Friends* 1.9.15 (SB 20).

57. On Clodius's prosecution of Milo, see Cicero, *Letters to Quintus* 2.3.1–4 (SB 7), 2.6.4 (SB 10), *For Sestius* 95; Asconius, *Commentaries* 48C; Cassius Dio, *Roman History* 39.18–19.

58. For the proceedings of February 7, I quote from Cicero, *Letters to Quintus* 2.3.1–4 (SB 7); and also Plutarch, *Pompey* 48.7.

59. Cassius Dio, *Roman History* 39.20; Cicero, *On the Answers of the Haruspices* 20.

60. The response is partly preserved in Cicero's speech *On the Answers of the Haruspices* and can be found reconstructed in two excellent articles on the speech: Anthony Corbeill, "The Function of a Divinely Inspired Text in Cicero's *De haruspium responsis*," in *Form and Function in Roman Oratory*, ed. D. H. Berry and Andrew Erskine (Cambridge, UK: Cambridge University Press, 2010), 139–154; Mary Beard, "Cicero's 'Response of the Haruspices' and the Voice of the Gods," *Journal of Roman Studies* 102 (2012): 20–39.

61. Cicero, *On the Answers of the Haruspices* 8–9, 55; Cassius Dio, *Roman History* 39.20.3; Anthony Corbeill, "Clodius' *Contio de haruspicum responsis*," in *Reading Republican Oratory: Reconstructions, Contexts, Receptions*, ed. Christa Gray, Andrea Balbo, Richard M. A. Marshall, and Catherine E. W. Steel (Oxford, UK: Oxford University Press, 2018), 171–190.

62. Cicero, *On the Answers of the Haruspices* 31–32 (sacred places), 22–29 (games), 37–39 (profaned rites).

63. Cicero, *On the Answers of the Haruspices* 8–9, 59.

64. Cicero, *On the Answers of the Haruspices* 37.

65. Cicero, *On the Answers of the Haruspices* 39.

66. Cicero, *On the Answers of the Haruspices* 40.

### Chapter 10: The Hidden Hand

1. Cicero, *For Caelius* 18, 27, 77, *Brutus* 273; Quintilian, *Orator's Education* 6.3.69, 10.1.115. The major sources for Caelius's life are Cicero's speech *For Caelius* and the many letters he and Cicero exchanged, preserved in Cicero's *Letters to His Friends*. Valuable modern accounts are given by R. G. Austin, *M. Tulli Ciceronis pro M. Caelio Oratio*, 3rd ed. (Oxford, UK: Clarendon Press, 1960), v–xvi (hereafter Austin, *Pro M. Caelio*); T. P. Wiseman, *Catullus and His World* (Cambridge, UK: Cambridge University Press, 1985), 54–91.

2. Pliny, *Natural History* 27.4. For a valuable collection of testimony and fragments of Caelius's oratory, see Gesine Manuwald, *Fragmentary Republican Latin: Oratory, Part 3* (Cambridge, MA: Harvard University Press, 2019), 275–303.

3. Cicero, *For Caelius* 9–11; for his likely year of birth (probably misdated by Pliny, *Natural History* 7.165), see, e.g., Wiseman, *Catullus and His World*, 62.

4. The charges are discussed below. Major works of scholarship I have drawn on throughout my account of the trial in this chapter are Austin, *Pro M. Caelio*; Wiseman, *Catullus and His World*, 54–91; Katherine A. Geffcken, *Comedy in the "Pro Caelio": With an Appendix on the "In Clodium et Curionem"* (Leiden: Brill, 1973); D. H. Berry, *Cicero: Defence Speeches* (Oxford, UK: Oxford University Press, 2000), 122–161; Michael C. Alexander, *The Case for the Prosecution in the Ciceronian Era* (Ann Arbor: University of Michigan Press, 2002), 218–243; Matthew Leigh, "The *Pro Caelio* and Comedy," *Classical Philology* 99, no. 4 (2004): 300–335; James E. G. Zetzel, *Marcus Tullius Cicero: Ten Speeches* (Indianapolis: Hackett, 2009). Marilyn B. Skinner, *Clodia Metelli: The Tribune's Sister* (Oxford, UK: Oxford University Press, 2011); Andrew R. Dyck, *Cicero: "Pro Marco Caelio"* (Cambridge, UK: Cambridge University Press, 2013). My translations of *For Caelius* are much indebted to Austin, Berry, and Zetzel. A marvelous novel based on the trial of Caelius is Steven Saylor, *The Venus Throw* (New York: St. Martin's Press, 1995).

5. In starting my account with Alexandria, I follow the excellent discussion of Wiseman, *Catullus and His World*, 54–62, on which I draw.

6. Diodorus Siculus, *Library of History* 1.50.6–7, 17.52; Strabo, *Geography* 17.1.6–13; Judith McKenzie, *The Architecture of Alexandria and Egypt, 300 B.C.—A.D. 700* (New Haven, CT: Yale University Press, 2011).

7. On Ptolemy XI, see Appian, *Civil War* 1.102; also the fragment of the lost historian Porphyry of Tyre, *Jacoby Online* no. 260, frag. 2.11 (https://scholarlyeditions.brill.com/bnjo/).

8. See especially Strabo, *Geography* 17.1.11; Suetonius, *Divine Julius* 54.3; Plutarch, *Cato the Younger* 34.2–35; Cassius Dio, *Roman History* 39.12.

9. See especially Cicero, *For Rabirius Postumus* 4–6, *Letters to His Friends* 7.17.1 (SB 31); Cassius Dio, *Roman History* 39.14.2–3. For detailed discussions of the Ptolemy XII affair, see Mary Siani-Davies, *Cicero's Speech "Pro Rabirio Postumo"* (Oxford, UK: Clarendon Press, 2001); Kit Morrell, "'Who Wants to Go to Alexandria?': Pompey, Ptolemy, and Public Opinion, 57–56 BC," in *Communicating Public Opinion in the Roman Republic*, ed. Cristina Rosillo López (Stuttgart: Franz Steiner, 2019), 151–74.

10. Strabo, *Geography* 17.1.11; Cassius Dio, *Roman History* 39.57.1–2.

11. Cassius Dio, *Roman History* 39.13.1, 39.14.2.

12. Cicero, *Letters to His Friends* 5.12.4 (SB 22).

13. Cassius Dio, *Roman History* 39.13.2–14.3; also Cicero, *For Caelius* 23–24, 51–55, *On the Responses of the Haruspices* 34.

14. Cassius Dio, *Roman History* 39.15.2.

15. Cicero, *Letters to His Friends* 1.1.1–2 (SB 12), *Letters to Quintus* 2.2.3 (SB 6).

16. For the complex political maneuvering, described in letters of Cicero, *Letters to His Friends* 1.1–6 (SB 12–17, 56), *Letters to Quintus* 2.2, 3.2 (SB 6, 22); see also, e.g., Morrell, "Who Wants to Go to Alexandria?"

17. Cassius Dio, *Roman History* 39.14.3–4, 39.16.3; on Asicius and his trial, see Cicero, *Letters to Quintus* 2.9.2 (SB 12), *For Caelius* 23–24.

18. Cicero, *For Caelius* 3–14, 39, 72–77. On his birthplace, see Austin, *Pro M. Caelio*, 146–147; Wiseman, *Catullus and His World*, 62.

19. Quintilian, *Orator's Education* 6.3.69.

20. For Caelius's nicknames, see Quintilian, *Orator's Education* 1.5.61, 8.6.53 (discussed below); cf. Cicero, *Letters to His Friends* 8.15.2 (SB 149).

21. Cicero, *For Caelius* 27, 35; for Caelius as dancer, see Macrobius, *Saturnalia* 3.14.15.

22. Martial, *Epigrams* 1.62. For the Bay of Naples in the late Republican period, see John H. D'Arms, *Romans on the Bay of Naples: A Social and Cultural Study of the Villas and Their Owners from 150 BC to AD 400* (Cambridge, MA: Harvard University Press, 1970), 39–72.

23. Quintilian, *Orator's Education* 4.2.123–124. On the trial, see, e.g., Erich S. Gruen, *The Last Generation of the Roman Republic* (Berkeley: University of California Press, 1974), 287–289; on Cicero's understanding with Antonius, see especially Cicero, *Letters to Atticus* 1.12.1–2 (SB 12), *Letters to His Friends* 5.5 (SB 5).

24. Cicero, *For Caelius* 17–18, 77.

25. Cicero, *For Caelius* 76, *Letters to Quintus* 2.3.6 (SB 7); for this and other trials in the early months of 56 BC, see Gruen, *Last Generation*, 300–309.

26. Cicero, *For Caelius* 26.
27. Cicero, *For Caelius* 1, 56, 76, 78.
28. Cicero, *For Caelius* 1.
29. Cicero, *For Caelius* 17, 36, 38.
30. On the date of the trial, see, e.g., Dyck, *Cicero: "Pro Marco Caelio,"* 4.
31. On the Great Mother's Games, see, e.g., Wiseman, *Catullus and His World*, 198–206.
32. Ennius, *Tragedies* frag. 89, as quoted in Sander M. Goldberg and Gesine Manuwald, *Fragmentary Republican Latin: "Ennius"; Dramatic Fragments, Minor Works* (Cambridge, MA: Harvard University Press, 2018). A good, illustrated introduction to Roman drama is Timothy J. Moore, *Roman Theatre* (Cambridge, UK: Cambridge University Press, 2012).
33. In addition to Moore, *Roman Theatre*, 7–89, see Erich Segal, *The Death of Comedy* (Cambridge, MA: Harvard University Press, 2001), esp. 153–204.
34. Moore, *Roman Theatre*, 97–111; Wiseman, *Catullus and His World*, 28–30.
35. Cicero, *For Caelius* 27; on the case for the prosecution, see further Wiseman, *Catullus and His World*, 69–74; Alexander, *Case for the Prosecution*, 218–243; Jean-Michel David, *Le patronat judiciaire au dernier siècle de la République romaine* (Rome: École française de Rome, 1992), 564–565.
36. Atratinus's speech is discussed by Cicero, *For Caelius* 2–22.
37. Jason: Fortunatianus, *Art of Rhetoric* 3.7, with Wiseman, *Catullus and His World*, 72; Xerxes: Velleius Paterculus, *Roman History* 2.33.4; Ulysses: Suetonius, *Gaius* 23.2; Cassandra: Petronius, *Satyricon* 74.14.
38. For his speech, see Cicero, *For Caelius* 23–25, 27.
39. Cicero, *For Caelius* 35; for his speech, 25–69 passim; for his style, 25, 27.
40. Quintilian, *Orator's Education* 11.1.51.
41. Suetonius, *On Rhetoricians* 2.
42. Quintilian, *Orator's Education* 1.5.61.
43. Quintilian, *Orator's Education* 8.6.53.
44. Plutarch, *Cicero* 29.5. Clodia would have gained notoriety as well if she were the real woman behind the "Lesbia" of the contemporary poet Catullus ("Lesbia" was a pseudonym for the poet's lover, inspired by the birthplace of the love poet Sappho). For one discussion, see Skinner, *Clodia Metelli*, 121–144.
45. Quintilian, *Orator's Education* 6.3.25; Cicero's "most obscene story": *For Caelius* 69; the see-through silk dress: Quintilian, *Orator's Education* 8.6.53.
46. On Crassus's speech, see Cicero, *For Caelius* 18, 23; on Caelius's time with him, 9.
47. Cicero, *For Caelius* 1.
48. Cicero, *For Caelius* 2, 6, 14.
49. Cicero, *For Caelius* 17, 18.
50. Cicero, *For Caelius* 20, translated by Berry, *Cicero: Defence Speeches*, slightly modified.
51. Cicero, *For Caelius* 30, 31.
52. Cicero, *For Caelius* 31, 32.
53. Wiseman, *Catullus and His World*, 74. But some scholars, e.g., Dyck, *Cicero, "Pro Marco Caelio,"* 14, suggest Cicero might have invented the affair.
54. Cicero, *For Caelius* 70.

55. Cicero, *For Caelius* 33–34.

56. Cicero, *For Caelius* 36.

57. Cicero, *For Caelius* 37–38.

58. See, above all, the groundbreaking study of Geffcken, *Comedy in the "Pro Caelio"*; also Leigh, *"Pro Caelio* and Comedy."

59. Allegedly even the stern moralist Cato the Elder approved of the practice: Horace, *Satires* 1.2.31–35, with the commentary by the ancient scholiast on the passage.

60. Cicero, *For Caelius* 51–60.

61. Cicero, *For Caelius* 61–64.

62. Cicero, *For Caelius* 65–69 (with much borrowing from Austin, *Pro M. Caelio*, in my translations).

63. Cicero, *For Caelius* 70–80.

64. Cicero, *For Caelius* 50.

65. This emerges from a letter Cicero wrote to Terentia, *Letters to His Friends* 14.2.2 (SB 7); on Terentia's experience during Cicero's exile, see Susan Treggiari, *Terentia, Tullia and Publilia: The Women of Cicero's Family* (London: Routledge, 2007), 56–70.

66. Allegedly, the wife of a conspirator executed in 63 BC had to beg Terentia for the recovery of her husband's body (Plutarch, *Antony* 2.2); for the general principle of women helping women, see Appian, *Civil Wars* 4.32.

67. The major source is Cassius Dio, *Roman History* 39.55–58, with details added by other sources, e.g., Cicero's speech *For Rabirius Postumus*, 19–21; Plutarch, *Antony* 3; see also Siani-Davies, *Cicero's Speech "Pro Rabirio Postumo,"* 26–32.

68. Cassius Dio, *Roman History* 39.59.3–60.4, 39.61.4. Cicero's speeches from the time are full of attacks on Gabinius, e.g., *Against Piso* 48–50.

69. Cicero, *Letters to Quintus* 3.1.24 (SB 21), 3.2.2 (SB 22); Cassius Dio, *Roman History* 39.62.1–2; for a fuller account of the "trials and tribulations of A. Gabinius," see Gruen, *Last Generation*, 322–331.

70. Cicero, *Letters to Quintus* 3.3.3 (SB 23), 3.4.1 (SB 24); Cassius Dio, *Roman History* 39.55.4–5, 39.62 (which contains some inaccuracies).

71. Cicero, *Letters to Quintus* 3.5.8 (SB 25), citing Homer, *Iliad* 16.385–388; on the flood, see also Cassius Dio, *Roman History* 39.61. The translation of Homer is from Richmond Lattimore, *The Iliad of Homer* (Chicago: University of Chicago Press, 1951).

72. Cassius Dio, *Roman History* 39.55.5–6, 39.63.

73. Cicero, *Letters to Quintus* 3.7.2 (SB 27).

## Chapter 11: Accident

1. The main source for the discovery of Clodius's body and what followed is Asconius, *Commentaries* 31–33C, 42C; details are added by Cassius Dio, *Roman History* 40.48.2–49.3.

2. Scholarship on Cicero's defense of Milo, the events leading up to it, and the aftermath of the trial that I rely on in this chapter includes Andrew W. Lintott, "Cicero and Milo," *Journal of Roman Studies* 64 (1974): 62–78; Erich S. Gruen, *The Last Generation of the Roman Republic* (Berkeley: University of California Press, 1974), 337–350; James S. Ruebel, "The Trial of Milo in 52 BC: A Chronological Study," *Transactions of the American Philological*

*Association* 109 (1979): 231–249; A. M. Stone, "*Pro Milone*: Cicero's Second Thoughts," *Antichthon* 14 (1980): 88–111; Andrew R. Dyck, "Narrative Obfuscation, Philosophical Topoi, and Tragic Patterning in Cicero's *Pro Milone*," *Harvard Studies in Classical Philology* 98 (1998): 219–241; D. H. Berry, *Cicero: Defence Speeches* (Oxford, UK: Oxford University Press, 2000), 162–223; John T. Ramsey, "How and Why Was Pompey Made Sole Consul in 52 BC?," *Historia* 65, no. 3 (2016): 298–324 (with an important chronological table, 319–322); Kit Morrell, "Cato, Pompey's Third Consulship, and the Politics of Milo's Trial," in *Institutions and Ideology in Republican Rome: Speech, Audience, and Decision*, ed. Henriette van der Blom, Christa Gray, and Catherine Steel (Cambridge, UK: Cambridge University Press, 2018), 165–180; Thomas J. Keeline, *Cicero: "Pro Milone"* (Cambridge, UK: Cambridge University Press, 2021). A superb novel from which I have gained many insights is Steven Saylor, *A Murder on the Appian Way* (New York: St. Martin's Press, 1996).

3. On events of 53 and early 52 BC, see especially Asconius, *Commentaries* 30–31C, 48C; also Cicero, *For Milo* 25–26, 33, 41, 87; Cassius Dio, *Roman History* 40.46.1–48.2; on the elections for 54 BC, see Josiah Osgood, *Uncommon Wrath: How Caesar and Cato's Deadly Rivalry Destroyed the Roman Republic* (New York: Basic Books, 2022), 191–194.

4. Cicero, *Letters to Atticus* 4.13.1 (SB 87); Asconius, *Commentaries* 28C.

5. Macrobius, *Saturnalia* 2.2.9.

6. Celia E. Schultz, "*Debuit in te officiosior esse*: Power, Place, and Accusations of Prostitution in Late Republican Rome," *American Journal of Philology* (forthcoming).

7. Cicero, *Letters to Quintus* 3.6.6 (SB 26); on Milo's games, see also *Letters to Quintus* 3.7.2 (SB 27); *For Milo* 95; Asconius, *Commentaries* 31C; on Cicero's lobbying, see Cicero, *Letters to His Friends* 2.6.3 (SB 50).

8. Asconius, *Commentaries* 31C.

9. Kit Morrell, "P. Clodius Pulcher and the Praetorship That Never Was," *Historia* 72, no. 1 (2023): 29–57; on Clodius's proposed reforms, see especially Cicero, *For Milo* 33, 87–89; Asconius, *Commentaries* 52C.

10. Fragments of Cicero's speech are preserved in the *Scholia Bobiensia*, in Thomas Stangl, *Ciceronis Orationum Scholiastae* (Hildesheim: Georg Olms, 1964), 169–174.

11. Asconius, *Commentaries* 31C.

12. Cicero, *For Milo* 27, 28, 48; Asconius, *Commentaries* 31C.

13. Cicero, *For Milo* 27–29, 55–56; Asconius, *Commentaries* 31–32C; on the musicians, see Keeline, *Cicero: "Pro Milone,"* 247.

14. Cassius Dio, *Roman History* 40.49.2–5; Asconius, *Commentaries* 43C; Ramsey, "How and Why Was Pompey Made Sole Consul," 300–303.

15. Asconius, *Commentaries* 33C; Cassius Dio, *Roman History* 40.49.3; for the rumors on Milo, see Cicero, *For Milo* 62–64.

16. My sketch of Pompey's career draws from Josiah Osgood, *Rome and the Making of a World State, 150 BCE–20 CE* (Cambridge, UK: Cambridge University Press, 2018), esp. 108–123. Not to be missed is Cicero's account of Pompey's shows in 55 BC in *Letters to His Friends* 7.1 (SB 24).

17. Plutarch, *Pompey* 54.2–3; Cassius Dio, *Roman History* 40.45–46.1.

18. Asconius, *Commentaries* 33C; Cassius Dio, *Roman History* 40.49.4–5.

19. Asconius, *Commentaries* 43C.

20. Asconius, *Commentaries* 51C.

21. Asconius, *Commentaries* 50–51C.

22. Note Cicero, *Letters to Quintus* 2.12.2 (SB 16).

23. Asconius, *Commentaries* 33C.

24. Appian, *Civil War* 2.22 (probably Cicero refers to the violence, too, at *For Milo* 91).

25. Cicero, *For Milo* 70; Asconius, *Commentaries* 34C; Cassius Dio, *Roman History* 49.5.5 (misdated).

26. Asconius, *Commentaries* 34C; Cassius Dio, *Roman History* 49.50.1–2.

27. Asconius, *Commentaries* 34–35C.

28. I follow a key argument of Ramsey, "How and Why Pompey Was Made Sole Consul," esp. 313–318.

29. Asconius, *Commentaries* 51–52C, together with Cicero, *For Milo* 65; for Sallust and Fausta, see Aulus Gellius, *Attic Nights* 17.18.

30. On the three tribunes' meetings and Pompey's claims, see Asconius, *Commentaries* 51–52C.

31. On this and what follows, see Asconius, *Commentaries* 34C; Lintott, "Cicero and Milo," 71.

32. Ramsey, "How and Why Pompey Was Made Sole Consul," 310–312. For more on Caesar and Cato at this time, see Osgood, *Uncommon Wrath*, 196–201.

33. See especially Asconius, *Commentaries* 35–36C; Plutarch, *Pompey* 54.4–6; Ramsey, "How and Why Pompey Was Made Sole Consul."

34. Asconius, *Commentaries* 36C, 44C.

35. For the contents of the laws, see especially Asconius, *Commentaries* 36C, 38C, 39C; Plutarch, *Pompey* 55.4; Cassius Dio, *Roman History* 40.52; Gruen, *Last Generation*, 233–239, noting that the *lex Plautia de vi* and *lex Licinia de sodaliciis* stayed in effect.

36. Asconius, *Commentaries* 44–45C, with Cicero, *For Milo* 14.

37. Asconius, *Commentaries* 36C.

38. Cicero, *For Milo* 66; Asconius, *Commentaries* 36C, 50C.

39. Asconius, *Commentaries* 37C.

40. Cicero, *For Milo* 12, 47; Asconius, *Commentaries* 37–38C.

41. On these developments, see Asconius, *Commentaries* 38–39C; also Cicero, *For Milo* 21–22.

42. Asconius, *Commentaries* 39C.

43. Cicero, *For Milo* 59–60.

44. Asconius, *Commentaries* 41–42C; Quintilian, *Orator's Education* 4.2.25, 4.3.17; Cassius Dio, *Roman History* 40.54.2–3; *Scholia Bobiensia*, in Stangl, *Ciceronis Orationum Scholiastae*, 112; for a good discussion, see Keeline, *Cicero: "Pro Milone,"* 37–44.

45. Asconius, *Commentaries* 41C.

46. See, e.g., Stone, "Cicero's *Pro Milone*"; Berry, *Cicero: Defence Speeches*, 169–171; Keeline, *Cicero: "Pro Milone,"* 41–43.

47. Asconius, *Commentaries* 41C; Quintilian, *Orator's Education* 6.3.49; also important for the prosecution case is Cicero, *For Milo* 17–18, 46–48. The time Quintilian reports is

"before the ninth hour"; the Roman day, from sunrise to sunset, was divided into twelve hours, and throughout this chapter I give approximations; see further Keeline, *Cicero: "Pro Milone,"* 168–169.

48. Asconius, *Commentaries* 40–41C, 52C.

49. Cicero, *For Milo* 1–3, 92, 105; Asconius, *Commentaries* 40–41C; Plutarch, *Cicero* 35.2–5; Cassius Dio, *Roman History* 40.54.2, with discussion by Lynn S. Fotheringham, "Plutarch and Dio on Cicero at the Trial of Milo," in *Fame and Infamy: Essays on Characterization in Greek and Roman Biography and Historiography*, ed. Rhiannon Ash, Judith Mossman, and Frances B. Titchener (Oxford, UK: Oxford University Press, 2015), 194–207.

50. Asconius, *Commentaries* 41C; on Antony's appearance, see Plutarch, *Antony* 4.1–2.

51. Asconius, *Commentaries* 42C; Plutarch, *Cicero* 35.5.

52. Keeline, *Cicero: "Pro Milone,"* 24n91 rightly points out that both the prosecution and the defense cases were limited by the months of public debate that preceded the trial.

53. Cicero, *For Milo* 6–11.

54. Cicero, *For Milo* 24–29.

55. I draw on good discussions of Cicero's strategy in his narrative by Dyck, "Narrative Obfuscation," 222–227; Keeline, *Cicero: "Pro Milone,"* 153–173, esp. 167–168.

56. Cicero, *For Milo* 29 ("around the eleventh hour or not far off it").

57. Stone, "Cicero's *Pro Milone*," 89n12, citing the passage from *On the Ideal Orator* (2.294) I mention here.

58. Cicero, *For Milo* 32–66 (*cui bono*: 32; Clodius as woman: 55).

59. For what follows, see Asconius, *Commentaries* 31–32C.

60. Cicero, *Letters to Atticus* 4.3.5 (SB 75).

61. Keeline, *Cicero: "Pro Milone,"* 24n91.

62. Asconius, *Commentaries* 53C.

63. Asconius, *Commentaries* 54C; Cicero, *Letters to Atticus* 5.8.2–3 (SB 101).

64. Asconius, *Commentaries* 54–55C.

65. Asconius, *Commentaries* 55C.

66. On the divergent fates of Scipio and Hypsaeus, see, e.g., Plutarch, *Pompey* 55; Cassius Dio, *Roman History* 40.51.3, 40.53.1–2.

67. Valerius Maximus, *Memorable Deeds and Sayings* 9.5.3.

68. Tacitus, *Annals* 3.28.1.

69. Cloelius: Asconius, *Commentaries* 55–56C. Pompeius Rufus: Valerius Maximus, *Memorable Deeds and Sayings* 4.2.7; Cassius Dio, *Roman History* 40.55.1.

70. Cicero, *Letters to His Friends* 7.2.2–4 (SB 52), quoted again below.

71. See, e.g., Valerius Maximus, *Memorable Deeds and Sayings* 6.2.5; Plutarch, *Pompey* 55.5, *Cato the Younger* 48.4–5; Morrell, "Cato, Pompey's Third Consulship, and the Politics of Milo's Trial," 174–175. For the verdict in this trial, see Cicero, *Philippics* 6.10.

72. Cicero, *Letters to His Friends* 7.2.2–4 (SB 52).

73. Stone, "Cicero's *Pro Milone*," 102–111.

74. Cicero, *For Milo* 77.

75. Cicero, *For Milo*, 86, with Dyck, "Narrative Obfuscation," 233–239, on which I draw.

76. Cassius Dio, *Roman History* 40.54.3–4.

77. Asconius, *Commentaries* 41C; Quintilian, *Orator's Education* 3.6.93, 10.1.23, 10.5.20.

78. On this law, see especially Kit Morrell, *Pompey, Cato, and the Governance of the Roman Empire* (Oxford, UK: Oxford University Press, 2017), 204–236.

**Chapter 12: Vengeance**

1. Modern biographies of Cicero, which I have drawn on in this chapter, tell the story of his final years in more detail: H. J. Haskell, *This Was Cicero: Modern Politics in a Roman Toga* (New York: Alfred A. Knopf, 1942), 268–358; D. L. Stockton, *Cicero: A Political Biography* (London: Oxford University Press, 1971), 227–335; Elizabeth Rawson, *Cicero: A Portrait* (Ithaca, NY: Cornell University Press, 1975), 164–308; see also Andrew Lintott, *Cicero as Evidence: A Historian's Companion* (Oxford, UK: Oxford University Press, 2008), 253–424.

2. "Gigantic bore": Cicero, *Letters to Atticus* 5.2.3 (SB 95). Caelius's advice: *Letters to His Friends* 8.5.1 (SB 83). I discuss Cicero's governorship in Josiah Osgood, *Rome and the Making of a World State, 150 BCE–20 CE* (Cambridge, UK: Cambridge University Press, 2018), 144–159.

3. Caelius's letters can be found using the index of D. R. Shackleton Bailey's Loeb edition, *Cicero: Letters to His Friends*, 3 vols. (Cambridge, MA: Harvard University Press, 2001). Spectacle in Rome: *Letters to His Friends* 8.14.1 (SB 97); Cicero's murder: *Letters to His Friends* 8.1.4 (SB 77).

4. Cicero, *Letters to His Friends* 2.11.2 (SB 90); for Caelius's requests, see, e.g., 8.2.2 (SB 78), *Letters to Atticus* 6.1.21 (SB 115).

5. The main source on Brutus's loan is Cicero, *Letters to Atticus* 5.21.10–13 (SB 114), 6.1.3–8 (SB 115), 6.2.7–9 (SB 116). On Brutus, I draw on Plutarch's biography, as well as Kathryn Tempest, *Brutus: The Noble Conspirator* (New Haven, CT: Yale University Press, 2017), with helpful chronologies; and Susan Treggiari, *Servilia and Her Family* (Oxford, UK: Oxford University Press, 2019).

6. Cicero, *Letters to Atticus* 6.1.7 (SB 115).

7. Cicero, *Letters to His Friends* 2.12.2 (SB 95).

8. Cicero, *Letters to His Friends* 8.14 (SB 97). For a fuller discussion of the outbreak of the war, see Josiah Osgood, *Uncommon Wrath: How Caesar and Cato's Deadly Rivalry Destroyed the Roman Republic* (New York: Basic Books, 2022), 191–210.

9. Cicero, *Letters to His Friends* 8.14.3 (SB 97).

10. On Cicero's developing relationship with Caesar, see further Josiah Osgood, "The Pen and the Sword: Writing and Conquest in Caesar's Gaul," *Classical Antiquity* 28, no. 2 (2009): 328–358; on the course of the civil war see Osgood, *Uncommon Wrath*, 211–252.

11. Cicero, *Letters to Atticus* 10.9A.5 (SB 200A). Cicero's vacillations are recoverable in the extraordinary series of letters to Atticus from this time, on which see P. A. Brunt, "Cicero's *Officium* in the Civil War," *Journal of Roman Studies* 76 (1986): 12–32. The impact of war on Cicero's family is highlighted by Susan Treggiari, *Terentia, Tullia and Publilia: The Women of Cicero's Family* (London: Routledge, 2007), 100–154.

12. Plutarch, *Cicero* 38; see also Macrobius, *Saturnalia* 2.3.7–8.

13. For what follows, see Caelius's last letter to Cicero, *Letters to His Friends* 8.17 (SB 156); Caesar, *Civil War* 3.20–22; Velleius Paterculus, *Roman History* 2.68.1–3; Cassius Dio, *Roman History* 42.22–25.

14. For Cicero after Pharsalus, see especially Cicero, *Letters to Atticus* 11.7.2 (SB 218); Plutarch, *Cicero* 39.1–2; on Marcus junior at Pharsalus, Cicero, *On Duties* 2.45.

15. Cicero, *Letters to Atticus* 11.6.5 (SB 217). Cicero's letters, especially those to Atticus, are the main source for his life in this difficult period.

16. Plutarch, *Pompey* 77–80.

17. Cicero, *On Divination* 2.22.

18. Cicero, *Letters to Atticus* 11.8.2 (SB 219).

19. Cicero, *Letters to Atticus* 11.23.3 (SB 232).

20. See, e.g., Cicero, *Letters to His Friends* 14.8, 14.11, 14.21 (SB 164–166).

21. Cicero, *Letters to Atticus* 11.24.3 (SB 234); cf. Plutarch, *Cicero* 41.2–4, with further discussion by Treggiari, *Terentia, Tullia and Publilia*, 118–135.

22. Cicero, *Letters to His Friends* 14.20 (SB 173).

23. For Brutus's *On Virtue*, see Cicero, *Brutus* 11–12, 250, 330. See further Katharina Volk, *The Roman Republic of Letters: Scholarship, Philosophy, and Politics in the Age of Cicero and Caesar* (Princeton, NJ: Princeton University Press, 2021), 115–116, for the importance of this work.

24. Cicero, *Brutus* 13–21. On Atticus's *Liber annalis*, see Cornelius Nepos, *Atticus* 18.1–2.

25. Cicero, *Brutus* 6, 331. On Cicero's cultivation of Brutus, see the important paper by Kathryn Welch, "Cicero and Brutus in 45," in *Ancient History in a Modern University: The Ancient Near East, Greece, and Rome*, ed. T. W. Hillard, R. A. Kearsley, C. E. V. Nixon, and A. M. Nobbs (Grand Rapids, MI: Eerdmans, 1998), 244–256.

26. *Academica* 1.34. Excellent surveys of Cicero's philosophical program from this time are given by Rawson, *Cicero*, 230–247; Lintott, *Cicero as Evidence*, 301–407 passim. For the broader picture, see Volk, *Roman Republic of Letters*, esp. 111–180.

27. Cicero, *Tusculan Disputations* 1.101.

28. See, e.g., Cicero, *On Ends* 2.66, *Tusculan Disputations* 1.89, 4.2; Welch, "Cicero and Brutus in 45."

29. Plutarch, *Cicero* 41.4–6; Cassius Dio, *Roman History* 46.18.3, with discussion by Treggiari, *Terentia, Tullia and Publilia*, 133–135.

30. Cicero, *Letters to Atticus* 12.15 (SB 252). On the death of Tullia and Cicero's grief, see Treggiari, *Terentia, Tullia and Publilia*, 136–142; Josiah Osgood, *Turia: A Roman Woman's Civil War* (Oxford, UK: Oxford University Press, 2014), 95–99.

31. Cicero, *Letters to Atticus* 12.13.1 (SB 250), 12.20.1 (SB 258), 12.21.5 (SB 260), 12.32.1 (SB 271), 12.38a.1 (SB 279), *Letters to His Friends* 4.6.1 (SB 249); Plutarch, *Cicero* 41.7–8.

32. For more on Caesar's final years, see Osgood, *Uncommon Wrath*, 253–270. On the conspiracy against Caesar and the aftermath, an excellent account is given by Barry Strauss, *The Death of Caesar: The Story of History's Most Famous Assassination* (New York: Simon & Schuster, 2015); Peter Stothard's *The Lost Assassin: The Hunt for the Killers of Julius Caesar* (Oxford, UK: Oxford University Press, 2021) evokes the whole period brilliantly.

33. Cicero, *Letters to Atticus* 13.37.2 (SB 346), *Letters to His Friends* 6.19.2 (SB 262).

34. Cicero, *Letters to His Friends* 7.30.2 (SB 265).

35. See especially Suetonius, *Divine Julius* 79.3, 80.2.

36. Plutarch, *Brutus* 9.6–7; Appian, *Civil War* 2.112; Cassius Dio, *Roman History* 44.12.

37. For the planned meeting of March 15, see Cicero, *Philippics* 2.88. On Antony, Dolabella, and Fulvia, see Kathryn Welch, "Antony, Fulvia, and the Ghost of Clodius in 47 BC," *Greece and Rome* 42, no. 2 (1995): 182–201.

38. My account of the conspiracy, the assassination, and the days that followed, leading up to the funeral, is based on Nicolaus of Damascus, *Life of Augustus* 80–106; Suetonius, *Divine Julius* 78–87; Plutarch, *Caesar* 63–67, *Brutus* 8–20, *Antony* 12–14; Appian, *Civil War* 2.111–154; Cassius Dio, *Roman History* 44.11–52; Strauss, *Death of Caesar*; and the works cited above (nn. 1, 5). I have gained insights from a fine novel about Caesar's murder, Steven Saylor, *The Throne of Caesar* (New York: St. Martin's Press, 2018).

39. See the sources cited in the previous note.

40. See, e.g., Cicero, *Philippics* 1.1, 2.89; Plutarch, *Cicero* 42.3.

41. Quintilian, *Orator's Education* 6.1.31, with translation, modified, from Donald A. Russell, *Quintilian: "The Orator's Education,"* 5 vols. (Cambridge, MA: Harvard University Press, 2001). For problems in reconstructing Antony's speech, see, e.g., Josiah Osgood, *Caesar's Legacy: Civil War and the Emergence of the Roman Empire* (Cambridge, UK: Cambridge University Press, 2006), 12–13; Jon Hall, *Cicero's Use of Judicial Theater* (Ann Arbor: University of Michigan Press, 2014), 134–140; Kathryn Welch, "History Wars: Who Avenged Caesar and Why Does It Matter," in *Augustus and the Destruction of History*, ed. Ingo Gildenhard, Ulrich Gotter, Wolfgang Havener, and Louise Hodgson (Cambridge, UK: Cambridge Philological Society, 2019), 59–79.

42. See, e.g., Osgood, *Caesar's Legacy*, 12–61, for a fuller account of the year and a half following the Ides of March, with important new observations in Welch, "History Wars."

43. Cicero, *Letters to Atticus* 14.12.2 (SB 366), and see also *Philippics* 2.91; for complaints on Antony and Fulvia, see, e.g., *Letters to Atticus* 14.10.1 (SB 364), 14.12.1 (SB 366), 14.13.6 (SB 367).

44. For the military developments of 44 and 43 BC, see, e.g., Strauss, *Death of Caesar*, 185–228; Tempest, *Brutus*, 105–172; also the important study of Kathryn Welch, *Magnus Pius: Sextus Pompeius and the Transformation of the Roman Republic* (Swansea: Classical Press of Wales, 2012), 121–202.

45. See especially Cicero, *Letters to Atticus* 16.7 (SB 415), *Philippics* 1.1–10.

46. Cicero, *Philippics* 1.11–13; Plutarch, *Cicero* 43.5–7.

47. For what follows, see especially Cicero, *Philippics* 2.3–42 passim. I draw on an excellent translation and introduction to this speech in D. H. Berry, *Cicero: Political Speeches* (Oxford, UK: Oxford University Press, 2006), 222–270; and the excellent commentary by John T. Ramsey, *Cicero: "Philippics" I–II* (Cambridge, UK: Cambridge University Press, 2003).

48. Cicero, *Philippics* 2.39.

49. Cicero's scathing review of Antony's career is given at *Philippics* 2.44–111; on the crime of wishing to see Caesar killed, see 2.29, 2.34.

50. Cicero, *Philippics* 2.34.

51. Cicero, *Philippics* 3.35.

52. Cicero, *Letters to Brutus* 1.4.3 (SB 10).

53. Appian, *Civil Wars* 3.26. Cicero's response to the news, with a somewhat different version of Trebonius's death, can be found in *Philippics* 11.

54. Quoted in Cicero, *Philippics* 13.22. On Antony's rhetoric, see Welch, "History Wars."

55. Appian, *Civil Wars* 3.92.

56. On the Pedian law, see Augustus, *Achievements* 2.1; Livy, *Periochae* 120; Velleius Paterculus, *Roman History* 2.69.5; Plutarch, *Brutus* 27.4–5; Appian, *Civil Wars* 3.95, 4.27, 5.61; Cassius Dio, *Roman History* 46.48–49; Kathryn Welch, "The *Lex Pedia* of 43 BCE and Its Aftermath," *Hermathena*, no. 196/197 (Winter 2014): 137–162.

57. See, e.g., Velleius Paterculus, *Roman History* 2.64.1–2; Valerius Maximus, *Memorable Deeds and Sayings* 4.7.6, 9.13.3; Appian, *Civil Wars* 3.97–98.

58. On the establishment of the triumvirate and the proscriptions, see Osgood, *Caesar's Legacy*, 62–107; Carsten Hjort Lange, *Res Publica Constituta: Actium, Apollo, and the Accomplishment of the Triumviral Assignment* (Leiden: Brill, 2009), 13–48. For Verres, see Pliny, *Natural History* 34.6; Seneca, *Suasoriae* 6.3; Lactantius, *Divine Institutes* 2.4.37.

59. Major accounts are given by Plutarch, *Cicero* 47–49; *Antony* 20; Appian, *Civil War* 4.19–20; Livy, as quoted by Seneca, *Suasoriae* 6.17; Cassius Dio, *Roman History* 47.8.3–4, 47.11.1–2, with full discussions by Matthew B. Roller, "*Color*-Blindness: Cicero's Death, Declamation, and the Production of History," *Classical Philology* 92, no. 2 (1997): 109–130; Andrew Wright, "The Death of Cicero. Forming a Tradition: The Contamination of History," *Historia* 50, no. 4 (2001): 436–452.

60. Livy's account is quoted at Seneca, *Suasoriae* 6.17; Plutarch, *Cicero* 48.3–5, is similar.

61. Cassius Dio, *Roman History* 47.8.4; for Antony, see, e.g., Plutarch, *Antony* 20.4; Cassius Dio, *Roman History* 47.8.3.

## Conclusion: "White Toga Crime"

1. Cicero, *On Duties* 2.27.

2. Appian, *Civil Wars* 1.57.

3. *Speech of Hon. Charles Sumner in the Senate of the United States, 19th and 20th May, 1856* (Boston: John P. Jewett & Company, 1856), 7, 9, 95.

4. Quoted by Seneca, *Suasoriae* 6.22.

# INDEX

Index

Index